An AMERICAN HERITAGE Guide

NATURAL WONDERS
of
AMERICA

An AMERICAN HERITAGE Guide

NATURAL WONDERS
of
AMERICA

BY THE EDITORS OF
AMERICAN HERITAGE
The Magazine of History

EDITOR IN CHARGE
BEVERLEY DA COSTA

INTRODUCTION BY
ALVIN M. JOSEPHY, JR.

PUBLISHED BY American Heritage Publishing Co., Inc., New York

Staff for this Book

EDITOR IN CHARGE
Beverley Da Costa

ASSOCIATE EDITORS
Susan E. Green
Angela H. Weldon

ART DIRECTOR
Scott Chelius

PICTURE EDITOR
Alfred Baman

CONTRIBUTING EDITOR
Margot Brill

American Heritage
Publishing Co., Inc.

PRESIDENT AND PUBLISHER
Paul Gottlieb

EDITOR-IN-CHIEF
Joseph J. Thorndike

SENIOR EDITOR,
BOOK DIVISION
Alvin M. Josephy, Jr.

EDITORIAL ART DIRECTOR
Murray Belsky

GENERAL MANAGER,
BOOK DIVISION
Kenneth W. Leish

Introduction

The American experience has been an awesome one. There was a continent, unscarred, unspoiled, unexploited, wide open for the taking. To be sure, there were Indians to be got out of the way and a wilderness to be conquered. But what a wilderness! Enough forests with enough lumber to fill man's needs till the end of time. Enough wealth from the earth—iron and copper, coal and gold—to create the richest empires in history. There were animals with furs and animals for food, land for homes and land for flocks and herds, and farmlands with the deepest, most fertile loam that stretched on and on to the horizon. There were rushing rivers and great lakes with fish, and waterfalls for power, and potters' clay and salt licks and petroleum for lamps—and fields of flowers and birds in infinite variety. All for the taking.

It was taken, and from its bounty, America was built. But the conquest had its human side, and from the beginning the record shows a counterpull on the American soul—the lure of untouched and uncorrupted nature. To the first colonists, the Atlantic shore, from Massachusetts to Florida, was a Garden of Eden. Fur trappers, adventurers, soldiers, and runaways who moved inland, to Kentucky, Ohio, Missouri, Oregon, and California, wrote with stars in their eyes about the majestic forests, prairies, and granite mountains on which they came, and settlers who followed them agreed that nowhere in the world, save where they were establishing their new homes, was there a land so sweet, so fair, so wondrous.

As long as there was a frontier, there was always a pull—to leave the towns and cities and works of man and move on beyond the crowd, to climb a ridge and see what lay on the other side, to go where it was quiet, where the pressures (or boredoms) of civilization fell away and disappeared, where a family could drink deeply of nature's works, and, in freedom and peace, find renewal. The pull never died. The continent was exploited, and man moved back from the Pacific, searching out the nooks and wilderness holes that had been left. A century ago it dawned on Americans that one day even these bypassed areas would be gone, and then there would be no Eden for their children and children's children. In March, 1872, the nation pulled up short and established Yellowstone National Park, more than two million acres of wilderness and natural wonders set aside to be left forever as nature created them. Yellowstone was unique, not only the first national park in the world, but a people's testament to the strength of the counterpull against their headlong, materialistic rush to conquer and use up their natural resources.

Ever since then, the two strains have been in contest. As industries rose and cities grew, as technological installations, real estate developments, dams, roads, and other man-made facilities spread across the land, the one national park grew into a far-flung system of many national parks, monuments, seashores, recreation areas, and wild river preserves. Local and state parks, some of them older than Yellowstone, proliferated, as did national forests, primitive and wilderness areas, wild game, fish, and bird sanctuaries, wetlands, and even lowly "vest pocket parks" that provided islands of rest and escape in crowded urban centers. And the race goes on—to save what can be saved of the America that was, and miraculously still is, before development and the symbols of "progress" overrun it forever.

By and large, what have been saved are the nation's great natural wonders—the physical and geological features that provide drama to the American landscape, as well as the remnants of the wildlife that once teemed on the continent. The miracle at first was that there were so many different wonders—stirring, awe-inspiring, and at the same time peculiarly comforting because they had a way of bringing man down to proper size and reminding him of the primordial bond that, after all is said and done, continues to make him a part of nature. But the second miracle was that the American people through the years have been able to thrust aside the exploiters' grasp and save for posterity so many of the wonders. They are all in this guidebook, state by state—the forests, mountains, seashores, geysers, lakes, caves, buttes, canyons, and other natural spectacles of the American land, to which our ancestors once journeyed to live among, and to which we now journey in increasing millions each year to visit. They provide enjoyment, recreation, education, and insights to the past, present, and future. Some of them, particularly the wilderness and primitive areas, offer the same challenges that helped to shape and sustain the American character during its formative stages. Others, easily accessible and gentle, demand less of the visitor. From all of them, however, flow inspiration, added appreciation of the variety and richness of the natural resources of the nation, and a renewal of one's own spiritual strength.   ALVIN M. JOSEPHY, JR.

The editors of this guidebook have attempted to give in a compact, portable format, a representative sampling of the natural wonders in each state. We have included a brief description of the physical features and flora and fauna of National Park Service properties: parks, lakeshores, seashores, recreation areas, riverways, trails, parkways, and scenic monuments and memorials. (A map showing the location of these federally-administered sites and an accompanying list can be found on pages 316–19.) All 155 national forests, with their wilderness and primitive areas, are also described in this volume. We have indicated which properties are in *The National Registry of Natural Landmarks*—sites containing geological, ecological, or other natural features illustrating the natural history of the United States. Those state, county, and municipal parks and forests with extraordinary scenic features are also listed, as are outstanding sites that are privately owned but open to the public. The locations of all entries are given immediately following their names. At the end of each entry is information on the hours and admission fees; in the case of federal properties, where fees vary according to several factors, a mailing address for more specific data is given. Because of space limitations, many beautiful and interesting sites could not be included. We hope, however, that you will find your favorite spot within.

B.D.C.

Half title page: mountain laurel in the Southern highlands. Title page: view of the Snake River and the Tetons from Yellowstone National Park. Copyright page: centuryplant in bloom in Arizona desert. Opposite: Otter Cliffs in Acadia National Park, Maine

ALABAMA

BANKHEAD NATIONAL FOREST
northwest Alabama, headquarters in Hayleyville and Double Springs

Situated in the northwestern part of the state, in a land of streams and lakes, the forest encompasses about 179,000 acres. The picturesque rock bluffs that border the waters of **Lake Lewis Smith** and rise from the deep canyons along the **Sipsey River** are examples of the rugged beauty to be found in the Bankhead.

The **Bee Branch Scenic Area** includes a virgin hardwood forest, interesting ferns and flowers, the largest yellow poplar—80 inches in diameter—known in the state, a rock-rimmed canyon with towering walls, and a small waterfall. The **Brushy Lake Area** has a scenic trail under high rock bluffs on the shore of a 33-acre lake. The **Corinth Area** abuts 21,000-acre Lake Lewis Smith which is surrounded by forest and sheer rock bluffs. A scenic trail along the picturesque bluffs leads to towering **Natural Bridge,** the longest natural bridge east of the Rockies. Two sandstone arches, formed by erosion millions of years ago, vault 148 feet across a ravine filled with wild flowers, lacy ferns, and magnolias. In the **Sipsey Area** there are scenic trails along the **Sipsey Fork of the Black Warrior River** that meander under bluffs and through stands of hardwoods. *For further information write: Box 40, Montgomery, Ala. 36101*

CATHEDRAL CAVERNS
Grant vicinity, off U.S. 72 and U.S. 431

These immense caverns are deep enough to contain a 12-story

Left: the Sipsey River in Bankhead National Forest. Right: Cathedral Caverns

building. There are fascinating calcite formations, including one that resembles a frozen waterfall, and a forest of brilliantly colored stalagmites. **Goliath,** a giant stalagmite, measures 200 feet at its base and is 60 feet tall.
Open June–Sept: daily 8:30–6; Oct–May: daily 9:30–4:30. Admission: adults $2.50, children (5–12) $1.00

CHEAHA STATE PARK
29 miles south of Anniston on State 21 and 49
The highest peak in Alabama—the 2,407-foot **Cheaha Mountain**—is located in Cheaha State Park. An observation tower at the summit of the scrub-covered slope affords a panoramic view.

CONECUH NATIONAL FOREST
southcentral Alabama, headquarters in Andalusia
Situated on the flat, sandy coastal plain in the southern part of the state, this forest covers almost 84,000 acres along the Alabama-Florida border. Highways run through the lush pine forests affording travelers views of the semitropical vegetation and the streams that meander through the forest. There are beautiful natural lakes (**Blue Pond** and **Open Pond**) and a wildlife management area for deer, turkey, and small game.
For further information write: Box 310, Andalusia, Ala. 36420

DAUPHIN ISLAND
35 miles south of Mobile on State 163
A barrier beach lying in the Gulf Stream at the entrance to **Mobile Bay,** Dauphin Island was the base in 1699 for the beginning of French colonization of Louisiana and the site of a fort that was part of the Battle of Mobile Bay in 1864. Today this 18-mile-long island is a tourist resort attracting sportsmen to its annual deep-sea fishing "rodeo." The north side of the island faces **Mississippi Sound,** while miles of white sandy beach and dunes on the south side overlook the **Gulf of Mexico.** Other noteworthy features of the island are its giant oaks, Indian shell mounds, and a bird sanctuary.

DESOTO STATE PARK
11 miles northeast of Fort Payne on U.S. 59
This 4,825-acre park with its luxuriant cover of wild azalea, mountain laurel, and rhododendron is noted for its scenic beauty. Spectacular **Desoto Falls** leaps 110 feet into a rock basin, and above it a lake offers recreational facilities. **Little River Canyon,** formed of sheer rock 500 to 800 feet deep, has been called the Grand Canyon of the South. The **Little River** is formed from underground springs on top of a mountain and meanders down across the floor of the canyon. A chairlift takes visitors down into the gorge where there are many hiking trails. A 20-mile scenic drive has been constructed along the west rim; an 8-mile drive passes along the south end. On the east rim there is a large state game reserve where deer, turkey, and other wild animals are protected.

DISMALS GARDENS
Phil Campbell vicinity, off U.S. 43
In a deep, tree-shaded gorge, a sunken natural garden thrives amidst brooks, waterfalls, and unusual rock formations. The names given to the rocks suggest their shapes: **Indian Chief, Pulpit Rock, Hogarth's Curve,** and **Dance Hall.** The latter is a large flat rock used by Chickasaw Indians for ceremonial dances. Nature trails

ALABAMA

wind across the garden's 80 acres of primeval vegetation, permitting close looks at the great variety of trees, herbs, mosses, ferns, and wildflowers. During the warm weather the rocks glow at night, due to tiny, twinkling phosphorescent worms called dismalites.
Open daily: 8–sunset. Admission: adults 90¢, children (6–12) 50¢

GUNTERSVILLE CAVERNS
9 miles south of Guntersville on State 79

Like other fascinating caves in Alabama, this one is spangled with multicolored flowstone and contains calcite formations and onyx deposits. There are also interesting fossil imprints.
Open Apr 15–Labor Day: daily 9–6; winter: daily 9–4. Admission: adults $1.50, children (5–12) 75¢

HURRICANE CREEK PARK
8 miles north of Cullman on U.S. 31

A deep and scenic gorge with an inviting swimming hole can be reached via a winding, 1½-mile-long nature trail. On the way down, one passes a swinging bridge, a natural spiral staircase, several waterfalls, and interesting foliage and rock formations. A small cable car is available for the ascent to the top.
Open daily: sunrise–sunset. Admission: adults 75¢, children 50¢

KYMULGA ONYX CAVE
5 miles east of Childersburg on State 76

Used as a dwelling by prehistoric man, this remarkably beautiful cavern, with its fascinating bright onyx formations, later became sacred to the Creek Indians. Today's visitors are shown trenches and wells made by Confederate soldiers, who were mining saltpeter for gunpowder, and an excavation of an ancient Indian burial site.
Open daily: 8–8. Admission: adults $1.50, children (6–12) 95¢

MANITOU CAVE
Fort Payne, 6 blocks off U.S. 11

More than 7,000 years ago, this mammoth cavern sheltered the early Indian inhabitants of the region. Later, the Cherokees used the cave and left their artifacts. All along the walls, floors, and ceiling are multicolored calcite sculptures of all sizes and shapes—the largest being the 40-foot-high stalagmite called the **Haystack**.
Open summers: daily 7–8; winters: daily 8–5. Admission: adults $1.50, children (6–11) 75¢

NOCCALULA FALLS PARK
Gadsden, 3 miles from I-59

The main attraction in this municipal park is Noccalula Falls, which drops almost 100 feet from a limestone ledge into the gorge below.

RICKWOOD CAVERNS
5 miles north of Warrior off I-65

The underground caverns contain limestone formations thought to be about 260 million years old. Many-hued stalactites and stalagmites and underground streams may be viewed by visitors.
Open May–Sept: 8–8; Oct–Apr: 8–5. Admission: adults $1.50, children (6–11) 75¢

ROCK BRIDGE CANYON
2 miles northwest of Hodges on State 172

The best view of Rock Bridge Canyon, once the home of Creek Indians, is from the top of massive **Ball Rock**. This sandstone out-

cropping with quartz striations looms 285 feet above the canyon
floor. In the park below a nature trail winds past unusual rock formations, caves, waterfalls, fern gardens, and springs that maintain
a constant temperature of 55°. The visitor can also walk across the
82-foot-long **Natural Rock Bridge,** 100 feet above the canyon.
Open daily: sunrise–sunset. Admission: adults $1.00, children 50¢

RUSSELL CAVE NATIONAL MONUMENT
8 miles northwest of Bridgeport, County Roads 91 and 75
Located on a 310-acre site in northeastern Alabama, Russell Cave
contains an almost continuous record of 8,000 years of man's life
on this continent. Archaeologists can date the earliest arrivals from
about 6500 to 7000 B.C. in the Archaic period. The cave was a seasonal haven for these early people who lived by hunting and gathering for nearly 7,000 years. Changes in the shape and style of the
artifacts indicate a richer and more complex way of life in the Woodland period from 500 B.C. to A.D. 1000. Shortly after 1000, the Indians moved into settled villages and began to make less and less
use of the cave. Cherokee Indians lived in this region after 1500 and
left a few objects that have been found very close to the surface.
For further information write: Box 175, Bridgeport, Ala. 35740

SEQUOYAH CAVERNS
Valley Head vicinity, 6 miles north and 1 mile west of U.S. 11
This huge cave, named in honor of the inventor of the Cherokee
alphabet, served as a haven for Cherokees who refused to leave their
homeland in 1838 when the federal government moved the Indians
westward on the "Trail of Tears." Noted for the brilliant colors of
its salmon, blue, and black rock formations, the cave is encrusted
with fossils dating from the era when ocean covered the area. Today waterfalls and pools reflect such wonders as **Sam Houston
Column**—a huge stalagmite autographed by Houston in 1836 while
on a visit to court his future wife, one of Sequoyah's daughters.
*Open summers: daily 8–7; winters: daily 8–5. Admission: adults
$1.50, children (6–12) 75¢*

TALLADEGA NATIONAL FOREST
central Alabama, headquarters at Centreville, Haflin, and Talladega
The largest of Alabama's four national forests covers 357,808 acres
in the central part of the state at the southern end of the **Appalachian
Mountain** chain. This is a region of rock cliffs overlooking wooded
valleys, of scenic drives and trails, and of abundant wildlife.
Some main features of this large area are: **Cahaba Mountain,**
with a scenic drive and rewarding views of the surrounding country;
Coleman Lake, a 27-acre lake within the Choccolocco game management area; **Horn Mountain,** with a scenic drive overlooking the
Coosa and **Tallapoosa** river valleys. Other natural lakes are 20-
acre **Lake Chinnabee** and 110-acre **Payne Lake;** the latter is surrounded by pine forests and there is a nature trail at its north end.
For further information write: Box 35, Talladega, Ala. 35160

TUSKEGEE NATIONAL FOREST
eastcentral Alabama, headquarters at Tuskegee
This 10,777-acre forest lies midway between mountains and coast
in the rolling hills of the Piedmont upland belt. In a pine grove at
Taska may be found a replica of the log cabin birthplace of educa-
tor Booker T. Washington.
For further information write: Box 390, Tuskegee, Ala. 36084

ALASKA

ALASKA PENINSULA
southcentral Alaska

This peninsula extends almost 500 miles southward from the Alaskan mainland, from **Bristol Bay** of the **Bering Sea** on the northwest to the **Pacific Ocean** on the southeast. The **Aleutian Range** runs the length of the peninsula, which contains many volcanoes, including those in Katmai National Monument (*see*). Other major volcanoes on the Alaska Peninsula include 4,420-foot **Aniakchak Crater** and 8,400-foot **Mount Veniaminof** (both Registered Natural Landmarks) as well as 8,900-foot **Paviof Volcano**. Aniakchak Crater, an active volcano with a diameter of about 6 miles, is situated in a pristine setting of great natural beauty. Starting on May 1, 1931, and continuing for 11 days, Aniakchak hurled 15.4 cubic miles of ash and lava out of its core and scattered the material some 20 miles around the countryside. **Surprise Lake**, in the crater, is the source of the **Aniakchak River**—the largest river flowing into the Pacific from the Alaska Peninsula. Mount Veniaminof, an active volcano, situated about 60 miles south of Aniakchak Crater, contains the most extensive crater-glacier in the nation. The 25-square-mile icefield in the crater makes it the only known glacier on the continent with a volcanic vent in its center. Brown bears are abundant in the area, and the volcano's slopes are calving grounds for caribou.

ALEUTIAN ISLANDS
southcentral Alaska

The misty, fogbound Aleutians are actually partially submerged peaks of the **Aleutian Range** that extend some 1,100 miles southwestward from the western tip of the Alaska Peninsula (*see*). The islands are divided into 4 main groups—the **Fox, Andreanof, Rat,** and **Near islands**—and the chain contains countless islets and rocks. The Aleutian Islands separate the frigid **Bering Sea** and the warm **Pacific Ocean** and boast some of the world's most intensive volcanic activity as well as some of its worst weather. They are regularly lashed by fierce gales and no more than 25 clear days can be expected each year. Almost completely treeless because of the high winds, the Aleutians do have a luxuriant cover of grass, moss, and shrubs—the result of the relatively mild temperatures, heavy rains, and fog. They are also surprisingly rich in wildlife. All but 7 of the 207 islands are included in the **Aleutian Islands National Wildlife Refuge**, which covers 4,250 square miles. The islands are breeding grounds of the sea otter and the habitat of large numbers of brown bears, caribou, Steller's sea lions, wolves, wolverines, reindeer, and a multitude of birds. The chain also contains 2 Registered Natural Landmarks. Symmetrical, 9,387-foot **Shishaldin Volcano** on **Unimak Island** is one of the world's most perfect volcanic cones, rivaling Japan's Fujiyama in beauty, and is still active. At nearby **Bogoslof Island** at least 6 island masses have risen in the last 130 years; Bogoslof's current land mass is comprised of remnants of the last 3 eruptions. A community of 5,000 Steller's sea lions share the island with about 50,000 sea birds.

Discovered by Vitus Bering in 1741, the Aleutians were acquired from Russia as part of the Alaska Purchase in 1867. Several of the islands were the scene of bitter fighting during World War II, and some still serve as military bases. They are extremely difficult to

Top left: Sitka spruce in Tongass National Forest. Top right: Portage Glacier in Chugach National Forest. Center: polar bears on Arctic ice. Below: Mount McKinley and Wonder Lake in Mount McKinley National Park

reach because of their isolation. There are scheduled flights to several islands, including **Unalaska, Umnak, Shemya,** and **Attu,** where the United States maintains permanent bases. However, military clearance is needed to visit defense installations.
For further information write: Aleutian Islands National Wildlife Refuge, Cold Bay, Alaska 99571

BROOKS RANGE

So massive that it is virtually a separate region in itself, the Brooks Range is made up of several mountain chains that together wall off Alaska's Arctic Slope area from its Central Plateau. The Range, which is the northernmost part of the Rocky Mountains, extends some 600 miles across the state from the **Chukchi Sea** on the west to the Canadian border. The Brooks Range includes the **De Long, Baird, Endicott,** and **Davidson** mountain chains. Its highest peak is 9,239-foot **Mount Michelson,** in the northeast corner of the state. This 150-mile-wide range effectively isolates the ice- and snow-filled Arctic wilderness, making the North Slope largely inacessible by land transportation. One of the few existing corridors is **Anaktuvuk Pass** in the Endicott Mountains. Once a major passageway on man's historic migration route from Asia to North America, the pass was unused for centuries except by migrating caribou. Today, a small Eskimo village at the pass faces the end of its seclusion since it sits on the proposed oil pipeline route from the North Slope. Another area of interest in the Brooks Range is **Walker Lake,** a Registered Natural Landmark situated on the south slope of the Range, about 240 miles east of Kotzebue. The lake and its environs encompass a full range of ecological communities ranging from a lush white spruce forest on the lake's shores to the barren talus slopes 2,000 feet above its waters.

CHUGACH NATIONAL FOREST
southcentral Alaska, headquarters at Anchorage

The nation's second largest forest after Tongass (*see*), Chugach covers almost 5 million acres in 2 major divisions. Its largest portion encompasses a coastal strip and the islands of **Prince William Sound,** stretching from **Cape Suckling** on the east roughly to Seward on the west. The other portion of the forest is on **Afognak Island,** just southwest of the Kenai Peninsula (*see*). The forest's name is derived from the Chugach Eskimos, who made their home in the Prince William Sound area.

The Chugach is a region of mountain peaks—including those of the **Chugach Range**—glaciers, lakes, and streams. It is an area where dramatic geological events are constantly taking place. On March 27, 1964, the Good Friday Earthquake occurred. In a matter of minutes it reshaped a shoreline, built up new lands, submerged former dry land, and moved about countless masses of ice. Portage Glacier, about 50 miles southeast of Anchorage, was in the heart of forest area affected by the 1964 quake. It lies within the 8,600-acre **Portage Glacier Recreation Area,** which has a visitor center, camping facilities, nature trails, as well as an outstanding view of Portage Glacier and its melt lake, where it "calves" its huge icebergs. Some of the bergs that float in 600-foot-deep **Portage Lake** weigh as much as 2 million tons. The forest also encompasses the southern end of mammoth **Columbia Glacier,** whose 2.5-mile-wide face abuts **Columbia Bay,** west of Valdez. The second largest tidewater glacier in North America after Malaspina (*see*), Columbia stands 200 feet above the water and reaches to the bottom, 75 fathoms down. This

Left: Mount Shishaldin on Aleutian Islands. Right: Glacier Bay

makes an ice wall 650 feet high.

The Chugach National Forest is also known for the size and variety of the trophy animals that live within its far-flung borders. These include Kenai moose, Dall sheep, brown and black bears, mountain goats, and elk. The **Copper Delta Game Management Area,** just east of Cordova, contains the largest known concentration of trumpeter swans (once thought extinct) in North America, as well as Canada geese and other waterfowl, and shorebirds. The forest has many exceptional fishing areas on the Kenai Peninsula. *For further information: 555 Cordova St, Rm 504, Anchorage, 99501*

GLACIER BAY NATIONAL MONUMENT
southeast Alaska, headquarters at Bartlett Cove

Situated at the north end of the Inside Passage (*see*), Glacier Bay is a spectacular region of deep fiords and primeval forests, of snow-clad peaks and awesome glaciers. The largest of all areas administered by the National Park Service (2,803,840 acres), it extends from **Cross Sound** on the south to the Canadian boundary on the north. A unique wilderness of great scientific interest, the monument's ponderously advancing and retreating glaciers provide a record of rhythmic changes in the climate of our continent. As recently as 1794, when Captain George Vancouver sailed through Icy Strait, Glacier Bay was filled by a towering ice sheet extending 100 miles to the north. In the next century the ice retreated 40 miles, tidewaters invaded the basin and filled narrow fiords, and a spruce-hemlock forest took the place of the receding ice on land. By 1916 the terminus of **Grand Pacific Glacier** stood 65 miles from the mouth of Glacier Bay. Nowhere else have glaciers receded at such a rapid pace.

Today the monument encloses 16 active tidewater glaciers. They offer spectacular shows when great blocks of ice crash into the sea creating huge waves and massive icebergs. At a safe distance boaters can observe **Muir, Johns Hopkins,** and **Margerie glaciers** "calving" (discharging) great columns of ice into the bay. The sheer ice cliffs of **Crillon Glacier** rise almost 200 feet above **Crillon Lake** and are reflected in the chill waters below. Equally impressive are the rugged peaks of the **Fairweather Range,** dramatically visible from the upper reaches of the bay. The highest peak in the range is **Mount Fairweather** at 15,300 feet.

Land recently covered by ice is quickly reinvaded by plant life in successive stages, all of which are strikingly illustrated in the monument. Quite close to the glacier fronts, Alaska brown bear, black bears, and rare "blue" bears may be sighted. Lynx, wolves, and coyotes range the area, while Sitka deer, moose, otters, and mink inhabit the forest. In the bay waters are hair seals, sea lions, and porpoises. Waterfowl in large numbers frequent the inlets and bald eagles inhabit the shorelands.

There are no roads leading to the monument, and this spectacular region must be approached by air or by boat. There are scheduled and charter flights from Juneau, and tour boats operate daily from Glacier Bay Lodge at Bartlett Cove from May 15 to September 15.

For further information write: Box 1089, Juneau, Alaska 99801

INSIDE PASSAGE, or INLAND PASSAGE
southeast Alaska

One of the most beautiful sea trips on the North American continent is the voyage north from Seattle, Washington, to Skagway, Alaska. For about 950 miles, one can thread through the chain of forested islands known as the **Alexander Archipelago.** This marine highway, which is within the boundary of Tongass National Forest (*see*), is lined with towering snow-covered peaks rising from the sea, fiords, and glaciers. The waterway is sheltered from the storms of the Pacific and because of the Japanese current, the climate is much milder than generally believed. Heavy fog generally covers the area, and the air is filled with the sweet, winy scent of spruce.

In the late 1700s Russian, French, English, and Spanish explorers sailed these coastal waters and gave names reflecting their nationalities to the islands of the archipelago—**Chichagof, Baranof, Kupreanof, Prince of Wales,** and **Revillagigedo.** The Inside Passage was one of the most-used routes to the gold strikes at Juneau and later to the Klondike. Today, its waters teem with fishing vessels bringing in huge catches of salmon and halibut.

KATMAI NATIONAL MONUMENT
southcentral Alaska, headquarters at King Salmon

This national monument covers over 4,200 square miles on the northeastern end of the **Alaska Peninsula.** The monument includes about 100 miles of ocean bays, fiords, and lagoons on **Shelikof Strait.** These waterways are backed up by a range of glacier-covered peaks and crater lakes, and an interior wilderness of forests, streams, long lake chains, and rivers, all abounding in wild game and fish. One of the most fascinating areas of the monument is the **Valley of Ten Thousand Smokes.** In June, 1912, **Novarupta Volcano** exploded and spewed forth great masses of pumice and rock fragments. Then white-hot ash swept down adjacent valleys and buried nearly 40 square miles of the valley floor under glowing ash. Because of hot gases rising through cracks in the ash, scientists later named this region, Valley of Ten Thousand Smokes. At about the same time as the Novarupta eruption, a column of molten rock under **Mount Katmai Volcano,** 6 miles to the east, drained through the fissures of erupting Novarupta, causing the entire top of Katmai to cave in. Today, the crater caused by Katmai's collapse is filled with a lovely jade-green lake.

Since the 1950s **Mount Trident** has been the most active volcano in the monuments' volcanic field, which extends along its coastal area for over 80 miles; however, 6 other volcanoes have also been active. Today all but a few of the fumaroles of the Valley of Ten Thousand Smokes have cooled and are inactive. However, the valley is still of great interest because of its multicolored tuff (porous rock) and the hardy plants struggling to reestablish cover over the barren ground.

About 30 kinds of land mammals have been observed at Katmai, including brown bears, moose, foxes, lynx, wolves, and hares. The coastal area, with its rocky outcroppings, abounds in marine life such as the Steller's sea lion and the hair seal. Waterbirds are plentiful in the lakes region, northwest of the volcanic area, and along the seacoast. Some 40 species of songbirds can be seen during the short spring and summer season, and bald eagles are quite common. Fishing is excellent throughout the area.

Katmai has no rail or road approaches, and there is no commercial boat service to any part of the monument. There are commercial flights to King Salmon, the **Bristol Bay** side of the peninsula, and scheduled flights from there to the Brooks River campground on **Naknek Lake.** Charter flights (including float planes) to other parts of the monument may be arranged. There are jeep tours, accompanied by a monument naturalist, which leave from the Brooks River campground and go to the lower end of the Valley of Ten Thousand Smokes.

For further information write: Box 7, King Salmon, Alaska 99613

KENAI NATIONAL MOOSE RANGE
southcentral Alaska, on Kenai Peninsula, headquarters at Kenai

This 1,730,000-acre range was established in 1941 to protect the Kenai moose and other native wildlife species—Dall sheep, mountain goats, caribou, brown and black bears, and a variety of smaller animals. Although the range is now bisected by the Sterling Highway and other routes that provide access to recreational facilities, much of it remains a pristine wilderness with characteristic Alaskan terrain. This national area is a highly scenic district—over 90 miles long and between 20 and 50 miles wide—that is divided into a mountainous region and a forested lowland. The **Kenai Mountains** in the moose range's southeastern sector rise to 6,000 feet and are treeless above the 1,800-foot level. Behind these peaks lies the **Harding Ice Field,** which thrusts its numerous glaciers down the mountains. The lowland region is covered by a spruce-birch-aspen forest. The range also supports 146 species of birds, including grebes, loons, gulls, terns, and trumpeter swans. Approximately 1,040,000 acres have outstanding wilderness qualities and are being considered for inclusion in the National Wilderness system.

For further information write: Box 500, Kenai, Alaska 99611

KODIAK ISLAND
southcentral Alaska, off Kenai Peninsula, 200 miles southeast of Seward

The largest of Alaska's islands (100 miles long and 10 to 60 miles wide), Kodiak was discovered in 1763 by a Russian explorer who was searching for sea otters. Today, this mountainous, heavily forested island is famous for the salmon and king crab in its waters and as the home of the giant Kodiak or Alaska brown bear. The **Kodiak National Wildlife Refuge,** a 2,800-square-mile domain covering the southwestern part of the island, provides a natural habitat for the famous bears, which are the world's largest carnivores. The island may be reached by either air or ferry from Anchorage, Homer, and Seward.

For further information write: Box 825, Kodiak, Alaska 99615

ALASKA

KOTZEBUE
Arctic Alaska, about 180 miles northeast of Nome

This famous Eskimo village is situated at the northwest end of **Baldwin Peninsula**, which juts out into **Kotzebue Sound**. The town is 30 miles north of the Arctic Circle and visitors come to ride dogsleds, fish through the ice, and in March and April embark on polar bear and wolf hunts. During a 2-week period between mid-May and mid-June there is a spectacular ice breakup and in the wake of this there is excellent fishing for Arctic shee. This is also the season when the huge (between 12 and 17 feet in length) beluga whale is caught. Kotzebue, situated on the treeless tundra and inaccessible by highway, may be reached by daily flights from Anchorage, Nome, and Fairbanks.

MALASPINA GLACIER
southeast Alaska, on northern shore of Yakutat Bay

Malaspina, the largest glacier in North America, covers an area of 1,500 square miles and is bigger than all of Rhode Island. It is an outstanding example of a piedmont glacier—a glacier that has spread out onto level land at the point of emergence from a mountain valley. Malaspina is described and illustrated in geology texts as exhibiting classic examples of glacial movement. Registered Natural Landmark

MATANUSKA VALLEY
southcentral Alaska, 43 miles northeast of Anchorage

The richest agricultural area in Alaska, this fertile, 60-mile-long valley is ringed by the **Chugach** and **Talkeetna mountains** and drained by the **Matanuska River**. In 1935 the federal government resettled farmers here from the drought-stricken Midwest. Today, about half of the farmers in sparsely-populated Alaska are concentrated in Matanuska Valley. Their large, lush vegetables (such as giant 70-pound cabbages) and dairy products are shown at an annual fair at nearby Palmer. The pleasing patchwork vista of the farms separated by stands of willow and cottonwood trees can be seen by taking the aerial tramway to the top of 888-foot **Bodenburg Butte,** a humplike formation on the valley floor.

MOUNT MCKINLEY NATIONAL PARK
interior Alaska, 163 miles west of Paxson via Denali Highway

The nation's second largest national park after Yellowstone, Mount McKinley is a wilderness area of 3,030 square miles of mountain peaks, alpine tundra, spruce forests, glaciers, and glacial streams. The park is situated at the southwestern end of the **Alaska Range,** a 600-mile-long arc of mountains that extends across southcentral Alaska. The park segment of this range includes 20,320-foot Mount McKinley, the tallest mountain on the North American continent. The Athabascan Indians aptly named this majestic mountain Denali or "The High One," for in the entire Alaska Range fewer than 20 peaks exceed 10,000 feet. Four of these are within the park's boundaries: **Mount Foraker** (17,400 feet), **Mount Silverthrone** (13,220 feet), **Mount Crosson** (12,800 feet), and **Mount Mather** (12,123 feet). Mount McKinley's 2 major peaks may be seen from several vantage points, but one must be patient because the icy summit is shrouded in clouds and fog nearly 60 per cent of the time.

The park's landscape is largely the result of glacial activity during the Ice Age, when huge rivers of ice sculptured the peaks of the Alaskas, producing their sawtoothed spires and knife-edged ridges, as well as the broad, U-shaped glacial valleys, the moraines, and the kettle lakes which characterize this mountain area. There are more than a dozen active glaciers in the park today—the largest are on the south side of the Alaskas in the basin of the **Chulitna** and **Yentna** rivers. These valley glaciers originate high on the southern slope, where they are continually nourished by the moisture-laden winds of the Pacific Ocean. The park's loftiest mountains have snowfields at their higher elevations, and these fields are the birthplaces of the few large valley glaciers that flow down the north slope of the Alaska Range. These include **Herron Glacier**, which originates in Mount Foraker's snowfields; **Peters Glacier**, which circles Mount McKinley's northwest end; and 35-mile-long **Muldrow Glacier**, the largest northward-flowing glacier in Alaska.

The park is home to 132 species of birds and 37 species of mammals—some found nowhere else in the national park system. Dall sheep (relatives of the Rocky Mountain bighorn), caribou, moose, grizzly bear, red fox, lynx, timber wolf, and the wolverine are some of the animals that may be sighted on the icy cliffs and grassy hillsides, in the spruce forests, or on the open tundra.

Denali Highway, the only park road, leads some 90 miles into the heart of McKinley's most scenic areas. Alternating between forest and tundra and paralleling the Alaska Range, the road goes from the entrance on the eastern boundary to Camp Denali, near the semiabandoned mining town of Kantishna just outside the park's northern border. The highway crosses many rivers and climbs 4 passes. About 70 miles from the park entrance is Eielson Visitor Center with many fine exhibits and interpretive programs. Between this center and Camp Denali is oval-shaped **Wonder Lake**, the park's largest lake. There are many opportunities to view McKinley's peaks along the highway, which at one point passes within 27 miles of the summit. Nature walks are scheduled daily in summer from the McKinley Park Hotel over *Morino* and *Horseshoe Lake trails;* a ranger explains the geology and plant and animal life. Denali Highway and most park facilities are open only in summer. *For further information write: McKinley Park, Alaska 99755*

POINT BARROW
Arctic Alaska, 9 miles northeast of Barrow on Arctic Ocean
The northernmost point of Alaska, Point Barrow is some 350 miles

The Alaska Range and Yentna Glacier in McKinley National Park

ALASKA

north of the Arctic Circle and lies within 1,300 miles of the North Pole. The headland is situated on the **Arctic Ocean**. To its west lies Siberia; to its east, Arctic Canada and Greenland; behind it stretches the limitless Arctic tundra, covered with wildflowers in summer; and in front of it is the huge Arctic ice pack. All along the huge Arctic coast millions of tons of ice are pushed up on the beach forming a massive ice wall.

Point Barrow is also in the land of the midnight sun. Here the sun does not set for 82 days in summer and does not rise above the horizon for 51 days in the winter. A visit to the permafrost ice caves, a cruise on the Arctic Ocean in an oomiak (a sea-going walrus skin boat), or a ride by husky dogsled are some of the highlights of an Arctic visit. There are no roads to Barrow or the cape, but there are scheduled daily flights to the town. From Anchorage and Fairbanks air tours are available to other Arctic centers such as Kotzebue, Saint Lawrence Island, and Point Hope.

POINT HOPE
Arctic Alaska, on Chukchi Sea

This peninsula, the westernmost point on Alaska's **Arctic Slope** area, is inhabited primarily by Eskimos. The Ipuitak Site on the cape's tip is a National Historical Landmark containing the remains of an ancient Eskimo community.

PRIBILOF ISLANDS
southcentral Alaska, in Bering Sea north of Aleutian Islands

The Pribilof Islands are a group of 4 islands—**Saint Paul, Saint George, Walrus,** and **Otter**—that were named for a Russian navigator in search of furs. Since then British, French, Spanish, and American as well as Russian fur hunters have been lured to the Pribilofs, which are exceedingly rich in seals and foxes. Indiscriminate hunting threatened the seal herds, but the 1911 convention between the United States, Britain, Russia, and Japan saved the herds from extinction. Today, the Pribilof seal herds are flourishing, and the beaches of Saint Paul Island are the single greatest source of fur seals in the world. The Saint Paul Seal Rookeries are a National Historical Landmark.

SAINT ELIAS RANGE
southeast Alaska, 70 miles northwest of Yakutat

The first recorded visit of white men to the Alaska mainland was the expedition of Vitus Bering, a Danish explorer in the service of Russia. On July 16, 1741, St. Elias' Day, Bering sighted and named 18,000-foot, ice-sheathed **Mount Saint Elias.** Standing on the Alaska-Yukon international boundary, it is one of the peaks of the Saint Elias Range which extends some 200 miles from Alaska into Canada, and is notable for the extensive glacier system—the world's largest apart from the Polar ice caps—that fills the valleys between the peaks. The system is a mammoth expanse of unbroken ice several thousand feet deep. It extends from Mount Saint Elias over 230 miles eastward to the **Alsek River Valley.** Some of the famous glaciers that originate in this range are **Bering, Hubbard, Malaspina,** and **Seward.**

SAINT LAWRENCE ISLAND
Arctic Alaska, in Bering Sea, near entrance of Norton Sound

Only 45 miles from the coast of Siberia, this treeless, tundra-covered island lies under a blanket of snow for over half the year. It is

90 miles long and between 8 and 22 miles wide and is of volcanic origin. The principal activities of the Eskimo population are whaling, walrus and seal hunting, and fox trapping. The island was discovered by Vitus Bering on St. Lawrence's Day, 1728.

SEWARD PENINSULA
southcentral Alaska

This peninsula, which is 210 miles long and between 90 and 140 miles wide, is surrounded by **Chukchi Sea** and **Kotzebue Sound** on the north, by the **Bering Strait** on the west, and by **Norton Sound** of the **Bering Sea** on the south. **Cape Prince of Wales,** at the peninsula's western end, is the most westerly point of the North American mainland. Opposite the cape, only 55 miles across the Bering Strait, is **Cape Dezhnev,** Siberia. In the center of the strait are the 2 bleak, rockbound **Diomede Islands**—Russian-owned Big Diomede and American-owned Little Diomede. The USSR-US boundary and the international date line run between these 2 islands. When it is Sunday on the smaller one, it is Monday only 2½ miles away on the larger island. For food, the Diomede islanders look to the plentiful supply of seal, walrus, and birds that funnel through Bering Strait. One can reach Little Diomede from Shismaref, a tiny Eskimo village off the northern coast of Seward Peninsula. Nome, on the peninsula's southern coast, was the site of a famous gold rush in 1898. Today, visitors can still pan for gold on its beaches, and Nome is the major city on the peninsula. It is accessible by plane from Anchorage and Fairbanks, and bush aircraft and charter planes serve the entire area. Popular activities in the Nome region include sled riding, ice fishing, and snowmobile rides to a reindeer herd. Guided hunting trips for bear, walrus, and seal can be arranged.

TONGASS NATIONAL FOREST
southeast Alaska, headquarters at Juneau and Ketchikan

This vast, 16-million-acre forest, which blankets virtually the entire **Panhandle** region, is the largest forest in the national system. An incredibly beautiful region of mountains and sea, fiords and forests teeming with fish and wildlife, it looks much the same as it did when the Indians first settled here. The Tongass is divided into 2 units, the northern one administered from Juneau and the southern one from Ketchikan.

Tongass is a rain forest, with mosses carpeting the floors and festooning the tree branches. Sitka spruce and western hemlock, the dominant timber species, are both well suited to the wet climate of southeast Alaska. Cottonwood trees thrive near river bottoms and along streams, and bog areas known as muskegs are also common. The profusion of wildflowers is evidence of the influence of the Japanese current that bathes the southern shores of Alaska, causing surprisingly temperate winters.

In the Tongass one can still witness the same processes that shaped the land during the Ice Age. There are literally hundreds of glaciers carving, grinding, and sculpting the landscape. The source of many of these glaciers is the **Juneau Icefield,** a 1,500-square-mile mass of flowing ice, just outside the forest's boundary, extending from the **Skagway River** in the north for nearly 100 miles to the **Taku River.** Mendenhall Glacier, north of Juneau, is a great valley glacier—12 miles long and 1.5 miles wide—that originated in the Juneau Icefield about a century ago. Mendenhall's massive faces and deep crevasses can be seen from steep trails on both its sides. **Mendenhall Lake** (115 feet deep in some places) is fed from

Aerial view of Ford's Terror Fiord in the Tongass

the melting ice of the slowly retreating glacier. The **Mendenhall Glacier Recreation Area** has a visitor center and offers interpretive talks about the glacier. From Petersburg one can take a boat trip to awesome **Le Conte Glacier,** the most southerly tidewater glacier in Alaska. It may be seen discharging huge icebergs into **Le Conte Bay.** The spectacular fiords of the **Tracy Arm-Ford's Terror Scenic Area** can be reached by charter plane or boat from Juneau. Another major forest attraction is the **Granite Fiords Wilderness Study Area,** a potential 500,000-acre wilderness reserve. Here one can see where retreating glaciers of the Ice Age carved 2 deep valleys into the land. These were filled with seawater to become fiords that are now known as **Rudyerd Bay** and **Walker Cove.** In addition to these "granite fiords," the ice cut back into the mountains to form valleys that became the beds of the **Chickamin** and **Leduc rivers.** The huge proposed wilderness tract extends from the Canadian borders to the tides of Behm Canal. It includes sea-washed cliffs streaked with waterfalls, forested valleys, open meadows, and occasional muskegs filled with many-hued mosses and lichen-covered pines. During the warm summer months, the region is filled with blue grouse, scurrying ptarmigan, and soaring eagles; in the uplands, agile mountain goats share the terrain with Sitka deer and bears.

The bays, channels, and inlets throughout the forest are famous for good salmon, and the many lakes and streams yield numerous types of trout. The forest wildlife includes mountain goats, deer, brown bear, moose, eagle, and waterfowl. Much of the forest may be seen from the decks of the ferries and cruise boats that ply the Inside Passage (*see*). Sitka, on **Baranof Island,** is the site of the **Sitka National Monument,** which preserves the Indian stockade where, in 1804, members of the Tlingit tribe made their last stand against the Russian fur traders. On **Kruzof Island,** across Sitka Bay from the town of Sitka, is **Mount Edgecumbe,** an extinct, snow-capped volcano. A forest trail leads to its crater.

For further information: Box 1628, Juneau, Alaska 99801

ALASKA

VALDEZ AREA
southcentral Alaska, about 120 miles east of Anchorage

Valdez is called the "Switzerland" of Alaska, because of the ring of snow-capped **Chugach Mountains** that surrounds it. The town which was moved 4 miles west of its original site because of damage sustained after the 1964 earthquake) lies on Port Valdez, a deep fiord on the rugged coast of **Prince William Sound** that is Alaska's northernmost ice-free port. The Valdez area is noted for its many scenic splendors. Old Valdez is the southern terminus of Richardson Highway (State 4), which originated as a dogsled route into the interior, and which connects the port of Valdez with Fairbanks, 371 miles inland. The first 30 miles of the highway are noted for fine alpine scenery. Just outside of Valdez, the highway skirts **Valdez Glacier.** In the summer, salmon may be seen in the many streams formed from its melt. Then crossing the **Lowe River** and leaving the forests, the highway climbs to **Keystone Canyon** from whose perpendicular walls cascade **Horsetail Falls** and **Bridal Veil Falls,** both 300-foot waterfalls. It then continues on to cross the backbone of the Chugach Range at its highest point, 2,722-foot **Thompson Pass.** It then descends into the valley, and at 2,070 feet there is an overlook of **Worthington Glacier,** a registered Natural Landmark. This typical, small valley glacier (4 miles long and 1½ miles wide) is very accessible for study and observation as there is a trail leading right up to it.

YUKON RIVER
interior Alaska

The mighty, 1,979-mile-long Yukon River is the third largest in North America after the Mississippi-Missouri and Mackenzie river systems. It is formed by the confluence of the **Pelly** and **Lewes** rivers at Fort Selkirk, Canada, from streams rising in British Columbia and the Yukon Territory. Flowing northwest to Dawson, it crosses the Alaska border near Eagle and continues north to Fort Yukon, 1 mile above the Arctic Circle. Then, in a wide southwest swing it flows downstream through the interior of Alaska to empty into the **Bering Sea** through several channels south of **Norton Sound.** Its chief tributaries are the **White, Stewart, Klondike, Porcupine, Innoko, Koyukuk, Tanana,** and **Chandalar rivers.**

Most of the history, exploration, and development of Alaska centers in the river system. In 1831 the town of Saint Michael was built near the mouth of the Yukon by the Russians who then explored and mapped the lower reaches of the river. At about the same time, the Hudson's Bay Company sent out explorers to set up a fur post on the upper reaches of the river. Established in 1847, Fort Yukon is the oldest English-speaking settlement in Alaska; for over 20 years it served as a major trading post for the Hudson's Bay Company. Today Fort Yukon is the largest village and trading post on the Yukon. It is also the most northerly point on the river, and the midnight sun is clearly visible in late June.

By 1895 miners were already panning for gold along the river, but it was not until the great Klondike Gold Rush of 1898 that the Yukon became a legend. During the Gold Rush the term "Yukon" referred to the entire area drained by its headwaters. The all-water route from St. Michael then upriver to Dawson, the Klondike boomtown, was but one of several to the goldfields. Others chose arduous overland trails, such as those beginning at Skagway, Yakutat, or Valdez. By 1900 the rush had passed, but it had focused importance on the riches and potential of the Alaska Territory.

ARIZONA

APACHE NATIONAL FOREST
southeast Arizona, headquarters at Springerville
Located on the Arizona–New Mexico border this spruce-pine-aspen forest is said to include some of the states' most beautiful country. **Blue River, Big Lake, Crescent Lake,** and the **White Mountains** are among the attractions. Foremost of the many drives through the forest is the *Coronado Trail* (U.S. 666) commemorating portions of the route taken by Francisco Vásquez de Coronado in 1540; sections of the remote wilderness through which the trail passes have changed little since the days of the conquistador. **Blue Range Primitive Area** and **Mount Baldy Wilderness** are also here.
For further information: Box 460, Springerville, Ariz. 85938

APACHE TRAIL
central Arizona
Once the route of raiding Indian parties, this 76-mile road (State 88) extends from Apache Junction, 30 miles east of Phoenix, through Tonto National Forest *(see)* to Globe. Built in 1905 to transport equipment for the construction of Roosevelt Dam, the trail winds and twists through country rich with exotic scenery. A west-to-east route affords the driver the security of the inside rock walls; the only nonpaved portion is a narrow 25-mile stretch between Tortilla Flat and Roosevelt. Besides cactus forests, colorful rock formations, and unusual plant life, two of the major attractions along the trail are: **Superstition Mountains,** so-named by Indians who believed that the craggy peaks represented humans turned to stone, and **Fish Creek Canyon,** an almost perfect box canyon called Walls of Bronze for the splendid colors of its sheer vertical walls.

BARRINGER METEOR CRATER
Winslow vicinity, 19 miles west and 6 miles south of U.S. 66
Scientists estimate that this crater, the largest known of its kind in the United States, was caused about 22,000 years ago by a meteor ranging in size from 1 million to 10 million tons. The diameter of the 570-foot-deep crater is 4,150 feet at the rim. A museum and observatory are on the north rim. Registered Natural Landmark *Open daily during daylight hours. Admission: adults $1.25; children (13–18) 75¢, (6–12) 50¢*

CANYON DE CHELLY NATIONAL MONUMENT
Navajo Indian Reservation, 1 mile east of Chinle
Best known for the ruins of Indian cliff dwellings built into its walls, Canyon de Chelly is also a natural wonder of dramatic beauty. Sheer vertical walls of red sandstone, laid down more than 200 million years ago, stretch 30 to 1,000 feet above the **Rio de Chelly** and its tributaries. Ruins of several hundred Indian villages, most of them built between A.D. 350 and 1300, are scattered among Canyon de Chelly and **Canyon del Muerto,** the two principal canyons that with **Monument** and **Black Rock canyons** comprise the monument.
The ruins can be seen from 5 lookout points on a drive along the south rim of Canyon de Chelly. At the far end of the drive, at the junction of Canyon de Chelly and Monument canyon, one can look down 1,000 feet onto **Spider Rock,** a slender sandstone spire towering 800 feet above the canyon floor. A mile-long hiking trail leads from the drive to White House Ruin; this is the only place

Top left: descending the Grand Canyon by mule. Right: Saguaro National Monument. Below: Teepee formations in Petrified Forest National Park

where unescorted visitors are permitted into the canyons.
Visitor center open daily: winter 8–5, summer 8–6.
For further information write: Box 588, Chinle, Ariz. 86503

CHIRICAHUA NATIONAL MONUMENT
southeast Arizona, 36 miles southeast of Willcox

The weirdly shaped and precariously balanced volcanic rocks of Chiricahua National Monument represent billions of years of unending geological change. The result of volcanic eruptions, mountain building, and erosion by weather and water, these fantastic monoliths are still subject to the forces of nature. This field of grotesque rhyolite pinnacles sits high in the **Chiricahua Mountains,** once the home of the Apaches, who called this area Say Yahdesut (Point of Rocks). Now the mountains, with elevations ranging from 5,160 to 7,365 feet, are inhabited by Arizona white-tailed deer, coatis, peccaries, rodents, and many species of birds.

The monument is best viewed along the 15 miles of hiking (*Echo Canyon Trail*) and bridle trails where beds of the volcanic ash that formed the rocks can frequently be seen. Among the major formations are: **Cochise Head,** named for the Apache chief; **Punch and Judy; Album of Rocks,** a series of slender pillars; **Thor's Hammer;** and **Big Balanced Rock,** weighing about 1,000 tons and resting on a 4-foot-thick base. A paved drive also leads through **Bonita Canyon** to a lookout at *Massai Point*—named for the Apache warrior who, after escaping his white captors, made these mountains his hide-out for 3 years. **Sugarloaf Peak,** one of the highest points in the monument, offers exciting views in all directions. At the monument headquarters, a mile beyond the entrance, exhibits are set up to explain the natural history of the area.

For further information write: Dos Cabezas Star Route, Willcox, Ariz. 85643

COCONINO NATIONAL FOREST
central Arizona, headquarters at Flagstaff

This 1,800,738-acre pine forest located on a plateau in central Arizona varies in elevation from 3,500 to 12,670 feet. Many roads lead through the forest to its scenic attractions, including **Oak Creek Canyon,** considered to be one of the most beautiful canyons in the state. Highway 89A leads from the head of the canyon down red, white, and yellow rock walls dotted with pine, cypress, and juniper to the bottom 1,500 feet below. A drive in the northern end of the forest leads to **Humphrey's Peak,** one of the **San Francisco Peaks,** a series of extinct volcanoes. Reaching an altitude of 12,670 feet, it is the highest point in Arizona. The forest's other attractions include **Lake Mary,** and **Sycamore Canyon Primitive Area,** noted for vividly colored rocks and Indian ruins.

For further information write: Box 1268, Flagstaff, Ariz. 86006

COLOSSAL CAVE
22 miles southeast of Tucson on U.S. 10 and Old Spanish Trail Rd

Explorers have never been able to locate the end of this large underground cavern carved from a great vein of Escabrosa limestone. Here one can see interesting formations of stalagmites, stalactites, and calcite columns bearing such exotic names as **Frozen Waterfall, Kingdom of the Elves,** and **Praying Nuns.** The caves maintain a constant temperature of 72°; guided tours are available.
Open Mon–Sat 8–6, Sun and holidays 8–7

CORONADO NATIONAL FOREST
southeast Arizona, headquarters at Tucson

This forest covers nearly 1,800,000 acres in 12 widely scattered sections of Arizona and New Mexico. Because of the variance in elevation from 3,000 to 10,720 feet, one can pass in an hour's drive from barren desert to thick pine and fir forests. Scenic drives lead to some of the forest's many beautiful spots: *Hitchcock Highway* leads to **Mount Lemmon**—the southernmost ski area in the continental United States; *Swift Trail* to **Mount Graham**—the highest point in the forest; *Onion Saddle Road* through a section of the **Chiricahua Mountains.** Other features include **Cochise Stronghold,** a natural rock fortress, once used by the famed Indian chief; **Galiuro Wilderness;** and **Santa Catalina Mountains Recreation Area.** A visitor center is located at **Sabino Canyon.**
For further information write: Box 551, Tucson, Ariz. 85702

GLEN CANYON NATIONAL RECREATION AREA. *See* UTAH

GRAND CANYON NATIONAL PARK
headquarters at Grand Canyon Village on South Rim

One of the world's outstanding scenic and geological attractions, Grand Canyon is a 1-mile-deep, 217-mile-long gorge measuring from 4 to 18 miles in width. As a tourist site it is perhaps unrivaled for its spectacular multicolored peaks and walls, incredible beauty, and awesome magnitude; and as a geological phenomenon it is without equal. Begun as a gully, the canyon was "dug out" by the downcutting of the **Colorado River** and its tributaries and widened by various types of weathering and by an erosional process called "mass wasting." The canyon is constantly being deepened and widened by these same forces, although the change is imperceptible. What has been exposed is a huge slice of the earth's crust representing 2 billion years of geological development. Here scientists can observe layer upon layer of rock ranging from the Precambrian to Recent epochs. Because of the variations in elevation—from 2,000 feet above sea level at the river to nearly 9,000 feet on the North Rim—plant and animal life indigenous to areas from northern Mexico to southern Canada can be found.

The park is divided by the canyon span into 2 sections, the **North Rim** and the **South Rim,** each affording spectacular views from

Oak Creek Canyon in Coconino National Forest

scenic roads and trails. In addition, many arduous trails lead from the rims of the canyon to the Colorado River below. The South Rim, some 7,000 feet above sea level on the **Coconino Plateau,** is accessible year round by 2 drives. Among the best observation points along 8-mile *West Rim Drive* are *Hopi* and *Mohave points.* The canyon is best seen from here at dusk when the setting sun casts its glowing tones. *East Rim Drive,* a 25-mile road, ends at *Desert View* where the Watchtower offers an excellent panorama not only of the river and the canyon but of the Painted Desert and Kaibab National Forest (*see both*) beyond. Fine vistas are available to hikers from *West Rim Trail* and *Canyon Rim Trail.* The North Rim on the **Kaibab Plateau** can be reached by a scenic road or along a network of trails leading from the South Rim down into the canyon. Because the North Rim is 2,000 feet higher than the South, it is usually snowbound in winter and its 2 drives are closed from mid-October to mid-May. *Cape Royal,* another excellent viewing place, lies at the end of a 26-mile road; en route is *Point Imperial* (8,801 feet)—the highest spot on the canyon rim. A somewhat primitive road leads through the Kaibab National Forest to *Point Sublime,* where one is afforded the best view of the spectacular **Inner Gorge.** Among the trails that lead along the North Rim are *Cape Royal Trail* and *Bright Angel Point Trail,* a short self-guided walk from which the visitor can look across the South Rim to the **San Francisco Peaks** beyond.

Adjacent to the park is the **Grand Canyon National Monument,** a 310-square-mile primitive area, one of the most remote in northern Arizona. Perhaps the best view of the canyon is visible here from *Toroweap Point* where one can look straight down the steep walls to the Inner Gorge of the Colorado River 3,000 feet below.

For further information write: Box 129, Grand Canyon, Ariz. 86023

GRANITE DELLS
6 miles north of Prescott on U.S. 89

Also called **Point of Rocks,** this lovely scenic area is noted for the imposing granite formations that line the highway here for two miles. Many picturesque lakes are dotted among these weirdly shaped pink, gray, brown, and red stone walls.

HUALAPAI VALLEY JOSHUA TREES
45 miles north of Kingman on U.S. 93

This dense stand of Joshua trees is considered to be the best extant display of the species. Some of the trees are 25 to 30 feet high and measure up to 3 feet in diameter. Here too ecologists have a fine example of the **Mojave Desert** ecosystem. Eligible Registered Natural Landmark

KAIBAB NATIONAL FOREST
northcentral Arizona, headquarters at Williams

Divided into 4 sections, this forest contains the **Grand Canyon Game Preserve,** home of the famous North Kaibab deer herd and wild buffalo herd. This is also the only habitat of the Kaibab squirrel. In addition to scenic drives through pine, spruce, and aspen forests dotted with open meadows, other points of interest include **Bill Williams Mountain, Cataract Lake, Whitehorse Lake,** and **Sycamore Canyon Primitive Area,** noted for vividly colored cliffs and interesting Indian ruins.

For further information write: Box 817, Williams, Ariz. 86046

LAKE MEAD NATIONAL RECREATION AREA
visitor center, 4 miles east of Boulder City, Nevada

Extending for about 240 miles along the Arizona–Nevada border, this recreation area is made up of **Lakes Mead** and **Mohave** and the surrounding scenic country—a variety of desert, plateaus, and canyons. Created by the construction of Hoover Dam, Lake Mead is one of the world's largest artificial lakes. It is 115 miles long, has a 550-mile shoreline, and is 589 feet deep. Lake Mohave, backed up by Davis Dam, is 67 miles long and, like Lake Mead, offers a wide variety of water sports and other recreational facilities.

An especially scenic spot within the park is Pierce Ferry, Arizona, about 50 miles northeast of Hoover Dam. From here, in the **Grand Wash Cliffs**, one can see **Iceberg**, **Virgin**, and **Boulder** canyons to the west, and to the east the lower gorge of the **Colorado River** where Lake Mead meets the **Grand Canyon.** Shivwits Plateau, a 7,000-foot mesa, lies to the north. At Hoover Dam, one of the most spectacular man-made wonders in the world, guided tours and exhibits are offered.

For further information: 601 Nevada Hway, Boulder City, Nev. 89005

MARBLE CANYON NATIONAL MONUMENT
north of Grand Canyon, off U.S. 89

This awesome canyon, cut out by the mighty **Colorado River,** is famous for its imposing, 3,000-foot vertical walls of red standstone and white limestone. Lying between **Glen Canyon** and **Grand Canyon,** of which it is in fact a northern extension, it completes protection of a continuous 300-mile boating route on the Colorado. Among the famous rapids included in this 50-mile stretch of river are those at **Badger Creek, Soap Creek, Sheer Wall, House Rock,** and **President Harding.** Bounded by Kaibab National Forest, Grand Canyon National Park, (*see both*), Navajo Indian Reservation, and Glen Canyon National Recreation Area (*see Utah*), this small but spectacular monument is truly one of the world's great scenic wonders. There are fine views of Marble Canyon from the rims and from Navajo Bridge (U.S. 89A), which crosses the canyon.

For further information: Grand Canyon National Park, Box 129, Grand Canyon, Ariz. 86023

MOGOLLON RIM
74 miles southeast of Flagstaff via Long Valley

This ridge forms a natural barrier across 200 miles of central Arizona and marks the boundary of the **Coconino Plateau.** *Mogollon Rim Drive* leads along the 2,000-foot-high forested cliff and offers views of Coconino, Sitgreaves, and Tonto National Forests (*see all*).

MONTEZUMA CASTLE NATIONAL MONUMENT
5 miles northeast of Camp Verde on State 79

When early white settlers first saw this 20-room, 5-story dwelling sitting in a natural cave high on a limestone cliff, they thought it had been built by Aztecs and mistakenly named it for the famed Indian leader. The castle and the many other ruins here were in fact built by farming Indians who moved into the area in the 12th century.

The bluffs that house these dwellings sit on the north side of **Beaver Creek,** a tributary of the **Verde River.** They were formed millions of years ago when a lava flow dammed the mouth of the river creating a large lake. Subsequently the Verde and its tributaries deposited great quantities of limy mud in the lake. About 2 million years ago, after the lava dam had been worn away, the lake drained.

ARIZONA

The rivers then cut channels into the dried-out sediment thereby creating the limestone cliffs; further erosion widened the valleys.

Seven miles northeast in a separate section of the national monument is a limestone sink 470 feet in diameter and 70 feet deep. Many dwellings surround this well, which was used as a source for irrigation. Because the lime in the soil cemented the irrigation ditches the Indians built, they are still visible today.

Open May–Sept: daily 7–7. Oct–Apr: daily 8–5.

For further information write: Box 218, Camp Verde, Ariz. 86322

MONUMENT VALLEY NAVAJO TRIBAL PARK
Navajo Indian Reservation, Navajo Route 18

This vast area stretching for miles across northern Arizona and southern Utah is located within the Navajo Reservation and is famous for the huge blocks of red sandstone that loom as high as 1,000 feet above the valley floor. Carved into spires, pillars, and other unusual formations by the forces of erosion, these red monuments have been compared to the ruins of ancient Greek temples. One such "temple," **Agathla Peak,** has a spire 1,255 feet above its base. Once an isolated area the Tribal Park, which also includes **Mystery** and **Cane valleys,** is now open to the public. An excellent overview of the valley is available at the visitor center, 4 miles southeast of Utah State 47.

OAK CREEK CANYON. *See* COCONINO NATIONAL FOREST

ORGAN PIPE CACTUS NATIONAL MONUMENT
southwest Arizona, 140 miles south of Phoenix

Situated on the Arizona–Mexico border, this national monument was established in 1937 to preserve a segment of the **Sonoran Desert** which provides a stark, but beautiful, background for the organ pipe cactus and other desert plants found only in this section of the country. The organ pipe cactus takes its name from the shape of its tubular arms which grow to 20 feet or more forming clusters of branches resembling organ pipes.

The monument can be seen by driving along two scenic routes or by hiking along several nature trails. The 20-mile *Ajo Mountain Drive* passes along the steep canyons of the **Ajo Mountains** and includes many of the tallest stands of the organ pipes. The 51-mile *Puerto Blanco Drive* parallels the historic Camino del Diablo, a hazardous desert route established by the Spanish about 1700. The road skirts the **Puerto Blanco Mountains** and the Mexican border. Side roads lead from this drive to **Dripping Springs,** to a man-made oasis at Quitobaquito, and to **Senita Basin,** where the senita cactus grows. Hiking trails include *Desert View Nature Trail*, a mile-long road leading to a ridge overlooking the **Sonoyta Valley,** a 1½-mile trail to **Bull Pasture,** and a ¼-mile road to Dripping Springs. All visitors are advised to register at the visitor center where both scenic drives begin.

For further information write: Box 38, Ajo, Ariz. 85321

PAINTED DESERT

Extending for 300 miles from the edge of the **Grand Canyon** along the **Colorado** and **Little Colorado** rivers to the **Petrified Forest,** the Painted Desert is a kaleidoscope of color and a maze of intricately woven ravines, crests, and peaks. These badlands are the result of widespread erosion from torrential rains in an area devoid of vegetation. The spectacular colors, for which the region is legendary,

Rock formations in Monument Valley

are caused by mineral impurities in the volcanic ash left by eruptions millions of years ago. The colors are most vivid in the early morning and late afternoon, especially after a shower. Petrified Forest National Park (*see*), **Navajo National Monument,** and **Wupatki National Monument** are located in the desert.

PAINTED ROCKS STATE HISTORIC PARK
Gila Bend, 10 miles north of I-8 on Painted Rocks Rd
These 40-to-50-foot dark gray boulders are believed to have marked a boundary and commemorated a permanent peace treaty between the Yuma and Maricopa Indians. Covered with primitive drawings of men and animals, the Painted Rocks were a landmark to early travelers in the Arizona desert.

PETRIFIED FOREST NATIONAL PARK
26 miles east of Holbrook on U.S. 66 or 19 miles east on U.S. 180
This spectacular display of petrified wood—the largest in the world —covers 94,189 acres, partially in the eroded badlands of Arizona's Painted Desert (*see*). Over 180 million years ago, the area was a low-lying basin of streams and trees; in successive ages the trees were felled, buried under layers of mud and volcanic ash, and permeated by a water solution containing silica, thereby creating the colorful quartz for which the park is famous. Finally lifted by the processes of mountain building and exposed by erosion, the "trees" emerged as multicolored stone logs. The park is divided into 6 major forests, each noted for some outstanding feature: **Long Logs,** where some specimens are more than 100 feet long; **Jasper Forest,** famous for its particular opaque variety of reddish-brown and yellow quartz; **Crystal Forest,** boasting perfectly formed crystals of pure quartz and amethyst; **Black Forest,** an inaccessible area of dark-colored

stones; **Rainbow Forest,** the largest fossil area in the park; and **Blue Mesa,** featuring interesting combinations of petrified wood and soft clay. The Petrified Forest also features some 300 archaeological sites dating from A.D. 300 to 400, when Indians of the Pueblo and other cultures lived in the region.

The spectacular sites here are best viewed from the 28-mile scenic route that extends from the Painted Desert to the Rainbow Forest. In addition to the major forests, some interesting points along the route are: *Kachina Point,* a lookout offering a panoramic view of the Painted Desert; **Newspaper Rock,** a huge sandstone boulder covered with Indian petroglyphs; **The Teepees,** a series of peaks showing erosion of soft clay deposits; **Agate Bridge,** a natural bridge created by a 100-foot log embedded in sandstone spanning a 40-foot-wide ravine; *Jasper Forest Overlook;* and **The Flattops,** large sandstone-capped mesas and buttes that have not succumbed to erosion. Rainbow Forest Museum offers many interesting exhibits and displays some of the longest logs in the park.

For further information write: Holbrook, Ariz. 86025

PRESCOTT NATIONAL FOREST
central Arizona, headquarters at Prescott

With elevations increasing from 3,000 to 8,000 feet, this forest features plant life adaptable to its changing altitudes—grassland at lower elevations, piñon and juniper trees at middle ranges, and ponderosa pine at the heights. Scenic highlights include **Thumb Butte,** a granite formation eroded into the shape of a giant lion; **Mingus Mountain,** a 7,600-foot volcanic plateau; **Granite Mountain** and many scenic but primitive drives winding through the forest. **Sycamore Canyon** and **Pine Mountain primitive areas** are two unspoiled regions accessible by foot or on horseback.

For further information write: 344 S Cortez, Prescott, Ariz. 86301

SAGUARO NATIONAL MONUMENT
visitor center, 17 miles east of Tucson

Reaching heights of up to 50 feet, weighing from 6 to 10 tons, and sometimes living 200 years, the giant saguaros of the **Sonoran Desert** stand in two **Cactus Forests** of this national monument. The plant, unique to this region, is composed of a stem of spongy tissue supported by slender ribs. During the rainy seasons, water is soaked up through the root system and stored in the spongy tissue; a mature plant can absorb as much as a ton of water, which it lives on in dry periods. Known as the apartment house of the desert, the giant saguaro provides homes for such desert birds as the Gila woodpecker, the great horned owl, and the gilded flicker. Birds and insects are also attracted to the nectar of the creamy-white flowers, Arizona's state flower, that bloom on the cactus in May and June.

The National Monument is located in 2 separate areas: the **Rincon Mountain** section and the **Tucson Mountain** section, lying east and west of Tucson. A 9-mile loop road with short side trails winds through the larger Rincon Forest, where peccaries, the little wild pigs of the desert, can be seen. Beyond the forest are the **Tanque Verdes Mountains** and the Rincons; trails lead to the mountain tops. The Tucson section of the Monument, located 15 miles west of the city, features a dense forest of young saguaros. Many animals native only to this region can be seen along the dirt roads and hiking trails here.

Visitor center open daily 8–5.

For further information write: Box 17210, Tucson, Ariz. 85710

SITGREAVES NATIONAL FOREST
central Arizona, headquarters at Holbrook

Smallest of the national forests in the Southwest, Sitgreaves covers less than 800,000 acres of the ponderosa pine forest of the **Colorado Plateau**. The drive along **Mogollon Rim** (*see*) here affords beautiful views of **Pleasant Valley** and the Fort Apache Indian Reservation below. Eight beautiful lakes provide excellent trout fishing.
For further information write: Box 908, Holbrook, Ariz. 86025

SOUTH MOUNTAIN PARK
8 miles south of downtown Phoenix on Central Ave

Except for a few developed areas, this large, municipally owned desert park of 14,817 acres has been preserved in its natural state. Among the interesting rock formations, canyons, and desert terrain one can find over 300 plant specimens and many species of animals and birds. Forty miles of hiking and saddle trails—the most popular is to **Hidden Valley**—lead to the park's natural wonders. One of the most scenic drives winds to *Dobbin's Lookout* and **Mount Suppoa**, (elevation 2,660 feet) which offers views of Phoenix, the **Salt River Valley, Squaw Peak,** and the **Camelback Mountains.**
Open daily: 8–midnight

SUNSET CRATER NATIONAL MONUMENT
16 miles northeast of Flagstaff off U.S. 89

Sunset Crater, a 1,000-foot-high truncated cone, is the result of the most recent eruption of a member of the **San Francisco Peaks** volcanic field that covers 3,000 square miles of northern Arizona. In about A.D. 1065 when the great eruption occurred, volcanic ash, molten lava, and cinders were spread over the area. Later, minerals deposited around the rim of the crater by vapors escaping from vents near the base stained the cinders and produced the glowing sunset colors for which this national monument is named. Dark at the

Superstition Mountains in Tonto National Forest (see page 34)

bottom and gradually changing from rosy tones to yellow, the now-extinct volcano seems to be in a state of perpetual sunset.

Except for trees and other plant life that have sprung up among the lava and cinders, Sunset Crater looks almost exactly as it did when the volcano erupted over 900 years ago. The spots of interest within the monument—such as some of the lava flow and a lava cave —can be seen along *Lava Flow Nature Trail*. An 18-mile paved road leads through the cinder-covered hills of Coconino National Forest (*see*) to **Wupatki National Monument,** where the ruins of the villages of the Indians who inhabited the area until the 13th century can be seen.

Visitor center open daily: winter 8–5; summer 8–7.

For further information: Tuba Star Route, Flagstaff, Ariz. 86001

TONTO NATIONAL FOREST
central Arizona, headquarters at Phoenix

Although much of this forest of nearly 3 million acres is inaccessible, many of its physical attractions can be seen along such scenic roads as the *Apache Trail, Mogollon Rim Drive* (*see both*), and *Beeline Highway*. In addition over 16,000 acres here are composed of man-made lakes—**Apache, Canyon,** and **Saguaro lakes** on the **Salt River** and **Bartlett** and **Horseshoe lakes** on the **Verde River.** Other attractions are the **Mazatzal Wilderness,** which embraces the north end of the **Mazatzal Range;** the **Sierra Ancha Wilderness,** whose rough mountains have precipitous box canyons and high vertical cliffs; and **Superstition Wilderness,** which is the site of the inhospitable **Superstition Mountains** and the legendary Lost Dutchman Gold Mine. The **Pine Mountain Primitive Area,** which extends into Prescott National Forest (*see*), contains islands of ponderosa pine surrounded by desert mountains with hot, dry mesas and deep canyons.

For further information write: Room 6208, Federal Building, 230 N First Ave, Phoenix, Ariz. 85025

TONTO NATURAL BRIDGE
12 miles northwest of Payson off the Pine–Payson Rd

Spanning the intricate maze of grottoes and caves of **Pine Creek Canyon,** this natural bridge rises 128 feet above the creek at one end and 150 at the other. A massive arch of travertine on limestone walls, it extends over an opening 150 feet wide and 400 feet long. Evidence has been found of prehistoric habitation among the stalagmites and stalactites of the caves below.

Admission: adults $1.00, children (12–17) 50¢

WALNUT CANYON NATIONAL MONUMENT
7½ miles east of Flagstaff, 3 miles south off U.S. 66 or I-40

Now the site of the ruins of more than 300 cliff rooms, this area was settled by the Sinagua Indians in the 12th century following the eruption of the volcano (*see* **Sunset Crater**) that transformed this arid land into rich farming soil. The 400-foot-deep canyon provided a foundation for the dwellings which were built into the long, shallow cavelike recesses created in the limestone walls when soft layers of stone eroded faster than the harder layers. A paved trail leads to 25 of the cliff rooms; along the trail many of the plants and animals important in the lives of these early Indians can still be seen. Another trail leads along the canyon rim and offers fine views of the surrounding scenery.

Open May–Sept: daily 7–7. Oct–Apr: daily 8–5.

For further information: Route 1, Box 790, Flagstaff, Ariz. 86001

ARKANSAS

BLUE SPRING
7 miles west of Eureka Springs on State 62

One of the world's largest, this natural spring in the **Ozarks** produces 38 million gallons of water daily. It is located near Eureka Springs, a town boasting 63 natural springs within its limits. Near Blue Spring is **Pivot Rock**, a large balanced rock 15 times larger at its top than at its base.

BUFFALO RIVER STATE PARK
17 miles south of Yellville on State 14 and 3 miles east on State 268

The National Park Service has called the Buffalo River "one of the few rivers still possessing exceptional wilderness value." Located in the **Ozark Mountains** the river passes through some of the state's wildest and most scenic country. Most oustanding is the portion included in Buffalo River State Park, a 2,160-acre site noted for its rugged terrain and many caves, waterfalls, springs, and unusual rock formations. Floating trips by canoe or flatbottom johnboat are very popular on the Buffalo. One of the best trips, through the river's wildest section, is the 5-day run from the state park to its junction with the **White River**. A highlight on the river is **Hemmed-In Hollow**, a box canyon with a 200-foot, free-falling waterfall.

BULL SHOALS CAVERNS
½ mile south of Bull Shoals off State 178

These underground caverns feature interesting displays of rock formations. Located in the **Ozarks,** the caverns are adjacent to a restored 1890 mountain village and near Bull Shoals Dam, one of the country's largest concrete dams. Near the caverns is **Bull Mountain** with an observation tower at its summit.
Open: Apr–Oct: daily 8–6. Admission: adults $1.50, children 75¢

Above: the White River and a mountain landscape in Ozark National Forest

ARKANSAS

DEVIL'S DEN STATE PARK
13 miles west of Winslow on State 74

Situated in a rugged, wooded section of the **Boston Mountains** in the **Ozarks**, this 4,320-acre park, the state's largest, is notable for the deep cracks and crevices caused by a folding of the earth's crust. **Devil's Den Cave** and **Ice Box Cave**, where temperatures never rise above 60°, are among the many scenic attractions.

HOT SPRINGS NATIONAL PARK

Set in a bustling resort city of the same name, Hot Springs was first recognized as a national wonder in 1832 when Congress created the Hot Springs Reservation. Now encompassing over 1,000 acres, it is still visited for the 47 thermal springs that miraculously produce more than a million gallons of water daily at an average temperature of 143°. Why the springs produce hot water is unknown, although various theories—such as chemical reactions, friction, compression, and masses of underground hot rocks—have been suggested. It is known that the springs lie along a fault in the earth's crust in the valley between **West** and **Hot Springs mountains**, 2 of the 5 mountains included in the park. (The others are **Sugarloaf, North,** and **Indian mountains.**) Of the 47 springs only 2 **Display Springs** are open so that visitors can see how the water emerges from the ground. The other 45 springs are sealed to prevent contamination, then the water is cooled, collected, and piped to reservoirs for use in the 17 bathhouses in the park and the city.

The self-guided, mile-long *Promenade Nature Trail* enables visitors to investigate the park's interesting geological and botanical features; regularly scheduled nature walks are conducted during the summer. Scenic drives and trails are also available.
Visitor center open daily 8–5; closed Christmas.
For further information write: Box 1219, Hot Springs, Ark. 71901

MOUNT NEBO STATE PARK
7 miles west of Dardanelle on State 155

From lookouts in the park on the top of this pine-grown 1,800-foot mountain, one can look down on the scenic **Arkansas River Valley.** The 2,000-mile-long river is the state's principal waterway.

OUACHITA NATIONAL FOREST
westcentral Arkansas and southeast Oklahoma, headquarters at Hot Springs

Located on the Arkansas–Oklahoma border, this forest covers more than 1½ million acres in the **Ouachita Mountains,** one of the few American ranges to run in an east-west direction rather than north-south. Some outstanding features here are **Caney Creek Back Country,** a 10,236-acre area of secluded forest characterized by clear streams and picturesque rock outcroppings accessible only by foot or on horseback; **Lake Ouachita,** a huge man-made lake, which can best be seen from a lookout on **Hickory Nut Mountain;** and the *Talimena Scenic Drive,* a 55-mile road from Mena, Arkansas, across the tops of **Rich** and **Winding Stair mountains** to Talihina, Oklahoma.
For further information write: Hot Springs, Ark. 71901

OZARK NATIONAL FOREST
northwest Arkansas, headquarters at Russellville

Set in the **Ozark** and **Boston mountains,** this forest of over a million

Display Springs in Hot Springs National Park

acres features many scenic attractions among its crystal-clear lakes and soaring rock bluffs. Some of the outstanding sites here are **Magazine Mountain** (elevation 2,753 feet), the highest point in the state; **Haw Creek Falls; Hurricane Creek Natural Bridge; Blanchard** and **Partee springs,** where thousands of gallons of water flow per day; **White Rock Mountain,** offering some of the most scenic views in the forest; the picturesque area at **Bayou Bluff;** and **Alum Cover Natural Bridge,** a 130-foot rock span. Scenic drives and hiking and saddle trails lead to these and other attractive areas.
For further information write: Box 340, Russellville, Ark. 72801

PETIT JEAN STATE PARK
6 miles south of Morrilton on State 9 and 15 miles south on State 154
Situated 800 feet above the **Arkansas River Valley** on **Petit Jean Mountain** (altitude 1,100 feet), this state park includes many scenic natural wonders. Outstanding are **Cedar Creek Canyon,** varying in depth from 200 to 400 feet; **Bear Cave,** a rock deposit with many twisted fissures; the **Palisades,** a cliff 500 feet above the **Petit Jean** and **Arkansas rivers; Indian Cave,** featuring primitive pictographs; and 70-foot-high **Petit Natural Bridge.**

SAINT FRANCIS NATIONAL FOREST
eastcentral Arkansas, headquarters at Russellville
One of the newest and smallest (20,611 acres) national forests, Saint Francis is named for the river that forms its eastern border. Located in the **Arkansas Delta** region, the forest is divided into rich bottomland and the rugged terrain of **Crowley's Ridge,** an area of narrow gullies, steep slopes, and wide valleys. The ridge runs for 200 miles from southern Missouri to Helena, Arkansas, on the **Mississippi River** and is a unique physical feature for this part of the country. Some of the attractions in the forest are located at **Bear Creek Lake,** a 625-acre lake atop Crowley's Ridge, and **Storm Creek Lake,** where stands of hardwood trees dot the 50-mile shoreline.
For further information write: Box 340, Russellville, Ark. 72801

CALIFORNIA

ANGELES NATIONAL FOREST
southern inland region, headquarters at Pasadena

The rugged terrain of this 691,000-acre forest covers a quarter of the land in Los Angeles County. The scenic *Angeles Crest Highway* (State Highway 2) traverses the forest from the foothills community of La Canada to the Big Pines Station high in the mountains. Along the way the wildlife and vegetation changes with the elevation from desert to alpine life zones. At key places along the highway lookout points offer panoramic vistas. From *Devil's Canyon Vista* one can see the 36,000-acre **San Gabriel Wilderness**, dedicated to recreation in a primitive environment, and the jagged **Twin Peaks**, both over 7,000 feet high. *Jarvis Memorial Vista* offers an excellent view of **Bear Canyon**. The viewfinder at *Inspiration Point* on **Blue Ridge** helps you locate several important peaks such as 10,064-foot **Mount Baldy** (the highest in the forest) and 9,399-foot **Mount Baden-Powell**, with its stand of 1,000- to 2,000-year-old trees in the **Ancient Limber Pine Forest**. The Angeles, which is crossed by a portion of the *Pacific Crest Trail*, also contains **Devil's Punchbowl** county park. *For further information: 1015 N Lake Ave, Pasadena, Calif. 91104*

ANZA–BORREGO STATE PARK
southern inland region, 30 miles west of Salton Sea

Occupying 488,000 acres, this vast sunny tract of **Colorado Desert** is the nation's largest state park. Some 700 miles of vehicle trails within the park lead to its varied attractions. At **Split Mountain** one can see perpendicular canyon walls rising up to 600 feet. Growing on a rocky slope a short distance away is a stand of rare, puffy-looking elephant trees. Only those with 4-wheel-drive vehicles are advised to make the tortuous descent into **Sandstone Canyon** or into the **Calcite Canyon Scenic Area** with its curious sandstone formations sculpted into fantastic shapes by millions of years of wind and rain. From the lookout at *Font's Point*, there is a spectacular vista of the barren **Borrego Badlands**, a stark network of steep-sided ravines and dry creek beds. Or, one can visit one of the park's many oases, including **Palm Springs**, **17 Palms**, and **Yaqui Well**.

BIG SUR
northern coastal region, 20 miles south of Carmel to Lucia on State 1

This incomparable stretch of rugged seacoast country, flanked by the steep slopes of the **Santa Lucia Range**, has long been a favorite haunt of artists and writers. A scenic section of State 1, known locally as the *Big Sur Highway*, provides superb views as it traverses long wave-terraces, crawls along cliffs 1,000 feet above the seething surf in deep granite coves, weaves for miles through high green ridges, and passes beaches where the rare sea otter may be sighted and roaring waterfalls descend from redwood canyons to the sea. The terrain in Pfeiffer Big Sur State Park ranges from the level valley of the **Big Sur River** to chaparral-covered mountain slopes.

CASTLE CRAGS STATE PARK
northern inland region, 25 miles north of Lake Shasta via I-5

Situated north of the Sacramento Valley, this 5,328-acre forested mountain park (elevations from 2,000 to 6,000 feet) is surrounded by primitive back country. Presiding regally above the upper **Sacramento River** are castlelike spires of ancient granite. These glacier-

Top left: sea elephants on Channel Islands National Monument. Right: bristlecone pine in Inyo National Forest. Below: Mount Whitney

polished crags were formed about 225 million years ago beneath the earth's crust and were later pushed up as a result of faulting. Comprising the crest of **Flume Creek Ridge**, a weathered slab of greenstone and slate—**Grey Rocks**—is another interesting formation that appears to be thrust over sideways. Other scenic landmarks include **Castle Dome**, accessible by *Crags Trail*, and **Battle Rock**, the scene of an Indian battle with the white man.

CHANNEL ISLANDS NATIONAL MONUMENT

Of the 8 Channel Islands, extending in a chain in the **Pacific Ocean** for about 150 miles between the latitudes of San Diego and Los Angeles, the 2 smallest—**Anacapa** and **Santa Barbara**—covering 18,167 acres, comprise this national monument. Millions of years ago the islands were originally a part of the southern California mainland; however, volcanic forces eventually submerged an enormous land mass, leaving only 8 mountaintops protruding above the water's surface. As a result of geographical isolation, these windswept cliff-bound islands have, over the years, developed species of plants and animals quite different from their mainland relatives; on Santa Barbara and Anacapa alone there are 45 endemic varieties of plants. These islands also serve as sanctuaries for numerous marine animals and nesting birds. Dotted with caves, rock bridges, offshore pillars, small rocky bays, and picturesque sandy beaches, Santa Barbara is home to a large rookery of sea lions. Anacapa, actually a slender chain of islands with many steep cliffs and canyon walls, is a favorite refuge of nesting seabirds that include California brown pelicans and Farallon cormorants. Other animals occasionally spotted are rare sea mammals, such as the sea otter, sea elephant, and Guadalupe fur seal. There are no permanent structures on either island and no public transportation to them. *For further information write: Box 1388, Oxnard, Calif. 93030*

CLEVELAND NATIONAL FOREST

southern coastal and inland regions, headquarters at San Diego

The 3 sections of the southernmost national forest in California stretch in an arc between the ocean and the desert roughly from Santa Ana to San Diego. Within its 567,000 acres lie the peaks of the **Santa Ana Mountains, Palomar Mountain**, with its world-famed observatory, **Laguna Mountain Recreation Area**, Capitan Grande Indian Reservation, and the **Agua Tibia Primitive Area**—

limited to winter use due to fire hazard. This beautiful mountain-
and canyon-filled forest is traversed by the *Pacific Crest Trail*.
For further information: 3211 Fifth Ave, San Diego, Calif. 92103

DEATH VALLEY NATIONAL MONUMENT
southern inland region, headquarters and visitor center at Furnace Creek

Nestled on the California–Nevada border between the **Panamint
Range** to the west and the **Amargosa Range** to the east, this great
desert basin—about 140 miles long and from 4 to 16 miles wide—
features a wealth of geological phenomena, plant and wildlife, and
historic ruins. This land of wind-whipped dunes and ever-shifting
lights and colors was named by fortyniners, who made a nearly
disastrous trek across it on their way to the California gold fields.
The valley's brief boom occurred in the 1880s with the production
of borax, "the white gold of the desert." Of the region's approximately 3,000 square miles, 550 are below sea level. From the
Black Mountain lookout, *Dantes View*, one is offered a unique
opportunity to see both **Badwater,** which at 280 feet below sea
level is the lowest point in the western hemisphere, and **Mount
Whitney** (*see Sequoia and Kings Canyon National Parks*), the highest peak in the contiguous United States. Other fine vistas are provided at **Zabriskie Point** in the Black Mountains, and at 11,049-foot
Telescope Peak, the highest point in the monument. The colorful
central section of the valley can be explored via the scenic *Artists
Drive*, which leads to such wonders as **Golden Canyon** and the
Devils Golf Course, with its crystal-like salt formations. State 190
offers access to **Stove Pipe Wells,** where desert springs were marked
with stovepipes, a 'patch of former salt marsh called **Devils Corn
Field,** and **Furnace Creek,** an emerald-green oasis and the valley's
chief settlement. Near the monument's northern boundary are
Ubehebe Crater, an 800-foot-deep volcanic cinder cone, and the
fabulous Spanish provincial residence—Scotty's Castle—built for
some 2 million dollars by Walter Scott, one of Buffalo Bill's cow-
boys. Tourists are advised to visit this area of fantastic heat, boasting
high summer temperatures of 120°, during the temperate winter
months between October and May. Death Valley supports over
26 mammal species, 200 bird species, and 600 plant varieties.
For further information write: Death Valley, Calif. 92328

Desert landscape in Death Valley National Monument

CALIFORNIA

Basaltic columns in Devils Postpile National Monument

DEVILS POSTPILE NATIONAL MONUMENT
Sierra region, 70 miles northeast of Fresno

This 798-acre tract is situated inside Inyo National Forest (*see*) on the eastern slope of the **Sierra Nevada** at an altitude of 7,600 feet. It features a sheer wall of blue-gray basaltic columns, rising from 40 to 60 feet on the face of a cliff, resembling the pipes of a gigantic organ. This cluster originated as a remnant of an ancient lava flow and was subsequently scoured smooth by glacial ice. An easy trail to its crest shows the exposed tops of the columns, whose polished surfaces look like inlaid tiles. The monument is one of the key points on the *John Muir Trail*, a 212-mile segment of the *Pacific Crest Trail* between **Yosemite** and **Sequoia** national parks. A 2-mile trail along the **Middle Fork of the San Joaquin River** leads to beautiful 140-foot **Rainbow Falls**. Evidence of recent volcanic activity is seen in various pumice deposits and hot springs.

For further information write: Yosemite National Park, Box 577, Yosemite Village, Calif. 95389

ELDORADO NATIONAL FOREST
Sierra region, headquarters at Placerville

Situated in the heart of the popular winter sports belt of the **Sierra Nevada**, this 886,000-acre forest includes a section of the **Mokelumne Wilderness** and a portion of the *Pacific Crest Trail*. It features picturesque camping spots around small alpine lakes, and abundant wildlife, including California mule deer, Columbian black-tailed deer, black bear, and occasional mountain lions in the highest reaches. Another major attraction, the **Desolation Mountain Primitive Area**, extends over the southwestern portion of **Lake Tahoe** basin and the mountainous terrain of granite peaks near the headwaters of the **Rubicon River. Pyramid Peak** is the tallest of 4 high summits which provide excellent vistas of one of the most northerly sections of the glaciated High Sierra-type lands. A 20-mile foot and horse trail runs the length of the region from **Echo Lake** to **Emerald Bay**, a Registered Natural Landmark, with its brilliant waters colored in variations of emerald and deep blue.

For further information: 100 Forni Rd, Placerville, Calif. 95667

INYO NATIONAL FOREST
Sierra region, headquarters at Bishop

Comprising more than 1,800,000 acres, Inyo is studded with wilderness areas and dozens of lofty peaks, including the **White Mountains** which rise to 14,000 feet. **Palisade Glacier,** the southernmost glacier in the United States, and the eastern escarpment of the **Sierra Nevada** are other awesome wonders. At **Mammoth Lakes** the visitor may take self-guided trails to a 60-foot-deep earthquake fissure or to the site of recent volcanic activity at **Crater Lakes.** The most fascinating feature of the forest is, perhaps, the 20,000-acre **Ancient Bristlecone Pine Forest** on the high, semiarid slopes of the White Mountains district. The short squat trees—no more than 25 feet tall with short needles tufted to stubby branches—are unique. Many have endured the hardships of mountain summers and winters for more than 4,000 years. Sculpted over the ages by fire, windblown sand, and ice particles, they are referred to as "living driftwood." From **Schulman Grove** a footpath leads to the **Pine Alpha Tree,** 4,300 years old, and another walk winds to the venerable **Methuselah,** which at 4,600 years is the oldest living tree known to exist.
For further information: 2957 Birch St, Bishop, Calif. 93514

JOSHUA TREE NATIONAL MONUMENT
southern inland region, 140 miles east of Los Angeles via I-10; headquarters and visitor center just off State 62 at Twentynine Palms

This 870-square-mile tract at the junction of the **Colorado** and **Mojave deserts**—with elevations ranging from 1,000 feet in the east to 5,750 feet in the **Little San Bernardino Mountains** to the west—preserves a rich variety of desert flora and contains striking granite formations. Found mostly above 3,000 feet in the central section of the monument, stands of the rapidly diminishing Joshua tree—a gigantic yucca belonging to the lily family—attain heights of 40 feet and bear cream-white blossoms in clusters 8 to 14 inches long. Other distinctive plants including the creosote bush, with its leaves covered with a waxy coating, the ocotillo, which loses its leaves during dry spells, and several varieties of cactus with no leaves are all adapted to this arid region where the average rainfall is less than 5 inches. Water-loving palms thrive at such oases as **Lost Palms Canyon,** the largest, **Fortynine Palms,** and **Canyon Cottonwood Spring.** *Salton View,* at 5,185 feet, commands a superb sweep of the **Coachella Valley** from the **Salton Sea** (at 241 feet below sea level, this is the lowest large body of water in the nation) at one end to Palm Springs at the other.
For further information: Box 875, Twentynine Palms, Calif. 92277

KLAMATH NATIONAL FOREST
northern inland region, headquarters at Yreka

Although a section of this 1,698,000-acre national forest extends into Oregon, the main body of this high mountainous country, dotted with lakes and streams, lies in the California **Coast Ranges.** Of the many forest roads and trails, the *Klamath River Highway* winds a particularly picturesque course parallel to the wild river which cuts through a deep canyon. The forest includes a segment of the **Salmon–Trinity Alps Primitive Area** *(see also Shasta–Trinity National Forest).* The **Marble Mountain Wilderness** takes its name from a mountain whose 700- to 1,000-foot-thick marble cap gives the impression of perpetual snow. The forest contains some of the finest specimens of Columbian black-tailed deer in California. And, among the varieties of flora in the region, the stands of rare Brewer's

CALIFORNIA

or weeping spruce are perhaps the most interesting.
For further information: 1215 S Main St, Yreka, Calif. 96097

LAKE TAHOE. *See* **TAHOE** and **ELDORADO NATIONAL FORESTS**

LASSEN NATIONAL FOREST
northern inland region, headquarters at Susanville

This 1,147,000-acre forest, which encircles Lassen Volcanic National Park (*see*), contains numerous lakes formed as a result of volcanic activity that took place millions of years ago. **Eagle Lake,** at an elevation of 5,100 feet, is one of the state's largest bodies of fresh water. Isolated since ancient geological times, with no known outlet, the lake has a high mineral content which may be the reason its fish grow to an unusual size. Nearly 20 million years old, **Lake Almanor** was formed when volcanic eruptions blocked and submerged a 500-square-mile area. Of particular interest are the **Subway Caves,** created within the past 2,000 years when molten lava spread over much of the **Hat Creek Valley** and formed large air pockets beneath the earth's surface. Offering excellent fishing is the **Thousand Lakes Wilderness,** which possesses 7 major lakes formed from potholes left by the eruption of an ancient volcano. Similar volcanic or glacial depressions have left the beautiful timber-lined lakes of the **Caribou Wilderness.**
For further information: 707 Nevada St, Susanville, Calif. 96130

LASSEN VOLCANIC NATIONAL PARK
northern inland region, headquarters ½ mile west of Mineral on State 36

Located in the middle of Lassen National Forest (*see*) at the southern tip of the **Cascades,** this park of 165 square miles contains a segment of the *Pacific Crest Trail* and a wealth of volcanic phenomena. It has over 50 mountain lakes as well as meadows and forests. Rising spectacularly at the park's west boundary, 10,457-foot **Lassen Peak** is the only recently active volcano in the conterminous United States; a series of eruptions between 1914 and 1921 buried much of this area under ash and lava. From Lassen's summit, reached by a 2.2-mile climb along the *Lassen Peak Trail,* there are magnificent views of the surrounding, cinder-covered terrain. The 30-mile-long *Lassen Park Road* traverses the park from the **Sulphur Works** entrance on the south to the visitor center at **Manzanita Lake** on the northwest. Situated just off this highway are such awesome wonders as the **Sulphur Springs Thermal Area.** The most impressive hydrothermal landscape in the park is, perhaps, the area beyond **Emerald Lake** named **Bumpass Hell.** In this strange barren land, volcanic forces millions of years old are still at work, as seen in the furious hot springs, gurgling mudpots, and jetting vents of steam and sulphur. At the northwest edge of the park, one can view the pink-toned **Chaos Crags,** lava plugs almost 2,000 feet high. Explosions from its base subsequently formed the **Chaos Jumbles,** among which a group of small coniferous trees—the **Dwarf Forest**—thrives. From **Butte Lake** a self-guiding trail leads to one of the park's most remarkable features, a 700-foot-high **Cinder Cone** created by lava flows that occurred as late as 1851. At its summit, one can gaze at a landscape of multicolored lava fields, dunes of volcanic ash, and **Soda Lake,** a carbonated body of water. A trail from **Warner Valley** leads to **Boiling Springs Lake,** which simmers at 125° and boasts a 2,000-foot shoreline.
For further information write: Superintendent, Mineral, Calif. 96063

Bumpass Hell area in Lassen Volcanic National Park

LAVA BEDS NATIONAL MONUMENT
northern inland region, about 60 miles northwest of Alturas on State 139

Situated near the Oregon border on a 46,162-acre mountain plateau, with elevations ranging from 4,000 to 5,700 feet, this is a rugged wasteland formed as a result of volcanic activity. Centuries ago, a group of flaming volcanoes spewed a blanket of molten, incandescent lava over the region; the lava cooled, hardened, and left a fascinating assortment of symmetrical cinder cones, deep chasms, steep basaltic cliffs, fumeroles and chimneys, and tubes or caves. A miniature volcano at the southern part of the monument, **Schonchin Butte,** is the largest of 17 cinder cones (100 to 500 feet high) created by gaseous-type eruptions. Explosions of superheated gas out of the earth produced fumeroles like the one at **Fleener Chimneys,** which has a 3-foot diameter and is about 130 feet deep. The 300 currently known caves in the monument were formed by fissure-type eruptions. *Cave Loop Road* provides access to **Sentinel Cave**—named for the stone figures adorning its passages—and **Catacombs Cave**—its wall niches resemble those in Rome. **Merrill Ice Cave** contains a frozen waterfall and river of ice, and **Skull Ice Cave,** the largest in the region, has a 75-foot-high domed roof. In addition to their geologic interest, the rock formations in this monument played a prominent part in the Modoc War of 1872–73 when the Modoc Indians made a last valiant effort to recover their homeland from the white man.

For further information write: Box 867, Tulelake, Calif. 96134

LOS PADRES NATIONAL FOREST
central coastal region, headquarters at Goleta

The 1,950,000 acres of land within this forest contain much of the mountainous area along the central coast of California. The main division stretches north of Santa Barbara to include the **Santa Ynez, San Rafael, Sierra Madre,** and **La Panza mountains.** The **Santa Lucia**

Mountains are included in the smaller division farther north. The elevation climbs from sea level at the Monterey coast to 9,000 feet at **Mount Pinos**. The rivers that originate within the forest—**Big Sur, Carmel, Salinas, Santa Maria, Santa Ynez, Santa Clara,** and **Ventura**—supply water for the coastal valley communities below. The scenic 143,000-acre **San Rafael Wilderness**, in the San Rafael and Sierra Madre mountains, is accessible by 125 miles of hiking and horseback trails. The 95,000-acre **Ventana Wilderness**—in the Santa Lucia Mountains of Monterey County—contains the unique Santa Lucia fir and is the southernmost limit of the coastal redwoods. Two sanctuaries have been established in the forest to protect the endangered California condors. Fire closures are usually in effect in the summer.

For further information write: 42 Aero Camino, Goleta, Calif. 93017

McARTHUR–BURNEY FALLS MEMORIAL STATE PARK
northern inland region, 64 miles northeast of Redding via State 299 and 89

Enclosed by the beautiful evergreen forests of the **Pit River** country, this 565-acre park features the falls Theodore Roosevelt once called the eighth wonder of the world. Emerging from its underground source, **Burney Creek** pours over a preliminary fall and then forms 2 equal cascades that hurtle over a 129-foot cliff into an emerald-colored pool below. Enhancing the spectacle are innumerable streams of white water issuing from the fern- and moss-covered rock behind Burney Falls.

MENDOCINO NATIONAL FOREST
northern inland region, headquarters at Willows

Covering more than a million acres of the **Coast Ranges**, Mendocino's southern boundary is about a 2-hour drive north from San Francisco. The elevations range from less than 1,000 feet to over 8,000 feet at the crest of the mountains. The **Yolla Bolly–Middle Eel Wilderness** offers opportunities for camping, hiking, fishing, and nature study. From **Anthony Peak** there is a fine view into the wilderness which is covered by snow from December through mid-March. Lakes **Pillsbury, Letts, Plaskett,** and **Hammerhorn** offer boating and trout fishing. The 4 self-guided auto routes and numerous trails give access to the many scenic spots such as **Black Butte, Grindstone Canyon, Snow, Sanhedrin,** and **Shutiron mountains**.

For further information: 420 E Laurel St, Willows, Calif. 95988

Left: California condor in Los Padres National Forest. Right: Monterey Peninsula

MITCHELL CAVERNS STATE RESERVE
southern inland region, about 80 miles east of Barstow via I-40

Located in the **Mojave Desert,** this 5,280-acre reserve occupies the eastern slope of the **Providence Mountains.** The subterranean caverns began to form some 12 million years ago as a result of the action of water, laden with carbonic acid, on limestone deposits, and took thousands of years to complete. Still more thousands of years were required to fill the caves' interiors with graceful stalactites and stalagmites. **El Pakiva** and **Tecopa caverns** are open to the public, but only experienced spelunkers are admitted to the **Winding Stair Cave,** which descends 350 feet in a series of free-fall drops ranging from 50 to 140 feet.

MODOC NATIONAL FOREST
northern inland region, headquarters at Alturas

Bounded on the north by Oregon and on the east by Nevada, Modoc National Forest comprises approximately 1,688,000 acres in the **Cascade Range.** In the rugged back country of the **South Warner Wilderness,** hunters and fishermen find abundant supplies of mule deer and trout. Access is provided by the 27-mile-long *Summit Trail* which extends from **Patterson Meadow** in the south to Porter Reservoir in the north. By following this route, one can view lush alpine settings at a 9,000-foot elevation, go around the western portion of **Eagle Peak**—dominating the region at 9,906 feet—pass **Patterson Lake,** nestled against a massive backdrop of cliffs that rise more than 800 feet to the top of **Warren Peak,** and skirt the summit of **Squaw Peak** (8,650 feet) which serves as a landmark at the wilderness' northern boundary.

For further information write: 441 N Main St, Alturas, Calif. 96101

MONTEREY PENINSULA
northern coastal region, from Pacific Grove to Carmel

The famed *Seventeen-mile Drive* has some of the finest vistas on the California coast with its shoreline of granite cliffs, white sand dunes, and clinging, twisted cypress trees native to this one area (*see also Point Lobos*). Off **Point Joe,** several conflicting ocean currents meet at the **Restless Sea.** Other points of interest include **Seal Rock** and **Bird Rock,** the breeding place of the sea lion and the raucous meeting place of sea birds; and **Cypress Point,** the finest lookout on the road. At **Point Pinos,** the northernmost point on the peninsula, there is a celebrated grove of pine trees. Each year, from late October through May, the trees are covered with thousands of Monarch butterflies, which migrate from Canada and Alaska to mate here.

MOUNT SHASTA. *See* SHASTA–TRINITY NATIONAL FORESTS

MOUNT WHITNEY. *See* SEQUOIA AND KINGS CANYON NATIONAL PARKS

MUIR WOODS NATIONAL MONUMENT
northern coastal region, 17 miles northwest of San Francisco via U.S. 101

This beautiful 503-acre tract lies in a canyon on the slopes of 2,604-foot **Mount Tamalpais.** It offers 6 miles of hiking trails through a grove of coastal redwoods, many of which are more than 2,000 years old. Unlike the giant sequoias in Sequoia and Kings Canyon National Parks (*see*), the trees here are comparatively slender, graceful, and tall—they are among the tallest of all living trees, with some majestic specimens soaring 240 feet above the forest floor. This primeval stand was named in honor of the conservationist John Muir, who devoted his life to establishing forest reserves where trees would be saved for their use as watersheds and "where nature may heal and cheer and give strength to body and soul alike." *For further information write: Mill Valley, Calif. 94941*

PALM SPRINGS
southern inland region, in the upper Colorado Desert

Nestled at the base of the 10,831-foot-high **San Jacinto Peak**, this oasis community is renowned for its dry, sunny winter climate and mineral springs. On the Agua Caliente Indian Reservation surrounding the town are such scenic points of interest as the **Andreas Canyon**, with its fascinating rock formations and caves formerly inhabited by the Indians, and the 20-mile-long **Palm Canyon**, with some 3,000 Washington palms—thought to be from 1,500 to 2,000 years old—lining its steep walls. A 1.4-mile walking trail descends **Tahquitz Canyon**, which contains a 60-foot waterfall. The biggest and longest single-span aerial lift in the world transports passengers from **Chino Canyon** a distance of some 13,200 feet to the 8,516-foot-high Mountain Station at the eastern edge of **Long Valley**.

PINNACLES NATIONAL MONUMENT
northern inland region, 35 miles south of Hollister off State 25

A rugged, relatively primitive region in the **Gabilan Range** (one of the **Coast Ranges**), this monument encompasses some 14,000 acres of colorful pinnacles and crags, narrow deep canyons, and caves. Created as a result of violent volcanic action, the majority of the monument's spirelike pinnacles—rising from 500 to 1,200 feet above a canyon floor—are situated on or flank a central ridge running from north to south. Flowing east across the ridge, 2 streams have carved out deep notches at **Bear Gulch** and the **Balconies** into which huge wedge boulders have fallen and formed covered canyons, or "caves." The monument's main attractions are reached by the *Chalone Peak, High Peaks,* and *Rim trails* and other footpaths. Besides its dramatic rock formations, the area also contains a variety of wildlife and the only examples of Coast Range chaparral. *For further information write: Paicines, Calif. 95043*

PLUMAS NATIONAL FOREST
Sierra region, headquarters at Quincy

The assorted natural attractions of this 1,148,000-acre forest include rushing rivers, lakes, mountains, valleys, and deep canyons. A major feature is the 640-foot-tall **Feather Falls**, the third highest known waterfall in the United States. The **Feather River Canyon** country extends for nearly 100 miles toward the Nevada border. (The **Middle Fork of the Feather** is part of the National Wild and Scenic Rivers system.) This land of pine and fir is reached by the *Feather River Highway* (State 70) which curves across the Sierras at **Beckwourth Pass** and zigzags along alternate sides of a picturesque gorge in a series of "leap-frog bridges." The forest is traversed by the *Pacific Crest Trail*, and visitors can pursue varied activities at **Frenchman Lake, Antelope** and **Little Grass** valleys. *For further information: 159 Lawrence St, Quincy, Calif. 95971*

POINT LOBOS STATE RESERVE
northern coastal region, just below Carmel off State 1

This 1,250-acre state reserve on the south shore of **Carmel Bay** is the habitat of one of the 2 remaining natural groves of Monterey cypress. Sprawling off fog-washed cliffs within ½ mile of high tide,

Left: Point Reyes National Seashore. Right: Redwood National Park

these fantastic trees were molded into twisted, stunted shapes by the unrelenting forces of nature. This tree-clad headland includes such interesting offshore rock formations as the **Sea Lion Rocks** where a herd of 30 rare, once nearly extinct, sea otters frolic with colonies of California and Steller's sea lions. Other rocks include **Bird Island,** a haven for thousands of shore and marine birds, and the **Pinnacles,** ceaselessly pounded by the action of the waves. Registered Natural Landmark

POINT REYES NATIONAL SEASHORE
northern coastal region, about 32 miles north of San Francisco via State 1

Located on the **Point Reyes Peninsula,** this picturesque and remote region embraces 100 square miles of high rocky headlands, long sandy beaches with spectacular surf, esteros (inlets) with sand dunes, lakes, woods, and meadows. Sir Francis Drake is believed to have landed beneath the tall white cliffs at the southern end of the peninsula in 1579. Today this natural harbor is known as **Drakes Bay.** Geologically, Point Reyes is separated from the California mainland by the San Andreas Fault (*see*). Beaches along the seashore can be reached via the *Sir Francis Drake Boulevard* and the *Coast Trail.* Inland, such trails as the popular *Bear Valley Trail* thread through grasslands and woods or wind into the high country of the **Inverness Ridge,** where a virgin stand of Douglas fir towers more than 1,000 feet over the Pacific.
For further information write: Point Reyes, Calif. 94956

RANCHO LA BREA
southern coastal region, Hancock Park, Wilshire Blvd, Los Angeles

This metropolitan park is renowned for its outstanding collection of Pleistocene fossils. While seeking fresh water, such prehistoric animals as the ground sloth, sabre-toothed tiger, and mammoth became entrapped in the sticky pits of natural asphalt tar once in this area. The pits were later discovered by the Spanish explorers of California. Registered Natural Landmark

REDWOOD NATIONAL PARK
northern coastal region, via U.S. 101 between Crescent City and Orick

Established in 1968, this 58,000-acre national park features some of the world's finest redwood groves. These tall, majestic trees

Palm Canyon near Palm Springs (see page 48)

evolved over 30 million years ago, and many of the specimens in this forest are thousands of years old. Weaving for some 35 miles southeast of Orick, the *Bald Hills Road*—also used by logging trucks—passes spectacular stands of redwoods and offers an excellent view of **Redwood Creek.** In addition to trees, this region encompasses some 40 miles of scenic, untamed coastline with steep descending beaches, rocky promontories jutting into the sea, salt marshes, and dunes to which access is provided by the *Klamath Beach Road* and numerous trails. Rookeries of birds, colonies of sea lions, and migrating whales can be seen on or near the off-shore rocks.

For further information: Drawer N, Crescent City, Calif. 95531

RUSSIAN GULCH STATE PARK
northern coastal region, 10 miles south of Fort Bragg on State 1

This 1,222-acre park features groves of second-growth coast redwoods and a high, rock-bound headland descending to a sandy beach, a popular base for skindivers in search of abalone. An example of a blowhole, a natural phenomenon along the Mendocino coast, occurs here. The **Devil's Punch Bowl** is a 200-foot-long sea-cut tunnel that has collapsed on its inland end and left a gaping hole 100 feet across and 60 feet deep. Inland the attractions are **Russian Gulch Creek Canyon,** with a scenic hiking trail, and the **Pygmy Forest,** featuring dwarf vegetation. Registered Natural Landmark

SALTON SEA STATE RECREATION AREA
southern inland region, south of Indio via State 111 or 86

Situated on the northeastern shore of the Salton Sea, this 16,500-acre recreation area lies in a hot, dry desert landscape bounded by the abruptly rising **Santa Rosa Mountains.** The body of water—more than 35 miles long and from 9 to 15 miles wide—is a remnant of the ancient Salton Sink, which 1,000 years ago filled the desert basin. Gradually the sea evaporated, leaving an expanse of white salt flats; in 1905 the **Colorado River** reflooded the basin and created the present Salton Sea.

SAN ANDREAS FAULT

One of the world's largest and most famous faults, the San Andreas forms a continuous fracture, at least 20 miles deep, in the earth's crust for about 600 miles from the coastal region of northern California southward to the **Cajon Pass.** A wrench-type fault in which blocks on opposite sides have slipped horizontally in relation to each other, the 100-million-year-old San Andreas may have an accumulated displacement as much as 350 miles. Such displacement has been the source of California's major earthquakes, including the San Francisco disaster of 1906. The movement of this intermittently active fault is illustrated at the private 10-acre Cienega winery at Hollister in San Benito County; specific groups or individuals will be admitted by permission when prior arrangements are made. Registered Natural Landmark

SAN BERNARDINO NATIONAL FOREST
southern inland region, headquarters at San Bernardino

Comprising 812,000 acres of the highest mountain areas in southern California (including 11,502-foot **San Gorgonio Peak**), this forest (which is traversed by the *Pacific Crest Trail*) offers a variety of activities. The northern section contains **Cucamonga Wilderness** and **San Gorgonio Wilderness** areas, **Lake Arrowhead** and **Big Bear Lake**—which provide excellent facilities for both winter and summer sports. The floor of **San Gorgonio Pass** (3–4 miles wide) separates the forest's sections; the southern part in the **San Jacinto Mountains** features **Black Mountain Scenic Area** and **San Jacinto Wilderness,** both outstanding for their primitive natural beauty. Magnificent **San Jacinto Peak** (10,831 feet) is actually in San Jacinto

Snow Valley in San Bernardino National Forest

State Park surrounded on 3 sides by the forest. State Highway 74, a scenic drive from Hemet to Palm Springs, traverses a variety of vegetative zones from pine forests to groves of date palms.
For further information: 144 Mountain View, San Bernardino, Calif. 92408

SAND HILLS
southern inland region, 15 miles west of Yuma, Arizona

The main attractions of the 90,000-acre area are hills formed from sand and fine pebbles that have been carried by the wind from a flat plain to the west to their present site near the Arizona border. The larger Sand Hills cover several acres and rise to elevations of about 300 feet. Growing here are unusual and hardy specimens of plants which have adjusted to the peculiar topographic conditions created by encroaching sand. Registered Natural Landmark

SEQUOIA AND KINGS CANYON NATIONAL PARKS
Sierra region, headquarters at Ash Mountain, on the Generals Highway, 6 miles above Three Rivers; visitor centers at Lodgepole and Grant Grove

Extending from the foothills of the **San Joaquin Valley** on the west to the crest of the **Sierra Nevada** on the east, these 2 adjoining parks, with a combined area of 1,324 square miles, preserve ancient groves of giant sequoia trees and contain some of the most spectacular untamed wilderness in North America. Among the chain of peaks rising from 12,000 to over 14,000 feet is the celebrated **Mount Whitney,** whose 14,495-foot elevation is the highest peak in the contiguous United States. Approached by either the *John Muir Trail* or the *High Sierra Trail,* Mount Whitney should be climbed only by experienced mountaineers. Although the high country is penetrated only by trails, the 47-mile-long *Generals Highway* connects both parks and provides convenient access to their scenic features. Passing through Kings Canyon National Park, the road leads to **General Grant Grove,** which houses the renowned **General Grant Tree.** Its 267-foot height and 107-foot girth makes it the second largest sequoia tree. Nearby **Redwood Mountain Grove,** the largest sequoia grove anywhere, boasts at least 3,000 trees 10 or more feet in diameter. Situated about 40 miles to the east, Kings Canyon, the steep-walled valley of the **South Fork of the Kings River,** possesses sheer granite walls, which in one place rise 8,000 feet. Sequoia National Park contains **Giant Forest,** site of the **General Sherman Tree,** the world's largest living tree at 272 feet high and 101 feet wide, and estimated to be 3,500 to 4,000 years old.
For further information write: Three Rivers, Calif. 93271

SEQUOIA NATIONAL FOREST
Sierra region, headquarters at Porterville

Situated just south of Sequoia National Park (*see*), this forest is crossed by the *Pacific Crest Trail* and covers 1,100,000 acres of mountains, lakes, and streams. Renowned for its groves of giant sequoia trees, the forest contains the 269-foot-high, 90-foot in circumference **Boole Tree.** Other outstanding arboreal specimens include the stands of redwood at **Balch Park** (at an elevation of 6,325 feet) and the 3 largest known foxtail pines, which can be reached in a 2-hour hike from **Mineral King Valley.** One of the forest's highlights is the **Dome Land Wilderness,** an open semiarid area named for its granite domes, monolithic rock outcroppings formed by erosion and weathering. Similarly, the **High Sierra Primitive Area** (*see also Sierra National Forest*)—possibly the wildest mountainous

High Sierra back country, Sequoia and Kings Canyon National Parks

region of California—features a variety of vegetation and wildlife zones. The *Needles* overlook offers a spectacular view of **Mount Whitney.** Taking the *Western Divide Highway,* one can visit **Dome Rock,** a massive monolith overlooking the **Kern River.**

For further information: 900 W Grand Ave, Porterville, Calif. 93257

SHASTA–TRINITY NATIONAL FORESTS
northern inland region, headquarters at Redding

These contiguous national forests encompass almost 2,800,000 acres in the California **Coast Ranges.** The outstanding attraction of the area is **Mount Shasta,** whose snow-capped summit at an elevation of 14,162 feet towers over the region and can be seen for many miles. Five permanent glaciers—**Whitney, Bolam, Hotlum, Wintun,** and **Knotwakiton**—reside on the slopes of this dormant volcano, which also is host to over 400 varieties of alpine plants. A fairly easy ascent can be made by starting at Sand Flat, progressing 1½ miles to Horse Camp, and then making a 4-hour climb to the summit. The forest, which is traversed by the *Pacific Crest Trail,* contains many picturesque lakes, such as **Shasta** with 350 miles of shoreline. Trails weave their way across the **Salmon-Trinity Alps Primitive Area,** a wild country of lakes, deep glacier-cut valleys, and high granite peaks. The similarly rugged **Yolla Bolly-Middle Eel Wilderness** received its name meaning "high snow-covered peaks" from the Wintun Indians.

For further information: 1615 Continental St, Redding, Calif. 96001

SIERRA NATIONAL FOREST
Sierra region, headquarters at Fresno

This 1,296,000-acre forest, which is traversed by the *Pacific Crest Trail,* is a true sportsman's paradise; it contains 7 herds of mule deer, black bear, and innumerable species of upland game and fish. The lands of the forest are carefully controlled to produce range for grazing animals, timber, and water—the vast watershed of the **San Joaquin River** rises in the heart of the forest and provides much-needed water for crop irrigation in the **San Joaquin Valley** below. Among the scenic attractions are the stands of giant sequoia trees at **Nelder** and **McKinley groves** and 5 large lakes, including **Mammoth Pool** and **Bass Lake.** Extending into Inyo National Forest (*see*) are the remote **John Muir Wilderness,** with its thousands of

lakes, and the **Minarets Wilderness,** whose rugged snow-capped peaks offer an exciting challenge to the experienced mountain climber. In the **High Sierra Primitive Area,** the **Tehipite Valley** approximates the scenic grandeur of **Yosemite Valley.**
For further information write: 1130 "O" St, Fresno, Calif. 93721

SIX RIVERS NATIONAL FOREST
northern coastal region, headquarters at Eureka

This 935,000-acre forest stretches 135 miles south from the Oregon border along the west slope of the **Coast Ranges** and lies due east of a section of California's renowned redwoods. The 6 primary rivers for which the forest was named originate in or flow through the region, and include, from north to south, the **Smith, Klamath, Trinity, Mad, Van Duzen,** and **Eel.** Access to this rugged undeveloped land is mainly by trail, and only a few major roads such as the *Klamath River Highway* penetrate its interior.
For further information write: 710 "E" St, Eureka, Calif. 95501

STANISLAUS NATIONAL FOREST
Sierra region, headquarters at Sonora

Bordering Yosemite National Park (*see*), this million-acre national forest ranges in altitude from 1,100 to 11,575 feet. By driving along the precarious but dramatic route of State 108, the tourist may visit the forest's deep canyons and gorges, undercut by the **Merced, Tuolumne, Stanislaus,** and **Mokelumne rivers,** forested mountain slopes, scarred by sluicing operations, and such historic landmarks as **Ebbetts** and **Sonora passes,** over which the prospectors trekked during the gold fever of '49. Accessible only by trail is the beautiful **Emigrant Basin Primitive Area** with its vast expanses of glaciated granite, steep-walled canyons, and massive lava-capped peaks— 11,575-foot **Leavitt Peak** at the crest of the **Sierra Nevada** being the highest point in the forest. The 50,000-acre **Mokelumne Wilderness,** extending into Eldorado National Forest (*see*), contains rugged mountains, dominated by the barren 9,371-foot **Mokelumne Peak.** The forest is traversed by a portion of the *Pacific Crest Trail.*
For further information: 175 S Fairview Lane, Sonora, Calif. 95370

TAHOE NATIONAL FOREST
Sierra region, headquarters at Nevada City

Covering approximately 695,000 acres in the mountains northeast of

Emerald Bay of Lake Tahoe

Trona pinnacles (see page 56)

Sacramento, this forest is crossed by the *Pacific Crest Trail*. Its foremost attraction, **Lake Tahoe**, with its brilliant clear-blue water and shoreline silhouetted by verdant forests and snow-capped peaks, is regarded as one of the most beautiful lakes in the world. It is 22 miles long, 8 to 12 miles wide, and so deep (1,650 feet) it never freezes. Daily boat trips offer excellent views of the lake and shore. Each year thousands of winter sports enthusiasts flock to such resorts as **Squaw Valley**—where the 1960 Winter Olympics were held—**Powder Bowl, Granlibakken, Sugar Bowl,** and **Boreal Ridge**. The *Donner Trail* leads to *Donner Summit*, a popular point overlooking **Donner Lake**, and to the site where an ill-fated party of 81 settlers camped during the winter of 1846 and 1847 and lost 36 of their members due to cold and starvation. The 7-mile-long *Pioneer Trail* along the southwest fringe of **Lake Valley** was originally a segment of the old Pony Express Route. In the **Upper Yuba Recreation Areas**, the *Alpha-Omega Overlook* offers views of the former gold mining communities.
For further information: Highway 49 & Coyote St, Nevada City, Calif. 95959

TOIYABE NATIONAL FOREST. *See* **NEVADA**

TORREY PINES STATE RESERVE
southern coastal region, just south of Del Mar
Occupying a wind-swept mesa on the crest of a high bluff overlooking the Pacific, this 877-acre park is the only natural habitat in the United States of the extremely rare Torrey pine. This grove of some 3,000 specimens possesses a peculiar grotesque beauty. Originally

symmetrical, the trees have been sculpted into twisted, gnarled, sprawling shapes by a combination of strong and steady winds and salt spray from the sea.

TRONA PINNACLES
southern inland region, 7 miles south of Argus

These spirelike tufa pinnacles were created in ancient glacial lakes that have now run dry. Composed of thick deposits of lime produced by the action of blue-green algae, these porous formations built up out of the water over thousands of years and eroded into the pinnacles that stand today. Registered Natural Landmark

WHISKEYTOWN–SHASTA–TRINITY NATIONAL RECREATION AREA
northern inland region, around Whiskeytown Lake, about 8 miles west of Redding

This area boasts some of the most breathtaking scenery in northern California. Lying on **Clear Creek,** a tributary of the **Sacramento River,** the dam-created **Whiskeytown Lake** is dotted with wooded isles and is enclosed by 36 miles of shoreline dominated by digger pines, ponderosas, and Douglas firs. The impounded lake is stocked with rainbow and brown trout, largemouth and smallmouth bass; it offers excellent beaches and boat-launching ramps, as well as numerous camping and picnicking sites. Some 50 miles of back-country roads lead to such points of interest as the 6,209-foot **Shasta Bally** or follow the picturesque Clear Creek as it meanders through gorges and rocky hills.
For further information write: Box 188, Whiskeytown, Calif. 96095

YOSEMITE NATIONAL PARK
Sierra region, headquarters and visitor center at Yosemite Village

Unsurpassed for its breathtaking combination of panoramic peaks, massive granite domes, steep-walled chasms, shimmering waterfalls, and luxuriant forests, Yosemite National Park covers approximately 1,200 square miles. Ever since the first tourists arrived. in **Yosemite Valley** in 1855, this 7-square-mile area in the very heart of the park has been the chief tourist attraction. Carved out by the **Merced River,** the "incomparable valley" is surrounded by an irregular-shaped rim which rises 2,000 to 4,000 feet from the valley

Left to right in Yosemite National Park: Yosemite Falls, a black bear, Cathedral Spires, El Capitan and Bridalveil Fall

floor. Within the valley's confines are exhibited an incredible variety of landforms, including 12 types of granite rock, sculpted over the ages by ice, running water, and weathering agents. Looming over the valley are such immense pinnacles as **El Capitan**— one of the world's largest exposed granite monoliths, the colossal **Sentinel Rock** which resembles a medieval fortress, and the **Royal Arches** carved on the face of a cliff. Dotting the landscape, also, are such helmet-shaped monoliths as **Half Dome,** a sheer-faced semidome considered to be one of Yosemite's most famous features. The valley is best known for its spectacular free-leaping waterfalls. One of the world's tallest waterfalls, **Upper Yosemite Fall** plummets 1,430 feet to its base, at which point the **Middle Cascade** descends another 675 feet, and finally the **Lower Yosemite Fall** drops still another 320 feet for a total distance of 2,425 feet. Equally awe-inspiring is the wind-whipped **Bridalveil Fall,** which makes an almost uninterrupted descent of 620 feet. Providing a far-flung vista of the entire valley is the famous lookout at *Glacier Point* on the south rim.

Access to Yosemite's numerous natural wonders is made possible by some 238 miles of primary roads, 98 miles of secondary roads, and 765 miles of trails. Reached via *Wawona Road* (State 41), **Mariposa Grove** features stands of giant sequoia trees—**Grizzly Giant** boasts a girth of 96.5 feet, a height of 209 feet, and is around 3,000 years old. Traversed by foot or horseback, the **Grand Canyon of the Tuolumne River** is a remote region where the river encounters shelves of rock with such force that arcs of water—known as **Waterwheel Falls**—are created. *Big Oak Flat* and *Tioga roads* wind into high country about 55 miles from Yosemite Valley, where the scenic **Tuolumne Meadows**—the largest subalpine meadow in the **High Sierra**—is situated at an elevation of 8,600 feet. This mountain garden is a broad basin with numerous spots for campsites and trout-stocked lakes such as **Tenaya,** whose shores have been polished to a glistening smoothness by ancient glaciers. Here is Yosemite's tallest peak, 13,114-foot **Mount Lyell,** whose slopes also shelter the park's largest glacier. The **Hetch Hetchy,** once as beautiful as Yosemite Valley, contains today a reservoir that impounds San Francisco's water supply. There are 220 species of birds and 75 species of mammals in the park.

For further information: Box 577, Yosemite Village, Calif. 95389

COLORADO

ARAPAHO NATIONAL FOREST
northcentral Colorado, headquarters at Golden

Straddling the Continental Divide, this million-acre forest is noted for the spectacular scenery of its mountains, ranging in elevation from 7,500 to 14,274 feet. Over half the forest is included in the **Gore Range–Eagles Nest Primitive Area,** a mountainous region accessible only by foot or on horseback. It features sharp ridges, natural lakes in cirques (steep-walled basins formed by glacial erosion), and high peaks ranging from 11,000 feet to the 13,534-foot **Mount Powell.** Dotted throughout the forest are ghost towns and rotted railroad beds, all that remain of the boom days when mining towns sprang up all along the Great Divide. A 4-hour self-guiding auto route, open from July through Labor Day, leads through the forest, crosses the Continental Divide at **Rollins Pass,** and continues through Roosevelt National Forest (*see*).

For further information write: 1010-10th St, Golden, Colo. 80401

BLACK CANYON OF THE GUNNISON NATIONAL MONUMENT
South Rim entrance, 11 miles northeast of Montrose

One of the world's greatest wild canyons, Black Canyon is the result of about 2 million years of erosion and downcutting by the **Gunnison River** and its tributaries. In its deepest section, which extends for 10 miles, the canyon varies in depth from 1,730 to 2,245 feet and in width from 1,300 feet at the rims to as narrow as 40 feet at the bottom. Downcutting by smaller tributaries has resulted in many side, or hanging, valleys that rise high above the canyon floor. Weathering and erosion have caused weirdly shaped pinnacles to form in some places and sheer cliffs to form in others. The canyon takes its name from the ancient lichen- and moss-covered rocks of dark schist, granite, and gneiss that give this marvel of nature a somber and startling effect. Old piñon and juniper trees growing on the rims—some estimated to be over 700 years old—accentuate the starkness. Drives with many observation points and foot trails lead along both sides of the canyon. *North Rim Drive*, an unpaved road, is usually closed from November to May.

Adjacent to the Black Canyon is **Curecanti National Recreation Area,** a complex of 3 dams—Blue Mesa, Morrow Point, and Crystal (proposed)—in the canyons of the Gunnison River. Although this section of the 50-mile gorge created by the river is not as spectacular as the national monument, it is still a beautiful site. Also noteworthy is **Blue Mesa Lake,** a 20-mile-long lake backed up by the dam.

For further information: Curecanti National Recreation Area, 334 S 10th St, Montrose, Colo. 81401

BOX CANYON PARK
Ouray vicinity

The steep granite walls of this beautiful gorge rise 285 feet above **Canyon Creek.** Only 20 feet wide, the canyon is spanned by a high bridge, near which the creek disappears into an underground passage. A trail leads to the bottom of Box Canyon, where the creek emerges from its subterranean channel as a foaming waterfall.

BRIDAL VEIL FALLS
2½ miles southeast of Telluride off State 145

This beautiful waterfall cascades 365 feet to **Bridal Veil Creek** below; it dissipates into a spray before it reaches the creek.

Top left: bighorn sheep in Rocky Mountains National Park. Center: cactus in bloom. Right: Dinosaur National Monument. Below: Garden of the Gods

COLORADO

CAVE OF THE WINDS
west of Manitou Springs on U.S. 24 to Serpentine Drive
This cave, carved by underground water, lies in the western wall of **Williams Canyon**, a rugged gorge of white sandstone and gray limestone walls. The cave, which can be reached along *Serpentine Drive*, a scenic route through Williams Canyon, is divided into 17 named chambers featuring intricate stalagmites and stalactites. *Open July–Labor Day: daily 8–7; rest of the year 9–5. Admission: adults $1.50, children (6–12) $1.00*

COLORADO NATIONAL MONUMENT
4 miles west of Grand Junction and 3½ miles south of Fruita
In 1911 President William Howard Taft set aside this 28-square-mile area of canyons, cliffs, rock formations, and looming monoliths as a national monument. Carved into the **Uncompahgre Highland**—a great upwarp in the earth's crust—by erosion, temperature variations, flooding and undercutting, these canyons represent billions of years of geological history. As the forces of erosion shaped the sandstone, so dinosaur bones, petrified wood, and relics of prehistoric Indian cultures were uncovered. Here, amongst the canyon walls and the piñon pine-Utah juniper forest that covers part of the region, is a geological and historical record of westcentral Colorado. The monument is a scenic wonder and can best be seen by following the 22-mile *Rim Rock Drive* from **No Thoroughfare Canyon** at the east entrance to **Fruita Canyon** at the west. Along the route, as it skirts **Columbus, Red, Ute,** and **Monument canyons,** such rock formations as **Coke Ovens, Balanced Rock, Sentinel Spire,** and the 1,000-foot **Independence Monument,** (the tallest monolith in the park) can be seen. Self-guided nature trails lead along the canyon rims; *Liberty Cap Motor Nature Trail* traverses **Monument Mesa.** *Visitor center open June–Aug: daily 8–8. Sept–May: daily 8–5. For further information write: Box 438, Fruita, Colo. 81521*

CURECANTI NATIONAL RECREATION AREA. *See* BLACK CANYON OF THE GUNNISON NATIONAL MONUMENT

DENVER MOUNTAIN PARKS SYSTEM
This 13,500-acre municipal park system that includes 27 recreational and scenic areas in the foothills of the **Rocky Mountains** is unique in the country. Connected by 100 miles of highway, it offers countless natural wonders. Among the highlights here are: **Lookout Mountain** (7,374 feet), featuring Buffalo Bill's tomb and the Cody Memorial Museum at the summit from which there is a beautiful sunset view of Denver; **Genesee Mountain** (8,274 feet) and the surrounding 2,403-acre park; the **Denver Mountain Park Game Preserve,** with elk, deer, and a herd of 60 buffalo; **Bear Creek,** where a dam has created a 55-acre lake and a beautiful waterfall; **Bear Creek Canyon,** a deep, rocky gorge; and **Morrison Mountain** (7,880 feet).

The most outstanding part of the system is the **Park of the Red Rocks** with its spectacular monoliths composed of Precambrian quartzitic sandstone with some shale and limestone. The chief formations found on the 600-acre site include **Picnic Rock, Rock of the Nine Parts, The Titanic and the Iceberg, Creation Rock,** and **Ship Rock.** But the park's main attraction is the red-hued natural amphitheater that boasts perfect acoustics. Ten thousand seats have been built into the mountainside facing the huge red standstone walls that form the backdrop of the stage.

Rafting on the Green River in Dinosaur National Monument

DINOSAUR NATIONAL MONUMENT
headquarters, 2½ miles east of Dinosaur on U.S. 40

The most remarkable dinosaur fossil deposit in the world is preserved in this national monument on the Colorado–Utah border. The **Dinosaur Quarry,** where petrified skeletons of dinosaurs, crocodiles, and turtles have been uncovered, was set aside as a monument in 1915. At the Quarry Visitor Center in Utah (6 miles north of Jensen on Utah 149) one can still see technicians working to expose more fossils.

In 1938 the boundaries of the monument were extended to include the spectacular region to the north and east where sedimentary rock has been carved into scenic canyons and steep gorges by the **Green** and **Yampa rivers.** Among the outstanding sites are **Lodore Canyon,** varying in depth from 1,000 to 3,300 feet above the Green River, and **Castle Park,** a picturesque area 7 miles above the confluence of the rivers. A primitive road, beginning outside the monument at Elk Spring, parallels the Yampa River and passes such great sandstone masses as **Echo Park** (5,080 feet), **Harpers Corner** (7,528 feet), and **Steamboat Rock** (6,066 feet). Self-guiding nature trails at **Red Rock, Plug Hat,** and Harpers Corner lead the visitor to the interesting animal and plant life of this semidesert environment. *Dinosaur Quarry visitor center open June–Labor Day: daily 7–9. Sept–May: daily 8–5. Headquarters open June–Labor Day: daily 8–6. For further information write: Box 101, Dinosaur, Colo. 81610*

FLORISSANT FOSSIL BEDS NATIONAL MONUMENT
25 miles west of Colorado Springs and 3 miles south of Florissant on State 143

Located at an altitude of 8,300 feet, this grassy forest of small trees covers the site of an ancient lake once 10 miles long and 2 miles wide. The lake was formed millions of years ago when volcanic eruptions blocked the drainage of the area. With succeeding eruptions, volcanic ash and dust settled over the lake trapping fish, leaves, insects, and other plant and animal life; what remains today are delicate fossils petrified in layers beneath the lakebed. Within the area stumps of trees that predate the lake abound. The petrified sequoia is the most unusual, but stumps and leaves of pine, willow, walnut, oak, and maple are also here. Unlike other fossil deposits known for the size of the remains, Florissant is remarkable for the thousands of delicate creatures embedded here.

Open daily during daylight hours. For further information: Rocky Mountain National Park, Estes Park, Colo. 80517

GARDEN OF THE GODS
Colorado Springs, northwest of U.S. 24

This 370-acre municipal park is in a hilly region famous for the rock formations of red sandstone with occasional upthrusts of gypsum found here. Reaching heights of 300 feet and called by such exotic names as **Gateway Rocks** and **Cathedral Spires,** these weird formations are only one section of an outcrop that extends for over 300 miles from Wyoming across Colorado.

GRAND MESA NATIONAL FOREST
westcentral Colorado, headquarters at Delta

Located on top of 10,500-foot-high Grand Mesa, the largest flat-topped mountain in the world, this forest contains 368,418 acres of outstanding scenery. The mesa itself was created when a thick lava flow covered softer sedimentary rock formations here giving them an armorlike protective coating. The surrounding area not protected by the lava succumbed to the forces of erosion and eventually the mesa was left like a "colossal island in the sky." But even on the mesa some places remained exposed, such as the **Lakes Country** of the national forest, where depressions were formed by glacial action and a weathering process called "slumping." Some of these depressions were later filled and used as reservoirs but others are natural lakes where water sports are available 2 miles above sea level.

The scenic wonders of the forest can be viewed from State highway 65 which crosses the mesa from north to south; a visitor center is located on the highway at the **Carp Lake** turn-off. At *Land's End,* on *Scenic Rim Drive Road,* one can overlook a 500-foot vertical drop, considered to be one of the most outstanding scenic views in the nation. *Crag Crest Trail* leads to a volcanic hogback that rises 1,000 feet above the mesa.

For further information write: 11th and Main, Delta, Colo. 81416

Wind-sculptured dunes in Great Sand Dunes National Monument

GREAT SAND DUNES NATIONAL MONUMENT
38 miles northeast of Alamosa on State 150

Visible for 70 miles, these huge sand dunes—the largest in the country—lie in the **San Juan Valley** at the western base of the **Sangre de Cristo Mountains.** In places the ever-shifting gray-brown dunes reach heights of 700 feet and stand in dramatic contrast to the 14,000-foot forested mountains behind them. The dunes change and grow as southwesterly winds pick up tons of sand in the arid **San Luis Valley** and carry them until the barrier created by the Sangre de Cristos prevents the sand from moving on. The dunes have been known to "walk" as much as 7 feet in a day, although the average change is 3 inches weekly. It is advisable to visit the monument in the early morning or at sunset, when the lovely soft colors can be seen to their best advantage.

Visitor center open daily 8–5. For further information write: Box 60, Alamosa, Colo. 81101

GUNNISON NATIONAL FOREST
central Colorado, headquarters at Gunnison

Located on the western slope of the **Rocky Mountains,** this forest features 27 peaks over 12,000 feet and many high lakes. Taylor Reservoir, one of the state's largest lakes, may be reached by following the **Taylor River** through a picturesque 20-mile canyon. The natural beauty of the region is preserved in **La Garita Wilderness,** a 49,000-acre area partially located across the Continental Divide in Rio Grande National Forest (*see*), and **West Elk Wild Area.** Elevations in West Elk vary from 8,000 to 12,920 feet above sea level; portions of many high ranges are located here including the **Beckwith Mountains, West Elk Range,** and the **Anthracite Range.** Here too is the world's largest blue spruce, a 126-foot-high tree measuring 15 feet 8 inches in circumference. Many hiking and saddle trails wind through both wilderness areas.

For further information write: Gunnison, Colo. 81230

MESA VERDE NATIONAL PARK
on U.S. 160, 10 miles east of Cortez and 9 miles west of Mancos

This flat-top mountain (mesa), slashed by canyons and covered with piñon and juniper trees, is believed to have been named the "green table" by Spaniards who first saw it about 1776. Rising 2,000 feet, the mesa overlooks **Montezuma Valley** to the west and the valley of the **Mancos River** to the east. Here some of the best-preserved Indian ruins in the country sit on the mesa top and inside the shallow caves that the forces of erosion have carved in the canyon walls. Indians occupied this area from around the opening of the Christian Era until the 14th century and their development is divided into 4 archaeological periods. The ruins for which Mesa Verde is renowned, such as Cliff Palace, Square Tower House, and Spruce Tree House, date from the last period (1100–1300).

A 21-mile road leads from the entrance in the **Mancos Valley** to park headquarters where a fine museum is located. Stops marked off on the road include the *Montezuma Valley Overlook* and *Mancos Valley Overlook* which offer panoramic scenic views. From *Park Point*, the highest spot on the mesa (8,572 feet), there is a desert-mountain view of the famous **Four Corners,** where Colorado, Utah, New Mexico, and Arizona meet. *Ruins Road*, a 12-mile drive consisting of two self-guided loops, winds around the mesa and in places skirts the canyon rims.

For further information: Mesa Verde National Park, Colo. 81330

COLORADO

MOUNT EVANS
35 miles west-southwest of Denver

A part of the **Front Range of the Rocky Mountains,** this 14,264-foot peak is reached by the *Mount Evans Scenic Drive*—said to be the highest paved auto route in the country. Beginning at Denver on U.S. 40, the road continues to State 74 and State 103. At this junction is **Echo Lake,** a particularly lovely lake set in a natural park crossed by scenic trails. From here the road continues to State 5 as it passes **Summit Lake,** a snow-fed glacial cirque surrounded by a variety of unusual arctic-alpine plants, some found nowhere outside the Arctic Circle. Considered to have the finest example of tundra in the conterminous United States, the lake is a Registered Natural Landmark. From here State 5 climbs along twisted hairpin turns to the top of Mount Evans. (The last few yards must be climbed on foot). From the summit there is a spectacular view of the entire Front Range and the **Great Plains** stretching eastward.

PIKE NATIONAL FOREST
central Colorado, headquarters at Colorado Springs

This 1,258,825-acre forest, with elevations ranging from 5,500 feet in the northeast section to 14,234 feet on **Mount Lincoln** in the northwest, is most famous as the site of **Pikes Peak** (*see*). But the forest boasts many other scenic attractions. One of its wildest and most beautiful spots is **Lost Creek Scenic Area,** a 15,000-acre region located in the **Tarryall Mountains,** part of the **Front Range of the Rockies.** Here are such impressive mountains as **Bison Peak** (12,400 feet) from which one can see Pikes Peak to the east, the **Tarryall River Valley** to the south, **Collegiate Range** to the west, and **Windy Peak** to the north. The area takes its name from **Lost Creek** which disappears at least 9 times into subterranean channels as deep as 175 feet below the granite surface. Action of this kind, though common in limestone, is almost unknown in granite. The entire scenic area is an Eligible Natural Registered Landmark. *For further information: 403 S Cascade, Colo. Springs, Colo. 80903*

PIKES PEAK
Pike National Forest

Although not the tallest mountain in the **Front Range of the Rockies,** Pikes Peak is one of the most famous. Surrounded by Indian legend and prominent in the history of the West, the 14,110-foot granite mountain stands in isolation on the edge of the **Great Plains.** Visible from the east for miles, it became a sentinel to westward-bound pioneers and prospectors—"Pikes Peak or Bust!" became a catch phrase of the gold rush of 1859. Zebulon Pike first spotted the peak in 1806 and because he thought it to be over 18,000 feet named it Great Peak. It was subsequently named James Peak and Highest Peak and did not appear on a map under its present name until 1835. Today the mountain is accessible by car or cog railroad from Manitou Springs. The 18-mile *Pikes Peak Highway,* recommended only for those highly experienced in mountain driving, offers scenic vistas as it climbs 7,309 feet from Cascade to the summit.

RIO GRANDE NATIONAL FOREST
southcentral Colorado, headquarters at Monte Vista

Situated between the **San Luis Valley** and the Continental Divide, this forest is named for the **Rio Grande,** the third longest river in the United States, which rises here. Among the oustanding sites in the forest is **Wheeler Monument,** made up of remarkable sandstone

Pikes Peak

formations carved by erosion into whimsical shapes and figures. More than 1,600 miles of road and 1,280 miles of foot and saddle trails lead to such attractions as **La Garita Wilderness,** a 49,000-acre primitive area straddling the divide and partially located in Gunnison National Forest (*see*). Dominated by **San Luis** and **Stewart peaks,** both over 14,000 feet high, the area features steep slopes, glacial rock deposits, and alpine streams. **Upper Rio Grande Primitive Area,** another scenic region, features 56,000 heavily forested acres along the Great Divide.
For further information write: Monte Vista, Colo. 81144

ROCKY MOUNTAIN NATIONAL PARK
headquarters near Estes Park, 65 miles west of Denver

The rugged terrain and varied landscape of the **Front Range of the Rockies** is the setting for this 410-square-mile national park. Here one can see examples of many of the geological components of the Rocky Mountains: flat summits (**Deer** and **Flattop mountains**), extinct volcanoes (**Specimen Mountain**), glacial moraines (**Bierstadt Ridge**), small glaciers (**Tyndall** and **Andrews glaciers**), glacial troughs (**Spruce Canyon**), cirques (**Chasm Lake**), and 84 named peaks with elevations exceeding 11,000 feet. The "crown jewel" is 14,256-foot **Longs Peak,** the highest point in the park.

Many of the outstanding sites can be seen by driving along *Trail Ridge Road,* one of the highest continuous auto routes in the United States. Eleven miles of this 50-mile road are above the timber line (about 11,500 feet) and more than 4 miles are at altitudes of 12,000 feet. Beginning at Deer Ridge Junction the road follows an old Indian trail across the mountains; at every turn and at each of the 6 observation lookouts there is an outstanding view of mountains (the snow-capped **Mummy Range**), meadows (**Horseshoe Park**), lakes (**Iceberg Lake**), and valleys (the **Colorado River Valley** at the end of the road). In addition, the park's many wonders can be seen along the 300 miles of trails available. Some of these trails are short strolls, some self-guided nature walks, and others arduous treks through difficult back country. Among the principal trails are the ½-mile *Tundra Trail* at *Rock Cut* lookout, 2 miles above sea level on the *Trail Ridge Road,* where unusual vegetation and effects of glaciation can be seen up close; *Bear Lake Nature Trail* at the base of the Front Range; and the rugged climb to Longs Peak. Many other trails lead to such spots as **Nymph Lake, Dream Lake, Glacier Gorge,** Flattop Mountain, and the ghost town at Lulu City. The park offers many scheduled programs including nature walks, longer hikes, and auto caravans. Information can be obtained at the Alpine and Moraine Park visitor centers and at park headquarters at Estes Park.

Because of the variance in elevation from about 8,000 feet above sea level to over 14,000 feet, plants and animals indigenous to several environments exist within the park. The tiny, but centuries-old tundra plants, found above the timber line are most unusual. Although the park is famous for its bighorn, or mountain sheep, they are seldom seen. More common are the elk, mule deer, and beaver; 215 kinds of birds have been spotted here.

Adjacent to the park at the southwest is **Shadow Mountain Recreation Area** made up of the "Great Lakes" of Colorado—Grand Lake, and the man-made reservoirs **Shadow Mountain Lake** and **Lake Granby.** In addition to water sports and fishing (the lakes boast 5 species of trout) the area offers the mountain scenery that makes Rocky Mountain one of our most beautiful national parks.

For further information: Rocky Mountain National Park, Box 1080, Estes Park, Colo. 80517

ROOSEVELT NATIONAL FOREST
northcentral Colorado, headquarters at Fort Collins

Named in honor of Theodore Roosevelt, one of the nation's first conservationists, this 790,000-acre forest features 17 varieties of conifer and broadleaf trees. Most noteworthy here is the **Rawah Wilderness**—a primitive area 14 miles long and 3 miles wide situated in the **Medicine Bow Mountains,** an extension of the **Front Range of the Rockies.** Accessible only by foot or on horseback, the wilderness boasts 75 miles of trails, 26 well-stocked alpine lakes, altitudes ranging from 9,500 to 13,000 feet, and rugged, unspoiled terrain, much of it above the timber line. A 4-hour self-guided auto tour crossing the Continental Divide at **Rollins Pass** leads through this forest and Arapaho National Forest *(see);* the road is open from July through Labor Day.

For further information write: Rocky Mountain Bank & Trust Building, 211 Canyon, Fort Collins, Colo. 80521

ROUTT NATIONAL FOREST
north Colorado, headquarters at Steamboat Springs

Named in honor of Colonel John N. Routt, the last territorial and first elected governor of Colorado, this 1,125,000-acre forest lies astride the Continental Divide in the **Park Range,** a section of the **Rocky Mountains.** The forest is famous for its trout streams, sparkling alpine lakes, and lofty mountains, including the 10,719-foot **Rabbit Ears Peak.** Popular here too is **Fish Creek Falls,** a spectacular cascade dropping 200 feet. Among the most scenic areas is **Mount Zirkel Wilderness,** a 72,000-acre region accessible by trail.

For further information: Hunt Building, Steamboat Springs, Colo. 80477

ROYAL GORGE PARK
about 10 miles northwest of Canon City

Known as the Grand Canyon of the Arkansas, this spectacular gorge of steep granite walls rises 1,000 feet above the **Arkansas River.** At one of the narrow points a suspension bridge, open to pedestrians and cars, spans the canyon opening. The world's highest suspension bridge, it rises 1,053 feet above the river and is 1,260 feet long. Beneath the bridge a scenic railroad runs along the river bed and an incline railroad near the visitor center on the north rim descends 1,500 feet at a 45° angle to the canyon floor. In addition a ½-mile-long aerial tramway hangs suspended above the gorge from one rim to the other. From *Point Sublime* on the south rim there is a particularly scenic view of the massive multicolored walls of the gorge. *Open daily during daylight hours. Bridge toll includes admission to the park: adults, $1.25; children (7–11) 50¢*

SAN ISABEL NATIONAL FOREST
southcentral Colorado, headquarters at Pueblo

This forest of fir, spruce, and ponderosa pine is best known for its imposing mountains. **Mount Elbert,** at 14,431 feet, is the highest peak in the state and the second highest peak in the 48 contiguous states. Moreover, of the 53 peaks in Colorado with elevations exceeding 14,000 feet, 20 are in San Isabel. Two fine examples are **Mount Massive** (14,418 feet)—with 70,000 acres above the timber line, unusual alpine vegetation, and the remnants of a glacier that remains throughout summer—and **Blanca Peak,** (14,363 feet)—the highest point in the **Sangre de Cristo Mountains,** the southernmost range of the Rockies. The **Spanish Peaks,** twin mountains rising 7,000 feet above the **Great Plains,** served as important landmarks to Indians and Spanish and French explorers. They are also geolog-

Suspension bridge over the Royal Gorge

ically significant as prime examples of "stocks"—massive rock formations created by the intrusion of igneous, or molten, rock into layers of softer sedimentary rocks. Here too are great walls called "dikes," that radiate out from the peaks in all directions. Exposed by erosion, some of these dikes (4,000 have been identified) are up to 100 feet wide, 14 miles long, and 100 feet high. The Spanish Peaks are the finest example of this combination of stocks and dikes. They and the other natural wonders of the forest can be seen along *Apishapa Scenic Drive* and the 700 miles of trails available here. *For further information write: Pueblo, Colo. 81002*

SAN JUAN NATIONAL FOREST
southwest Colorado, headquarters at Durango

Noted for its splendid scenery, alpine lakes, canyons, and waterfalls, this forest is located on **San Juan Mountains,** a range of the Rockies. One of the most scenic areas here is the **San Juan Primitive Area,** where 240 miles of trails wind through the 230,000 acres that have been set aside to preserve their natural setting and unspoiled beauty. Points of interest in the area, accessible only on foot or horseback, include **Mount Eolus** (14,079 feet), **Windom Peak** (14,091 feet), **Rio Grande Pyramid,** a 13,830-foot mountain resembling an Egyptian pyramid, **Weminuche Pass** (10,622 feet) on the Continental Divide, **Emerald Lake,** a glacial lake, and **Trinity Peaks,** 3 peaks each over 13,000 feet. In another section of the forest a ride on a narrow-gauge passenger railroad is available. The 44-mile trip from Durango to Silverton parallels the beautiful Animas River and passes such scenic areas as **Silver Falls, Needle Creek Canyon, Mountain View Crest,** and **Grand Turk Mountain.** *For further information: Oliger Building, Durango, Colo. 81301*

Crossing Weminuche Pass in San Juan National Forest

COLORADO

SHADOW MOUNTAIN RECREATION AREA. *See* **ROCKY MOUNTAIN NATIONAL PARK**

UNCOMPAHGRE NATIONAL FOREST
westcentral Colorado, headquarters at Delta

Proclaimed by Theodore Roosevelt in 1905, this 1,050,000-acre forest is located on the **Uncompahgre Plateau**—10,388-foot tableland stretching for nearly 60 miles. The outstanding **Scenic Region** covers almost 100,000 acres on the northern slopes of the **San Juan Mountains,** a range of the Rockies. The area is accessible by U.S. 550, the famous *Million Dollar Highway.* But because the terrain is so rugged and the internal roads unimproved, the sites here can be reached only along 100 miles of foot and saddle trails or 40 miles of road open only to vehicles with 4-wheel drive. Near Ouray, where the Million Dollar Highway begins, are 3 peaks over 14,000 feet—**Mount Sneffles** to the west, and **Uncompahgre** and **Wetterhorn peaks** to the east. *Horse Thief Trail,* an arduous mountain trek, leads from Ouray to the **Bridge of Heaven,** a narrow hogback, that slopes nearly 2,000 feet to the valley below. From here one can see **Uncompahgre Peak** to the east and **Red Mountain Pass** (11,018 feet) to the south. Other roads lead to such attractions as **East Ridge** (13,000 feet) and **Yankee Boy** and **Black Bear basins,** two glacier-formed basins named for once-active mines. Perhaps the most spectacular view of the region is from the 13,218-foot summit of **Engineer Mountain.** Accessible by a road that winds through **Poughkeepsie Gulch,** an imposing canyon, and an open meadow near **Miners Creek,** to the arctic-alpine zones as it ascends the mountain, it offers an unforgettable view.

For further information write: 11 and Main, Delta, Colo. 81416

WHITE RIVER NATIONAL FOREST
northcentral Colorado, headquarters at Glenwood Springs

This forest takes its name from the river that rises high in its mountains. Highlighting the attractions here is **Mount of the Holy Cross** (13,978 feet) named for the ravines that form a cross 1,500 feet long with arms extending 750 feet on the mountain's north face. The awesome site is best seen when snow drifts up to 80 feet deep fill the ravines. Among the many scenic regions in the forest is 66,380-acre **Maroon Bells-Snowmass Wilderness** in the **Elk Mountains,** a range of the Rockies. Dominating the skyline are such lofty peaks as **Capital, Snowmass, Maroon, Castle,** and **Pyramid,** all over 14,000 feet. Nearly 130 miles of foot and saddle trails lead to such lovely wilderness spots as **Capital Knife Edge,** where the apex of the northeast ridge of **Capital Peak** (14,000 feet) varies in width from 2 inches to less than an inch, **Conundrum Hot Springs,** a small spring near **Conundrum Creek** that gushes warm water, and **Maroon Lake,** one of the state's most photographed lakes, located near Aspen at the base of Maroon Peak. A unique feature in this forest is *Roaring Fork Braille Trail,* a ¼-mile trail located at 10,400 feet on **Independence Pass** just off State highway 82. The self-guiding trail provides 23 stations equipped with braille plaques explaining the natural history of the area. Except for the removal of extremely hazardous objects and the addition of a nylon cord to guide blind visitors, the trail has been left in its natural state.

For further information write: Federal Building, Ninth and Grand Ave, Glenwood Springs, Colo. 81601

CONNECTICUT

CAMPBELL FALLS STATE PARK
Norfolk vicinity, State 272 near the Massachusetts border

Campbell Falls, which actually lie in Massachusetts, are the main attraction in this scenic, 102-acre park. The falls spill some 50 feet down a wild ravine to the streams below. The rugged appearance of this rocky defile is due partly to the eroding action of the waters which, over the centuries, have forged a series of overhanging crags. It is possible to climb partway up the gray slate rocks of the roaring falls. From the Massachusetts parking and picnic area, there is a fairly steep descent to the falls and ravine through groves of pines and hemlocks. The park presents a colorful display of fall foliage.

CATHEDRAL, OR CALHOUN, PINES
about 5 miles south of Cornwall

Connecticut's most magnificent stand of trees, these giant white pines loom skyward as high as 125 feet in a silent forest. Although sometimes described as a primeval forest, the stand is probably second-growth timber that developed over 200 years ago in an early settler's clearing or in a vacancy in the original forest created by a fire or by a storm. Forming a dense canopy through which shafts of light occasionally penetrate, these sun-loving trees cast their deep shade on a rising generation of hemlock, beech, and maple. The forest has been privately owned for more than 80 years, but access is freely given to all who want to enjoy these venerable trees.

Left: Devil's Hopyard. Right: New London light on Long Island Sound

DEVIL'S HOPYARD STATE PARK
about 3 miles north of East Haddam off State 82

Chapman Falls are the most spectacular feature in the 860-acre park. These falls, on trout-filled Eight Mile River, cascade some 60 feet into a deep gorge called Devil's Hopyard, one of the loveliest in Connecticut. One side of the river is steep and has rugged, wooded trails. The strangely formed ledges and holes in the surrounding rocks are vivid examples of the forces of nature at work. The potholes are perfectly cylindrical and range in width and depth from several inches to several feet. An old folk tale maintains that the devil used to sit on a precipice above the falls and play the violin while the local witches brewed up black-magic potions in the potholes beside the falls. Actually, they were formed when water carried stones from upstream and trapped them in eddies where they spun around and around and wore depressions in the rock.

DINOSAUR TRACKWAY
Dinosaur State Park at Rocky Hill, ¾ miles east of Route I-91

The trackway was discovered in August, 1966, when a bulldozer operator noticed that he had uncovered a slab of rock bearing strangely shaped imprints. The markings proved to be the tracks of dinosaurs of the Triassic period, which lasted from about 225 to 180 million years ago. Although dinosaur tracks are fairly common in the red sandstone and shale of the Connecticut River Valley, those at Rocky Hill are the best preserved. The site, with over 1,000 tracks, is the largest known exposure on a single bedding plane, allowing scientists to study a reptile community as it actually lived. A large section of the trackway, with about 500 footprints, is on view in the exhibit building, which also contains a full-scale reconstruction of a Triassic dinosaur as it might have looked. Registered Natural Landmark
Open Apr–Nov: daily 10–5

HAMMONASSET BEACH PARK
Madison, 1½ miles south of Exit 62 on the Connecticut Turnpike

The largest of the state's shore parks, Hammonasset has 2 miles of frontage on Long Island Sound. With its outcroppings of rocks and marshland to the rear of the beach, the spot is characteristic of Connecticut's rock-bound shoreline. The whole coast is lapped by the sound—which long ago lost its oceanic flavor due to the protection of Long Island—and is dotted by a network of sandy beaches, estuaries, sand spits, small harbors, and intervening marshes.

HANGING HILLS
about 2 miles west of Meriden off U.S. 6A

This range is composed of 2 lava flows in 3 different hills. West Peak, the most westerly one, is also the highest, rising to 1,024 feet. Its summit, which may be reached by a highway, affords a breathtaking panorama of all of central Connecticut. In places the Hanging Hills provide unobstructed views as far as Long Island Sound and Massachusetts. They also house 900-acre Hubbard Park and 181-acre West Peak State Park and may be enjoyed via drives, paths, and nature walks such as the *Metacomet Trail.*

INDIAN WELL STATE PARK
2½ miles northwest of Shelton on State 110

Indian Well is actually a pool formed by erosion at the foot of a waterfall. The Indians believed that it was bottomless, but today it is quite shallow due to the build-up of silt deposits. Before reaching the well, the stream plummets over a spectacular cliff which has been gouged into a troughlike formation by the coursing waters. The park boasts two miles of wooded terrace along the **Housatonic River,** and offers hiking on the *Paugussett Trail.* In the springtime there is a profusion of striped maple and wildflowers.

KENT FALLS STATE PARK
4 miles northeast of Kent on U.S. 7

Reputed to be the most spectacular in Connecticut, Kent Falls rush down a 200-foot drop as they travel a quarter of a mile over a series of cascades. The brook, which is arched by stately hemlocks, passes over a series of marble and limestone ledges, where the eroding action of the water has scooped out numerous potholes. The wooded areas along the stream are ideal for hiking and short walks bring one to a view of the **Housatonic Valley.**

MACEDONIA BROOK STATE PARK
4 miles northwest of Kent off State 341

One of Connecticut's finest nature-study sites, this park occupies the largest area of any of its state parks—about 2,300 acres of hiking trails in a setting of rugged beauty. The visitor may see an abundance of animal life, plant life, and geological phenomena. Coursing through the park are about four miles of Macedonia Brook, which has been called a paradise for fishermen. Hikers can enjoy the *Appalachian Trail,* which passes through the park and leads to the peaks of **Cobble Mountain** and **Pine Hill.**

MOHAWK STATE FOREST AND MOHAWK MOUNTAIN STATE PARK
headquarters, southwest of Goshen on Toumey Road

This forest and park comprise 3,504 acres of magnificent woods traversed by several automobile roads and hiking trails, including a section of the *Appalachian.* Mohawk Mountain State Park contains Connecticut's largest ski area. On a clear day, one can see as far as the **Catskills** from the mountain's summit, which is accessible by road or by trail. The forest has scenic vantage points, interesting geological formations (such as glacial eskers, or gravel ridges known in New England as whalebacks or horsebacks), and many trails (*Great Gulf* and *Mattatuck*). Of particular interest are a large marsh with typical flora and fauna and **Black Spruce Bog.**

SLEEPING GIANT STATE PARK
3½ miles north of Hamden on State 10

One of the basalt ridges typical of the Connecticut Lowland, Sleeping Giant Hills are now encompassed in a park that contains a sampling of woods, streams, rocks, and views characteristic of the state. These five successive rolling hills, which resemble a prostrate cyclopean form, are most striking when viewed from **New Haven Harbor.** According to an Indian legend, the sprawling giant is the spirit Habbamock, who was condemned to eternal sleep for having diverted the waters of the **Connecticut River.** (That its waters were diverted has been confirmed by modern geologists.) The park also boasts 27 miles of nature trails, including a section of the *Quinnipiac. The Heaton Trail,* or *Tower Path,* rises some 739 feet through picturesque terrain to the "stomach," or highest elevation, of the giant. Here there is a lookout tower, from where one has a fine view of the **Hanging Hills** of Meriden (*see*) to the north and New Haven and **Long Island Sound** to the south.

DELAWARE

BLACKBIRD–APPOQUINIMINK SALT MARSHES
southeast New Castle County

Over 2,000 acres of coastal salt marsh on **Delaware Bay,** seriously threatened by heavy industry and drainage, have been preserved by a citizen conservation organization. These salt marshes are a favorite winter home or stopover for migratory waterfowl, such as Canada geese. They are a valuable natural resource and a vital link in the ecology of the region. Thomas Jefferson once referred to Delaware as "a jewel among the states." The salt marsh is an intrinsic part of its character and beauty.

BRANDYWINE CREEK STATE PARK
4 miles north of Wilmington off State 100

The terrain of this 433-acre park is typical of the northern counties of Delaware with its high-rolling meadows and woodlands sloping down to Brandywine Creek. For this reason a major portion of the park has been designated a nature-study area and is utilized by nature explorers the year round. Here, the Delaware Nature Education Center conducts such activities as bird migration counts, compilation of a catalogue of wildflowers native to the state, and tours over the nature trails in the park.
Open daily: 8–one hour after sunset

Left: Great Cypress Swamp. Right: Blackbird-Appoquinimink salt marshes

DELAWARE

CAPE HENLOPEN STATE PARK
1 mile east of Lewes on State 18

Cape Henlopen is the high sandy hook of land that marks the entrance to **Delaware Bay.** The ocean beach of steep, white sand and pounding surf has long made the area a popular recreation site. In addition, the Cape is of great interest to naturalists. Due to a predominating northwesterly winds, the sands of Delaware's ocean coast are constantly shifting. Over a period of time, this causes the dunes to "walk." The largest example of this phenomenon is the **Great Walking Dune.** Strange, rare plants are hidden among the dunes along with wind-dwarfed trees. Colonies of sea birds nest at the tip of the Cape, and many other species stop here during migration season. There are 2 nature trails in the park: *Pinelands Nature Trail* traverses the dunes, skirts cranberry bogs, and penetrates a pitch-pine forest. *Seaside Nature Trail* is routed through dense thickets and natural pine plantations.

GREAT CYPRESS SWAMP
Sussex County, west of Selbyville

A 3,500-acre tract on the Delaware–Maryland border is all that remains of a unique freshwater swamp that once covered much of the **Delmarva Peninsula.** Here, on the headwaters of the **Pocomoke River** and to the west, in the **Trap-Trusum ponds** area (*see*), is the northernmost stand of giant bald cypress trees in the country. Generations of farmers clearing land, shingle makers, and a great fire in 1930 reduced the swamp to the remnants found today. The lustrous hand-riven shingles of Pocomoke cypress can still be seen on many of the mossy old houses in the area.
For further information write: Delaware Wild Lands, Inc., 1011 Washington St, Wilmington, Del. 19801

TRAP POND STATE PARK
5 miles east of Laurel off State 24

The main feature of this wooded park is the stand of giant bald cypress trees at the headwaters of Trap Pond. Visitors can canoe through the clear, amber waters—stained by the tannic acid in the cypress roots—in boats available from the park. There is also a ¼-mile nature trail which presents a living museum of the south Delaware environment. West of the park, at **Trusum Pond,** Delaware Wild Lands has preserved another portion of this cypress-swamp landscape once called the Delaware Everglades.

Cape Henlopen

DISTRICT OF COLUMBIA

GREAT FALLS OF THE POTOMAC

15 miles northwest of Washington via George Washington Memorial Parkway

Forming the boundary between Virginia and Maryland, the Great Falls are a series of cascades and rapids in the historic **Potomac River**. Here, upstream from the nation's capital, the Potomac pours over picturesque falls (the highest is 35'feet) and swirls into thundering rapids (the deepest is the 200-foot-deep **Mather Gorge**). There are spectacular views of the falls from the state parks with scenic walks that are maintained on either side of the river. The Virginia park features the remnants of the 1785 Patowmack Canal associated with George Washington. In the Maryland park the restored Great Falls Tavern (1832) has natural exhibits of the area.

ROCK CREEK PARK

This 1,754-acre natural woodland park follows scenic Rock Creek and the rugged steep-walled gorge it cuts out to its confluence with the **Potomac River**. Among the park's attractions are many points of historical interest, the National Zoological Park, and the Rock Creek Nature Center, with a self-guided nature trail.

THEODORE ROOSEVELT ISLAND

off the George Washington Parkway above Theodore Roosevelt Bridge

This 88-acre wilderness island in the **Potomac River** was established as a memorial to President Theodore Roosevelt for his pioneering efforts in conservation. Maintained as a natural area, it features 50 species of trees and over 200 varieties of wildflowers amidst swamps, forests, and marshes. Accessible only by foot, the island is crisscrossed by 3½ miles of trails.

Left: memorial statue of Theodore Roosevelt. Right: Great Falls of the Potomac

FLORIDA

APALACHICOLA NATIONAL FOREST
west Florida, headquarters at Tallahassee

Extending west from Tallahassee to the **Apalachicola River**, this 556,500-acre forest abounds in wildlife including black bear and panther. Among the many scenic regions here are **Silver Lake**, a 23-acre lake set in a grove of oak, pine, cypress, and cedar; **Wright Lake**, an 8-acre natural lake surrounded by Spanish moss-draped cypress and pine; **Hitchcock** and **Whitehead lakes**, with beautiful hardwood hammocks on the backwaters of the **Ochlockonee River**. *For further information write: Box 9, Tallahassee, Fla. 32304*

BIG CYPRESS SWAMP
southwest Florida

Covering 2,400 square miles on the western edge of the **Everglades**, this area is a vast forest morass that has been described as a "green carpet drenched with a hose." Collier-Seminole State Park, 17 miles south of Naples, covers 6,432 acres of the swamp and can be reached by the historic Tamiami Trail (U.S. 41). Here too is the Seminole Indian Reservation. Another section of the swamp is **Big Cypress Bend**, which includes a 215-acre virgin cypress forest with many trees 100 feet high and over 5 feet in diameter, a 100-acre sawgrass prairie, and 100 acres of palmetto hammocks. The Bend is a Registered Natural Landmark.

THE BIG TREE
6 miles south and 2 miles west of Sanford off U.S. 17 and 92

This cypress tree—126 feet high, 17½ inches in diameter, with a circumference of 47 feet—is believed to be 3,500 years old. Named "the Senator" for State Senator M. O. Overstreet, who donated it and the surrounding land to the county, it is said to be the oldest and largest tree of its kind in the United States.

BISCAYNE NATIONAL MONUMENT
about 10 miles south of Miami metropolitan area

This tropical marine park comprises 96,000 acres of which only 4,000 are land areas—a chain of 25 islands or keys. Established to protect the subtropical coastal area, the monument stretches northeasterly from above the tip of Key Largo to Sands Key and extends seaward for 5 miles. It goes to a depth of 60 feet near the Florida Current (Gulf Stream) and includes what are considered to be the most northerly living coral reefs in the United States. Here is a rich and varied display of marine life. On the ocean side of the keys, in the treacherous reef waters, many species of coral, sea whips, and seafeathers abound along with over 250 species of marine fishes, including barracuda, shark, parrotfish, and Spanish hog fish. On the landward side of the keys, in **Biscayne Bay**, are many kinds of fish and shellfish, as well as the manatee, a large aquatic mammal.

Little remains of the original tropical hardwood forests that once covered the keys, although many other kinds of trees can still be found including mangrove, torchwood, Jamaica dogwood, and redberried eugenia. Rare specimens include mahoganies on Sands Key and a stand of Sargent palm, once considered extinct, on Elliott Key. Many south Florida and West Indian birds are found here, among them such rarities as the egret and short-tailed hawk. *For further information write: Box 279, Homestead, Fla. 33030*

Top left: reefs in John Pennekamp Coral Reef State Park. Right: Alexander Springs in Ocala National Forest. Below: Biscayne National Monument

FLORIDA

CALADESI ISLAND STATE PARK
off Dunedin in the Gulf of Mexico

Called "beautiful bayou" by the Spanish, this lovely island is located off the Florida panhandle and is washed by the **Gulf of Mexico** and **St. Josephs Bay**. It features 3 miles of beaches on the Gulf shore and dense mangrove thickets on the bay. A sandy ridge about 12 feet high runs down the center of the island to groves of oak and pine at the south end. The many natural attractions, including tropical birds, can be seen along 20 miles of canoe trails and from a 60-foot observation tower.

CORKSCREW SWAMP SANCTUARY
about 25 miles southeast of Fort Myers on State 82

This 6,080-acre swamp wilderness includes the largest remaining stand of virgin bald cypress in North America. Here among these majestic Spanish moss-draped cypress (dated at 700 years old and reaching heights of 130 feet), animals such as bobcats and alligators can be found along with more than 40 species of birds. A ⅞-mile-long boardwalk provides a dry self-guided trail through the sanctuary which is maintained by the National Audubon Society. Registered Natural Landmark

Open daily 9–5; closed July 4, Thanksgiving, Christmas, New Year's Day. Admission: adults $1.00

EVERGLADES NATIONAL PARK
headquarters, 12 miles west of Homestead on State 27; other entrances off the Tamiami Trail (U.S. 41)

Called "Pa-hay-okee" (grassy waters) by the Seminoles, the Everglades are a vast complex of marshy grasslands, murky swamps, open waterways, and islands of trees and bushes. Covering over 1,400,000 acres at the southern tip of the Florida peninsula, the park is the largest remaining subtropical wilderness in the United States. Here many unusual plants and animals—some found nowhere else in the country—exist in their natural environment. In the fresh and salt waters and on dry land are wild crocodiles and alligators, many kinds of reptiles, among them poisonous coral snakes and diamondback rattlers, turtles weighing up to 800 pounds, manatees and porpoises, many small mammals, including otters, foxes, and squirrels, and many larger ones, such as panthers, bobcats, and black bears. In addition the park boasts what is considered to be the largest and most unusual bird community in North America—nearly 300 species including the egret and roseate spoonbill, both close to extinction earlier in the century. Plant life in the Everglades occurs in 6 general types of areas—hammocks, bayheads, cypress heads, pinelands, mangrove swamps, and marshes—each with its distinctive type of vegetation. Hammocks—small elevated mounds or islands rising above the marshes of Jamaica sawgrass—support growths of moss, fern, orchids, and hardwood trees. Especially noteworthy is the royal palm, found only in this part of the continent. Unfortunately, a large part of the mangrove forest was destroyed by Hurricane Donna in 1960.

The park can be seen by boat, car, or on foot. A 38-mile drive goes from park headquarters at Royal Palm, near the Homestead entrance, across the southern section to Flamingo. From this drive and the spur roads and foot trails that lead off it, most of the park's major attractions can be seen. Among the points of interest are: *Anhinga Trail*, in the wet regions where alligators, birds, and other wildlife abound; *Gumbo Limbo Trail*, which leads through a

A *lagoon and 2 newly-hatched egrets in Everglades National Park*

tropical hardwood hammock; *Mahagony Hammock Trail,* featuring a rare stand of mahagony trees; and *West Lake Trail,* which skirts a mangrove swamp. At *Pa-hay-okee Overlook,* a boardwalk and observation tower offer panoramic views. The *Shark Valley Loop Road* in the northern section penetrates 15 miles into the Everglades, although it is closed in some seasons.

In addition there are 3 marked canoe trails in the vicinity of Flamingo and a spectacular 99-mile *Wilderness Waterway* from Flamingo through rivers, creeks, and bays to Everglades City. Because of the shallow water only small craft (less than 20 feet) should make the trip; all boaters must file a float plan. The Western Water Gateway at Everglades City leads into the **Gulf of Mexico** and the **Ten Thousand Islands,** a chain of islands within the park's boundaries. Covered with mangrove swamps and surrounded by clam beds, they are a fisherman's paradise. A nature trail on **Sandfly Island** offers a glimpse of the area's natural history.

Flamingo visitor center open daily 8:30–5. Royal Palm visitor center open Wed–Sun: 9–5. For further information write: Everglades National Park, Box 279, Homestead, Fla. 33030

FALLING WATERS STATE PARK
3 miles south of Chipley on State 77A

The hilly terrain in this 152-acre park is dotted with limestone caves, hardwood forests, and a beautiful waterfall, an unusual site in Florida. From a platform there is a lovely view of the flowing stream falling 80 feet into a limestone sink. Marked trails lead through the most scenic areas of this natural woodland.

FLORIDA CAVERNS STATE PARK
3 miles north of Marianna on State 167

This intricate network of limestone caves was long known to Indians of the region before they were first sighted by the Spanish in 1693. The interesting stalactite and stalagmite formations can be seen on a ¾-mile tour through lighted passageways. The park, located in the valley of the **Chipola River,** also features gardens, wildlife, and a natural rock garden.

Caverns open daily: 8–sunset. Admission: adults $1.55; children (6–12) 52¢

FLORIDA

GROSSMAN HAMMOCK STATE PARK
11 miles northwest of Homestead

An oasis of hardwood trees and springs amongst the sawgrass marshes of the **Everglades**, this 640-acre park is located 5 miles east of Everglades National Park (*see*). Also here is **Lake Chekika,** named for a leader of the Seminoles, and an Indian burial mound where excavations have unearthed artifacts 2,000 years old.

GULF ISLANDS NATIONAL SEASHORE. *See* MISSISSIPPI

HIGHLANDS HAMMOCK STATE PARK
6 miles west of Sebring off U.S. 27 on State 634

One of the outstanding scenic attractions in Florida, this 3,800-acre subtropical park is located in a beautiful jungle swamp and hardwood forest. Sabal palms, pines, sweet gums, and ancient oaks (some over 100 feet tall and 31 feet in circumference) are a few of the many trees that line 10 miles of foot trails and 2 miles of scenic driveways. In addition fascinating vegetation can be seen from the wooden walkways that lead through **Charley Bowlegs Cypress Swamp.** In the nature museum are displays of flora and fauna found in the park; guided tours are available.

HOMOSASSA SPRINGS
75 miles north of Tampa at junction of U.S. 19 and 98

This fresh-water spring flows at a rate of 6 million gallons an hour. Thousands of fresh- and salt-water fish (34 varieties have been spotted) can be seen from the large observatory that floats in the center of the spring. Other features include an alligator lagoon, a sea lion spring, deer and bird parks, and a rich display of orchids. Boats cruise through the waters.

Open daily 8–6. Admission: adults $2.75, children (6–12) $1.40

JOHN PENNEKAMP CORAL REEF STATE PARK
off Key Largo, entrance from U.S. 1

This fascinating state park, the only underwater one of its kind in the country, covers about 75 square miles of protected ocean water. It is 21 miles long and extends 6 miles into the **Atlantic** off Key Largo. From glass-bottom boats one can see this living coral reef with over 40 species of coral and hundreds of species of tropical fish. Recreational facilities are available on shore including a nature walk through the mangroves.

LAKE OKEECHOBEE
southcentral Florida
> The second largest fresh-water lake entirely within the boundaries of the United States, this awesome body of water is about 35 miles long, 30 miles wide, and at its deepest point is 15 feet. It is so shallow that a wading bird can be seen a mile from shore. Shrouded in mystery and legend (early Spanish explorers called it "Name of the Holy Ghost"), the lake is said to turn into a "cauldron of destruction" during a hurricane. To prevent its overflow, it has levees on three sides; the **Kissimmee River** flows into it from the north.

LONG KEY STATE PARK
off U.S. 1 at Layton, about 75 miles south of Miami
> This 291-acre park is located on one of the many beautiful **Florida Keys,** a chain of islands connected to the mainland by the Overseas Highway (U.S. 1). A sand-covered coral island, Long Key is dense with tropical vegetation—mangrove thickets are especially prevalent. Water sports and fishing are available in **Florida Bay** on the west side of the island as well as in the **Atlantic Ocean.**

OCALA NATIONAL FOREST
northcentral Florida, headquarters at Ocala
> This lush, junglelike forest situated between the **Oklawaha** and **St. Johns rivers,** contains the largest stand of sand pine in the world. Other trees in the 366,000-acre forest include longleaf, slash and other pine, cypress, and hardwoods. In addition the forest boasts 20,000 acres of lakes and ponds, over 50 miles of spring runs, and more than 150 miles of rivers. Two outstanding attractions are **Juniper Springs** and **Alexander Springs** recreation areas, both built around clear, bubbling springs that flow at a constant temperature of 72°. Juniper Springs produces 8.3 million gallons daily and Alexander Springs produces 76 million gallons daily. Other points of interest in the forest include **Clearwater** and **Halfmoon lakes, Johnson Field,** a large hammock adjacent to the Oklawaha River, and the **Ocala Wildlife Management Area,** home of one of the largest herds of deer in the state.
> *For further information write: Box 1206, Ocala, Fla. 32670*

OKEFENOKEE SWAMP. *See* **GEORGIA**

Lake Okeechobee

FLORIDA

OSCEOLA NATIONAL FOREST
north Florida, headquarters at Lake City

Named for an early 19th-century Seminole chief, this forest covers 157,000 acres of scenic flat land, swamps, creeks, and rivers. **Ocean Pond**, a 2,000-acre natural lake surrounded by cypress trees draped with Spanish moss, is typical of the misty, eerie atmosphere found in the forest. At Olustee, east of the Ocean Pond area, a monument commemorates the largest Civil War battle fought in Florida.
For further information write: P.O. Building, Lake City, Fla. 32055

RAINBOW SPRINGS
4 miles north of Dunnellon on U.S. 41

Thousands of individual springs producing 459 millions of gallons daily make up this scenic attraction. Here too are the 60-foot **Rainbow Falls**, one of the highest waterfalls in the state, and *Rainbow Trail*, a path winding through lush tropical greenery. Boats with cabins suspended 5 feet below the surface of the springs afford spectacular views of the underwater environment.
Open June 16–Labor Day: daily 9–7; Labor Day–June 15: daily 10–6

RAVINE GARDENS STATE PARK
about ¼ mile from Saint Johns River in Palatka, entrance on Twigg St

Over 100,000 azaleas and other flowering plants have been placed around the natural ravine in this beautifully landscaped, 85-acre park. Believed to have been dug out by water from over 10 underground springs here, the ravines (70 to 120 feet deep) are a rarity in Florida. A 5-mile scenic drive and paths lead through the grounds.

REED WILDERNESS SEASHORE SANCTUARY
8 miles south of Stuart off U.S. 1

This stretch of beach, typical of Florida's Atlantic coast, lies between the ocean and the sound known as **Peak Lake**. It is one of the last remaining undeveloped areas of its kind. Predominantly a mangrove swamp, some of the black mangroves are as large as 4 feet in diameter. The beach is an important nesting site of the Atlantic loggerhead turtle. Registered Natural Landmark

SILVER SPRINGS
5½ miles east of Ocala on State 40

This 100-acre park (Florida's Silver Springs) bordering the scenic **Silver River** is the site of 14 separate spring groups that produce a half a billion gallons of water daily at a uniform temperature of 72°. Hundreds of underwater plants and 35 varieties of fish can be seen in the spring, on the river, and in an aquarium. Glass-bottom boat rides through the springs and cruises on the river are available.

WAKULLA SPRINGS
15 miles south of Tallahassee off State 61

Clear water of an even temperature and near-constant flow runs year round in this 185-foot deep spring said to be the largest and deepest in the world. Named "Mysteries of Strange Waters" by the Indians, it is the source of the **Wakulla River,** an unspoiled waterway lined with Spanish moss-draped cypress and surrounded by a large hardwood hammock with 100-foot trees. The river and the spring are home to many fish, alligators, and turtles, and to various species of birds including rare limpkins and anhingas. Glass-bottom boat rides through the spring and "jungle cruises" on the river are available. Registered Natural Landmark
Open May–Labor Day: daily 9–7; Labor Day–Apr: daily 9–5

AMICALOLA FALLS STATE PARK
Juno, 16 miles northwest of Dawsonville via State 183 and 52

The main feature of this park is Amicalola Falls, the highest in the state. They are formed by a clear mountain creek plunging 729 feet in a series of 7 cascades. High in the **Blue Ridge Mountains,** the park includes some of Georgia's most beautiful scenery. The *Amicalola Falls Nature Trail* extends from the stream below the falls to the lake above them. Another hiking trail leads from the top of the falls 6.9 miles north to **Springer Mountain,** the southernmost peak of the Blue Ridge and the terminal of the *Appalachian Trail.*

BLACK ROCK MOUNTAIN STATE PARK
Mountain City, 3 miles north of Clayton on U.S. 441 and 23

The mountain, named for its humped shoulders and sheer cliff of dark granite, rises to an altitude of 3,600 feet. From its summit one can, on a clear day, see as far as 30 miles to areas of North and South Carolina as well as of Georgia

CHATTAHOOCHEE NATIONAL FOREST
north Georgia, headquarters at Gainesville

With its rivers, streams, and well-timbered rich, red soil, this 677,000-acre forest is typical of the southern **Appalachian Mountain** area. It rises abruptly in the foothills of the Piedmont, crosses over the **Blue Ridge,** and then slopes to the north, where it is bounded by North Carolina's Nantahala National Forest and by Tennessee's

Brasstown Bald and a typical pine stand in Chattahoochee National Forest

GEORGIA

Cherokee National Forest (*see both*). The forest is the source of several of the South's important rivers, including the **Coosa, Tennessee, Savannah,** and the **Chattahoochee** itself. It is also the home of a great many species of fish, birds, and animals, and boasts the greatest diversity—over 136 species—of trees in North America. The most prevalent are poplar, maple, pine, hemlock, basswood, cucumber, ash, white oak, and red oak. The forest is threaded by hundreds of miles of roads and trails, which are particularly attractive during the fall foliage and spring flowering seasons. It contains Georgia's highest mountain, 4,784-foot-high **Brasstown Bald,** and its highest body of water, **Lake Conasauga,** 3,200 feet above sea level. Among its many other scenic areas are **Sosebee Cove,** which boasts stands of towering yellow poplar and buckeye; **High Shoals,** with its 5 waterfalls and luxuriant flora; and **Anna Ruby Twin Falls,** which have drops of 153 and 50 feet. Another point of interest is 3,782-foot **Springer Mountain,** the southern terminus of the *Appalachian National Scenic Trail,* which extends for about 2,000 miles beginning on **Mount Katahdin** in Maine. This region has been immortalized by Sidney Lanier, one of Georgia's most famous poets.
For further information write: Box 1437, Gainesville, Ga. 30501

CROOKED RIVER STATE PARK
about 12 miles northeast of Kingsland

This park, which offers many recreational facilities, is located on the north bank of **Saint Marys River.** Its name derives from the fact that the river runs a very crooked course through southeast Georgia and northeast Florida. It is about 175 miles long, but a straight line from its source to its mouth would be only about 65 miles long.

MAGNOLIA SPRINGS STATE PARK
5 miles north of Millen on U.S. 25 and State 21

These crystal-clear springs, which literally bubble forth from the ground, flow at an estimated 9 million gallons per day. Because of the depth of the spring the water is ice cold. It forms a 12-to-15-foot-deep pool whose bottom is covered with easily visible marine plants. During the Civil War, the park was the site of Fort Lawton, a Confederate military prison.

OCONEE NATIONAL FOREST
central Georgia, headquarters at Gainesville

This forest, which is divided into 3 sections, comprises over 100,000 acres in the gently rolling hill country of the Piedmont. The **Oconee River** and 15,330-acre **Lake Sinclair** provide recreation and excellent fishing. The **Piedmont National Wildlife Refuge** abuts that portion of the forest bordered by the **Ocmulgee River.**
For further information write: Box 1437, Gainesville, Ga. 3051

OKEFENOKEE SWAMP
8 miles south of Waycross on U.S. 1 and 23

One of the largest freshwater swamps in the United States, and one of the most primitive, Okefenokee is famous for its weird, mysterious beauty. Most of its 660 square miles are in southeastern Georgia, but a portion lies in northeastern Florida. About ⅔ of the swamp is a national wildlife refuge, where there are heavy concentrations of bear, deer, bobcats, alligators, otters, and other creatures. The swamp is especially important as a haven for some 200 types of birds, notably the exotic white ibis and threatened species like the osprey, bald eagle, and Florida sand-hill crane. The only way to penetrate this eerie region of water, prairie, cypress, jungle, and spongy islands—some floating and some anchored—is by canoe. There are several marked trails through the lily-filled water. The Indians called the swamp Owaquaphenoga, which means "land of the trembling earth." In many places merely pressing down on the swamp floor makes the trees shake violently because the island bogs are made chiefly of a thick (up to 20 feet) deposit of peat only tenuously attached to the bottom by plant matter. Okefenokee is famous as the home of Pogo, the comicstrip character. In its dark waters rises the **Suwanee River,** which flows across Florida and empties into the **Gulf of Mexico.** Aside from the wildlife refuge, the swamp contains the Stephen C. Foster State Park, noted for its virgin stand of cypress, and Okefenokee Swamp Park, with its flower gardens, bird sanctuaries, alligator pools, and animal exhibits. *For further information: Okefenokee National Wildlife Refuge, Box 117, Waycross, Ga. 31501*

PROVIDENCE CANYONS
8 miles west of Lumpkin on U.S. 27 and State 27

These rainbow-hued canyons, some of which are 200 to 300 feet deep, are a phenomenon of land erosion. Apparently, below the topsoil of this region there was a 100-foot layer of loose-clay sand covering blue marl, a hard-clay limestone. For centuries, rainwater had been eating away at the marine sands formed when the area was part of the ocean's floor. Finally, about 150 years ago, the earth above began crumbling, and the "gobling monster" devoured more and more land, including farms, fields, and houses. Today the canyons cover about 3,000 acres.

Providence Canyons

Stone Mountain

RADIUM SPRINGS
about 2 miles south of Albany on State 3

Now the center of a well-known resort, these springs were called "skywater" by the Creek Indians, who believed that their blue waters had dropped from the sky. The main spring, with a flow of 70,000 gallons per minute, is the state's largest. It maintains a constant temperature of 68° and its source is unknown.

Open April–mid-Sept: daily 9–7

SEA ISLANDS
southeast Georgia, off the coast near Brunswick

Although there are several "sea islands" off the Georgia coast, the term refers essentially to **Saint Simons, Jekyll,** and **Sea Island** itself, all connected to the mainland by causeways. Formed by the vigorous currents that sweep the coast, and threaded by the Intracoastal Waterway, the "Golden Isles" are palm-fringed, semitropical paradises. Gulf Stream breezes ensure year-round vacation weather. Jekyll is now a state-owned public park. It features a 9½-mile-long ocean beach, a wildlife refuge, and excellent fishing conditions. Saint Simons is the site of **Fort Frederica National Monument,** which contains the ruins of an important British fortress during the War of Jenkins' Ear (1739–48). It is also famous for its 200-year-old live oaks festooned with Spanish moss. Sea Island, now a fashionable resort, offers a lovely setting of palms and pines and 5 miles of beach. The islands' terrain includes the boggy marshes characteristic of the whole Georgia coast, as well as heavily wooded areas. There is also a group of remarkably beautiful sea marshes between the coast and the islands.

STONE MOUNTAIN STATE PARK
16 miles east of Atlanta on U.S. 78

One of the largest solid masses of exposed granite on earth, Stone Mountain covers 583 acres and is 1,686 feet high. The mountain, probably some 200 million years old, is also the site of the world's largest sculptural work—a colossal equestrian carving of Generals Robert E. Lee and "Stonewall" Jackson and Confederate President Jefferson Davis. This Confederate Memorial Monument was designed in 1916 by Gutzon Borglum, sculptor of the Mount Rushmore Memorial *(see)* in South Dakota. Carving began in 1923, but problems ensued and the project was temporarily abandoned. It

was resumed recently and the monument on the mountain's steep north side is now almost completed. This 3,200-acre park has several hiking and nature trails. One of these, *Mountain Walk-Up Trail*, leads to Stone Mountain's summit, which affords a magnificent view. There are gardens and a lake with a canoe trail.
Open Labor Day–June: daily 10–5; summer 10–9

TALLULAH GORGE PARK
Tallulah Falls in northeast Georgia

This 1,000-foot-deep gorge is lushly vegetated—even its steep, rugged walls are covered with trees and shrubs. **Tallulah River,** which originally cut the deep crevice with its rushing torrents, was diverted in 1913 to provide power for a hydroelectric dam. Today only a trickle of water flows over what was once the scene of a beautiful waterfall. The park offers a trail around the gorge's rim.
Open daily Apr–Oct: 8–dark. Admission: 45¢

TOCCOA FALLS
2 miles northeast of Toccoa on grounds of Toccoa Falls Institute

Nestled in the foothills of the **Blue Ridge Mountains,** these falls are formed by **Toccoa Creek** as it plummets over a 186-foot-high precipice. The thin veil of mist tumbling over the moss-covered rocks is a beautiful sight. There is a path leading to the rocks behind the falls and a rustic stairway leading to the top of the falls.
Open: daily 7:30–7:30. Admission: 50¢

WARM SPRINGS

Located in a city of the same name in western Georgia, these gentle springs at the foot of **Pine Mountain** were made famous by President Franklin D. Roosevelt, who went there for physical therapy after contracting poliomyelitis. The springs, whose healing properties were known to the Indians, maintain a constant temperature of about 88° and flow at the rate of 800 gallons per minute. Geologists discovered that rain which falls on the top of Pine Mountain and on other high places in the vicinity penetrates the rock strata and travels at least 2,800 feet into the earth. A break in the rock strata under Warm Springs permits the water to reach the surface. The Little White House, Roosevelt's Georgia home and the scene of his death, is open to the public.

Live oak forest on Jekyll Island in the Sea Islands group

HAWAII

Island of Hawaii

AKAKA FALLS STATE PARK

Hamakua coast district, 10 miles north of Hilo, access off State 22
This 65-acre park is so densely canopied by its lush flora—notably giant gingers, ferns, azaleas, orchids, and bamboo—that the sunlight assumes a muted quality. Magnificent Akaka Falls, the state's largest easily accessible waterfall, plunges 420 feet over a moss-covered volcanic cliff into **Kolekole Stream.**

HAWAII VOLCANOES NATIONAL PARK

park headquarters, southwest of Hilo via Mamalohoa Highway (State 11)
With its unique volcanic formations, tropical rain forests, deserts, rare birds, and the only two active volcanoes in the Hawaiian Archipelago—**Mauna Loa** and **Kilauea**—this 344-square-mile park is one of the Aloha State's greatest attractions. Mauna Loa, believed to be the largest active volcano in the world and probably the biggest single mountain on earth, rises approximately 13,680 feet above sea level and over 30,000 feet from the ocean floor. At its summit is a large depression called **Mokuaweoweo Crater.** This is actually a caldera, a crater formed by the collapse of a volcanic cone. Kilauea, whose gentle slopes abut and merge with the slopes of Mauna Loa on the west and the north, is even more active. The 4,000-foot-high summit of the volcano has collapsed to form a broad, shallow caldera paved with recent lava flows. This is **Halemaumau,** Kilauea's most active vent and the traditional home of Pele, Polynesian goddess of volcanoes. Halemaumau's rim may be reached via self-guiding *Halemaumau Trail,* called the "world's weirdest walk." Beginning near the park headquarters, it traverses Kilauea caldera's scorched, scarred floor. The flora includes warped, grayish trees and plants, ash beds and rock, steam cracks, as well as lichens. In recent decades, Kilauea has averaged an eruption every 2 years. There is a visitor center and museum near headquarters that offer films on the eruptions.

Crater Rim Drive provides one of the best orientations to the park. Traveling clockwise from headquarters, this road leads to **Thurston Lava Tube,** which once conducted a flowing mass of hot, molten lava. When the outer crust hardened and the inner portion flowed away, a tunnel remained. It can be explored for about 500 feet. A short distance beyond is the **Tree Fern Jungle,** which contains 2 self-guiding trails. This huge, tropical forest is watered by rains carried by the northeast trade winds. It boasts many varieties of giant tree ferns shaded by ohia trees, which are related to the eucalyptus and have scarlet or yellow blossoms. The drive continues to an area of **Kilauea Crater** where there is an excellent view of Halemaumau firepit. South and west of Kilauea Crater, the road leads to the upper edge of the **Kau Desert,** which receives no rain from the trade winds, but only an occasional soaking from a heavy general storm. In harsh contrast to the fern forest, the desert is an arid region of crusted volcanic ash, pahoehoe lava (smooth surfaced and shaped like strands of twisted rope), and dunes of wind-blown ash and pumice. It may be explored via several hiking trails. Other sights along the Crater Rim Drive include **Steaming Bluff** and **Sulfur Banks.** *Mauna Loa Strip Road* (off State 11) leads to **Tree Molds,** some as wide as 5 feet across, formed when liquid lava cooled around tree trunks, burning the insides out and crusting

Top left: Lava trees on Hawaii. Top right: Silversword, Haleakala National Park on Maui. Center: Diamond Head on Oahu. Below: Wailua Falls on Maui

along the outsides. It continues to **Kipuka Puaula,** or Bird Park, which covers about 100 acres on a kipuka—an island of vegetation bypassed by older lava flows. Where such an area remains undisturbed by lava long enough, soil builds up and trees reach maximum growth. A self-guiding trail leads into a forested section of the park, where there are many native trees and birds. From Kipuka Puaula there is a 10-mile drive to an overlook partway up Mauna Loa at 6,662 feet. At the road's end there is an 18.2-mile hiking trail to Mauna Loa's summit. The *Chain of Craters Road* leads southeast of Kilauea Crater to the seacoast of Kalapana. It passes near the rims of 9 pit craters. Due to eruptions in 1969, 3 miles of this road were closed, but motorists may visit either end. One of the most recently completed drives in the park is the new 19-mile *Kalapana Road.* From **Makaopuhi Crater,** along Chain of Craters Road, it traverses ohia forests to the top of **Poliokeawe Pali,** a bluff from which there are sweeping views of the shoreline. On a clear day one can see **Ka Lae,** the southernmost point in the United States.

For further information write: Superintendent, Hawaii 96718

KAIMU BLACK SAND BEACH
Puna district, near Kalapana just southwest of junction of State 13 and 137
With its jet-black sand, white surf, and towering coconut palms, Kaimu Beach is an esthetic treat. The dark sand was formed when molten lava exploded into fine crystals as it hit the ocean and then was pulverized by the action of the waves.

KAPOHO CONE
Puna district, on State 137 near village of Pohoiki
This broad, green-cloaked mound was formed by an ancient volcanic eruption. A road leads to its low rim, from where one can walk down inside the cone. Here there is a 6-acre lake that appears green because of abundant algae and surrounding jungle growth.

KAUMANA CAVES
Hilo district, about 5 miles from downtown Hilo on State 20
These lava tubes and many branching caverns were formed during the 1881 eruption of **Mauna Loa** (*see Hawaii Volcanoes National Park*), when the flow lasted 9 months and came closer to Hilo than at any other recorded time. From a picnic area there is a stairway leading to a fern grotto between two facing lava tubes. The one pointed toward Hilo (2½ to 15 feet high and 10 to 60 feet wide) may be explored, but the other is too dangerous to enter.

KONA COAST
With its beaches that are ideal for surfing and its excellent facilities for deep-sea fishing, the Kona coast is one of the state's most famous resort areas. It also abounds in historic significance. Captain James Cook, who discovered the Hawaiian Islands, was killed here in **Kealakekua Bay** in 1779. The Kona area was also the birthplace in 1758 of Kamehameha I, who began a powerful dynasty that ruled the islands for 100 years. The south end of Kona contains **Mauna Loa's** last lava flows, 100,000-acre Honaunau Forest, and many orchards. On the south shore of **Honaunau Bay** is **City of Refuge National Historical Park**—the site of an important place of refuge.

LAVA TREE STATE PARK
Puna district, about 3 miles east of Pahoa on State 132
Located in the Nanawale Forest Preserve, this 17-acre park is the site of the "petrified Hawaiians," weird, lava-encrusted tree trunks.

The area was once occupied by a grove of large ohia trees, but this lush forest was engulfed by lava during an eruption, around 1790, from the east rift of **Kilauea** (*see Hawaii Volcanoes National Park*). The trees were completely buried, but there was enough moisture in their trunks to harden the lava into a rigid shell.

MAUNA KEA STATE PARK
Puhakuloa area, about 37 miles west of Hilo on State 20

Located on the slopes of majestic, 13,796-foot-high Mauna Kea Volcano—the state's highest peak—this park is divided into 2 areas. **Pohakuloa** camp is set in bird grasslands at 6,500 feet. Here there are Hawaiian trees and several types of native fowl, including the rare nene geese. **Hale Pohaku,** a timber-line camp at 9,200 feet, features emerald grasses carpeting cinder cones, grazing herds, and introduced game. Two routes lead to Mauna Kea's summit, a 6-mile hiking trail and a 4-wheel-drive road, whose use is controlled. The summit itself, a cluster of rainbow-hued cones, boasts the state s only snow skiing in season. From here there is a magnificent view of other volcanoes as well as fields of cinders and hardened lava. Other attractions on Mauna Kea include mysterious **Lake Waiau** (at 13,000 feet); because of an impervious bottom, the water does not seep away through the porous lava. At about 12,000 feet, at the end of a short footpath from the road, is **Keanakakoi Cave**—the world's most extensive primitive adz quarry.

POLULU VALLEY
Kohala district, about 1½ miles east of Niulii

This broad, green-carpeted valley lies between 5,505-foot **Kohala Mountain** and a coast of precipitous scenic gorges. Guided trips on mule-back may be made into Pololu and along the top of the cliffs overlooking its gorges. For hardy hikers, there is a 40-mile network of wet, slippery trails into this and other valleys named **Honokane-Nui, Hokokane-Iki, Honokea,** and **Honopue.** Advance arrangements with the Kohala Sugar Company are necessary.

WAILOA RIVER STATE PARK
in Hilo City at the north end of Piilani St

A landscaped river and lakeside area, this 146-acre park includes **Wailoa River, Waiakea Fishpond**—fed by freshwater springs—and **Waiolama Canal.** It offers excellent fishing opportunities.

Left: black sand beach at Honaunau Bay on Kona Coast. Right: Tree Fern Jungle in Hawaii Volcanoes National Park

HAWAII

WAILUKU RIVER STATE PARK
in Hilo City

Covering some 81 acres, this park comprises 2 areas: one centered at **Rainbow Falls**, the other at **Boiling Pots**. The waterfall, reached by Rainbow Drive off Waianuenue Street, pours its torrents over a lava ledge on the Wailuku River. It is noted for the rainbow often visible in the morning mist. Boiling Pots are a mile farther inland at the terminus of a foot trail from the corner of Wailuku and Peepee Falls drives. These pots are actually a series of deep, round pools between 20 and 50 feet wide that the Wailuku has cut into the ancient lava beds over which it flows.

WAIPIO VALLEY
Hamakua coast district, 9 miles northwest of center of Honokaa

Access to this awesome gap is through cane fields and tiny villages at 1,000 feet above sea level, via a rough-surfaced but paved road. It comes to a dead end at a 1,500-foot lookout point on Waipio's east rim. Below is the 6-mile-long valley, bounded by 2,000-foot-high walls, checkered with small taro patches, and threaded by a lazy stream. During rainy periods the cliffs are resplendent with waterfalls. The most notable of these are **Nanaue Falls**, which drop into a series of swimming pools, and 1000-foot **Hiilawe Falls**.

Island of Kauai

HANALEI VALLEY
north coast, Hanalei vicinity

Sometimes called Hano-hano, or most beautiful, this lush, green valley is considered by many to be the most lovely spot in Hawaii. It is bisected by the silvery **Hanalei River**, which runs to the sea through rice paddies and taro fields, and it is rimmed by precipitous green mountains. Neighboring **Waioli Valley**, its backdrop, is often laced with waterfalls.

KOKEE STATE PARK
southwest section, about 15 miles north of Kekaha on State 55

This forested mountain park covers about 4,640 acres adjacent to Waimea Canyon State Park (*see*). From 4,000-foot-high *Kalaulau Lookout*, there is a spectacular view through shifting clouds of serene **Kalaulau Valley** and the blue ocean at its mouth. Besides some 12 miles of dirt roads, this park offers about 80,000 feet of hiking and nature trails. *Iliau Loop*, a 10-minute nature walk where the native iliau tree blooms in spring, affords a vista of **Waimea Canyon** and **Waialae Falls** in the distance. Three-mile-long *Kukui Trail* leads to the floor of Waimea Canyon and continues to Waimea. Among the park's many other hikes are 3½-mile *Waimea Canyon Rim Trail*, 3½-mile *Alakai Swamp Trail*, which leads over the jungle and bog of **Alakai Swamp**, and *Pihea Trail* to the rim of Kalalau Valley.

MOUNT WAIALEALE

Located at the heart of the island, Mount Waialeale, some 5,000 feet high, is probably the wettest place in the world. Each year, clouds of the trade winds drench its summit with an average of 460 inches of rain, the greatest recorded precipitation on earth. These torrents have eroded gorges up to 3,000 feet deep along its flanks.

NA PALI COAST

On the spectacular northwest coast of Kauai, from **Barking Sands** to **Ke'e Beach,** a series of sheer cliffs rise 2,000 to 3,000 feet above the crashing sea. The **Na Pali Cliffs** are indented by a series of deep, jungled valleys, such as the lovely **Hanakapiai** and **Kalalau** (the largest), penetrable only by foot or horseback. The sandy beaches of this rugged coast are accessible from the sea by boat in fair weather or by helicopter excursion.

SLEEPING GIANT MOUNTAIN
east coast area, seen from State 56 between Wailua and Kapaa

Resembling the profile of a sleeping giant, this mountain (also called **Nonou Mountain**) rises to an altitude of 1,241 feet. It may be explored by several trails. One goes to a shelter on the giant's chest. The 2-mile east side trail begins at a marker on the upper end of Haleilio Road, which goes through Wailua Homesteads from State 56. To climb the west side, start from Kinalu Road off Kamalu Road in Wailua Homesteads; after 1½ miles this trail joins the other.

SPOUTING HORN
south shore area, 4½ miles south and west of Koloa

This spectacular fountain of salt spray and foam is formed by wave action forcing sea water through a hole in a shoreline lava tube. The spouting of the water is accompanied by a strange moan that legend attributes to a grotesque sea monster trapped inside.

WET AND DRY CAVES OF HAENA
north coast area, Haena vicinity

With its palm-studded beaches and mountain backdrops, the peaceful Haena region epitomizes the beauty of the South Seas. It is also steeped in legend. **Maniniholo Dry Cave** is actually an immense lava tube that extends for hundreds of yards from the sea to the top of a mountain. According to a local myth, it was made by menehune (a legendary race of dwarfs) as they dug for an evil spirit who had stolen their fish. **Waikapalae** and **Waikanaloa wet caves** are said to have been dug by Pele, Polynesian goddess of volcanoes, as she searched for a home. The Haena region is also the site of picturesque **Bali Ha'i Beach** in the movie *South Pacific.*

WAILUA RIVER STATE PARK
east coast area, about 6 miles north of Lihue on State 56

Containing 6 different areas centered around the Wailua River, this park offers viewpoints of waterfalls—notably **Opaekaa Falls**—jungle valleys, and the sea. Its highlights include the **Fern Grotto,** an unusual fern-clothed cave upstream from the mouth of the Wailua, which may be reached by an excursion boat. The **Wailua River Reserve** preserves the river's natural setting with its waterfalls, canyons, and heavy tropical growth.

WAIMEA CANYON STATE PARK
southwest section, about 12 miles north of Kekaha on State 55

Comprising 1,866 acres next to Kokee State Park (*see*), this park has 600 feet of hiking trails leading into deep, colorful Waimea Canyon. This canyon is a 10-mile series of gorges cut into the horizonal layers of old lava flows of the **Kokee Plateau.** At one point it is 2,857 feet deep. Sculpted chiefly by the **Waimea River,** this so-called Grand Canyon of the Pacific is brilliantly hued, its colors ranging from the blues and mossy greens of its dense vegetation to the reds and browns of its volcanic escarpment.

Iao Needle in Iao Valley

Island of Lanai

GARDEN OF THE GODS
northwest Lanai, about 7 miles from Lanai City

One of the most scenic sites on the "Pineapple Island" is a rainbow-hued canyon of windswept sand. It contains weird, black lava formations—remnants and results of erosion and coloration wrought on the lava by wind, rain, and sun. The "garden" may be reached via an unpaved road that passes through pineapple fields and an area of lantana, poha, Norfolk Island pines, and eucalyptus.

Island of Maui

HALEAKALA NATIONAL PARK
headquarters 27 miles southwest of Kahului Airport via State 37, 377, and 378

Cone-studded **Haleakala crater,** one of the largest on earth, is the major feature of this park. This huge pit, carved out of the dome of Haleakala (house of the sun) by centuries of erosion, is 7½ miles long and 2½ miles wide. Its floor covers 19 square miles and lies 3,000 feet beneath Haleakala's 10,023-foot summit. No volcanic activity has occurred within the crater for a few hundred years, but around 1790 there were 2 minor flows at lower elevations. Haleakala, officially classified as dormant, could erupt again. Although there are no roads leading into the crater, it can be explored on foot via 30 miles of well-marked trails. *Halemauu Trail* affords views of **Keanae Valley** and **Koolau Gap** among other sights. *Sliding Sands Trail,* along a terrain of fine-grained cinders and ash, passes many cinder cones and **Magnetic Peak.** A recent addition to the park, comprising some 4,300 acres, is an 80-mile stretch from the eastern edge of Haleakala crater across part of **Kipahulu Valley**—a great forested ravine—down to the **Seven Sacred Pools** at oceanside. Much of the valley, which is practically inaccessible, is covered by a dense rain forest that retains the same essential species composition that prevailed before western man arrived in the Hawaiian Islands. Its upper region, above 3,100 feet, will be preserved for scientific purposes. The 300 or more inches of rain that fall here each year cascade via waterfalls, gulches (notably **Waimoku Falls** and **Oheo Gulch**), and lava pools, until they empty into the Pacific via the Sacred Pools. The lower region, threaded by trails and roads, is a pastoral area of rolling grasslands accented by guava thickets. The park also contains many examples of the silversword (ahinahina), found nowhere else in the world in its natural habitat. This large yuccalike plant is best seen from 9,324-foot *Kalahaku Overlook* along the park's motor road (State 378) or on the *Silversword Loop Trail* within the crater. Rare birds native only to Hawaii, such as the iiwi, apapane, and amakihi, may be sighted along the trails. *Visitor center open daily 8:30–3:30. For further information: Haleakala National Park, Box 456, Kahuliu, Maui, Hawaii 96732*

IAO VALLEY
3 miles west of Wailuku on State 32

This spectacular gorge, traversed by a winding road, is hemmed in by densely forested walls almost a mile high. It contains 4-acre Iao Valley State Park, a mountain-canyon park with a scenic viewpoint of **Iao Needle**. This volcanic ridge, which rises 1,200 feet from the valley floor, is blanketed with vegetation. The park also boasts 1,300 feet of trails into a region famous for its native birdlife.

KEANAE STATE WAYSIDE
about 30 miles east of Kahului on State 36

This scenic overlook provides a panoramic vista in 2 directions. One can look down over Wailua to the sea as it breaks against the fertile **Keanae Peninsula** with its green flatlands of taro and banana groves. Or one can look up through **Keanae Valley** to **Koolau Gap** on the rim of Haleakala crater (*see Haleakala National Park*).

WAIANAPANAPA STATE PARK
4 miles north of Hana on State 36

With its legendary caves, rocky coast, and old Hawaiian coastline trails, this 120-acre park is well worth a visit. A footpath leads to **Waianapanapa** and **Waiomao caves**, two old lava tubes near the sea. The sound of the ocean sweeping in and out of Waianapanapa Cave is supposed to be the moans of a Hawaiian princess murdered there by her jealous husband. The park's shore is lined with a striking black, volcanic sand beach and wave-battered rock formations. These include a natural rock arch and blow hole, chasms, and cliffs where sea birds nest.

WAILUA FALLS
8 miles south of Hana off State 31

These mighty falls drop hundreds of feet over a high canyon wall into **Wailua Gulch**, which contains a kukui grove. The water comes from the slopes of Haleakala (*see Haleakala National Park*).

Haleakala crater

HAWAII

Island of Molokai

HALAWA VALLEY
northeast corner
> This scenic, green-carpeted valley—½-mile wide and 3 to 4 miles deep—is backed by towering cliffs. At its end 2 plunging waterfalls, **Moaula** and **Hipuapua**, feed a stream that meanders out to sea. They plummet with such force that the pools below are a mass of bubbles. To hike in this valley one needs permission from its owner, the Puu O Hoku Ranch. However, the country roads within it and the beach park in the south are publicly owned.

PALAAU STATE PARK
about 3 miles north of Kualapuu off State 47
> A forested mountain area of some 234 acres, this park features a lookout over pastoral hills, the Pacific, and **Kalaupapa Peninsula** (isolated by sheer 2,000-foot cliffs) some 1,600 feet below. It also offers 1,500 feet of winding trails and an arboretum containing 40 species of labeled indigenous and exotic trees. Of historical interest is **Kauleonanahoa**, a 6-foot phallic rock used in fertility rites.

PALI COAST
> The Pali Coast extends from **Halawa Valley** *(see)* westward to **Kalaupapa**, a tiny, 4½-square-mile peninsula isolated from the rest of the island by the north coast's fortresslike cliffs. The Pali, one of Hawaii's most spectacular coastlines, is made up of 2,000-foot-high green cliffs, honeycombed with caves and sprayed by mists of innumerable waterfalls. Many of the falls plunge all the way to the ocean, and several remote valleys—notably **Wailua, Pelekuna,** and **Waikolu**—break the towering cliffs. This windward shore is accessible only by plane or by boat from May until mid-September, when the sea is calm enough for the boats to land.

Island of Oahu

DIAMOND HEAD
10 miles from downtown Honolulu
> Jutting out over the **Pacific Ocean** at the south end of **Waikiki Beach,** this world-famed promontory has become the symbol of the Hawaiian Islands. The extinct crater is an outstanding example of a type of volcanic cone on which the character of the rock and the bedding structure has been exposed. The gullying on the slopes of Diamond Head is typical of the erosion of such cones. Registered Natural Landmark

KOKO HEAD AND KOKO CRATER
eastern end, rising at end of Maunalua Bay off State 72
> Koko Head (642 feet) and Koko Crater (1,208 feet) are prominent landmarks on Oahu's eastern end. Formed by volcanic action, they are said to have been created by Pele, Polynesian goddess of volcanoes, in her last attempts to forge a home on Oahu. Along the highway between the 2 craters are many scenic points, including a lookout onto 523-acre **Kuapa Pond,** which lies just west of Koko Head. The craters are also the center of a 1,260-acre park that includes natural and recreational areas, Hanauma Bay Beach Park, Koko Head Sandy Beach Park, as well as many roads and trails. Also within the regional park is **Halona Cove,** a narrow turbulent inlet

Surfing off Waikiki Beach

between sheer cliffs, and **Halona Blowhole,** nearby. This geyser-like phenomenon is activated by the waves forcing water up through a shoreline lava tube.

NUUANU PALI
about 7 miles from downtown Honolulu via Pali Highway

This spectacular mountain pass through the **Koolau Range,** above and behind Honolulu, is a 1,200-foot-high gap flanked by cliffs that rise 2,000 to 3,000 feet. Here is the famous *Nuuanu Pali Lookout,* a state wayside, from where one can admire a superb view of the windward coast of Oahu and the fluted mountain palisades.

PUU UALAKAA STATE PARK
off Round Top Drive on Maikiki Round Top

This park offers an outstanding overlook of about ⅓ of Oahu from the head of **Manoa Valley** to the **Waianae Mountains** on its leeward side. One can also see into the vast center of **Punchbowl Crater,** which houses the National Memorial Cemetery of the Pacific.

SACRED FALLS
Hauula vicinity, southwest off Kamehameha Highway (State 83)

A marker on this highway points the way to these falls, which drop 80 feet into a crisp, 50-foot-deep swimming hole at the head of **Kaliuwaa Valley.** This gorge may be reached by a 1½-mile hike along a muddy, cane-field road. Hardy hikers may climb a mile up a rocky mountain ravine to the falls themselves.

WAIMEA FALLS
½ mile inland from State 83 (Kamehameha Highway) on north coast

This natural pool and waterfall may be reached by the "Menehune Train," a narrated tour by wagon-train, or via a hiking trail. Other trails in the area penetrate deep into an unspoiled valley of koa wood, guava, orange trees, and fern grottoes.

IDAHO

BALANCED ROCK
16 miles southwest of Buhl off U.S. 30

Like a giant mushroom atop a tiny pedestal, Balanced Rock sits on the edge of **Salmon Falls Creek Canyon**. The main rock is 40 feet high and the base on which it rests is 1 foot by 1½ feet by 3 feet.

BRUNEAU CANYON
south of Bruneau in southwest Idaho

Running the entire length of the **Bruneau River,** this picturesque 67-mile-long canyon has walls of basaltic rock that rise almost vertically. The canyon rims vary in height from 450 to 2,000 feet.

BRUNEAU DUNES STATE PARK
7 miles northeast of Bruneau on State 51

Rising out of the desert here are huge sand dunes, some over 400 feet high, that have been shaped by the wind into pyramids with deep craters. Two of the largest cover 500 acres.

BOISE NATIONAL FOREST
southwest Idaho, headquarters at Boise

This 2,950,000-acre forest in the **Sawtooth Mountains** varies in elevation from 5,000 to 10,700 feet. An area of rugged terrain abounding in wildlife—black bear, mule deer, elk, bighorn sheep—the forest contains most of the headwaters of the **Boise, Payette,** and **Salmon rivers**. Here too are portions of the **Sawtooth** and **Idaho primitive areas,** unspoiled stretches of natural wonders; the Sawtooth Area features lofty peaks, deep gorges, glacial basins, and more than 100 well-stocked alpine lakes. The **Middle Fork of the Salmon River,** the famed **River of No Return,** runs through the Idaho Area, a region of imposing mountains, and scenic river back country.

CHALLIS NATIONAL FOREST
central Idaho, headquarters at Challis

An area of exceptional scenic beauty, this 2½-million-acre forest lies in the rugged terrain of the **Salmon River Mountains,** and the **Sawtooth, Lemhi,** and **Lost River ranges**. Here, amidst deep canyons, many natural hot springs, and sparkling lakes, streams, and rivers (including the **Big** and **Little Lost rivers**) is the state's highest mountain, 12,655-foot **Borah Peak**. An unimproved hiking trail leads to the summit. The forest includes portions of the **Sawtooth Primitive Area,** an unspoiled region in the jagged Sawtooth Range, and the **Idaho Primitive Area,** bisected by the turbulent and scenic **Middle Fork of the Salmon River**. Among the other noteworthy regions here are the **Stanley Basin Area,** featuring beautiful alpine lakes, meadows, and streams in the shadow of the Sawtooth Range; the **White Mountains Area,** an undeveloped region of glacial peaks and glacial cirques; and the **Pahsimeroi Valley,** home of one of the largest antelope herds in Idaho.
For further information write: Challis, Idaho 83226

CLEARWATER NATIONAL FOREST
northeast Idaho, headquarters at Orofino

This 1,677,000-acre forest features steep river canyons and vast stands of trees in the picturesque **Bitterroot Mountains** on the Idaho–Montana border. Crossed in the south by the **Lochsa River**

Top left: Balanced Rock. Right: Shoshone Falls of the Snake River. Below: Stanley Basin in Challis National Forest

IDAHO

(part of the National Wild and Scenic Rivers system) and in the north by the **North Fork of the Clearwater,** this forest has some 400 named creeks and 150 mountains and buttes (the highest is 8,810-foot **Ranger Peak**). Lewis and Clark Highway (U.S. 12) runs for 90 miles through the forest and roughly parallels the historical *Lolo Trail* followed by the explorers in 1805. The highway crosses the Bitterroots at its highest point—5,187-foot **Lolo Pass** (*see Nez Perce Historical Park*). Atop the range, near the pass, is **Packer Meadow,** a beautiful alpine meadow where Lewis and Clark camped. The **Bernard De Voto Memorial Grove,** an imposing stand of cedars dedicated to the famed historian-conservationist, and **Jerry Johnson Hot Springs,** natural springs named for an early miner and trapper, are 2 sites along the Lochsa (also known as the **Middle Fork of the Clearwater**). Sections of the vast Selway–Bitterroot Wilderness (*see*) and the **Mallard–Larkins Pioneer Area** are here. *For further information write: Orofino, Idaho 83544*

COEUR D'ALENE LAKE
north Idaho, reached by U.S. 95, 95A, and I-90

Considered one of the loveliest in the Northwest, this lake is 24 miles long and about 2½ miles wide. Fed by the **Saint Joe** and **Coeur d'Alene rivers,** and drained by the **Spokane River,** it features many scenic bays and inlets and a small island in its southern section. U.S. 95A follows the tree-lined lake for about 50 miles, but the most impressive view is from the *Mineral Ridge Trail* (between **Wolf Lodge Bay** and **Beauty Bay**), a 3-mile hike that ends at a point 715 feet above the lake.

CRATERS OF THE MOON NATIONAL MONUMENT
18 miles southwest of Arco on U.S. 20, 29, and 93A

Resembling a black moonscape, this monument in the **Snake River Lava Plain** is a pock-marked field of deep craters, cinder cones, spatter cones, and other lava formations. This terrain was formed not by the eruptions of single volcanoes but by fissure eruptions—millions of years of intermittent flows of lava at 2,000° through wide cracks in the earth's crust along the 40-mile **Great Rift** (*see*). Two distinct types of lava can be seen here: "pahoehoe," a hard, smooth rock found in ropelike lengths, and "aa," a sharp, spiny rock.

This 83-square-mile area is best seen from a 7-mile loop road and the 4 spur roads that lead off it to various trails. The first stop on the road is **North Crater Lava Flow,** a vast field of pahoehoe lava with aa lava at the edges. It is believed that the last activity here was about 1,600 years ago, making this one of the youngest flows in the monument. Farther along, the road skirts **Paisley Cone** and **Devils Orchard,** a group of weird cinder formations and crater-wall fragments; a ½-mile nature trail leads through this area. **Inferno Cone,** one of the most interesting stops on the road, offers a magnificent panorama from its summit—seemingly endless black lava fields, with the **Pioneer Mountains** rising to the north; **Big Butte,** called the sentinel of the Snake River Plains, to the east; and **Big Cinder Butte,** at 800 feet one of the world's largest purely basaltic cinder cones, to the south. Other points of interest along the loop road are **Big Craters–Spatter Cone Area,** from which a string of cones along the **Great Rift** can be seen, and the **Cave Area,** where trails lead to a series of lava tubes or caves. The principal sites here are **Indian Tunnel,** more than 830 feet long, and **Boy Scout Cave,** which has a floor of ice even in the summer. *For further information write: Box 29, Arco, Idaho 83213*

THE GREAT RIFT
25 miles northwest of American Falls off State 39

One of the longest volcanic rifts in the continental United States, the Great Rift is a 40-mile-long series of fissures that began as a weakness in the earth's crust and cracked under pressure allowing molten lava to escape. A fine example of the resulting outpouring of lava are the formations at the Craters of the Moon National Monument (*see*). The Great Rift has been explored to a depth of 800 feet and is said to be the deepest known open rift in the world. Visible here are such volcanic features as lava tubes or caves, spatter cones, and pahoehoe and "aa" lava, 2 types of volcanic rocks. Perhaps the most outstanding features here are the ice caves found along the rift walls. Although geologists do not precisely know how these caves were formed, most believe they are the result of steam exploding under pressure. In one of these, **Crystal Ice Cave,** there is a fascinating display of delicate ice crystals and imposing ice pillars on walls of lava. Stalagmites of ice rise as much as 16 feet above the cave floor. Accessible by a 1,200-foot tunnel, the cave is 150 feet below ground and has a constant temperature of 32°. It is located 22 miles west of State 39 and is the only fissure of its kind in the world to be open to the public. The Great Rift is a Registered Natural Landmark.

Crystal Ice Cave open May–Oct: daily 7–sunset. Admission: adults $1.50, children (6–12) 75¢

HELLS CANYON–SEVEN DEVILS SCENIC AREA
in Payette, Nezperce, and Wallowa–Whitman national forests

The **Grand Canyon of the Snake River**—Hells Canyon—is the deepest gorge in North America. For 125 miles the Snake has gouged out a twisted passage between the **Wallowa Mountains** in Oregon and the **Seven Devils Mountains** in Idaho, reaching a maximum depth of 7,900 feet and an average depth of 5,500 feet. A 26-mile section of this awesome gorge has been set aside in the Hells Canyon–Seven Devils Scenic Area, covering 130,000 acres and extending into 3 national forests—Payette and Nezperce in Idaho and Wallowa–Whitman in Oregon (*see all*). The Seven Devils Mountains, a volcanic range named from an old Indian legend, contrasts with the deep, wild gorge and forms its eastern wall. Dotted throughout the mountains are crystal-clear lakes (there are 40 on the Idaho side), meandering creeks, and grassy plateaus. This vast scenic area

Left: pahoehoe lava in Craters of the Moon National Monument. Right: Crystal Ice Cave (see The Great Rift)

offers countless vantage points from which to view the natural beauty. Among the loveliest on the Oregon side are *McGraw Lookout* (5,920 feet) and *Hat Point*, reached after a 27-mile hike, and in Idaho—*Kinney Point* (7,126 feet), *Horse Mountain Lookout* (6,887 feet), and **Sheep Rock**, a 6,4840-foot shelf overhanging a chasm. *Dry Diggins Lookout* (7,828 feet) between the **Snake** and the **Salmon rivers** near Pollack, Idaho, is difficult to reach but offers magnificent views of both canyons. For the fearless driver there are spectacular views offered along the *Kleinsmith Grade*, a twisting, 12-mile narrow road beginning at Cuprum, Idaho, that descends 2,600 feet in 6 miles. Trails lead throughout the area to the many major "devils"—the highest is **He Devil**, altitude 9,393 feet—and to lesser peaks. From the crests of many ridges there are unobstructed views of Idaho, Oregon, Montana, and Wyoming. In order to preserve the unspoiled quality of this region few roads have been improved and visitors are advised to make inquiries into conditions before starting out.

Hells Canyon Dam, third in a series of dams on the Snake River (the others are Brownlee and Oxbow dams), is in the scenic area and is accessible on State 71 from Weiser. Together these dams create 90 miles of reservoirs; a road connecting Brownlee and Hells Canyon dams skirts the Snake River Canyon.

For further information: Pacific Northwest Region Headquarters, USDA Forest Service, Box 3623, Portland, Ore. 97208

IDAHO FALLS OF THE SNAKE RIVER
city of Idaho Falls in southeast Idaho
Although not impressive for its height, this low waterfall in the **Snake River** rushes over a 1,500-foot-wide curved rim with such force that it turns a foamy white. The river and falls form a lovely setting for an adjacent park and gardens.

KANIKSU NATIONAL FOREST
north Idaho, west Montana, east Washington; headquarters at Sandpoint
Dominating this beautiful forest in the **Selkirk** and **Cabinet mountains** near the Canadian border is the 85,000 acres of **Pend Oreille Lake,** with its magnificent fiordlike bays, small islands, and 111-mile shoreline. Named by early French trappers, it is known for its scenic beauty as well as for the size of its fish. (A 37-pound Kamloops trout and a 32-pound Dolly Varden have been caught here.) Among the many other natural attractions in the forest are **Clark Fork River** that flows down from the Cabinet Mountains; **Upper Priest Lake Scenic Area,** an unspoiled 6,000-acre region where elevations range from 2,450 feet at the lake to 5,000 feet on **Plowboy Mountain; Cabinet Mountains Wilderness,** featuring glacial cirques, lakes, and **Snowshoe Peak,** at 8,712 feet the highest point in this range of the **Rockies;** and **Northwest Peak Scenic Area,** a 6,900-acre alpine primitive area. **Tepee Creek Natural Area** has been set aside to protect a stand of virgin white pine, and the **Roosevelt Grove of Ancient Cedars** preserves 800-year-old western red cedar.
For further information write: Sandpoint, Idaho 83864

MINNETONKA CAVE
9 miles west of Saint Charles on a gravel road in southeast Idaho
This ½-mile-long cave sits at an altitude of 7,700 feet in the **Bear River Range,** a branch of the **Wasatch Range** of the **Rocky Mountain** chain. Featuring 9 distinct chambers, each maintaining a constant temperature of 40°, the cave is famous for its intricate stalactites,

stalagmites, helictites, and for the many Paleozoic plant and animal fossils found on its walls, ceilings, and floors. Guided tours are conducted through the cave which is now maintained by Cache National Forest (*see*) in Utah.

Open June 15–Labor Day: daily 10–5. Admission: 50?

NEZPERCE NATIONAL FOREST
north Idaho, headquarters at Grangeville

Extending across northern Idaho from the **Bitterroot Mountains** on the Montana border down to the **Snake River** on the Oregon border, this forest features many scenic wonders and countless sites of historical importance to the Nez Perce Indians, whose homeland this once was. Sections of the forest are included in the Nez Perce Historical Park, Hells Canyon–Seven Devils Scenic Area, and the Selway–Bitterroot Wilderness (*see all*). This 2,196,043-acre forest is bounded on the north by the **Lochsa River** (the **Middle Fork of the Clearwater**) and on the south by the famed **Salmon River.** A 40-mile stretch of the Salmon through a wild rugged canyon has been set aside in the **Salmon River Breaks Primitive Area**—an unspoiled roadless section on the river's north bank. Another scenic preserve is the **Buffalo Hump–Gospel Lakes Area,** featuring high ridges and many lovely mountain lakes. Four rivers all part of the mighty **Columbia River** system—the Salmon, Snake, **Selway,** and **South Fork of the Clearwater**—begin or pass through the forest. A particularly scenic attraction is **Selway Falls,** a huge cascade created when an ancient landslide blocked the Selway River. These and the forest's other attractions are accessible by networks of thousands of miles of roads and trails.

For further information write: Grangeville, Idaho 83530

NEZ PERCE NATIONAL HISTORICAL PARK
north Idaho, headquarters at Spaulding

A new concept, this park is made up of 23 separate sites and is constantly being expanded. Covering 12,000 square miles in the homeland of the Nez Perce Indians, it extends roughly from east of Lewiston within sight of the **Clearwater Mountains** to **Lolo Pass,**

Shiras moose in Selway–Bitterroot Wilderness (see page 105)

high in the **Bitterroot Mountains** on the Montana border. Among the sites here are some natural wonders that have played an important role in the historical and cultural life of the Nez Perce. **Coyote's Fishnet**, east of Lewiston on U.S. 95-12, a natural rock formation on the face of the bluffs on the south side of the **Clearwater River**, is named for Coyote, a principal figure in Nez Perce legend and mythology. High in the hills on the opposite shore of the river is an outcropping called the **Bear**. Nearby is another formation, the **Ant and Yellow Jacket**, created, according to legend, when a fight took place here which so enraged Coyote that he turned both into stone. At the East Kamiah site, west of U.S. 12 on the Clearwater River, is the **Heart of the Monster**, a 30-foot rock said to be all that remains of a monster killed by Coyote. It is believed that from the monster's blood Coyote created the Nez Perce people. Northeast at the **Wieppe Prairie**, for generations a favorite gathering place, a lookout offers an especially scenic view of the surrounding country. Extending east from Wieppe for about 150 miles is the Idaho section of the historic *Lolo Trail*. Developed by the Nez Perce as an access route over the Bitterroot Mountains to the buffalo in Montana, it is now paralleled by U.S. 12—the Lewis and Clark Highway. Lolo Pass (5,187 feet), at the crest of the mountains, is the pass Lewis and Clark crossed in their 1805 expedition.
For further information write: Box 39, Spaulding, Idaho 83551

PAYETTE NATIONAL FOREST
west Idaho, headquarters at McCall

This 2½-million-acre forest is located in 2 sections: one on the **Snake River**, overlooking **Hells Canyon**, and partially included in the Hells Canyon–Seven Devils Scenic Area (*see*), and the other on the **Salmon River**. Elevations vary in Payette from 1,500 feet on the Snake to 9,524 feet atop **Mormon Peak** near the **Middle Fork of the Salmon**. The forest includes about half of the **Idaho Primitive Area**, which extends into Boise, Challis, and Salmon national forests. The 106-mile-long Middle Fork of the Salmon, which flows through this 1¼ million-acre area, has been designated part of the National Wild and Scenic Rivers system. Payette forest encompasses most of the **North Fork of the Payette** and the **South Fork of the Salmon**.
For further information write: McCall, Idaho 83638

SAINT JOE NATIONAL FOREST
northeast Idaho, headquarters at Saint Maries

Dominated by stately stands of white pine and crossed by the **Saint Joe River**, this 865,000-acre forest lies in the scenic **Bitterroot Mountains**. Among the many natural features here are **Snow Peak**, a pyramid-shaped, granite mountain accessible by trail; **Elk Falls**, 3 beautiful waterfalls ranging from 20 to 75 feet in the narrow basalt rock gorge of **Elk Creek**; and **Hobo Cedar Grove Botanical Area**, a 240-acre natural preserve. Also here is a large portion of the **Mallard–Larkins Pioneer Area**, covering 30,500 acres between the **North** and **Little North Fork of the Clearwater River**. This unspoiled area features elevations ranging from 2,600 feet at **Mallard Peak** to over 7,000 feet atop **Black Mountain** and can be seen only on foot or on horseback. Two unusual features of the forest are **Emerald Creek Garnet Area**, where digging and collecting in rich gem garnet deposits is permitted in certain sections along the **East Fork of the Emerald Creek**, and **Willow Creek Vista**, where one can see the complete cycle of timber production.
For further information write: Saint Maries, Idaho 83861

SALMON NATIONAL FOREST
northcentral Idaho, headquarters at Salmon

This rugged, unspoiled 1,790,944-acre forest lies along the western slopes of the **Continental Divide** at the Idaho–Montana line. It contains part of the **Idaho Primitive Area** (*see Payette National Forest*), and is traversed by portions of the **Middle Fork of the Salmon** and the main **Salmon rivers**. Fishing and hunting are good.

For further information write: Box 729, Salmon, Idaho 83467

SANCTUARY OF BIRDS OF PREY
southwest Idaho, 30 miles southwest of Boise

An area of exceptional, if desolate, beauty, the **Swan Falls** reach of the **Snake River Canyon** combines cliffs, desert, and river in the 25,255-acre "nature area" set aside here as a sanctuary for rare birds of prey. With cliffs ranging from 30 to 800 feet above the canyon floor, this terrain is a perfect setting for the perpetuation of such threatened species as the golden eagle and the prairie falcon, who can exist and multiply here almost free from danger. Visitors to the sanctuary can view the birds and the lovely scenery, especially around **Sinker** and **Castle creeks.**

SAWTOOTH NATIONAL FOREST
southcentral Idaho, headquarters at Twin Falls

Named for its jagged peaks, the **Sawtooth Mountains** form the western boundary of this 1.8 million-acre forest. The range, part of the **Rocky Mountain** chain, bisects the **Sawtooth Primitive Area,** an unspoiled scenic preserve of more than 170 picturesque glacial lakes and rugged mountains, partially located in the forest's western section. A host of scenic attractions can be found in Sawtooth. Among them are **Boulder Basin,** a 500-acre subalpine glacial cirque at 9,000 feet in **Boulder Mountains; Redfish Lake** and **Redfish Creek,** where a visitor center features natural and historical displays; and **Fishhook Creek,** a meandering stream fed by 10 glacial lakes, which can be reached from the visitor center by a self-guided nature trail.

Many scenic drives lead throughout the forest, especially in the Ketchum district near famed **Sun Valley.** A highlight here is the ski lift up **Bald Mountain,** a 3-mile trip to the 9,200-foot summit, from which there is a magnificent view of the surrounding mountains—the **Pioneer, Boulder, Smoky,** and **Sawtooth ranges.** Other features include **Trail Creek Summit** (7,900 feet) and **Trail Creek Falls,** a 60-foot cascade, accessible by a scenic drive cut from the side of a canyon wall; and **Galena Summit** (8,701 feet), where from an overlook 1 mile beyond there is a spectacular view of the **Sawtooth Valley.** The main attraction in the southern section of the forest, which extends into Utah, is the **Silent City of Rocks,** a fantastic outcropping of strangely eroded granite formations that served as a landmark to early settlers. Below is **Emigrant Valley,** through which hundreds of pioneers trudged on their way west.

For further information write: 1525 Addison Ave, E, Twin Falls, Idaho 83301

SELWAY–BITTERROOT WILDERNESS
eastern Idaho, western Montana

The largest classified wilderness area in the United States, this 1,238,335 preserve lies on both sides of the **Bitterroot Mountains** and extends into 4 national forests—Nezperce and Clearwater in Idaho and Bitterroot and Lolo in Montana (*see all*). An area of unsurpassed beauty with countless mountain lakes, streams, and rivers,

IDAHO

and such majestic peaks as **Blodgett Mountain** and **Trapper Peak,** it looks almost as it did when Lewis and Clark came here in 1805. The wilderness includes large parts of the **Lochsa (Middle Fork of the Clearwater)** and **Selway river** drainages on the western side of the mountains, and the **Bitterroot River** drainage on the eastern side in Montana. The Selway provides a scenic waterway by which to see this wilderness where elk, moose, and bear roam free. *For further information write to individual forests.*

SHOSHONE FALLS
4½ miles northeast of Twin Falls off U.S. 93

These falls, higher than Niagara, are formed as the **Snake River** crashes over a 1,000-foot-wide horseshoe-shaped rim here and drops 212 feet. Because so much of the river is used for irrigation, very little water ever reaches the basaltic rim and only in the late spring do the falls attain their natural grandeur.

SHOSHONE INDIAN ICE CAVES
17 miles north of Shoshone on U.S. 93

These caves are actually a series of craters lying against walls of lava. They contain pits, potholes, natural bridges, and vaulted chambers and maintain a very low temperature year round. The caves are especially beautiful in the autumn when dripping water from the ceiling freezes to create a whimsical ice world. A museum displays Indian artifacts and minerals. *Caves open: May–Oct 15: daily 7:30–½ hour before sunset. Admission for tours: adults $1.25, children (7–12) 60¢*

TARGHEE NATIONAL FOREST
east Idaho and west Wyoming, headquarters at Saint Anthony, Idaho

Extending in a semicircle around the headwaters of the **Snake River,** this 1.7-million-acre forest features vast stands of lodgepole pine and Douglas fir. The forest runs north and south from the Continental Divide to the **Upper Snake River Valley** and is bounded on the east by the **Teton Range,** a branch of the **Rocky Mountains.** Included here are such scenic waterways as the **Warm River** and **Henrys Fork of the Snake River** with its 2 lovely waterfalls—the 65-foot **Lower Mesa Falls** and **Upper Mesa Falls,** a 114-foot cascade. Nearby is **Big Springs,** a particularly scenic and impressive spring which is the main source of Henrys Fork. A forest of deep canyons, picturesque mountains, and lovely streams, reservoirs, and lakes (such as **Henrys Lake,** lying at 6,000 feet), Targhee is also the home of some of Idaho's largest antelope and moose herds. While the grizzly bear and bighorn sheep are less evident, they too can be seen in remote regions. The **Island Park** area is one of the most important wintering places in the United States for trumpeter swan. *For further information: 421 N Bridge St, Saint Anthony, Idaho 83445*

THOUSAND SPRINGS
north of Buhl on U.S. 30

Cascading down the lava walls of the **Snake River Canyon,** these waters are believed to be the re-emergence of the **Big and Little Lost rivers** that disappear into the desert 150 miles to the northeast. The springs appear intermittently for about 2 miles and gush out of the side of the cliff with such force that they become fine white spray before splashing into the Snake River below.

YELLOWSTONE NATIONAL PARK. *See* WYOMING

APPLE CREEK CANYON STATE PARK
northwest of Stockton off State 78

This 157-acre park is famous for the scenic canyons and imposing
high bluffs created by the **Apple River** as it cut into the limestone,
shale, and dolomite here. Widened by erosion, these cliffs offer
lovely views of the surrounding area, including 1,241-foot **Charles
Mound,** the highest point in the state. Because the glacier that
covered the rest of Illinois did not touch this section, many fossil
remains can still be seen along the canyons and cliffs.

BEALL WOODS NATURE PRESERVE
7 miles south of Mount Carmel near Keensburg off State 1

Also known as the **Forest of the Wabash,** this 270-acre preserve is
the largest single, untouched tract of deciduous trees left in the
United States. Lying along the right bank of the **Wabash River,** the
forest includes both river bottomland and upland ecological communities. This diversity has produced 60 different identified species of
trees as well as an abundance of native wildlife. Here too is the
largest Shumard oak in the country (over 150 years old and measuring 61½ inches in diameter) and nearly 300 trees with diameters
greater than 30 inches. Five self-guiding nature trails and 7 miles
of rustic trails lead through the forest. Registered Natural Landmark

BUFFALO ROCK STATE PARK
4 miles west of Ottawa off U.S. 6

This fortresslike sandstone bluff, commanding a lovely view of the
Illinois River, was once an island during the time the great river
was a lake in this region. The "hump" of this "buffalo" sits 100 feet
above the north bank and is covered with oak, cedar, and pine.

Left: Starved Rock State Park. Right: waterfall in Shawnee National Forest

107

ILLINOIS

CAVE-IN-ROCK STATE PARK
8 miles east of Elizabethtown on State 1

Occupying a narrow strip of land on a steep bluff overlooking the **Ohio River,** this park takes its name from a cave that for many years was the headquarters of gangs of outlaws and river pirates. The cave, halfway up the face of the 60-foot bluff, extends for 108 feet and has an average width of 40 feet; its arched opening is 55 feet wide. Trails wind throughout the park and afford beautiful views of the Ohio River below.

DIXON SPRINGS STATE PARK
10 miles west of Golconda on State 146

This 400-acre park sits atop a gigantic block of rock in the Illinois **Ozarks.** Because of erosion the rock has been exposed in some places; in others it has slumped down producing cliffs and canyons, including one 60 feet deep. During rainy periods, more than 1,500 waterfalls pour down over rocks and boulders covered with fern, ivy, lichen, and moss. Rock formations in the park bear such exotic names as **Devil's Workshop, Album Rock,** and the **Chain of Rocks.**

FERNE CLYFFE STATE PARK
12 miles south of Marion on State 37

Located in the Illinois **Ozarks,** this 1,073-acre park has a deep central valley from which canyons, gorges, and other lovely scenic spots radiate. Highlights here include an unspoiled area at the foot of **Round Bluff,** featuring a variety of native wildlife and a man-made lake; **Honeycomb Rock,** a peculiarly eroded boulder; and **Hawks' Cave,** a 150-foot-long cavern eroded into a sheer cliff of sandstone by wind and water. Because of its fine natural acoustics, the cave is used for Easter sunrise and other religious services.

GIANT CITY STATE PARK
12 miles south of Carbondale off U.S. 51

This scenic park in the Illinois **Ozarks** takes its name from the central section where massive sandstone rocks have been eroded and separated from each other forming orderly passageways resembling city streets. Rising 30 to 40 feet, these multicolored walls are so perpendicular as to seem man-made. Also noteworthy here is the "Old Stone Fort," an ancient Indian wall of unquarried stone built atop an 80-foot sandstone bluff. The 1,672-acre park features 75 different kinds of trees, including sweet gum, winged elm, and cucumber, and over 800 varieties of ferns and flowering plants. Nearby peach and apple orchards are a lovely sight in the spring.

MATTHIESSEN STATE PARK NATURE AREA
7 miles southwest of La Salle off State 178

Set aside to preserve the natural beauty and wildlife here, this scenic area is covered with canyons, dells, waterfalls, and unusual rock formations. In the park geologists can study Paleozoic limestone and sandstone usually found only at great depths, which has been exposed by the enormous upthrust known as the La Salle Anticline. The principal canyon in the park, part of the **Vermilion River Valley,** is 200 feet deep and varies in width from 50 to 150 feet; a waterfall cascades 55 feet. Nature trails lead to the many interesting rock formations including **Devil's Paint Box, Giant's Bathtub,** and **Strawberry Rock.** The park also boasts varied plant life, over 50 species of birds (cardinals, crows, owls), many small animals (rabbits, raccoons, opossums), and a herd of deer.

MISSISSIPPI PALISADES STATE PARK
2 miles north of Savanna on State 84

Sharply rising 250 feet and commanding an inspiring view of the majestic **Mississippi River,** these wooded bluffs were named for the famous **Palisades of the Hudson** that they resemble so much. This 1,560-acre rugged, natural area is crisscrossed by 15 miles of foot trails that lead from the base of the cliffs up the fern-covered slopes marked by deep ravines to the summit. Among the many interesting features here are unusual rock formations.

SHAWNEE NATIONAL FOREST
south Illinois, headquarters at Harrisburg

Covering over 240,000 acres stretching from the **Mississippi** to the **Ohio rivers,** this forest features dense woods, lakes, rolling hills, and unusual rock formations. Among the numerous scenic and recreational areas here are **Oakwood Bottoms Greentree Reservoir,** a bird refuge and oak forest that is partially flooded from October to February; **Lake of Egypt Recreational Area,** a 2,300-acre man-made lake system surrounded by wooded shorelines; and the **LaRue–Pine Hills Ecological Area,** where animals and rare plants are preserved in their natural environment. Here too are *Pine Hills Scenic Drive,* a 7-mile road offering a broad view of the **Mississippi Valley,** and *Inspiration Point Forest Trail, a ¾-mile* walk through deep canyons and ridges to *Inspiration Point.* The view from here is considered to be the best in the Midwest—a sweeping panorama of the forest, the Missouri **Ozarks,** the Mississippi valley and river. Perhaps the most unusual feature of the forest is the **Garden of the Gods**—an area of fantastically eroded rock formations.
For further information: 317 E Poplar St, Harrisburg, Ill. 62946

STARVED ROCK STATE PARK
5½ miles southeast of La Salle on State 71

This 1,451-acre park sits atop a bluff overlooking the **Illinois River.** It takes its name from a 125-foot-high promontory on which a band of Illinois Indians, according to legend, were starved into surrender by its enemies in 1769. Most of the exposed rock in the park is St. Peter's sandstone dating from the Paleozoic era. Usually found only at great depths, the sandstone was exposed by the massive upthrust known as the La Salle Anticline. The rock was subsequently carved by glacial actions and erosion producing the many deep canyons and unusual formations. Among the most interesting sites are **Horseshoe Canyon,** an especially scenic area; **Council Cave,** an Indian meeting place; and **Skeleton Cave,** a burial site.

Palisades of the Mississippi River

INDIANA

BLACK ROCK
midway between Attica and Lafayette, via South River Road

Lying amidst rugged terrain on the north bank of the **Wabash**, this 160-foot bluff juts into the river. From its level summit there are spectacular views of the Wabash winding in both directions.

BROWN COUNTY STATE PARK
just south of Nashville on State 46 and 35

Covering 15,492 acres of wooded, steep-sloped hills, Brown County is noted for its lakes and streams and its many miles of drives and forest trails. One of the most popular is *Lafe Bud Trail* to 1,167-foot **Weedpatch Hill**, the highest of the southern Indiana hills.

CLIFTY FALLS STATE PARK
about 1½ miles west of Madison via State 56 and 107

Situated on the crest of a high bluff overlooking the **Ohio River**, this park offers a breathtaking view of the river and the hazy hills on its Kentucky shore. Its scenic attractions include **Clifty Falls** and **Clifty Canyon**.

FALLS OF THE OHIO (OHIO RIVER CORAL REEFS)
Floyd Co, Indiana; Jefferson Co, Kentucky—Louisville vicinity

These falls are no longer spectacularly beautiful due to the industrialization and canalization of the Ohio River. What is significant about them is the variety and abundance of well-preserved corals in several thin limestone areas exposed in the river's bed and banks. This site is a classic example of a coral community dating from

Left: fishing on the Tippecanoe River. Right: Indiana Dunes landscape

periods during which land plants and then forests and amphibians appeared. Registered Natural Landmark

HOOSIER NATIONAL FOREST
south Indiana, headquarters at Bedford
Covering 155,000 stream- and river-filled acres, this forest lies in the southern Indiana region of rolling hills and steep river bluffs. It is an area of hardwoods—maples, oaks, hickories, beeches, and yellow poplars—all rising against a backdrop of pines. Hoosier contains 16 recreation sites, including **Hemlock Cliffs** with a forest trail and 2 waterfalls, active only in the spring. **Pioneer Mothers Memorial Forest** contains 80 acres of virgin woods and peaceful trails, and *Buzzard Roost Overlook* offers a trail and a lookout with sweeping vistas of the **Ohio River.** **Saddle Lake Recreation Area** boasts a forest trail, as does **German Ridge Recreation Area.** Other park attractions include **Indian Lake** and **Lake Celina,** connected by a 2½-mile scenic drive.
For further information write: 1615 J St, Bedford, Ind. 47421

INDIANA DUNES NATIONAL LAKESHORE PROJECT
headquarters at junction of U.S. 12 and Kemil Rd, east of State Park
The projected national lakeshore will preserve about 8,000 acres of dunes, bogs, and marshes along **Lake Michigan's** southern shore between Gary and Michigan City. Thus the clean, sandy beaches backed by enormous dunes will be saved from development. All the land for this lakeshore, except that within Indiana Dunes State Park (*see*), is in private hands and will have to be purchased by the federal government. It will include **Cowles Bog,** near the state park, and **Pinhook Bog,** 6 miles south of Michigan City, both Registered Natural Landmarks. These 2 areas are interesting for the variety of wetland plants and animals they contain.
For further information write: Box 12, Chesterton, Ind. 46304

INDIANA DUNES STATE PARK
about 10 miles west of Michigan City at U.S. 12 and State 49
Boasting 3 miles of wide, white sand beach on **Lake Michigan,** this park covers 2,182 acres. It features some of the world's largest sand dunes, some fixed and some imperceptibly moving. Rising as high as 190 feet, they are backed by densely forested areas that include a large section of marshland. The 3 highest dunes, **Mounts Tom, Jackson,** and **Holden,** provide a panoramic view of the area. The park also has an extremely varied plant life.

JUG ROCK PARK
less than 1 mile north of Shoals on the White River
This regional park contains a remarkable pillar of natural rock (60 feet tall and 15 feet in diameter) that resembles a very large jug. Other features are **Pinnacle Rock,** a moss-covered cliff towering some 150 feet above the **White River,** and nearby **McBrides Bluffs,** a range of lofty cliffs rising about 175 feet over the river.

MARENGO CAVE
¾ *mile north of Marengo, ¼ mile northeast of State 66–64 junction*
This limestone cave, whose greatest depth is 286 feet, contains many caverns with stalactites and stalagmites of pure calcium carbonate, which transmit a pearly glow when illuminated.
Open Apr–Oct: daily 9–5; Nov–Mar: weekends. Admission: adults $1.85, children (6–12) 90¢

INDIANA

PINE HILLS NATURAL AREA
15 miles southwest of Crawfordsville adjoining Shades State Park

This 600-acre natural area contains a number of plant species that are probably Pleistocene relicts. The most conspicuous of these are groves of hemlock and white pine with an understory of Canadian yew. The land here is sharply dissected with deep, stream-carved canyons. Between the meanders of the former streams are narrow ridges, or backbones. Those formed by **Indian Creek** are considered the most remarkable examples of incised meanders in the eastern United States. Registered Natural Landmark

SPRING MILL STATE PARK
3 miles east of Mitchell on State 60

Aside from its famous reconstructed pioneer village, this park boasts numerous natural wonders, including miles of wooded trails and about 100 acres of virgin woodland with extremely large specimens of white oak and tulip poplar. It also contains several caves that are part of the complicated limestone drainage system underlying the Indiana and Kentucky cavern region. **Twin Cave** and **Donaldson Cave**, with its underground river containing a rare species of blind fish; both offer subterranean boat rides.

TIPPECANOE RIVER STATE PARK
just north of Winamac on U.S. 35

Covering 2,744 acres, this park stretches for some 8 miles along the **Tippecanoe**, one of northern Indiana's most picturesque rivers. Three hiking trails thread the park; near its entrance an 80-foot tower provides a view of rolling fields, green forests, and the bends and lagoons of the river.

TURKEY RUN STATE PARK
2½ miles north of Marshall on State 47

Dissected by **Sugar Creek** and abounding in deep, rock-walled canyons and scenic gorges formed in prehistoric times, this park boasts 13½ miles of foot trails. It also has large tracts of virgin timberland and numerous yew trees, rare in the Midwest.

WYANDOTTE CAVES
Wyandotte, about 10 miles west of Corydon on U.S. 460

One of the largest on the North American continent, Wyandotte Caves has 5 distinct floor levels, many caverns with notable formations, and about 23 miles of explored passages. Many of its walls and ceilings are mottled and striped with variegated strata of limestone separated by bands of black flint. Its 135-foot **Monumental Mountain** is said to be the world's highest underground mountain. **Little Wyandotte Cave,** 700 feet to the south, may possibly be an extension of the larger one.
Open daily: summer 8–6, winter 8–5. Admission: adults $1.50, children 75¢; slightly higher for longer tours

IOWA

BACKBONE STATE PARK
4 miles southwest of Strawberry Point via State 410

This park covers 1,411 acres within the horseshoe bend of the upper **Maquoketa River.** The **Devil's Backbone** is a long, narrow ridge of rugged limestone bluffs that rise 90 to 140 feet above the curve of the river; an observation tower is on the top. The park also contains many hiking and nature trails, which give access to scenic caverns, springs, and woods.

BELLEVUE STATE PARK
just south of Bellevue on U.S. 52 and 67

Situated on a plateau overlooking the **Mississippi River,** this 148-acre park offers some spectacular views of the sluggish "Father of Waters," of the nearby sand dunes, and of the area's rugged woods. Perpendicular cliffs rise some 400 feet from the river to the plateau, and serpentine trails lead from the park down the east face of the bluff past unusual rock formations.

BIXBY STATE PARK
2 miles north of Edgewood via county road

This rugged park features a waterfall, flowing springs, a profusion of wildflowers, and a phenomenal ice cave. Although **Bixby Cave** is smaller than **Decorah Ice Cave** (*see*), its ice is more abundant. Its temperature rarely rises above the freezing point.

CAYLER PRAIRIE STATE PRESERVE
10 miles southwest of Spirit Lake in northwest Iowa

This 120-acre virgin tract allows one to see the prairie much as the

Top: Ocheyedan Mound. Bottom: Cedar River. Right: White Pine Hollow Preserve

113

pioneers did. Its terrain permits variety in vegetation—265 species in 53 plant families. Registered Natural Landmark

CRYSTAL LAKE CAVE
6 miles southeast of Dubuque off U.S. 52 and 67

Nearly 1 mile long, this cave contains an underground lake of crystal-clear water and sparkling stalactites and stalagmites resting on onyx marble foundations. Artificial lights enhance the rock formations, and the temperature of 48° to 50° is refreshing.

Open June–Aug: daily 8–6; May, Sept, Oct: weekends 8–5. Admission: adults $1.20, children (6–12) 60¢

DECORAH ICE CAVE
slightly northeast of Decorah in northeast Iowa

Set in a high, rocky bluff overlooking the **Upper Iowa River,** this cave is over 200 feet deep, but only about 75 feet are open to visitors. The cave's walls are limestone honeycombed with fissures that retain cold temperatures even in warm weather. When moisture-filled spring and summer air enters the cave, it condenses to ice, but by late fall, enough warm air has entered to melt the ice. Thus the cave is ice-coated in summer and warm in winter. A pathway leads from the cave up the side of the cliff to a rocky promontory, where there is a fine view.

DOLLIVER MEMORIAL STATE PARK
3 miles northwest of Lehigh off State 50

Covering 613 acres on the **Des Moines River,** this park features deep ravines, wooded hills, trails, and Indian mounds. Sandstone cliffs, impregnated with iron, rise above the banks of **Prairie Creek,** bordering the west side of the park. Adjacent to Dolliver is **Woodman's Hollow,** a deep gorge carved into the sandstone by the river.

GITCHIE MANITOU STATE PRESERVE
9 miles northwest of Larchwood, near State 9

Bordering **Big Sioux River,** this preserve of prairie and brushland is noted for wild grasses that elsewhere have been replaced by domestic varieties. Other outstanding features are **Jasper Pool** and the pink stone outcrops of ancient Sioux quartzite.

HAYDEN PRAIRIE STATE PRESERVE
5½ miles west of Lime Springs in northeast Iowa

This 200-acre virgin area is a remnant of the true prairie that once covered most of the state. It contains at least 149 species of prairie plants. Registered Natural Landmark

KALSOW PRAIRIE STATE PRESERVE
3 miles north and 1 mile west of Manson via county road

Covering 160 acres, this area protects a fine example of virgin prairie which is rapidly disappearing from the state's landscape. At least 230 species of plants occur here.

MAQUOKETA CAVES STATE PARK
7 miles northwest of Maquoketa via State 130

Noted for its large limestone caves, a natural bridge that arches some 50 feet above the valley floor, and a 17-ton balanced rock perched atop a cliff, this park covers 152 well-wooded acres in eastern Iowa. Several caves were inhabited by prehistoric man, and evidence for their occupation has been found.

IOWA

OCHEYEDAN MOUND
2 miles south of State 9, near Ocheyedan

Rising an impressive 170 feet above the surrounding plain and at an altitude of 1,675 feet, Ocheyedan Mound is the highest point in this generally flat state. Long thought to have been an Indian burial ground, it is actually a kame—a small conical hill of roughly sorted sand and gravel, deposited by a glacier in a mass of stagnating ice or in angles of ice. It may have been used by the Indians as a place of mourning, hence its name, which is a Sioux word meaning "spot where they weep."

PIKES PEAK STATE PARK
3 miles southeast of McGregor via State 13 and 340

This 140-acre park is situated atop a thickly wooded 500-foot bluff overlooking the **Mississippi River**. It was named by Zebulon Pike, discoverer of the more famous **Pikes Peak** in Colorado (*see*). Other attractions include fossil-rich sandstone and limestone walls and **Pictured Rock Canyon** with its strangely shaped colored sands. A trail from the top of the bluff down to the canyon winds through rugged terrain and passes beneath **Bridal Veil Falls**.

PILOT KNOB STATE PARK
4 miles east, 1 mile south of Forest City via U.S. 9 and State 332

Occupying a heavily wooded tract in northern Iowa, this park features Pilot Knob, a glacial formation rising some 300 feet above the prairie. In pioneer days this hill served as a landmark for westbound travelers. From a lookout on its crest, there is a panorama of green cornfields, meadows, woods, and, on a clear day, the hills of Minnesota over 200 miles to the north. The park also includes a scenic road, trails, and spring-fed **Dead Man's Lake**.

SPOOK CAVE
7 miles west of McGregor on U.S. 18, and 2 miles north on State 13

This rock-ribbed underground river cavern may be explored only by boats. It maintains a constant temperature of 47°.
Open Apr, May, Sept, Oct: daily 8–5; June–Aug: 8–6. Admission: adults $1.50, children 75¢

STONE STATE PARK
northwestern corner of Sioux City in western Iowa

Located on the **Big Sioux River**, this 875-acre park lies in the heart of the rolling, glacially produced hills that border the **Missouri** and **Big Sioux river valleys**. Hiking trails and drives lead to observation points overlooking the plains of South Dakota.

WAPSIPINICON STATE PARK
at the southern edge of Anamosa on U.S. 151

Situated along the west bank of the Wapsipinicon River, this park features high, rocky cliffs, meadows, wooded hills, several caves, and a spring-fed stream. The river flows past dark, limestone cliffs festooned with ferns and mosses, giving a wilderness atmosphere.

WHITE PINE HOLLOW PRESERVE
1 mile north and 2 miles west of Luxemburg via State 3

This rough, forested terrain contains the largest stand of native white pine remaining in Iowa—many are over 200 years old. The pines predominate, but the hollow also contains oak, maple, hickory, basswood, and elm trees. Registered Natural Landmark

115

KANSAS

BIG BASIN
13 miles west of Ashland off U.S. 160, 283
> This mile-wide sinkhole is a 100-foot-deep natural depression covering 2,000 acres in southwest Kansas. The caverns, created when subterranean water dissolved supporting rock strata, collapsed to form the basin. **Little Basin,** a smaller sinkhole ½ mile to the east, contains **St. Jacob's Well,** a lovely natural pool of water accessible by a path from the southern rim of the Big Basin.

CASTLE ROCK
22 miles southeast of Quinter off I-70
> This 7-foot chalk spire, carved by erosion, rises above the **Smoky Hill River Valley.** A famous state landmark, it is visible for miles.

FLINT HILLS REGION
eastern Kansas, northeast of Manhattan
> Extending for about 200 miles between the **Arkansas River** in Oklahoma and the **Kansas River** in Kansas, the Flint Hills are a limestone escarpment rising 300 to 500 feet above the **Great Plains.** Because the rock underlying these low, rolling hills has proved impervious to farming, this area of prairie—probably the largest remaining stretch in the United States—has remained unspoiled. In order to further insure its protection, a small but particularly scenic area in eastern Kansas has been proposed as the **Prairie National Park.** In this 7-by-13-mile strip, covering approximately 57,000 acres north and east of the Kansas and Blue rivers, are grass-covered hills (bluestem grass is especially prevalent) and many meandering creeks. **Cedar, McIntire, Carnahan,** and **Booth creeks** generally flow north by south into **Blue River,** and **Camp Creek** flows east into **Rock Creek,** a tributary of the Kansas. *State Highway 13,* paralleling Cedar Creek, offers a scenic drive across this beautiful grassland.

Left: Castle Rock. Right: buffalo in the Smoky Hill River Valley

MONUMENT ROCKS
27 miles southeast of Oakley off U.S. 40

Rising sharply above the flat **Smoky Hill River Valley**, these chalk pinnacles and spires are also known as the **Kansas Pyramids**. They are the remains of shale and chalk beds in the sea that once covered the area during the Cretaceous geologic period. The chalk beds contain the richest deposits of cretaceous marine fossils found in the United States. A wall less than a foot thick, which is slowly giving way to the wind and rain, connects the rocks here, some of which reach 60 feet. Of particular interest is the **Sphinx**, an isolated formation whose stern face was carved by the elements. Registered Natural Landmark

OLD MAID'S POOL
5 miles northwest of Sharon Springs off U.S. 40

This 200-foot-deep pool fills a large sinkhole—a natural depression formed by the collapse of underground caverns. The pool, said to have never gone dry, was used as a watering place by early settlers and wagon trains on their way west.

PAWNEE ROCK
¼ mile north of Pawnee on U.S. 56, Pawnee State Monument

This huge promontory of Dakota sandstone was one of the most famous landmarks on the Santa Fe Trail. A camping and rendezvous site for scouts and Indians alike, many fights between the Indians and pioneers in wagon trains occurred here. Now a state monument, it offers a sweeping view of the **Arkansas, Ash,** and **Walnut rivers.**

ROCK CITY
2½ miles southwest of Minneapolis off State 106

Over 200 unusual sandstone formations—some perfectly rounded, some elliptical, and others eroded into interesting shapes—cover this area. Called concretions, rounded masses of minerals found in sedimentary rock, these formations vary from 8 to 27 feet in diameter. According to Indian legend, the rocks were rolled here by the Great Spirit, who predicted that when the wind had carried the rocks to the sea, and the waves had dissolved them into sand and washed the grains on the shore, the white man would return to his European homeland.

Stand of black walnut near Neosho River

KENTUCKY

BREAKS INTERSTATE PARK

7 miles from Elkhorn, Kentucky; 8 miles from Haysi, Virginia, on I-80

This beautiful park on the Virginia-Kentucky border covers 2,500 acres of scenic woodlands and mountains. The deepest canyon east of the Mississippi—more than 5 miles long and 1,600 feet deep—has been carved here by the **Russell Fork River,** a tributary of the **Big Sandy.** Scenic overlooks offer lovely views of the sheer vertical walls, rapids, and pools of the twisting gorge. Of the many interesting rock formations, the most famous is the **Towers,** a pyramidlike series of rocks, ½ mile long and ⅓ mile wide.

CARTER CAVES STATE RESORT

35 miles west of Ashland on State 182

This park, located in the state's northeast mountain region, is famous for a series of caverns, rock cliffs, and natural bridges. Three caves with interesting and colorful rock formations are open to the public. Other natural attractions include well-stocked, 45-acre **Smoky Valley Lake** and **Cascade Caves,** with limestone, iron, and salt formations, and underground rivers and waterfalls.

Cascade Caves open June–Labor Day: daily 8–6. Admission: adults 75¢, children 35¢

CRYSTAL ONYX CAVE

2½ miles southwest of Cave City on U.S. 31W

In the center of the Kentucky cave area, this cavern contains unusual onyx formations, underground waterfalls, and a lake.

Open Memorial Day–Labor Day: daily 7–7. Admission: adults $2.00, children (7–11) 50¢

Left: Natural Bridge. Top: Bluegrass country. Below: Cumberland Gap

CUDJO CAVE
on U.S. 25E, in Cumberland Gap National Historical Park
This privately owned limestone cave is actually a series of rooms connected by a mile-long winding hallway. Originally called Soldier's Cave, it was discovered by a Confederate soldier while he was digging a rifle pit. Guided tours are available.
Open May–Sept: daily 8–6; rest of the year: daily 9–5. Admission: adults $1.50, children (6–12) 75¢

CUMBERLAND FALLS STATE RESORT PARK
18 miles southwest of Corbin on State 90, in Daniel Boone National Forest
Called the Niagara of the South, this impressive cascade is the largest east of the Rockies and south of Niagara. Here the scenic **Cumberland River** plunges 68 feet over a precipice 150 feet wide into a rock-strewn gorge. Many observation points overlook the gorge in this 1,098-acre park. A moonbow created by mist from the falls— the only known one of its kind besides that at Victoria Falls in South Africa—is visible here during a full moon.

CUMBERLAND GAP NATIONAL HISTORICAL PARK
visitor center southeast of Middlesboro on U.S. 25E or 58
Located close to the meeting point of Kentucky, Virginia, and Tennessee, this gap is a natural pass in the **Cumberland Mountains,** the southernmost branch in the **Appalachian** chain. Such notches, or wind gaps, occur frequently in the Appalachians and are caused by a combination of stream activity, rock fracturing, and erosion. This historic pass across what had been an unbreachable barrier was first discovered by Dr. Thomas Walker in 1750. But it was not until 1775, with the opening of Daniel Boone's Wilderness Road, that the great transmontane migration began. Hacked out of virgin land, the road passed through the Gap and allowed for the settlement of Kentucky. It is estimated that about 12,000 settlers had entered the Kentucky Territory by the end of the Revolution, most of them via the Cumberland Gap.

Today this important area is preserved in a 20,169-acre park offering a wide range of historical and scenic attractions. Among the natural sites here are **The Pinnacle,** on *Skyland Road,* a high shoulder about 1,000 feet above the saddle, or lowpoint, of the gap; **Tri-State Peak,** reached from U.S. 25E, where Tennessee, Kentucky, and Virginia meet; **Sand Cave,** on the *Ridge Trail,* a shallow sandstone cave with an opening span 240 feet wide and 80 feet high; **White Rocks,** 400-to-600-foot vertical cliffs rising 3,451 feet above sea level and visible from U.S. 58; and Cudjo Cave (*see*). Many hiking trails wind through the area, including a ¼-mile remnant of the Wilderness Road. Among the many lookouts on the park's drives offering unspoiled views are *Wilderness Overlook,* on the Skyland Road, and *Sugar Run Overlook,* on Kentucky 988.
Park open: summer 8–7; rest of the year 8:30–5. For further information write: Box 840, Middlesboro, Ky. 40965

DANIEL BOONE NATIONAL FOREST
eastern Kentucky, headquarters at Winchester
Originally called Cumberland National Forest, this scenic area of nearly 500,000 acres was renamed to honor Kentucky's most famous frontiersman. Here in a region of mountains, forests, and streams are high sandstone cliffs, deep gorges, and natural bridges. Among the forest's highlights are **Red River Gorge,** a picturesque rock-strewn canyon in the Red River; **Sky Bridge,** a natural sandstone

KENTUCKY

arch; **Yahoo Falls,** an impressive 113-foot waterfall on **Lake Cumberland,** a huge man-made lake impounded by Wolf Creek Dam; and **Rock Bridge,** an unusual stone bridge spanning **Swift Camp Creek.** Of the many scenic drives here, two of the most beautiful are *Mountain Parkway* and the *Red River Gorge Scenic Drive,* a 30-mile loop road through rugged back country that follows the river for 8 miles. Countless trails, lookout points, and scenic areas are scattered about the forest. Particularly spectacular views are offered from *Stearns Tower,* atop a 1,400-foot-high wooded knoll, *Triangle Tower,* a lookout atop a 1,386-foot pinnacle, and from **Koomer Ridge,** known for its rock bridges. **Natural Arch Scenic Area,** a 945-acre preserve, features cliffs, canyons, and a lovely sandstone arch. *For further information write: 27 Carol Road, Winchester, Ky. 40391*

DIAMOND CAVERNS
1½ miles north of Park City on State 255

Although one of the smaller caves in the area, this is among the most beautiful with its interesting stalactites and stalagmites.
Open Memorial Day–Labor Day: daily 7:30–6; rest of the year: daily 8–4. Admission: adults $2.00, children (12–16) $1.00

FALLS OF THE OHIO (OHIO CORAL REEF). See INDIANA

JEFFERSON NATIONAL FOREST. See VIRGINIA

JESSE JAMES AND HUNDRED DOME CAVES
1¼ miles west of Park City on U.S. 31W

These caverns feature rock formations—huge stalactites and stalagmites, and interesting helictites—which have been lighted. Prehistoric Indian skeletons have been discovered here.
Open daily 8–4. Admission: adults $2.00, children (6–12) $1.00

MAMMOTH CAVE NATIONAL PARK
headquarters north of Park City on State 225; west of Cave City on State 70

These fantastic caverns—extending for 7 miles—were formed as underground waterways dissolved a bed of limestone, creating a large sinkhole. This was followed by an upthrust of the earth's crust in this region which drained the caves of the subterranean rivers and lowered the watertable. Subsequently the caverns were enlarged and modified by erosion and by downcutting of surface waters, mainly by the **Green River** and its underground tributaries—**Echo River** flows here 300 feet below the earth's surface. The initial stage of development created large barren rooms, but the secondary stage brought with it the formation of dripstone deposits of gypsum and travertine stalagmites, stalactites, helictites, and other grotesque and beautiful creations. What remains is considered one of the world's greatest natural wonders—an underground maze of lakes, rivers, corridors, and chambers covered with intriguing formations resembling draperies, flowers, needles, and snowballs.

Trips through this fantastic subterranean world, where the temperature remains a constant 54° and the humidity 87 per cent, vary from a short, ¾-mile trip to **Frozen Niagara**—a massive flowstone deposit 75 feet high and 45 feet wide—to an all-day tour of the 150 miles of explored corridors and passageways. At every turn within these corridors there is some formation that could be considered a highlight. The domes and pits for which these caves are famous (such as the 130-foot **Roosevelt Dome** and the 95-foot-deep **Silo Pit**) can be found in many areas. **Crystal Lake,** one of the many underground bodies of water, can be seen 60 feet below Frozen Niagara, and there is an unusual boat trip on Echo River, which includes a walk through a corridor so low, narrow, and tortuous that it is called **Fat Man's Misery.** A 4½-mile Scenic Trip includes such wonders as **Diamond Grotto,** where sparkling gypsum deposits decorate the ceiling, and **Grand Canyon,** a deep gorge formed when the floor of one passageway dropped through the ceiling of another. In addition there is a Historic Trip that takes the visitor along a route used by man for centuries. Artifacts have been uncovered revealing that pre-Columbian Indians lived and hunted here; the mummified body of a man believed to be about 2,000 years old, now called Lost John, can be seen near the spot where he was discovered. The most interesting living creatures in the caves are the famous blind fish, who have lost their sight as an adaption to their underground environment; other cave-dwelling animals include bats, cave crickets, and spiders.

Above ground, this park is made up of nearly 52,000 acres of thick forest. Here, among the oaks, hickories, and maples, one can find such animals as skunks, foxes, and rabbits, as well as over 170 species of birds. Roads with scenic overlooks and 2 self-guiding trails are featured here: *Sunset Point Nature Trail,* which affords an excellent view of the Green River, and *Cave Island Natural Trail,* leading to the old forest in the Green River bottomland where huge sycamores and beeches grow and underground rivers emerge. From May through October, one can take an hour-long ride on the scenic Green River. A museum is included at the visitor center near the natural Old or Historic entrance.

For further information write: Mammoth Cave, Ky. 42259

MAMMOTH ONYX CAVE
central Kentucky at Horse Cave on I-65
This large cavern contains unusual onyx formations, stalactites, stalagmites, and hanging bridges. In underground pools, such as **Martha's Pool,** are "eyeless" or blind, fish. Tours are conducted in the cave, where the temperature is always 60°.
Open daily: summer 7–6, winter 8–5. Admission: adults $2.10, children (6–11) $1.05

NATURAL BRIDGE STATE RESORT PARK
on Highway 11 near Slade in Daniel Boone National Forest
This 1,337-acre park in the scenic **Red River Valley** takes its name from the massive arch that has been carved out by wind and water. The sandstone bridge is 65 feet high and has an opening 78 feet wide. A skylift to the top of the bridge, 1,560 feet above sea level, provides a spectacular view of the surrounding valleys, cliffs, streams, and mountains. Many wooded trails lead throughout the park to other attractions, such as **Devil's Gulch, Balanced Rock,** and **Mill Creek Lake.** This bridge is the largest of 12 such arches in Daniel Boone National Forest (*see*).

OTTER CREEK PARK
west of Muldraugh off State 1638, 30 miles southwest of Louisville
This 2,427-acre preserve on the **Ohio River** was set aside by the National Park Service in 1939 as a reforestation area and a wildlife sanctuary. Here the scenic Otter Creek emerges from underground caverns and winds through wooded hills and valleys once owned by the Boone family.

LOUISIANA

AVERY ISLAND
9 miles southwest of New Iberia

Completely surrounded by sea marshes, this largest of the **Five Islands** overlies a coastal salt dome. Rock salt, which in places reaches to within 12 feet of the surface, has been mined here since 1791. From the highest point on the "island," almost 200 feet above sea level, there is a vista of woodlands, cypress swamps, the diverse coastal vegetation, and far to the south **Vermillion Bay.** Also on the island is tropical Jungle Garden, featuring a bird sanctuary.

BOGUE FALAYA STATE PARK
near Covington on U.S. 190

This 13-acre park occupies a scenic spot on the sandy banks of **Bogue Falaya,** a clear stream that flows into the **Tchefuncta River.**

CHEMIN-A-HAUT STATE PARK
10 miles north of Bastrop off State 139

This beautiful park is located in the pine forests of northeast Louisiana. Here, **Bayous Bartholomew** and **Chemin-a-Haut** flow together and provide an unspoiled setting for this 550-acre preserve.

CHICOT STATE PARK
8 miles north of Ville Platte off U.S. 167

Set in the rolling, wooded hills of southern Louisiana, this 6,480-acre park features a picturesque, well-stocked, 2,500-acre lake. A 301-acre arboretum here is crossed by many winding scenic trails.

Left: waterfowl on Mississippi River Delta. Right: cypress swamp with water hyacinths

KISATCHIE NATIONAL FOREST
central and northern Louisiana, headquarters at Pineville

Divided into 6 units covering about 600,000 acres, this forest of pine and hardwood trees draped with Spanish moss includes many scenic regions of bayous, lakes, and streams. Among the highlights here is the **Kisatchie Hills Scenic Area,** a region of rocky, flat-topped mesas rising about 350 feet, one of the highest points in the state. The region is best viewed from the *Longleaf Trail Vista,* the last stop on the 15-mile *Longleaf Auto Tour* which crosses the Kisatchie Hills. Other scenic areas include **Gum Springs,** a small, spring-fed pool; **Corney Lake,** a 2,100-acre well-stocked lake lined with trees; and **Saline Bayou,** which flows into **Saline Lake** and then on to the **Red River.**

For further information write: Pineville, La. 71360

LAKE BRUIN STATE PARK
4 miles north of Saint Joseph off U.S. 604

This 12-mile-long lake—one of the state's most beautiful—is shaped like an oxbow. Formed by a cutoff of the **Mississippi,** it is a wildlife sanctuary where many kinds of waterfowl can be seen in winter. The state park, located on the lake's shore, features a lovely stand of huge, old cypress trees.

LAKE PONTCHARTRAIN
southeast Louisiana

This large, shallow lake (41 miles long, 25 miles wide, and about 10 to 16 feet deep), played an important role in the historic Battle of New Orleans in 1815. Today the lake is connected by channels to **Lake Maurepas,** the **Mississippi River, Lake Borgne,** and through it to the **Gulf of Mexico.** The world's longest overwater highway, a section of the *Greater New Orleans Expressway,* crosses the lake north from New Orleans; for 8 miles passengers are out of sight of any land. Fontainebleau State Park, with many scenic trails, covers 5 miles of the lake's north shore near Mandeville.

MISSISSIPPI RIVER DELTA AND MOUTH

The famed Delta extends from just below the mouth of the **Red River** to the mouth of the Mississippi itself. It is an area of swamps, salt marshes and low-lying alluvial tracts built up by the sediment collected by the river in its more than 2,500-mile journey south from **Lake Itasca** (*see*) in northern Minnesota. Crossing the Delta region are the rivers and bayous lined with trees draped in Spanish moss—such as the **Atchafalaya River** and **Bayou Lafourche**—which typify this part of southern Louisiana. The river winds and twists its way past New Orleans to empty into the **Gulf of Mexico,** about 100 miles farther southeast, through a series of small channels or "passes" that cross a narrow neck of land jutting into the water. Among the main channels are **Southwest, South,** and **North passes, Pass a Loutre**—site of a 66,000-acre state shooting ground—and **Main Pass,** site of the **Delta Migratory Waterfowl Refuge,** a large government-owned winter sanctuary for waterfowl.

SAM HOUSTON STATE PARK
north of Lake Charles on State 378, off U.S. 171

Located on the tree-lined banks of the scenic **Calcasieu River,** a 215-mile waterway that flows into **Lake Charles** and **Calcasieu Lake,** this park features over 1,000 acres of wooded and open land.

MAINE

ACADIA NATIONAL PARK
headquarters and visitor center at Hulls Cove, Mount Desert Island

Surrounded by the sea, Acadia combines a rich mixture of scenic beauty—mountains and lakes, forests and streams, chasms and caves. It covers 41,634 acres and is spread over **Mount Desert Island, Isle au Haut, Schoodic Peninsula,** and several smaller islands. Its network of over 100 miles of trails reaches nearly every summit and valley in the park. Acadia occupies over 40 square miles of Mount Desert, the largest of Maine's myriad islands. In 1604 French explorer Samuel de Champlain first sighted it and named it Isle des Monts Déserts because of its chain of bare, granite peaks.

A good introduction to the island's east side is via *Park Loop Road,* which includes *Ocean Drive.* Beginning at **Sieur de Monts Spring,** it then passes **Champlain Mountain** overlook with its magnificent ocean view—the 1,058-foot summit may be reached by *Precipice Trail.* A spur road leads to **Anemone Cave,** a sea cave that waves have eroded in the granite, and rejoins the Loop near **Sand Beach,** a sand bar deposited across what was once a cove, and **Thunder Hole,** where wave action creates thunderlike sounds. **Otter Cliffs,** which drop steeply into the Atlantic 107 feet below, provide a sweeping view of **Frenchman Bay.** From here the *Seashore Trail* leads to the rocky shore through a forest of spruce and fir. The Loop then passes **Otter Cove, Western Point, Black Woods,** and **Hunter's Head.** From here it goes inland to **Jordan Pond** (originally scooped out by a glacial ice sheet), which is surrounded by stands of birch, beech, and ash with liberal sprinklings of evergreens. This is a fine area in which to study the effects of glacial erosion. There is a natural amphitheater carved by the glacier that overwhelmed the island less than 20,000 years ago; **The Bubbles,** 2 peaks formed by glacial action; and, on the east slope of South Bubble, a glacial erratic—a large boulder transported a considerable distance from its original source. Continuing on the Loop's northern segment, one comes to a spur road that climbs 1,530-foot **Cadillac Mountain,** the highest point on the **Atlantic Coast.** From here there is a panoramic view of the ocean studded with islands, including the **Cranberries** and **Porcupines.** The road continues to the park entrance or east to Bar Harbor, once a fashionable resort. *Sargent Drive,* leading to the island's center, follows the east shore of **Somes Sound.** According to many geologists, this is the only true fiord on the Atlantic Coast of the United States. *Long Pond* and *Western Fire gravel roads* lead to the mountains (**Beech Mountains**) and lakes (**Echo Lake**) of the island's west side. Among the picturesque coves and harbors here, the **Seawall** section is notable for its shoreline of a natural wall of boulders cast up by the sea.

Schoodic Peninsula, the only mainland section of Acadia Park, lies on the eastern side of Frenchman Bay and is reached by State 186. A park road follows the peninsula's rugged coastline and leads to **Schoodic Head,** a 440-foot rock headland offering a panoramic vista of this section of the park and the sea beyond.

Isle au Haut, a spruce-covered island south of **Deer Isle,** is reached by mailboat from Stonington. Half of this island, which has a remote, unspoiled quality, is administered by the National Park Service. Its spectacular scenery includes towering cliffs at its northern end, **Mount Champlain** and **Jerusalem Mountain.**

For further information write: Box 338, Bar Harbor, Me. 04609

Left and right: typical coastal and inland lake landscapes. Center: Mount Katahdin in Baxter State Park. Below: Schoodic Point in Acadia National Park

Canoeing on the Allagash River

ALLAGASH WILDERNESS WATERWAY
northwest of Baxter State Park in northern Maine
> This 92-mile-long corridor through the forest of Maine's northern
> wilderness encompasses some 200,000 acres. With its many lakes,
> streams, and ponds—notably **Chamberlain Lake** and the swift-
> flowing **Allagash River** with its rapids—it is one of the state's favor-
> ite canoeing areas. The longest canoe trip is from **Telos Lake** to
> **West Twin Falls**, where the waterway ends. One can detour to the
> northwest and paddle in the solitude and silence of **Allagash Lake**
> in the shadow of 1400-foot **Allagash Mountain**.

AROOSTOOK STATE PARK
U.S. 1, 4 miles south of Presque Isle
> Located in the heart of Maine's famous potato district, this park is
> on the shores of **Echo Lake**, where trout may be caught. In the back-
> ground is **Quoggy Joe Mountain** which rises only 600 feet above
> the lake but still offers an excellent view of the countryside.
> *Open daily May 15–Oct 15*

BAXTER STATE PARK
about 16 miles north of headquarters at Millinocket via Park Road
> One of the largest and most superb natural areas in the eastern
> United States, this park covers over 200,000 acres of wilderness.
> It features mountainous woodlands, ponds, streams, wildlife pre-
> serves, and 83 miles of hiking trails. Baxter's 46 mountain peaks and
> ridges are dominated by **Mount Katahdin**, a Registered Natural
> Landmark. **Baxter Peak**, at 5,267 feet above sea level, is the state's
> highest point. Each day, the first rays of sunlight to strike the United
> States fall on this mountain. The other peak on Katahdin's crest is
> **Pamola**. Between Baxter and Pamola is the famous **Knife Edge
> Ridge**—less than 3 feet wide in places, it drops 1,500 feet almost
> straight down on both sides. Baxter Park is also the northern termi-
> nus of the *Appalachian National Scenic Trail,* which extends 2,000
> miles through 14 states to its southern terminus in Georgia. Ten
> miles of this trail are in this park. Baxter is divided into distinct
> forest and alpine vegetation zones. The alpine zone is limited to the
> upper slopes and tableland of Mount Katahdin, which has many
> arctic plants and shrubs. A small section of the park is covered with
> northern hardwood forest, but most of it is northern coniferous
> forest, heavily dominated by black spruce and balsam fir trees. The

park has 7 major campgrounds which give access to its many hiking trails. From Abol campground on the park's southern side, *Abol Trail* provides a direct ascent to Katahdin's summit via the tableland. The **Katahdin Stream** campground, also on the park's southeast side, is traversed by the Appalachian Trail, which also goes through the tableland to Baxter Peak. One mile up this trail are beautiful **Katahdin Falls. South Branch Pond** campground in the northern portion of the park boasts an impressive view toward Katahdin and is the base for a climb of **Traveler Mountain.** The whole park is rich in animal life such as moose, bear, and caribou which roam in their natural habitat.
Open daily May 15–Oct 15

DESERT OF MAINE
2 miles west of Freeport on Desert Rd, off junction of I-95 and U.S. 1
Fine-textured sand deserts, like this one, are common coastal phenomena. The glint of mica in its drifting sand dunes indicates that the Desert of Maine, which began in the 19th century, probably covers the bed of an ancient lake formed by the glaciers.
Open May–Nov: daily 8–8. Admission: $1.25, children under 13 free

CAMDEN HILLS
Camden, on the coast of southern Maine
These towering mountains rise almost at the ocean's edge and form a semicircle around Camden, one of the state's loveliest coastal towns. The group includes 800-foot **Mount Battie;** 1,380-foot **Mount Megunticook;** 1,272-foot **Bald Mountain;** and 1,300-foot **Ragged Mountain.** Camden Hills State Park, 2 miles north of Camden on U.S. 1, covers over 5,000 acres and has 25 miles of nature trails that thread Mount Megunticook. A park road leads to the summit of Mount Battie. From here there is an excellent view of Camden and its harbor, the ocean, and the many islands of **Penobscot Bay.**

COBSCOOK BAY STATE PARK
6 miles south of Dennysville on U.S. 1
Surrounded on 3 sides by Cobscook Bay (Indian for "boiling tides"), this park covers 868 acres and includes subalpine spruce and fir forests. The name aptly describes the effect created by the bay's waters as they fluctuate with every tide.
Open daily May 15–Oct 15

GRAFTON NOTCH STATE PARK
State 26 between Upton and Newry in western Maine
One of Maine's most interesting state parks, Grafton Notch is traversed by the *Mahoosuc Trail,* part of the *Appalachian Trail.* The notch itself is formed by 4,180-foot-high **Old Speck Mountain** and 3,812-foot-high **Baldpate Mountain.** The park also contains **Screw Augur Falls,** where the swirling water of **Bear River** has worn holes up to 25 feet deep in the rock of the riverbed. **Old Jail,** a chasm 75 feet long and 25 feet wide, is another of the park's scenic attractions. A path into the woods leads to **Moose Cave,** a deep gorge on the Bear River formed by rocks that have broken off Baldpate Mountain. The cave is cold even on the hottest days.

GULF HAGAS
about 25 miles northwest of Brownville in central Maine
Gulf Hagas is a breathtaking gorge formed by the west branch of the **Pleasant River** as it twists through mountain foothills and cuts

its course 100 feet below sheer walls of slate deposits to form a natural chasm. The gorge is about 3 miles long and covers some 850 acres. In this stretch the river drops over 500 feet, creating many falls and rapids with such names as **Stair Falls, Buttermilk Falls,** and **Billings Falls.** The walls of the gorge are covered with an excellent spruce-pine forest with some specimens of white pine, hemlock, and white cedar. Gulf Hagas is truly one of nature's last strongholds; it is privately owned by paper companies that have dedicated themselves to the preservation of its natural values. The most direct automobile route to Gulf Hagas is by gravel road from Route 11, a few miles north of Brownville, to Katahdin Iron Works, now a state park. From here one can hike about 6 miles to the Gulf, or travel over rough road by jeep. Registered Natural Landmark
Tollgate fees: $1.00 per day per car, $1.50 per day per trailer

KENNEBUNKPORT
3 miles southeast of Kennebunk

Situated at the mouth of tidal **Kennebunk River,** this elm-shaded resort village is typical of the many ports that dot Maine's rocky sea-drowned coast. Its shoreline rock formations are noteworthy for their magnificent displays of surf. At **Spouting Rock** and **Blowing Cave,** slightly north of the port, a geyser is formed as the incoming tide forces water through cavernous rock formations.

MONHEGAN ISLAND
about 10 miles south of Port Clyde in the Atlantic Ocean

Remote Monhegan, the home of seafarers, fishermen, and artists, is about 1 mile long and ½ mile wide. It has the highest cliffs on the New England coast, rising, on the seaward side, to headlands as high as 160 feet. Directly in the path of storm waves, these unsheltered cliffs are often drenched with spray. In winter, at **White Head Cliff,** water from a nearby spring freezes into gold-colored ice. The northern half of the island is nearly completely covered with essentially virgin forest. Here are the famous **Cathedral Woods,** dense stands of almost pure red spruce, some of which are over 90 years old. Registered Natural Landmark

MOOSEHEAD LAKE
north of Greenville in northcentral Maine

Cutting through an unspoiled, nearly trackless wilderness, this lake is surrounded by rugged mountains and virgin forests. It is in one of the last primitive areas where deer, moose, and other animals roam in their natural habitat. The state's largest lake and the source of the **Kennebec River,** irregularly shaped Moosehead covers 120 square miles. It is 40 miles long, from 1 to 20 miles wide, and has many large and small islands—notably **Deer, Moose,** and **Sugar**—as well as sheltered inlets and coves. Midway along its east shore, **Mount Kineo,** a solid mass of flint, rises abruptly 1,806 feet above sea level. The southern shore is dominated by **Lily Bay** and by **Baker** and **Big** and **Little Squaw mountains.**

MOUNT BLUE STATE PARK
north and southwest of Weld, at junction of State 142 and 156

In a beautiful setting of lakes, streams, and mountains, this park covers 1,273 acres. One section is on the west shore of **Lake Webb,** the other slightly northeast of the lake. The park offers excellent fishing and ample hiking trails. There is also a road to the top of **Center Hill** (1,600 feet) from where there is a magnificent view of

the surrounding countryside. For another panoramic view one can climb 3,187-foot **Mount Blue.**
Open daily May 30–Oct 15

OGUNQUIT
on coast of southeastern Maine

With its verdant setting and seaside charm, Ogunquit is a well-known art center and summer resort. Its most scenic area is *Marginal Way*, a mile-long footpath that follows the rockbound coast from the mouth of the **Ogunquit River** to Perkins Cove, an artists' colony to the south. The path, bordered by bayberry, juniper, cedar, and other vegetation, offers long views and close-ups of minerals, tidal pools, and marine life. The shore road continues on past the cove to 100-foot-high **Bald Head Cliff,** which extends 300 feet into the ocean. The pounding of the sea often creates sprays that rebound off the cliff 100 feet into the air.

RANGELEY LAKES
Rangeley vicinity on New Hampshire border

In the heart of a richly forested region of western Maine, this famous chain of 6 stream-linked lakes lies between rugged, evergreen-clad hills and mountains abounding in wild game. These lakes, noted for their trout and salmon fishing, cover about 80 square miles and range in altitude from 1,256 to 1,511 feet. They are **Rangeley** or **Oquossoc, Mooselookmeguntic; Molechunkamunk** or **Upper Richardson; Welokennebacook** or **Lower Richardson; Cupsuptic;** and **Umbabog,** on the New Hampshire line. Mooselookmeguntic, about 13 miles long, is the longest of the chain. Recreational facilities are available at nearby Rangeley State Park. There is superb skiing at Saddleback Mountain, also in the lake region.

Bobcat in the Moosehead Lake area

MAINE

REVERSING FALLS
northeastern Maine at West Pembroke

These salt-water falls occur when the incoming tidal current passes between **Mahar's Point** on **Leighton's Neck** in West Pembroke, and **Falls Island,** a few hundred yards distant. This current alternately fills and empties both **Dennys** and **Whiting bays.** The phenomenon is caused as the water, flowing swiftly at 25 knots, strikes rock projections along its course and creates a set of falls. This unique natural wonder may be appreciated from a 140-acre regional park on Leighton's Neck.

SEBAGO LAKE
about 30 miles northwest of Portland in southwestern Maine

Maine's second largest lake after Moosehead (*see*), Sebago is 4 miles long and 11 miles wide. It is connected to **Long Lake** in the north via the famous canal lock on **Songo River.** In this region, which covers hundreds of square miles, there are some 32 sparkling lakes and ponds offering excellent fishing and recreation opportunities. Sebago Lake State Park, on the lake's northern side, offers recreation and hikes on nature trails.

TWO LIGHTS STATE PARK
Cape Elizabeth, off State 77 in southern Maine

On the very tip of **Cape Elizabeth,** this park offers a spectacular view of **Casco Bay** and the open **Atlantic.** Its rocky, steep shoreline is characteristic of Maine's coast in general. Swimming is available at nearby Crescent Beach State Park.

Open daily Apr 15–Dec 15

WEST QUODDY HEAD
Lubec, in northeastern Maine

The most easterly point in the United States, West Quoddy Head is the site of new, 400-acre Quoddy Head State Park. Here, spruce- and pine-covered rock ledges rise 50 or more feet from the ocean, some tapering to 190 feet. From these high cliffs one can witness the nation's highest tides—ranging from 20 to 28 feet—and admire spectacular vistas of smashing surf and the rugged headlands of nearby Canadian islands of **Campobello** and **Grand Manan.** Adjacent to the park is the candy-striped West Quoddy Lighthouse, a famous navigational landmark. About 1 mile from the light, on the left of a dirt road leading back to Lubec, is a boglike area called **Carrying Place Cove.** This flatland, formerly a lake bed left by retreating glacial ice, contains excellent samples of true arctic tundra and rare insectivorous pitcher and sundew plants. A bridge connects Lubec with Campobello Island, New Brunswick, where one may visit the summer home of President Franklin D. Roosevelt.

WHITE MOUNTAIN NATIONAL FOREST. *See* **NEW HAMPSHIRE**

MARYLAND

ASSATEAGUE ISLAND NATIONAL SEASHORE

8 miles south of Ocean City, Maryland, via State 376 or 611; 2 miles east of Chincoteague, Virginia, via State 175

This narrow barrier island—an unspoiled combination of 14-foot sand dunes, salt marshes, and magnificent white sand beaches—is part of the barrier reef that extends along the Atlantic coast from Massachusetts to Florida. Until 1933 when a storm cut an inlet just below Ocean City, the island extended north to Delaware. Today Assateague is just less than 35 miles long and varies in width from ⅓ of a mile to slightly more than a mile. Paralleling the Virginia-Maryland coasts, it is separated from them by **Chincoteague** and **Sinepuxent** bays. The National Seashore is made up of 39,500 acres of land and water (19,000 acres are on Assateague and adjacent small islands). A 680-acre section of the Maryland portion of the island comprises Assateague State Park, and almost all of the Virginia section of the island is devoted to the **Chincoteague National Wildlife Refuge.** Because the refuge occupies the highest ground on the island and combines a setting of oak and pine woods with freshwater ponds and salt marshes, it attracts the migratory birds of the Atlantic flyway in early spring and autumn. (A nature trail winds through this scenic preserve.) The island also is home to some 40 species of shore birds. Living in the grassy marshes are perhaps the most famous animals on Assateague—wild ponies whose ancestors, according to legend, were left here by a shipwrecked Spanish galleon. Other animals (deer, foxes, raccoons) inhabit the pines and shrubs that provide a substantial plant cover behind the shifting dunes anchored only by grasses. The bay and ocean waters abound in shellfish and other marine life. At present there are no roads on

Left: wild ponies on Assateague Island. Below: Point Lookout extending into Chesapeake Bay. Right: Catoctin Mountain forest

Assateague, although one is planned that will connect the Maryland and Virginia bridges at either end. Visitor centers are maintained in both states.

For further information write: Route 2, Box 111, Berlin, Md. 21811

BATTLE CREEK CYPRESS SWAMP
on State 506 between Bowens and Port Republic

Located on a narrow neck of land bounded on the east by Chesapeake Bay (*see*) and on the west by the **Patuxent River,** this is one of the most northerly cypress swamps in the country. Cypress up to 100 feet tall and from 10 to 48 inches in diameter can be found here along with such other swamp and river-bottom trees as tupelo, holly, red maple, sweet gum, and pawpaw. The swamp abounds in fascinating indigenous animal life. Registered Natural Landmark

CATOCTIN MOUNTAIN PARK
headquarters and visitor center, 2 miles west of Thurmont on State 77

Catoctin Mountain—the east prong of the **Blue Ridge Mountains** in Maryland—extends about 37 miles south-southwest across Maryland to Virginia and descends from 1,900 to 500 feet. This park covers 5,769 acres of scenic woods and includes many points of historical and geological interest. Many of the components that went into the formation of the mountain can still be seen; the green rock (Catoctin greenstone) on *Hog Rock Trail* is the remnant of a lava flow millions of years ago. The Weaverton quartzite visible on **Wolf Rock** (1,400 feet) and **Chimney Rock** (1,420 feet) was compacted on the floor of the inland sea that once covered this area. Also located within the park is Camp David, the private presidential retreat established here during World War II by F.D.R., who called it "Shangri-La."

Several roads and 12 miles of hiking trails wind through the park. Hog Rock and *Deerfield* are 2 self-guiding nature trails. Among the trees found here are black locust, wild cherry, sassafras, and yellow poplar in the mountain valleys, and chestnut, oak, and hickory on the eastern slope. Small animals as well as ruffed grouse, barred owl, turkey vultures, and many other varieties of birds may be spotted.

For further information write: Thurmont, Md. 21788

CHESAPEAKE BAY

One of the great arms of the **Atlantic Ocean,** Chesapeake Bay is about 195 miles long and from 3 to 30 miles wide; its entrance from the ocean is the 13 miles between **Capes Charles** and **Henry** in Virginia. It is separated from the Atlantic by the **Delmarva Peninsula,** the so-called **Eastern Shore** on the bay side. The picturesque Chesapeake shoreline is so indented with rivers and inlets (48 rivers and a total of 150 bodies of water empty into the bay) that if it were straightened out it would run more than 5,000 miles. An area of great historical interest, countless scenic wonders can be found along its shores and in its waters. Examples of the varied attractions available here are **Tilghman Island,** a picturesque fishing resort at the mouth of **Choptank River; Point Lookout,** with a state park at the tip of the peninsula where the **Potomac River** empties into the bay; and the **Calvert Cliffs,** 30 miles of bluffs as high as 100 feet, featuring marine fossils from the Miocene period. One of the most famous sea-food producing areas in the country, Chesapeake Bay is also a favorite landing place for migrating birds. The formerly remote Eastern Shore is now accessible by the beautiful 7-mile-long Chesapeake Bay Bridge.

CUMBERLAND NARROWS
northwest of Cumberland on U.S. 40

A natural east-west passage across the **Appalachians**, this gap is a 1,000-foot-deep scenic gorge cut into **Wills Mountain** by **Wills Creek**. After General Braddock's army cleared the way in 1755, the Narrows provided a "gateway to the west" for colonial settlers. U.S. 40, once the historic Cumberland or National Road, passes through it.

DANS ROCK
about 5 miles northeast of Lonaconing

Rising to 2,898 feet, this peak is the highest point on **Dans Mountain**—part of the east escarpment of the **Alleghenies**—which runs for about 30 miles from northwest Maryland to southern Pennsylvania. The top offers a splendid panorama of the **Potomac River Valley, Big Savage Mountain,** and the surrounding wooded ridges.

ELK NECK STATE PARK
9 miles south of Northeast City on State 272

Located at the northern end of Chesapeake Bay (*see*) on a narrow neck of land between the **Northeast** and **Elk rivers,** this park includes in its 1,055 acres sandy beaches, marshy swamplands, and heavily wooded bluffs rising 1,000 feet. The entire park is a wildlife sanctuary and abounds in white-tailed deer, small mammals, and reptiles. Songbirds fill the woods, and seabirds thrive in the coastal waters here.

GAMBRILL STATE PARK
6 miles northwest of Frederick via U.S. 40

Located on **Catoctin Mountain,** this 1,141-acre park offers beautiful views and scenic trails in an area steeped in history. Highlighting the attractions here is the view from the 1,600-foot summit of **High Knob.** From 3 native-stone overlooks atop this mountain midway between the Mason-Dixon Line and the **Potomac River,** there is a panorama of the **Monocacy** and **Middletown valleys,** through which

View of Middletown Valley from High Knob in Gambrill State Park

armies from the French and Indian, Revolutionary, and Civil wars marched. There are 5 miles of wooded trails, including the self-guided *Lost Chestnut Nature Trail*, all rich in plant and animal life.

GREAT FALLS OF THE POTOMAC. *See* **DISTRICT OF COLUMBIA**

POCOMOKE STATE FOREST
between Snow Hill and Pocomoke City on U.S. 113

Made up of 10 separate tracts comprising 12,251 acres, this forest occupies a rather flat area south of the Delaware border. Located mainly along the Pocomoke ("black waters") River, it is noted for its stand of loblolly pine (this tree provides about half the timber cut in Maryland) and the mysterious cypress swamps that border the river. Rising in the Great Cypress Swamp in Delaware (*see*), the river flows southwesterly for 45 miles through the junglelike swampland of Maryland, until it reaches **Pocomoke Sound,** where it empties into Chesapeake Bay (*see*). The **Pocomoke River Swamp,** 30 miles long and from $\frac{1}{2}$ to 2 miles wide, supports 72 families of plant life. Bordering the river are southern white cedar and the bald cypress with its gnarled "cypress knees," root extensions that protrude above the water line. Wildlife abound in the forest, and nearly 200 varieties of birds have been spotted here.

SAVAGE RIVER STATE FOREST
east of Grantsville and 5 miles south of U.S. 40

The 2 sections of this 52,770-acre forest in the **Alleghenies** are located along the Savage River between **Meadow** and **Big Savage mountains** and on **Negro Mountain.** Elevations vary from 1,488 feet on the river to 2,991 feet on **St. John's Rock.** An important watershed, the forest is the source of the **Savage** and **Casselman rivers.** The Savage flows south into the **Potomac,** while the Casselman flows north into the **Ohio** and **Mississippi rivers.** The forest has many attractions, including what is believed to be the largest tree in the state—a 240-year-old white pine (off Savage River Road), 136 feet tall with a 40.9-inch diameter.

SWALLOW FALLS STATE PARK
9 miles northwest of Oakland on Garrett County Route 20

Located on the highest plateau (altitude 2,500 feet) of Maryland's **Allegheny Mountains,** this park in the Swallow Falls State Forest includes the last stand of virgin hemlock and white pine left in the state. Covering 40 acres, the trees reach as high as 120 feet, have trunks up to 40 inches thick, and are about 300 years old. Many other scenic attractions in this 257-acre park include **Swallow Falls** and **Lower Falls,** 2 cascades in the **Youghiogheny River,** and **Muddy Creek Falls,** a 51-foot drop near the confluence of the creek and the river. Many interesting rock formations, some embedded with fossils, cover this area. *Canyon Trail,* a scenic trek over high cliffs, connects the falls; a swinging bridge, accessible by a picturesque 100-foot trail, crosses Muddy Creek above the falls.

THE WYE OAK STATE PARK
near Wye Mills on State 622

This park preserves a mighty white oak, rated as the largest and finest specimen of its kind in the country. The impressive tree, estimated to be about 400 years old, measures 50 feet in circumference at its widest point; its total height is 95 feet and its branch spread is 165 feet.

MASSACHUSETTS

ALTAR ROCK
northeast section of Nantucket Island
> At an altitude of 102 feet, this rock is Nantucket's highest point. From it, one can gaze over the undulating green moors, harbors, small ponds, and gleaming white beaches. Like **Martha's Vineyard,** Nantucket was once a glacial outwash plain, but it is now a broad, grassy heath. Much of its picturesque charm dates back to the early 1800s when it was the world's leading whaling port.

BASH BISH FALLS STATE FOREST
follow markers from junction of State 23 and 41 in South Egremont
> Named for the state's most spectacular waterfall, this forest contains many hiking and climbing trails, including one leading to New York's Taconic State Park *(see)*. The falls are formed by **Bash Bish Brook,** which rushes down a heavily wooded, rocky gorge to take a final 60-foot plunge.

BEARTOWN STATE FOREST
east of Great Barrington off State 23
> Noted for its varied topography, this 8,207-acre forest encompasses parts of the **Housatonic Valley** in the north as well as **Mount Wilcox** (2,155 feet), **Livermore Peak** (1,863 feet), **Sky Peak** (1,947 feet), and **Barrington Mountain** (1,865 feet). Its many trails, including a segment of the *Appalachian Trail,* lead to panoramic vistas of the **Taconic Mountains** on the New York State border.

Left: Windsor Jambs gorge. Right: Gay Head Cliffs on Martha's Vineyard

MASSACHUSETTS

CAPE ANN
northeast coast of Massachusetts

Marking the southern end of **Ipswich Bay**, Cape Ann is characteristic of the state's rocky coastline with its granite boulders and barren, rock-strewn pastures. It is, in fact, one of the rockiest places in New England, its boulders having been torn loose, broken up, and in some cases brought there by the ice sheets of the great glaciers. The arm of land jutting out into the **Atlantic Ocean** is also famous for the fishing port of Gloucester. There is a state reservation at **Halibut Point**, the 12-mile-long rocky promontory on the cape's northeastern tip. There is also a reservation at 270-foot **Mount Ann**, the highest point on the cape. From here there is a magnificent panorama that sweeps from Maine, across **Massachusetts Bay,** southward to the **Blue Hills.**

CAPE COD NATIONAL SEASHORE
headquarters at Marconi Station Area, South Wellfleet

Cape Cod, where the *Mayflower* Pilgrims first landed in 1620, extends 65 miles out to sea in a fishhook-shaped formation—farther out than any other portion of our Atlantic coast. It is surrounded by **Buzzard's Bay, Nantucket Sound, the Atlantic Ocean,** and **Cape Cod Bay.** A creation of the glaciers, it has been considerably reshaped by wind and waves as have been the nearby islands of **Martha's Vineyard, Nantucket,** and the 16 **Elizabeth Islands.** This national seashore, stretching for more than 35 miles along the ocean (between the Chatham vicinity on Nantucket Sound and Long Point on Cape Cod Bay), and for 5 miles along the bay in the Wellfleet area, will ultimately encompass 27,000 acres. One of the last expanses of uninterrupted natural landscape along the Atlantic coast, it comprises an extremely varied terrain. The glacier-hewn shoreline contains banks and cliffs, of continental glacier sand, gravel, and clay, rising as high as 175 feet from the beach. But back of the pounding surf, the cliffs, and the dunes are numerous calm glacier ponds, luxuriant forests, salt- and fresh-water marshes, woodlands, and bays. This national seashore contains 6 beaches and 4 main areas, all accessible by road from U.S. 6. The **Province Lands Area,** at the tip of the cape, contains a visitor center and several miles of spectacular dunes. It also features guided walks into a beech forest and pond area. The **Pilgrim Heights Area,** north of North Truro, is noted for the pitch-pine forests dotting its highlands. Other attractions include a self-guiding nature trail leading into a large azalea-covered kettlehole formed by melting glacial ice. Another goes to a spring that the Pilgrims probably used. Along the ocean, across from South Wellfleet, is the **Marconi Station Area** with its nature trail heading inland to **White Cedar Swamp,** an unusual type of swamp for the region. **Wellfleet Bay Wildlife Sanctuary** is also accessible from here. The **Nauset Area,** in the Chatham vicinity, contains Salt Pond Visitor Center, **Nauset Marsh,** and self-guiding trails into **Red Maple Swamp** and **Salt Pond.**
For further information write: South Wellfleet, Mass. 02663

GAY HEAD CLIFFS
southwest point of Martha's Vineyard

Resisting the Atlantic's pounding waves, these varicolored cliffs rise as high as 150 feet above the sea. They are composed of white, red, gray, black, and yellow sands, clays, gravels, and lignites, and contain many fossil deposits. Registered Natural Landmark

JOSEPH ALLEN SKINNER STATE PARK
3 miles north of South Hadley on State 47

Covering 375 acres on 954-foot **Mount Holyoke,** this park provides a magnificent 70-mile vista of the broad **Connecticut Valley** and of nearby **Mount Tom.** It contains many unusual rock formations, such as **Titan's Piazza,** consisting of overhanging volcanic rock columns, and the **Devil's Football,** a 300-ton magnetic boulder.

MOHAWK TRAIL STATE FOREST
west of Charlemont on State 2

Noted for one of the finest natural stands of pine in the Northeast—with many trees over 100 feet—this forest also boasts red pine, spruce, hemlock, gray birch, maple, beech, and oak. It is bisected by State 2, known as the *Mohawk Trail,* and there are many hiking trails, some along the **Deerfield River,** and others leading into the mountains. Spectacular viewpoints may be reached by *Old Indian Trail* and by a path to *Totem Lookout.*

MOUNT GREYLOCK STATE RESERVATION
about 1½ miles west of North Adams

The main feature here is serene, cragless Mount Greylock, the highest peak in the state with an altitude of 3,491 feet. It is part of the **Berkshire Hills,** a continuation of Vermont's **Green Mountains.** A paved road leads to its summit, where there is a view of 4 states: Massachusetts, New York, Vermont, and New Hampshire. There is another lookout at *Stony Ledge,* lower down on the mountain, below the **Hopper**—a natural amphitheater, 1 mile square and 1,500 feet high, that eroded from the mountain's western face millions of years ago. The entire 8,660-acre reservation is crossed by 35 miles of trails, on Mount Greylock and on **Mounts Fitch, Williams, Prospect,** and **Saddle Ball.** The *Appalachian Trail* traverses most of the peaks in the area.

MOUNT SUGARLOAF STATE RESERVATION
just east of center of South Deerfield on State 116

Here, evergreen-clad Mount Sugarloaf rises some 500 feet above the surrounding farmland to an altitude of 720 feet above sea level. Directly on the **Connecticut River,** it is composed of an unusual type of red sandstone, more coarse than regular sandstone, known as

Left: Green Mountains vista from Mohawk Trail. Right: Cape Cod

Sugarloaf Arkose. A hiking trail leads to the summit, where there is a panoramic view of the Connecticut Valley.
Open Memorial Day–Oct: daily during daylight hours

PLUM ISLAND
northeast Massachusetts, about 6 miles southeast of Newburyport
Extending south about 8 miles along the Atlantic coast from the mouth of the **Merrimack River,** Plum Island is a long, natural expanse of beaches and dunes, except for some summer cottages on its northern end. Most of its southern end is occupied by the **Parker River National Wildlife Reservation,** which has a public recreation area. From the island's southern tip one can see the tidal marshes of the **Ipswich River.**
Wildlife refuge open May–Oct 15: daily 6–9

PLYMOUTH ROCK
Plymouth, at foot of Cole's Hill, Carver Street
Plymouth Rock is the legendary boulder that served as the Pilgrims' stepping stone in **Plymouth Harbor** when they disembarked from the *Mayflower* on December 21, 1620. Most of it is underground, and the rest is surrounded by a protective granite portico. The rock lies at the foot of **Cole's Hill,** traditionally considered the burial place of the colonists who died during the first winter, 1620–21. National Historic Landmark

PURGATORY CHASM STATE RESERVATION
about 4 miles southeast of Sutton and ¼ mile north of State 146
This 188-acre reservation features Purgatory Chasm, a huge fissure about 1½ miles long and between 40 and 70 feet deep.

SANDISFIELD STATE FOREST
east of New Marlboro on State 57, then south on side road
Cowles Hill, on the eastern border of this 2,725-acre forest, affords a superb view of the **Farmington River Valley.** Just outside the forest, near Southfield, is **Tipping Rock,** a 40-ton boulder left by a retreating glacier. It is so gingerly balanced that a mere touch of the hand will rock but not dislodge it.

WALDEN POND
1½ miles south of Concord on State 126
A state reservation preserves what is one of the best-known lakes in America, Walden Pond, made famous by philosopher-naturalist Henry David Thoreau. For 2 years in the mid-1840s, he lived on the pond's north shore in a log cabin he built with his own hands. Surrounded by woodlands, this 64-acre pond is in a kettlehole—a bowl-shaped depression formed by the melting process of a large mass of ice detached from a melting glacier and buried by gravel from meltwater streams. National Historic Landmark

WINDSOR STATE FOREST
between Savor and West Cummingham, off State 9
The main attraction of this 1,616-acre forest is **Windsor Jambs,** a 70-foot-deep rocky gorge. **Boundary Brook,** a tempestuous mountain stream, runs through the gorge and cascades some 50 feet, finally emerging alongside an evergreen-coated ridge. A trail leads from the upper falls, down the rapids, to the bottom of the ravine.

MICHIGAN

DRUMMOND ISLAND
Upper Peninsula, east of DeTour

This lovely wilderness, just east of the mouth of **Saint Marys River,** is the only one of the **Manitoulin Islands** in the United States. Resting on the Canadian border between **North Channel** and the main body of **Lake Huron,** the 20-mile-long and 11-mile-wide island can be reached by ferry from DeTour. It has 34 inland lakes and 30 bays and coves teeming with bass, northern pike, and walleyes.

HIAWATHA NATIONAL FOREST
Upper Peninsula, headquarters at Escanaba

This forest of cedar, spruce, pine, and aspen is located in 2 sections of a narrow neck of land bounded by **Lakes Superior, Huron,** and **Michigan.** Here, in the country immortalized by Henry Wadsworth Longfellow, are countless scenic wonders. Among the highlights are **Round** and **Government islands,** 2 unspoiled forest wilderness areas in Lake Huron; the **Land of the Big-Sea-Water,** an area of unsurpassed beauty featuring emerald-green water and pine and balsam forests (at night the northern lights are reflected here); and the *Whitefish River Way,* a plowed road along the **East Branch of the Whitefish River,** following an historic trail through frozen swamps and stands of hardwood and pine. The *Orgontz Natureway* offers a beautiful self-guided auto tour through the forest; another scenic highway is being built in the **Whitefish Bay Area** of the Big-Sea-Water, where hiking and saddle trails, overlooks, and vast wilderness areas are also being planned. A 40-mile canoe trip is offered on the **Indian River.**

For further information write: Escanaba, Mich. 49829

Left: aerial view of Isle Royale National Park. Right: wooded bridal path on Mackinac Island

139

MICHIGAN

HURON NATIONAL FOREST
east Michigan, headquarters at Cadillac

This 415,000-acre pine forest bordering **Lake Huron** boasts 650 miles of streams, dominated by the **Au Sable River.** Here too are such interesting features as the 4,010-acre **Kirtland Warbler Management Area,** set aside to protect a part of the world's dwindling population of this rare songbird; the **Tuttle Marsh Wildlife Area,** providing waterholes and food for a wide variety of animals; and the *Shore-to-Shore Trail,* a 22-mile trek through this beautiful forest from Lake Huron to **Lake Michigan.** Also here is the *Lumberman's Monument Auto Tour,* a scenic self-guided drive, with various side roads, through a miniature forest from the Au Sable to **Gordon Creek.**
For further information: Supervisor, Cadillac, Mich. 49601

ISLE ROYALE NATIONAL PARK
northwest rim of Lake Superior; 73 miles from headquarters at Houghton

One of the true wilderness areas in the country, this national park is located on an archipelago in **Lake Superior,** the largest freshwater lake in the world. The park includes 210 square miles of land on Isle Royale, an island about 45 miles long and 9 miles wide, and nearly 200 smaller islands. Accessible only by boat or float-plane, Isle Royale is actually closer to the Canadian border than to Michigan. (Only boats over 20 feet should attempt to cross the often rough waters to the island.)

The rock formations of Isle Royale are composed mainly of Precambrian lava flows layered with sandstone, siltstone, and conglomerate. Glaciers subsequently covered the island and dug out basins and valleys in the softer rock. Between the valleys, ridges of the harder volcanic rock are exposed such as **Greenstone Ridge,** which extends the entire length of the island and forms its backbone.

An area of unspoiled and serene beauty, covered with hardwood and evergreen forests, the park can be seen only on foot or by boat. There are countless harbors, over 30 inland lakes, and 25 miles of trout streams. (The principal ones are **Washington** and **Grace creeks,** and **Little** and **Big Siskiwit rivers.**) The park is crisscrossed by 120 miles of trails, including the 42-mile *Greenstone Ridge Trail,* which offers spectacular views of the surrounding forests, harbors, and islands, especially from 1,394-foot **Mount Desor,** the highest point in the park. Other interesting routes include *Feldtman Ridge Trail,* along which one can see excellent examples of Precambrian red sandstone and conglomerate; *Ishpeming Trail,* a 7-mile walk passing **Siskiwit Lake,** the largest in Isle Royale, and **Mount Ishpeming** (1,377 feet), the second highest peak in the park; *Lookout Louise Trail,* which offers fine views of **Monument Rock,** a 70-foot pinnacle carved by water and ice; and *Rock Harbor Trail,* a difficult 10-mile trek to scenic **Moskey Basin.**

Among the other interesting features of the park are the moose herds that can be seen everywhere. Recent arrivals to the island, they either swam or walked across the ice from Canada sometime after 1900. Rarely seen are the wolves that prey upon the moose and keep the herds to a size that the island can support. Other animals include red squirrel, snowshoe hare, and red fox; over 200 varieties of birds have been spotted here.
For further information: 87 N Ripley St, Houghton, Mich. 49931

LES CHENEAUX ISLANDS
Upper Peninsula, south of Cedarville

Located in one of the most scenic regions in the state, these 35 small islands (covered with thick forests and dotted with bays) lie in **Lake Huron** off the southeastern shore of the Upper Peninsula. Known locally as "the Snows," these tiny islands (the largest is **Marquette Island,** about 5 miles long) are popular fishing resorts. **Government Island,** now part of Hiawatha National Forest (*see*), is the only one of this beautiful chain in public ownership.

MACKINAC ISLAND

This small island (about 3 miles long and 2 miles wide) sits in the **Straits of Mackinac** between **Lakes Huron** and **Michigan.** It was called Michilimackinac, or Great Turtle, by the Indians who believed it had been created by supernatural powers; its name was later shortened. Most of this island, which is a limestone outcrop marked by cliffs, ravines, caves, and natural bridges, is a state park accessible by ferry from Mackinaw City and Saint Ignace. Among its many attractions are **Arch Rock,** a natural bridge 149 feet above Lake Huron; **Sugar Loaf Rock,** a limestone pinnacle; and **Cass Cliff,** which offers a spectacular view of the surrounding lakes.

MANISTEE NATIONAL FOREST
west Michigan, headquarters at Cadillac

Named for a Chippewa god—the Spirit of the Woods—this 474,000-acre forest is located on the eastern shore of Lake Michigan. It boasts fine beaches on its many lakes (including the **Lake Michigan Recreational Area**) and miles of well-stocked scenic rivers, such as the **Manistee, White, Big Sable,** and **Pere Marquette.** Picturesque drives with many overlooks wind through the forest past stands of white and jack pine and red, white, and black oak.

For further information write: Supervisor, Cadillac, Mich. 49601

OTTAWA NATIONAL FOREST
Upper Peninsula, headquarters at Ironwood

Located on the northwest tip of the Upper Peninsula, Ottawa is a 1,505,000-acre hardwood forest, consisting mainly of maple, birch, and mountain ash, with some stands of pine. Famous for its chain of lakes and rivers abounding with trout, bass, and pike, it also boasts 32 waterfalls. Although most of the falls are accessible only by hiking and saddle trails, some (such as **Sturgeon River Falls** on the scenic Sturgeon River) can be reached by road. Others accessible by car include **Potawatomi** and **Gorge falls** on the **Black River** and **Agate Falls** near **Trout Creek.** A 17-mile road, partially located within the forest, follows the course of the winding Black River to **Lake Superior; Rainbow, Sandstone,** and **Conglomerate falls** are located a short distance from this road. Porcupine Mountains State Park (*see*) and Lake Gogebic State Park lie within the forest.

For further information write: Supervisor, Ironwood, Mich. 49938

PICTURED ROCKS NATIONAL LAKESHORE
Upper Peninsula, 5 miles north of Munising

Extending for 15 miles along the shore of **Lake Superior,** the Pictured Rocks are multicolored sandstone cliffs with an average height of 50 to 80 feet, but some rise as high as 200 feet above the lake. These fantastic cliffs, which have been eroded by wind and weather into caves, pillars, and other unusual formations, are visible from a boat. (Scenic cruises are available from Munising.) Only **Miners Castle,** lying at the end of *Pictured Rocks Trail,* can be approached by land. In addition to the cliffs, the national lakeshore features **12-Mile Beach,** an unspoiled stretch of sand-and-pebble beach bordered by a 30-foot-high sand bluff. Other highlights include **Grand Sable Dunes and Banks**, 85-foot sand dunes atop the 275-foot-high bank of an ancient lake, and **Munising Falls**, which cascade 50 feet over a sandstone bluff into a natural amphitheater. A cave in back of the falls enables the visitor to walk behind the gushing water without getting wet.

Black bear, porcupine, and mink are among the animals found in the forest region behind the shoreline. Many varieties of water and shore birds can be sighted, and fish abound in Lake Superior, **Little Beaver Lake,** and the many other streams, rivers, and lakes included within the seashore. Most of the attractions here can be reached by roads and trails that are not passable in winter.

For further information write: Box 32, Munising, Mich. 49862

PORCUPINE MOUNTAINS STATE PARK
Upper Peninsula, 20 miles west of Ontonagon on State 107

This 58,324-acre park in Ottawa National Forest (*see*) is located in the Porcupine Mountains, the highest range in the Midwest. The park has such splendid natural wonders as **Lake of the Clouds, Mirror Lake,** parts of the **Big** and **Little Carp rivers,** and several miles of **Lake Superior** shoreline. Scenic drives and intriguing trails lead through vast stretches of pine and hardwood forests. One of the most beautiful drives in the state is the road along the park's southern boundary connecting the east and west entrances; hiking trails lead from the highway to various points of interest. A separate section of the park is located at the mouth of the **Presque Isle River** off Lake Superior (16 miles north of Wakefield on County road 519). Here a scenic drive through a virgin forest skirts the swirling river and offers magnificent views of **Iagoo, Nowadama, Manido,** and **Presque Isle falls.**

SLEEPING BEAR DUNES NATIONAL LAKESHORE
south of Glen Haven, off State 109

Covering 34 miles on the eastern shoreline of scenic **Lake Michigan,** this newly proclaimed national area contains beaches, forests, glacial lakes, and massive sand dunes. According to an Indian legend, a bear and her two cubs attempted to swim across the lake from Wisconsin. The mother bear, arriving first, climbed atop a bluff to await her cubs, who never were able to complete the

Pictured Rocks sandstone cliffs on Lake Superior

Sleeping Bear Dunes beach scene

journey. The "mother" is now the large, solitary Sleeping Bear dune and the "cubs" are **North** and **South Manitou islands,** lying a few miles offshore within the national area. One of the largest shifting dunes in the world, the Sleeping Bear towers 450 feet above Lake Michigan at **Sleeping Bear Point** and "walks" eastward toward **Glen Lake** at a rate of about 6 feet yearly. D.H. Day State Park, a 2,050-acre scenic area of sand dunes and beach bordering Lake Michigan, is also located here. Open only in summer, the park features "dunesmobiles," which make a 12-mile trip over the shifting sands.

TAHQUAMENON FALLS STATE PARK
Upper Peninsula, northeast of Newberry on State 123

This scenic park along the beautiful **Tahquamenon River** is known for its spectacular Upper and Lower Falls. Upper Falls, also known as Big Falls, takes a steep 40-foot drop that is 200 feet wide at the crest. The Lower Falls, divided by an island, are actually a series of cascades and rapids in the river. State 123 skirts the river and offers a lovely view of the falls; Upper Falls can also be seen by regularly scheduled boat trips from Soo Junction and a landing northwest of Hulbert. Once a vast wilderness, this 19,188-acre park also includes some virgin hemlock, spruce, and pine. A separate section of the park—the Rivermouth Unit—is located on scenic **Whitefish Bay** at the mouth of the Tahquamenon.

WARREN DUNES STATE PARK
17 miles south of Saint Joseph, off I-94

Extending for 2 miles along **Lake Michigan,** this park features a beautiful beach backed by spectacular wooded and barren sand dunes, including Warren Dune, **Tower Hill,** and **Pikes Peak.** It includes the **Warren Woods Natural Area,** an Eligible Natural Landmark. Here is a stand of virgin beech-maple forest, with fine specimens of individual sycamore, beech, maple, and other hardwoods, including some nearly 5 feet in diameter and 125 feet tall. Typical of the trees that once covered southern Michigan, this stand is the last tract of its kind left in the state.

143

MINNESOTA

ANCIENT RIVER WARREN CHANNEL
near Browns Valley in west Minnesota and east South Dakota
The **Minnesota River,** crossing the state from west to east, flows through a tremendous valley, once the bed of ancient glacial River Warren, which drained Lake Agassiz. River Warren cut a channel 50 to 90 feet below the present level of the Minnesota River in the vicinity of **Browns Valley.** When the ice sheet receded, and the **Red River of the North** could once again flow northward, the waters of River Warren dried up, leaving the sediment-covered channel that is still in existence today. Registered Natural Landmark

BANNING STATE PARK
2 miles north of Sandstone, off State 23
Here one can hike on 4 miles of trails and enjoy the **Kettle River** flowing through scenic gorges. At nearby Sandstone are quarries famous for sandstone which varies from pink to dark red.

CHIPPEWA NATIONAL FOREST
northcentral Minnesota, headquarters at Cass Lake
Covering 640,000 acres, this national forest features 499 major lakes including **Winnibigoshish, Leech,** and **Cass,** 3 of the biggest in the state. Its waters are well-stocked with fish. White, Norway, and jack pines grow in the forest's sandy areas; its heavy soils abound in white pine, balsam fir, white spruce, aspen, yellow birch, paper birch, elm, basswood, and oak; and its swamplands support black spruce, northern white cedar, and tamarack. The Chippewa abounds in wildlife and is a major nesting place of the bald eagle. There are also 42 recreational sites, many with scenic views and interpretive trails. A scenic road encircling **Pike Bay** goes through a pine forest characteristic of the growth that once covered much of northern Minnesota. Other attractions include the **Avenue of Pines** along State 46. Red pines, many over 100 years old, predominate.
For further information write: Supervisor, Cass Lake, Minn. 56633

DALLES OF THE SAINT CROIX
in Interstate State Park, 1 mile south of Taylors Falls
The Dalles (French for flagstone or slab of rock) extend along both sides of the **Saint Croix River** and are thus in Wisconsin as well as in Minnesota. These rocky cliffs, rising some 200 feet, were formed by lava flows and eroded by the river during the glacial period. They are crowned with pine and a dense undergrowth of bushes and vines. Also of interest in these ledges are the potholes, varying in diameter from a few inches to some 30 feet.

FORT SNELLING STATE PARK
south of Minneapolis via Hiawatha and Minnehaha avenues
Covering some 1,125 acres, this park is located on a steep bluff overhanging the junction of the **Minnesota** and **Mississippi rivers.** The fort, begun in 1819, is the oldest building in the state and was instrumental in opening the territory for settlement.

GRAND PORTAGE NATIONAL MONUMENT
38 miles north of Grand Marais via U.S. 61
Just south of the Canadian border, this 770-acre monument pre-

Top: bald eagle in Chippewa National Forest. Center: lady's slipper. Right: Pigeon River Falls in Grand Portage National Monument. Below: Boundary Waters Canoe Area in Superior National Forest

serves what was once a vital link in the 3,000-mile trade route from Montreal into the far Northwest. Grand Portage was a 9-mile trail from the north shore of **Lake Superior** to the navigable waters beginning at the mouth of the **Pigeon River.** To the fur traders, or voyageurs, who made the great journey it represented the end of travel on the **Great Lakes** and the beginning of the interior river and lake route.

For further information write: Box 666, Grand Marais, Minn. 55604

ITASCA STATE PARK AND NATURAL AREA
28 miles north of Park Rapids, just west of U.S. 71

Covering almost 30,000 acres, this park contains 157 lakes. The most important of these is **Lake Itasca,** the source of the **Mississippi River,** which winds its way 2,552 miles south to empty into the **Gulf of Mexico.** The park also features 20 miles of trails, fine forest land, and a scenic road. A portion of it, designated **Itasca Natural Area,** is a Registered Natural Landmark. It preserves some of the finest remaining stands of virgin red pine in the state. About a third of this forest cover is estimated to be red and white pine—with red predominating—between 100 and 300 years old. Another third of the forest cover consists of spruce and balsam, and the remainder is maple, basswood, and aspen.

JAY COOKE STATE PARK
2 miles west of Duluth via State 210 or 39

Like all the environs of Duluth, this area was once a smouldering mass of live volcanoes. This 8,920-acre park, on the shore of the **Saint Louis River,** preserves a section of the volcanic lava, which the river has exposed. The Saint Louis runs through a gorge, which drops some 395 feet within a few miles and which is cut deep into the dusky-colored rock. The park's spectacular terrain—rugged woods, rocks, evergreens—may be appreciated from its 26 miles of trail or from States 23 and 29, which traverse it.

LAC QUI PARLE STATE PARK
about 10 miles northwest of Montevideo off U.S. 59

Situated at the junction of historic **Lac qui Parle** and **Minnesota rivers,** this park embraces 455 acres. It has 4½ miles of trails and is heavily forested with hardwoods.

Gorge of the Saint Louis River in Jay Cooke State Park

LAKE AGASSIZ PEATLANDS
30 miles south of International Falls
When the glacial ice was retreating from Minnesota, the northward flow of the **Red River of the North** was blocked by a continental glacial ice sheet. The waters of the Red River were backed up to form huge Lake Agassiz, presumed to have been the largest temporary lake on the North American continent. It was, at its maximum, about 700 miles long and 250 miles wide and covered the northwestern sector of Minnesota as well as parts of the Dakotas and Canada. After the ice retreated to **Hudson Bay**, most of the water in Lake Agassiz drained northward once more. The glacial lake soon disappeared, leaving only scattered remnants in the form of small lakes and ponds. The Lake Agassiz Peatlands cover 22,000 acres and are a splendid example of the peatlands that cover most of the bed of Lake Agassiz. **Myrtle Lake Bog,** in the landmark's southern portion, represents an unusual phenomenon. As the bog surface around the lake expanded upward, the lake's water table also rose about 12 feet. Thus Myrtle Lake still exists contrary to the usual process whereby the lake would fill up to become a bog. About 5,000 acres in the northern part of the landmark is occupied by a raised bog, a bog type characterized by an elevated peat dome. About 3,500 acres of the landmark's drainage ways are occupied by string bogs—characterized by elongated boggy ridges covered with shrubs and tamaracks, alternating with treeless, sedge-covered hollows. Registered Natural Landmark

LAKE BEMIDJI STATE PARK
6 miles northeast of Bemidji off U.S. 71
On the sandy, north shore of Lake Bemidji, this park features a virgin pine forest and has 2 miles of hiking trails.

LAKE OF THE WOODS
north Minnesota, on Canadian border
Shared by both the United States and Canada, this irregularly shaped lake, about 70 miles long and 60 miles wide, is the state's largest lake. It is studded with over 14,000 islands; most are beautifully forested with pine and spruce. On its northwest shore, jutting into the lake is the famous **Northwest Angle,** the northernmost portion of land in the United States except for Alaska. It is completely separated from the rest of the state by the waters of the lake and is accessible by land only across the wilds of southeastern Manitoba. There are no roads in the Angle, which is a state forest.

LAKE VERMILION
northeast Minnesota, west of Ely
A maze of bays, inlets, and islands, Vermilion boasts a shoreline of over 1,000 miles. The lake, 35 miles long with over 365 islands, is surrounded by coniferous trees and rolling hills of solid granite. It is the largest lake in the famed **Arrowhead** region, the northeastern segment of Minnesota shaped like an arrowhead. Tower Soudan State Park, on Vermilion's southern shore, contains the state's oldest and deepest iron-ore mine.

MILLE LACS LAKE
eastcentral Minnesota
One of the state's largest and loveliest lakes, it has 150 miles of shoreline, which may be appreciated by a scenic drive combining State 18 and U.S. 169. On Mille Lacs southeastern shore is Father

Hennepin State Memorial Wayside, boasting a deciduous forest and trails. On its southwestern shore is Mille Lacs Kathio State Park, with 6,900 acres of hills, meadows, and forest.

MINNEHAHA PARK
Minneapolis, just off Minnehaha Parkway, below 46th Street

This park preserves and surrounds **Minnehaha Falls,** immortalized by Henry Wadsworth Longfellow in *Song of Hiawatha*. Minnehaha is an Indian word meaning "laughing waters." The falls are formed by **Minnehaha Creek** as it tumbles 93 feet over a limestone ledge.

MYSTERY CAVE
3 miles east of Spring Valley on U.S. 16, then 5 miles south

This cave features a magnificent underground lake as well as stalactites, stalagmites, and rare helictites, irregular stalactites with branching convolutions or spines. Two miles east is **Minnesota Caverns,** a larger underground cave.

Open Apr–Oct: daily 8–6. Admission: adults $1.50, children 75¢

NIAGARA CAVE
2 miles south of Harmony on State 139, then 2 miles west

Noted for its unusual formations in crystal, stalactites, stalagmites, and fossils, this lighted cave has 5 miles of passageways on 3 levels. Its most spectacular feature is the 60-foot subterranean waterfall which cascades into a river 200 feet below the earth's surface.

Open summer: daily 8–7; rest of year (closed Dec): 10–4. Admission: adults $1.85, children (6–12) 95¢

NORTH SHORE DRIVE (U.S. 61)
along north shore of Lake Superior between Duluth and Canada

Following **Lake Superior's** north shore some 150 miles between Duluth and the frontier, this scenic highway passes through a region of cascading rivers, towering cliffs, and fragrant, second-growth pines. It passes through parts of Superior National Forest (*see*) and provides access to many state parks and waysides. Heading northward from Duluth, one first reaches Flood Bay Wayside, with a sand beach and sheltered harbor on the lake; Gooseberry Falls Park, which features a stream with a series of falls and rapids; and Split Rock Lighthouse Park, featuring a trail leading up a gorge to **Baptism River Falls,** the state's highest waterfall. These are followed by Caribou Falls Wayside, boasting a craggy gorge and waterfalls. Then comes Temperance River Park, which has a rocky

river gorge with huge potholes, and Cross River Wayside, with its deep gorge. Farther on are Ray Berglund Wayside, noted for its cascades on the **Onion River;** and Cascade River Park, set in a mountainous, rock-bound area along the lake. Devil's Track Wayside, featuring falls and cascades, and Kodonce River Wayside with a rocky gorge and waterfalls come next. The last state park before the border is Judge C. R. Magny, famous for its waterfalls and boiling rapids on **Brule River.**

NORTHWEST ANGLE. *See* LAKE OF THE WOODS

PIPESTONE NATIONAL MONUMENT
about 1 mile north of Pipestone via U.S. 75 and States 23 and 30
This 283-acre national monument preserves the famous pipestone quarries where the Plains Indians used to obtain red stone for their peace pipes. The raw material is now reserved exclusively for Indians of all tribes. The monument also contains quartzite ledges, virgin prairie, grassland, flowering plants, and many birds. One of the best ways to visit it is via the self-guiding *Circle Trail*, a ¾-mile walk which passes points of interest such as the quarries, **Winnewissa Falls, Lake Hiawatha,** and **Leaping Rock,** where Indians used to test the strength of young men.
Open May 30–Labor Day: daily 8–9; rest of year: daily 8–5

SAINT CROIX STATE PARK
20 miles east of Hinckley on U.S. 61 and State 48
Pine, spruce, hardwoods, and wildlife abound in this 31,550-acre tract. A portion of the Saint Croix and several smaller rivers flow through the park, which also has 127 miles of foot trails.

SCENIC STATE PARK
7 miles southeast of Big Fork, then 1½ miles north on County 7
One of the most primitive parks in the state, Scenic covers 2,120 acres and has 4 miles of foot trails. It is noted for its virgin stand of Norway pine and its 4 unspoiled lakes.

SKYLINE DRIVE, DULUTH
Clinging to the shoreline bluffs overlooking Duluth, this 27-mile skyline drive affords a series of scenic lookouts over **Lake Superior.** On the southwest it connects with State 39 and Jay Cooke State Park (*see*). On the northeast it connects with magnificent North Shore Drive, or U.S. 61 (*see*).

Left to right: Lake Superior Palisades; paper birch in Superior National Forest; lake country in Voyageurs National Park

MINNESOTA

SUGAR LOAF

southeastern edge of Winona, 1¾ miles from city center
> This truncated limestone monolith is perched atop a 500-foot bluff.
> It can be reached by foot trail; from its crest the hiker has a magnifi-
> cent view of the **Mississippi River Valley**. The Indians used it for
> ceremonial and signaling purposes.

SUPERIOR NATIONAL FOREST

northeast Minnesota, headquarters at Ely
> One of the greatest wilderness areas in the United States, Superior
> covers some 3 million acres. On the north, it parallels the Canadian
> border for about 150 miles and in part of this stretch adjoins a similar
> Canadian preserve known as the Quetico Provincial Park. Both are
> matchless canoe regions, filled with cold, crystal-clear lakes and
> streams. The forest area was ravaged by 3 glaciers, which formed
> its innumerable valleys and ridges and its over 5,000 lakes. A good
> orientation is available at the Voyageur Visitor Center, 2 miles east
> of Ely on State 169. Superior's northern third is occupied by the
> famous **Boundary Waters Canoe Area**, which extends some 200
> miles along the Minnesota-Ontario line. It boasts 12,000 miles of
> canoe routes, most of which remain as they were when frequented
> by the voyageurs of the 17th, 18th, and 19th centuries. The forest,
> especially the canoe area, is underlaid with the continent's oldest
> rocks. Its land sections are almost completely forested, the principal
> conifers being pines (jack, white, and red). However, white and
> black spruce, balsam fir, northern white cedar, and tamarack are
> also common. The main broad-leaved trees are quaking aspen and
> paper birch. Near the **Moose River** northwest of Ely is the world's
> largest black spruce. It is 94 feet high and has a circumference of
> 52.5 inches. The forest also has some largest known white spruce
> and jack pine. There are 49 recreation sites, several scenic roads,
> and many foot trails. Among the trails are the *Echo, Sawbill, Cari-
> bou,* and the *Gunflint.* The flora is varied and includes many sub-
> arctic species, and the wildlife is plentiful. Superior is the haunt of
> the last substantial population of timber wolves, which are on the
> endangered list in the United States.
> *For further information write: Box 338, Duluth, Minn. 55801*

VOYAGEURS NATIONAL PARK

temporary headquarters west of park at International Falls
> Situated in the forested lake country along the Minnesota-Ontario
> border, this national park is still under development. It offers a
> setting reminiscent of that known to the voyageurs of the fur-trading
> era and will eventually encompass about 219,400 acres, of which
> some 80,000 are water. The main body of land is on **Kabetogama
> Peninsula**, a heavily forested tract of about 75,000 acres. Shaped by
> the glaciers into a wilderness of internal waterways and forests, it
> is covered with stands of fir, spruce, pine, aspen, and birch, which
> reach down to the water's edge. The shoreline also contains bogs,
> sand beaches, and cliffs and is broken by many small bays and hid-
> den coves, accented by promontories and rocky points. The island-
> dotted waters surrounding the peninsula include **Namakan, Kabe-
> togama**, and **Rainy lakes**, and several narrows, each less than 100
> feet in width. Although the government has authorized the creation
> of this park, the National Park Service has not yet provided visitor
> facilities. Private and state facilities are open throughout the year
> for the many people who come here.

MISSISSIPPI

BIENVILLE NATIONAL FOREST
central Mississippi, district offices at Forest and Raleigh

This 175,000-acre pine and hardwood forest has a lovely scenic area with the largest known tract of old pines in the state. Here, in the **Bienville Pines Scenic Area** are 100-to-200-year-old virgin loblolly and shortleaf pine; a 2-mile nature trail winds through the area. The forest also contains **Raworth, Shongelo,** and **Marathon lakes,** all offering excellent fishing.

For further information write: Box 1291, Jackson, Miss. 39205

CLARKCO STATE PARK
northeast of Quitman off U.S. 45

This 792-acre park is located in a region of gently rolling hills dotted with loblolly pine, white oak, and dogwood. Picturesque nature trails lead throughout the park.

DE SOTO NATIONAL FOREST
southeast Mississippi, district offices at Laurel, Wiggins, Hattiesburg, and Gulfport

Divided in 2 sections, this 500,000-acre forest features many scenic regions. Highlights include Big Biloxi Area, a stretch of hardwoods along the banks of the **Big Biloxi River;** 2 lovely spots along **Black Creek** at Cypress Creek and Janice; **Miles Branch,** a 4-acre lake with a white-sand bottom; **Red Creek;** and **Ashe Lake,** a 14-acre well-stocked lake. The most outstanding attractions offered in De Soto are a 24-mile float trip down **Black Creek** and **Beaver Dam Creek** and the 10-mile *Tuxachanie Trail,* a developed hiking route in a region of meandering streams, beautiful piney woods, and scenic hardwood-covered bottomland.

For further information write: Box 1291, Jackson, Miss. 39205

Left: Gulf Islands National Seashore. Right: a section of the Natchez Trace

151

MISSISSIPPI

GULF ISLANDS NATIONAL SEASHORE

Covering 163,200 acres of land and water, this newly authorized (January, 1971) national seashore stretches across the **Gulf of Mexico** from Florida to Mississippi. It includes 52 miles of sparkling sand beaches backed by scenic dunes and dotted with indigenous plant life on **Santa Rosa Island** and eastern **Perdido Key** off Pensacola, Florida, and **Petit Bois, Horn** and **Ship islands** off the Mississippi coast in the **Mississippi Sound.** Also featured here are the sites of 5 forts (among them Fort Pickens on Santa Rosa Island and Fort Massachusetts on Ship Island) spanning the history of the area from the time of the Spanish conquest to the Civil War. Modern missile sites and structures dating from World War II can also be seen within the seashore boundaries. There are not yet any National Park Service facilities.

HOLLY SPRINGS NATIONAL FOREST
north Mississippi, district offices at Oxford and Holly Springs

This lovely forest of oak, shortleaf pine, and beech covers 143,000 acres around Holly Springs, a typical antebellum town with fine old houses. The forest attractions are highlighted by the **Chewalla Lake Recreational Area,** made up of the 260-acre Chewalla Lake and a restored Choctaw burial mound. (The Choctaws believed that this was sanctified land.) Other points of interest in the forest include **Puskus** and **Tillatoba** lakes.
For further information write: Box 1291, Jackson, Miss. 39205

HOMOCHITTO NATIONAL FOREST
southwest Mississippi, district offices at Meadville and Gloster

The first national forest to be established in Mississippi, Homochitto contains 190,000 acres dominated by loblolly pines. Following the course of the scenic **Homochitto River,** this forest features a 13-acre lake and interesting nature trails at the **Clear Springs Recreational Area** and **Pipe's Lake,** a 26-acre spring-fed lake in a picturesque setting.
For further information write: Box 1291, Jackson, Miss. 39205

J. P. COLEMAN STATE PARK
12 miles northeast of Iuka off State 25

Situated in one of the state's most scenic areas, this 1,468-acre park is located on a bend in the **Tennessee River** and on beautiful **Indian Creek.** Crisscrossing the area are acres of spectacular lakes, miles of streams, and lovely waterfalls. Nature trails offer breathtaking views of this outstanding park.

Left: oak draped in Spanish moss. Right: Mississippi Delta

LEROY PERCY STATE PARK
south of Hollandale on U.S. 61

Located near the **Mississippi River Delta**, this 2,422-acre park includes dense stands of stately hardwood trees. Shady bayous wind through the park and provide a picturesque setting.

MAGNOLIA STATE PARK
northeast of Ocean Springs off U.S. 90

Located off the **Gulf of Mexico**, this park features the terrain for which Mississippi is known. Here Spanish moss-draped trees line the quiet bays and bayous that wind through the grounds.

NATCHEZ TRACE PARKWAY

One of the nation's most scenic highways, this road through a stretch of protected forest, meadow, and field will extend 450 miles when completed from Mississippi through Alabama to Tennessee. Originally an Indian trail, the Trace was developed first by pioneers traveling from Natchez to Nashville; it soon became an official government post route. From 1800 to 1820 the Trace was the most heavily traveled road in the old Southwest and was a vital link to the East. Today, the Parkway, being developed by the National Park Service, roughly parallels the Old Trace. Included here are such points of historical interest as Mount Locust, a Spanish-period house museum; Emerald Mound, one of the largest ceremonial Indian mounds in the country (both are near Natchez); and a log-cabin museum in Meriwether Lewis Park east of Hohenwald, Tennessee.

As the Parkway passes through scenic southern countryside, including Tombigbee National Forest (*see*), there are many beautiful vistas. Some interesting sites along the route in Mississippi include **Little Mountain** (at Jeff Busby Park, 73 miles south of Tupelo), where nature trails, unusual rock formations, natural springs, and an outstanding view from 600 feet above the parkway are offered; **Cole Creek** and **Hurricane Creek**, 2 lovely nature spots with winding trails, farther south; and *Red Dog Trail* (17 miles south of Kosciusko), an early 19th-century trail named for a Choctaw chief. The visitor center is located at Tupelo.

For further information write: NT 143, Tupelo, Miss. 38801

PETRIFIED FOREST
17 miles north of Jackson, off U.S. 49 at Flora

Varying in length from 3 to 20 feet, these orange-colored logs make up a forest of stone "trees"—one of the few accumulations of petrified wood to be found east of the Mississippi River. The trees (thus far firs and maples have been identified) are believed to have been buried during the Pleistocene period after they had been carried into the region by turbulent streams. As no roots or stumps have been found, it is assumed that the trees did not grow here. Nature trails and a museum are also featured. Registered Natural Landmark

Open daily 8–sunset. Admission: adults $1.00, children 50¢

TOMBIGBEE NATIONAL FOREST
east Mississippi, district offices at Ackerman and Houston

This 65,000-acre pine and hardwood forest near the Natchez Trace Parkway (*see*) includes such interesting attractions as 300-acre **Davis Lake** and the 100-acre, tree-lined **Choctaw Lake**. The highlight is Owl Creek Indian Mounds, 2 reconstructed mounds near the site of conquistador Hernando De Soto's 1540–41 winter camp.

For further information write: Box 1291, Jackson, Miss. 39205

MISSOURI

BENNET SPRING STATE PARK
12 miles west of Lebanon on State 64

Located around a beautiful spring that produces 71 million gallons of water daily, this 756-acre park on the **Niangua River** is known for its trout hatchery and excellent fishing. Also featured here is a fine museum, the Nature Interpretive Center, with exhibits of indigenous Ozark plant and animal life.
Center open summer: daily 9–6; winter Tues–Sun: 9–5

BIG OAK TREE STATE PARK
25 miles south of Charleston on State 77

This 1,013-acre park located on the **Mississippi River** is a botanical preserve, established to protect virgin timber. Nature trails wind throughout the park.

BRIDAL CAVE
3½ miles northwest of Camdenton off State 5 on Lake Road 5–88

This cave, noted for the variety of color in its formations, is one of the most beautiful caverns in the state. Its many onyx formations can be viewed from illuminated concrete walkways.
Open daily: summer 9–7; spring and fall 9–6; winter 9–5. Admission: adults $1.75, children (6–11) 75¢

CLARK NATIONAL FOREST
southeast Missouri, headquarters at Rolla

Straddling the **Ozark Plateau**, this pine-and-oak forest includes the headwaters of the **Current, Gasconade, Meramec, Black,** and **Saint Francis rivers.** It features topography ranging from gentle slopes to steep cliffs. Outstanding among the many attractions here are the **Saint Francis Mountains,** in the forest's eastern section. Lovely views are offered from lookouts on **Bell, Crane, Little Grass,** and **Cottoner mountains;** from atop **Johnston Mountain** there is a fine

Left: Bridal Cave. Right: Eleven Point Scenic River in Mark Twain National Forest

view of the state's highest peak—1,772-foot **Taum Sauk Mountain.** Other features in the forest include scenic **Paddy Creek,** an area rich in plant life; **Marble Creek,** a beautiful rushing stream through the Saint Francis Mountains; and **Markham Spring,** which gushes 4½ million gallons of water daily. Among the many hiking and saddle trails included in the forest are the 23-mile *Berryman Trail* and the 17-mile *Big Piney Trail.* Both offer close-up views of the 2,000 species of plants and 700 kinds of animals to be found here. *For further information write: Supervisor, Rolla, Mo. 65401*

GRAHAM CAVE STATE PARK
2 miles west of Danville off I-70 and County TT
　　This 251-acre park is famous for the sandstone cave where archaeologists have discovered what is believed to be evidence of the earliest known habitation of Indians in Missouri.

JOHNSON SHUT-INS STATE PARK
8 miles north of Lesterville on County Road M
　　This 2,478-acre park features a beautiful gorge carved by the east fork of the **Black River** and winding nature trails.

LOOKOUT POINT
Pinnacle Park in Clarksville on State 79
　　This bluff is the highest point between Saint Paul and New Orleans on the **Mississippi River.** Accessible only by skylift, the bluff rises 600 feet above the river and offers a spectacular view of the surrounding hills and valleys. It is located in a 24-acre park which also features a museum, a replica frontier town, an Indian burial mound, and a 50-foot observation tower.
　　Skylift fare: adults $1.50, children (under 12) 75¢

MARK TWAIN CAVE
2 miles southeast of Hannibal on State 79
　　This cave was first discovered in 1819–20 by hunter Jack Sims, who named it Big Saltpeter Cave for the large quantity of rock salt found there. It was later made famous by Mark Twain as the cave where Tom Sawyer and Becky Thatcher were lost and where Injun Joe died. Guided tours are led through lighted passageways, where the temperature is a constant 50°.
　　Open daily: Apr–Oct 8–8; Nov–Mar 8–5. Admission: adults $1.50, children (5–11) 75¢

MARK TWAIN NATIONAL FOREST
south Missouri, headquarters at Springfield
　　Named for one of the state's most famous sons, the forest covers nearly 620,000 acres in 6 sections of the scenic **Missouri Ozarks.** A rugged region of springs, rivers, glades, knolls, and caves, the forest features many outstanding attractions. A highlight is a float trip on the **Eleven Point Scenic River,** covering almost half of this quiet, 100-mile-long waterway. Gently flowing through unspoiled wooded countryside, abundant with wildlife, the river is fed by over 30 springs. Among the loveliest are **Greer,** the third largest in the state; **Graveyard,** a series of 7 springs; and **Blue Spring,** a large azure spring off the **North Fork River.** Other attractions in the forest include the **Current River** (*see Ozark National Scenic Riverways*), *Blue Ridge* and *Devereaux horse trails, Blue Spring* and *Woodchuck forest trails,* and a scenic drive on the *Glade Top Trail.*
　　For further information write: Supervisor, Springfield, Mo. 65802

MISSOURI

MARVEL CAVE
9 miles west of Branson on State 76

This limestone cave features 32 miles of passageways and a room 400 feet long and about 20 stories high. Located beneath Silver Dollar City, a replica pioneer settlement, the cave includes a massive rock formation called **Pike's Peak**.
Open daily: winter 9–6; summer 9–9. Tours conducted hourly

MERAMEC CAVERNS
3 miles south of Stanton off I-44 and U.S. 66

This cave features 5 separate floors of unusual formations and maintains a constant temperature of 60°. Located in a 110-acre park, the cave was used as a hide-out by Jesse James.
Open daily: summer 8–sunset; winter 8:30–sunset; closed Christmas. Admission: adults $2.50, children (6–12) $1.00

MERAMEC SPRINGS
6 miles south of Saint James on State 8

Gushing about 100 million gallons of water daily, this lively spring is located near the site of an ironworks established here in 1826. It is now part of a recreational area and wildlife refuge.
Open Mar–Sept: daily 5 A.M.–9; Nov–Feb: daily 7–7

MERAMEC STATE PARK
4 miles east of Sullivan off U.S. 66

This 7,153-acre park in the **Ozarks** is noted for its heavily wooded areas and many scenic sites. This beautiful park features the gorge of the **Meramec River,** many springs, winding nature trails, and more than 20 caves. **Fisher's Cave**, said to be the first large cave discovered west of the Mississippi, extends for about ½ mile and contains countless large stalactites. It varies in temperature, the coldest room being the 50° **Ice Box.**

MONTAUK STATE PARK
21 miles southwest of Salem via State 32 and 119

Located at the headwaters of the **Current River** (*see Ozark National Scenic Riverways*), this 1,096-acre park is in a heavily forested area dominated by oak and hickory trees. It features **Montauk Springs**, which emerge from an open valley here, and is one of the state's 3 trout-fishing parks; tours of the hatchery are available.

ONONDAGA CAVE
4 miles from Leasburg, off U.S. 66 and I-44, on County Road H

Located in Daniel Boone Park and said to have been discovered by the frontiersman, this cave is one of the largest in the state. It features colorful rock formations (red, brown, tan, and white) ranging from delicate lacy creations to huge onyx blocks weighing several tons. The cave has a huge central room and maintains a constant temperature of 60°. Guided tours are conducted through lighted concrete passageways.
Open daily summer: 8–sunset; winter: 8:30–sunset. Admission: adults $2.50, children (6–12) $1.00

OZARK NATIONAL SCENIC RIVERWAYS
southeast Missouri, headquarters at Van Buren

Extending for about 140 miles through the scenic **Ozark Mountains,** this national riverway, the first of its kind to be established, is made up of stretches of the beautiful **Current** and **Jacks Fork rivers**. (Strips of land adjacent to the rivers are also included in the national area.) Remnants of an ancient mountain chain, the Ozarks provide an unspoiled backdrop to these 2 free-flowing wild rivers. Float trips down the riverways or walks along the banks offer a close-up glimpse of this wonder of nature. Forests, predominantly oak-hickory and oak-pine, line ¾ of the riverways. Because of the range in elevation and the location of the Ozarks on the continent, botanical life indigenous to many different regions can·be found here; about 1,500 varieties of plants have been identified. Wildlife is abundant and nearly 200 kinds of birds can be seen. The rivers themselves teem with fish and are considered the best smallmouth bass streams in the state. Because of the geological make-up of the mountains, the area is dotted with countless springs and caves. Among the largest and most beautiful springs, each producing 65 million gallons daily or more, are **Welch** and **Blue springs** on the Current River, and **Alley Springs** on the Jacks Fork. **Big Spring,** south of Van Buren, is one of the largest spring outlets in the country, with a flow of 840 million gallons a day. Of the many caves in the area, the largest charted is **Round Spring Cavern,** with over 6,000 feet of passageways decorated with intriguing dripstone formations. Running through Mark Twain and Clark National Forests, the riverway is bordered on the north by Montauk State Park (*see all*); there is a visitor center at **Powder Mill Creek** just below the confluence of the 2 rivers. In addition to float trips and fishing, there are facilities for other water sports, camping, as well as hiking and saddle trails.

For further information write: Box 448, Van Buren, Mo. 63965

ROARING RIVER STATE PARK
7 miles south of Cassville on State 112
This 3,332-acre park in the **Ozarks** is situated on heavily wooded land first explored by the Spanish in the 16th century. The park takes its name from a spring that flows noisily through underground canyons until it emerges from beneath a high cliff. The spring gushes 28 million gallons a day. One of the state's 3 trout-fishing parks, it also features nature trails and bridle paths.

STARK CAVERNS
4 miles south of Eldon on U.S. 54
Located in an area famous for its caves, this underground cavern boasts unusual, illuminated dripstone formations. An ancient Indian burial ground is included on the site.
Open Apr–Nov: daily 8–7. Admission: adults $1.50, children 50¢

TALKING ROCK CAVE
5 miles south of Reeds Spring on State 13
One of the most unusual caves in the area, this cavern is notable for its drapery helictites and other rare formations, which may be viewed from lighted, concrete walkways.
Open daily: Memorial Day–Labor Day 8–6; Sept–May 9–5. Admission: adults $1.50, children (6–12) 75¢

TRAIL OF TEARS STATE PARK
10 miles north of Cape Girardeau on State 177
This 3,268-acre park sits on a wooded bluff overlooking the **Mississippi River.** The beautiful hills and valleys of this area were crossed by the Cherokees on their "Trail of Tears"—the enforced trek from their homeland in Tennessee and North Carolina to Oklahoma. Nature trails wind throughout the park.

MONTANA

ANACONDA-PINTLAR WILDERNESS
in the Beaverhead, Bitterroot, and Deerlodge National forests
This 157,803-acre tract of rugged mountains lies atop the **Continental Divide** in 3 national forests (*see above*). It is accessible by trails from **Big Hole, Bitterroot, Rock Creek,** and **Warm Springs Creek valleys.** It features glacial cirques, alpine lakes and meadows, and unusual stands of alpine larch. This roadless wilderness, where mountain goats make their home on lofty peaks, has many trails.

BEAVERHEAD NATIONAL FOREST
southwest Montana, headquarters at Dillon
Bordered on the west by the **Bitterroot Range** and on the east by **Madison Range,** this forest covers over 2 million acres in several sections. It boasts a varied landscape ranging from semidesert areas to large forests of lodgepole pine, Douglas fir, and Englemann spruce. Elevations vary from about 5,000 feet to 11,316 feet at **Hilgard Peak** in the Madison Range. Roads and trails lead to scenic viewpoints where one can appreciate many mountains, valleys, rocky peaks, timbered slopes, open meadows, lakes, and streams. Among Beaverhead's many special features are a section of the Anaconda-Pintlar Wilderness (*see*), the **Pioneer, Gravelly, Snowcrest, Greenhorn, Anaconda,** and **Tobacco Root mountains;** the **Ruby, Beaverhead,** and **Big Hole rivers;** and 2,310-acre **Cliff Lake Natural Area.** Also within the forest is 7,373-foot **Lemhi Pass,** a National Historic Landmark that has been designated Sacajawea Memorial Area. It is the point where the Lewis and Clark expedition crossed the **Continental Divide,** and where the party left the United States and entered Oregon territory. The forest is named for **Beaverhead Rock,** located outside its limits, 12 miles south of Twin Bridges. This natural landmark was of great help to Sacajawea, the Indian woman who guided Lewis and Clark on their historic trek to the Pacific Ocean.
For information: Skihi St and Highway 91, Dillon, Mont. 59725

BIGHORN CANYON NATIONAL RECREATION AREA
south Montana and north Wyoming, headquarters at Hardin, Montana
This 63,000-acre area features spectacular **Bighorn Lake,** a 71-mile-long reservoir created by the Yellowtail Dam across the **Bighorn River** near Fort Smith. The lake's lower 47 miles lie between a rugged, steep-walled canyon hundreds of feet deep, cut through the **Pryor** and **Bighorn mountains.** Every twist of this canyon is filled with scenic wonders. In it one can see where the earth's forces have distorted and bowed once-level rock into enormous swells called anticlines. Bighorn, the largest of these, extends southward from the dam and rises to form the Bighorn Mountains. Just upstream from the dam, the Bighorn River cuts through spectacular cliffs that loom almost ½ mile above it. These and other colorful bluffs along the entire canyon are rich in fossils.
For further information write: Box 458 YRS, Hardin, Mont. 59035

BITTERROOT NATIONAL FOREST
west Montana and east Idaho, headquarters at Hamilton, Montana
Covering 1,115,095 acres in Montana and 460,812 acres in Idaho, this forest encompasses a varied terrain of mountains, valleys, meadows, and a multitude of hot springs and alpine lakes. It is

Left: cougar. Right: Medicine Rocks State Park. Center: riding in Bob Marshall Wilderness. Below: alpine larch and lake in Anaconda-Pintlar Wilderness

bisected by the **Bitterroot River** and includes a large segment of the **Bitterroot Mountains.** Elevations range from some 3,000 feet to 10,131 feet at **Trapper Peak,** the highest point in the Bitterroots. Within its borders are portions of the Selway-Bitterroot Wilderness (*see Idaho*) and the Anaconda-Pintlar Wilderness (*see*). Among the forest's many other scenic attractions are **Painted Rocks Lake; Skalkaho Falls** near 7,258-foot **Sapphire Mountains Divide; Lake Como,** circled by a scenic trail; and in the Idaho sector, the rough, roadless **Salmon River Breaks Primitive Area,** a region Lewis and Clark found inpenetrable in 1805.

For further information: 316 Third St, Hamilton, Mont. 59840

BOB MARSHALL WILDERNESS
northwest Montana, in Flathead and Lewis and Clark National Forests

Noted for its outstanding scenery, hunting, and fishing, this 950,000-acre tract spills over the **Continental Divide** from Lewis and Clark into Flathead National Forest (*see both*). The Continental Divide extends for over 60 miles through the wilderness, where mountain ramparts tower above amphitheater cirques and wide valley troughs. Glaciated canyons, pulverized rock, and eroded limestone characterize the terrain, but the most interesting geological formation is the 1,000-foot-high **Chinese Wall,** a spectacular limestone reef that stretches for about 12 miles along the Great Divide. Other attractions in this trail-filled area include **Kevan** and **Sentinel mountains,** which abound in fossils; **Bullet Nose Mountain** and nearby caves that contain ice all year; **Sun River Canyon;** and rugged **Prairie Reef,** an 8,868-foot peak that affords a superb view of the Chinese Wall and Lower Sun River Canyon. **Haystack Mountain** on the Divide also offers a good view of the Chinese Wall to its north. From 8,097-foot **Shale Peak** one can appreciate the **Flathead Alps,** an offshoot of the Continental Divide near **Junction Mountain. Big Salmon** is the largest lake in the wilderness.

CUSTER NATIONAL FOREST
southeast Montana, headquarters at Billings

Covering 1,097,784 acres in Montana and extending into North and South Dakota, this forest has an extremely varied landscape. It contains the pine-clad hills and brake country of southeast Montana, as well as the rolling and flat prairie of the **Little Missouri River Grasslands** in North Dakota, and the timbered hills and lush grass of the **Grand River** and **Cedar National Grasslands** in northeast South Dakota. In the western, or Beartooth, division one can find fossils, see ice caves, enjoy the view from *Rock Creek Vista Point* on the Beartooth Highway, or explore **Beartooth Primitive Area,** which extends into Montana's Gallatin National Forest and Wyoming's Shoshone National Forest (*see both*). Here one can admire 12,799-foot **Granite Peak,** Montana's highest point; some 300 lakes; scores of waterfalls and glaciers; and the famous pink snow, whose color is due to microscopic plant life on its surface. On the area's southern edge is **Grasshopper Glacier,** one of America's largest icefields, 1 mile long, ½ mile wide; it is so named because of the millions of grasshoppers trapped in its depths.

For further information: 1015 Broadwater, Billings, Mont. 59102

DEERLODGE NATIONAL FOREST
southwest Montana, headquarters at Butte, access via U.S. 10

A realm of gentle foothills, green mountain valleys, timbered slopes, spectacular snow-capped peaks, and cool, alpine streams and lakes,

Deerlodge covers over 1,300,000 acres. It straddles the **Continental Divide** and elevations range from about 4,600 feet near the town of Deer Lodge to 10,635 feet on top of **Mount Evans** in the **Pintlar Range.** It also comprises such scenic areas as the **Flint Creek Range** and the **Highland, Tobacco Root, Sapphire,** and **John Long mountains.** Part of the Anaconda-Pintlar Wilderness (*see*) is here.
For further information write: 107 E Granite St, Butte, Mont. 59701

FLATHEAD LAKE
northwest Montana, about 8 miles south of Kalispell on U.S. 93

Scooped from the valley by the action of the great glaciers, Flathead is the largest freshwater lake west of the **Mississippi River.** It is 28 miles long, between 5 and 15 miles wide, and has an average depth of 220 feet. On the east it is shadowed by the splendid, rugged **Mission Range** and on the west by the foothills of the **Cabinet Mountains.** The lake offers excellent fishing and is flanked by scenic highways. Its shores are dotted with several state recreation areas, including West Shore and Yellow Bay areas.

FLATHEAD NATIONAL FOREST
northwest Montana, headquarters at Kalispell

One of the most scenic areas in the United States, this is a 2,336,400-acre region filled with majestic, timbered mountains, hanging valleys, glaciers, waterfalls, numerous lakes, miles of streams, and a vast network of roads and trails. **Mission Mountains Primitive Area,** covering 73,340 acres, features entrance trails through glorious stands of virgin spruce, western larch, and fir. A portion of the forest abuts Flathead Lake (*see*). This forest, which also includes part of Bob Marshall Wilderness (*see*), is one of the few remaining retreats of the grizzly bear.
For further information write: 290 N Main, Kalispell, Mont. 59901

Aerial view of the Chinese Wall in Bob Marshall Wilderness

Left: petrified stumps in Gallatin National Forest. Right: mountain goat in Glacier National Park

GALLATIN NATIONAL FOREST
south Montana, headquarters at Bozeman

The varied landscape in Gallatin's 1,700,166 acres ranges from 400-foot valley floors to 12,000-foot, snow-clad mountain peaks. Pine forests, trails, wildlife, over 200 lakes, and thousands of miles of clear mountain streams are some of its attractions. Bisected by the **Yellowstone River,** this forest includes parts of the **Bridger, Madison, Gallatin, Absaroka,** and **Crazy mountains.** Its main timber species are lodgepole pine, Douglas fir, and Engelmann spruce. The 37,800-acre **Madison River Canyon Earthquake Area** is one of its special features. The scene of a violent earthquake in August, 1959, this tract now has **Hebgen Lake** and **Earthquake Lake,** which were created by the quake. The forest also includes **Absaroka Primitive Area,** featuring varied wild game; and **Spanish Peaks Primitive Area,** offering a remarkable view of the surrounding **Gallatin River Valley.** It contains a part of **Beartooth Primitive Area,** which extends into Custer National Forest and Wyoming's Shoshone National Forest (*see both*).

For further information: Federal Building, Bozeman, Mont. 59715

GIANT SPRINGS
4½ miles northeast of Great Falls, on south bank of Missouri River

This is one of the world's largest freshwater springs. The water maintains a constant temperature of 52° and flows at a rate of 388,800,000 gallons per day.

GLACIER NATIONAL PARK
northwest Montana, headquarters at West Glacier off U.S. 2

Situated in the **Rocky Mountains,** this park contains nearly 1,600 square miles of America's finest mountain country. Together with Canada's adjoining Waterton National Park it forms the Waterton–Glacier International Peace Park. Glacier is a land of lofty, angular peaks, knife-edged ridges, and dense forests. Nestled in its higher peaks are some 50 small alpine glaciers—notably **Sperry, Kintla,** and **Grinnell**—lying at the heads of ice-carved valleys, and some 200 lakes. The park is bisected by the **Continental Divide**—streams flow northward into **Hudson Bay,** eastward to the **Gulf of Mexico,** and westward to the **Pacific.** The park is filled with many kinds of wildlife (moose, elk, mountain goat, black and grizzly bear) and varied plant life (natural alpine gardens). Within the park are the **Livingston** and **Lewis mountain ranges;** the highest peak is 10,448-foot **Mount Cleveland.** The park also boasts at least 1,000 miles of wilderness trails and several excellent highways. Foremost among these is *Going-to-the-Sun Road* (Glacier Route 1), an outstanding scenic road about 50 miles long that connects the park's east and west sides and crosses the Continental Divide through 6,664-foot **Logan Pass.** Some of the natural wonders it passes (from west to east) are **Lake McDonald,** which mirrors **Mount Cannon; McDonald Creek;** Logan Pass; and **Pollock, Piegan,** and **Going-to-the-Sun mountains.** It then continues through a spectacular section to **Saint Mary Lake,** rimmed with glacier-covered peaks. Here it joins *Blackfeet Highway* (State 49 and U.S. 89), which leads along the east side of the park from U.S. 2 to the Canadian border. Two of the park's best-known walks originate in the Logan Pass area. The 2-mile *Hidden Lake Overlook Trail* leads to a point about 800 feet above **Hidden Lake.** Plants, wildlife, fossil algae, and a U-shaped glacial valley are some of the features. The Garden Wall hike from Logan Pass to Granite Park follows the face of the famous **Garden Wall,** a sharp, narrow, jagged ridge along the face of **Mount Gould.** Visitor centers, ranger stations, campgrounds, hotels, lodges, and cabins are available within the park.

For further information write: West Glacier, Mont. 59936

GREAT FALLS PORTAGE
southeast of Great Falls at junction of U.S. 97, 89, and 91

On June 13, 1805, Captain Meriwether Lewis and a small party became the first white men to see the **Great Falls of the Missouri.** Their turbulence necessitated an 18-mile portage which took 31 days and was one of the greatest ordeals of the expedition. The falls are now harnessed for hydroelectric power and only a small amount of water trickles down. However, the sheaf of jagged rocks and the rugged landscape remain. National Historic Landmark

HELENA NATIONAL FOREST
west Montana, headquarters at Helena, access via U.S. 12, 41

Towering cliffs, glaciated valleys, mountain streams, lakes, quiet trails, and forest roads through the **Rocky Mountains** and along the **Missouri River**—these are some of the attractions of this 966,600-acre forest. Straddling the **Continental Divide** from the headwaters of the **Blackfoot River** in the south to the headwaters of **Prickly Pear Creek** in the north, Helena embraces the **Big Belt, Elkhorn,** and **Dry mountain ranges.** Its cover varies from dry areas to moist spruce country. Of special interest is *Figure-8 Route,* a scenic 75-mile drive that starts at Helena and goes through the Big Belt Mountains to the northeast. It passes through spectacular **Trout Creek** and **Beaver Creek canyons** and crosses the Missouri twice. At Helena itself one can see the main street, famous Last Chance Gulch, where some $20 million in gold was panned and sluiced during the late 1800s. The forest also includes the ghost towns of Diamond City, Marysville, and Crow Creek Falls. Another point of interest is 6,500-foot-high **Macdonald Pass,** the main route over the Continental Divide, 16 miles west of Helena. Another fascinating section is roadless, 28,562-acre **Gates of the Mountains Wilderness.** Here magnificent 2,000-foot limestone walls line the canyon, where the Missouri River crosses the Big Belt Range. The Gates were named by Captain Meriwether Lewis as he passed through on July 19, 1805. An illusion of nature seems to open gates on either side of the river. The wilderness, which is accessible by trails or by boat, contains many hiking trails. Fossils and interesting rock formations are among its natural features.

For further information write: 616 Helena Ave, Helena, Mont. 59601

KANIKSU NATIONAL FOREST. *See* IDAHO

KOOTENAI NATIONAL FOREST
northwest corner of Montana and east Idaho, headquarters at Libby

Covering some 1,800,000 acres, this forest features rolling, timbered hills, towering trees, and shimmering lakes and streams. It is named for the Kutenai Indians who inhabited the region before white men arrived. Its many attractions include portions of the **Cabinet, Purcell,** and **Flathead mountain ranges;** the **Yaak** and **Fisher rivers;** blue-green **Kootenai River** with spectacular **Kootenai Falls; Kootenai Canyon;** and **Vermiculite Mountain,** which contains the world's largest deposit of vermiculite. Other attractions include **Ten Lakes Scenic Area**—a beautiful, high, subalpine mountain ridge with small, glacially formed lakes and meadows. **Northwest Peak Scenic Area,** another subalpine mountain ridge, contains 7 small lakes and gnarled alpine larch. The **Ross Creek Scenic Area** has a 100-acre grove of ancient western red cedar trees and is traversed by a self-guiding trail. Also within this forest is the **Cabinet Mountains Wilderness,** a roadless, 94,272-acre tract along the Cabinet Mountains Divide. It extends also into Kaniksu National Forest (*see Idaho*) and features a series of prominent snowy peaks, glacial lakes, and waterfalls.

For further information: 418 Mineral Ave, Libby, Mont. 59923

LEWIS AND CLARK CAVERNS STATE PARK
18 miles east of Whitehall on U.S. 10

Nestled right in the heart of the **Rocky Mountains,** this park features the largest known limestone cave in the Pacific Northwest. Once known as Morrison Cave, the caverns are housed in 5,840-foot **Cave Mountain.** Formed an estimated 220 million years ago, the caverns boast stalagmites; stalactites; clusterites, which resemble a bunch of grapes; carpetlike flowstones; and many other delicate, multicolored formations. A novel jeep-railway and tram-lift combination transports visitors from the parking lot to the cave's entrance at 5,595 feet. From here they can enjoy a ¾-mile guided tour through the vaulted caverns. Outside, there is a panoramic vista of **Jefferson River Canyon** and the **Madison** and **Gallatin mountain ranges.**

Open June 15–Labor Day: daily 8–8; May–June 15 and Labor Day–Sept 30: daily 8–5. Admission: adults $1.00, children (6–12) 50¢

LEWIS AND CLARK NATIONAL FOREST
central Montana, headquarters at Great Falls

This forest, astride the **Continental Divide** and covering some 1.8 million acres, contains part of the Bob Marshall Wilderness (*see*), as well as portions of the **Highwood, Little Belt, Crazy, Big** and **Little Snowy mountain ranges.** Its many scenic attractions include **Smith River Canyon;** the **South Fork of the Judith River,** which flows through magnificent limestone canyons; and the **Ice Cave** on top of the west end of the Big Snowy Mountains. Also of note is 5,216-foot **Marias Pass** over the Continental Divide, which served the Blackfoot and Flathead Indians as a gateway across the Rockies. Another attraction is **Scapegoat Mountain-Half Moon Park,** a backcountry recreation area. Mountain goats are a frequent sight on the steep east face of 9,185-foot Mount Scapegoat. Just north of this area is **Cigarette Rock,** 5 feet in diameter and about 30 feet high. The main cover in the forest is lodgepole pine, but Douglas fir, ponderosa pine, and spruce are also present.

For further information: Federal Building, Great Falls, Mont. 59401

LOLO NATIONAL FOREST
west Montana, headquarters at Missoula

An extensive trail system leads through Lolo's many ridges, canyons, alpine meadows, and snow-capped peaks. Covering 2,076,641 acres, this forest includes a section of the famous Selway-Bitterroot Wilderness (*see Idaho*), the **Seeley Lake** chain, and portions of the **Rattlesnake, Bitterroot, Swan, Sapphire,** and **Coeur d'Alene mountain** ranges. It takes its name from **Lolo Creek,** which flows into the **Bitterroot River** about 12 miles south of Missoula. The Lewis and Clark expedition followed the northern Nez Perce Indian trail across the Bitterroot Mountains; it subsequently became known as the Lolo Trail. West of Lolo, within the forest, is a tree-lined section of Lewis and Clark Highway (U.S. 12) that parallels the route the explorers took to approach 5,187-foot **Lolo Pass** over the Bitterroots.

For further information write: 2801 Russell, Missoula, Mont. 59801

MAKOSHIKA STATE PARK
3 miles south of Glendive off U.S. 10

Makoshika, a Sioux Indian word for "hell cooled over," is an appropriate name for the badlands area of eastern Montana. Centuries of weathering have eroded limestone cliffs into the strange, vividly colored buttes, gullies, and spires within this park. Its sandstone rocks contain wonderful fossil specimens and semiprecious stones, notably beautiful moss agates.

MEDICINE ROCKS STATE PARK
12 miles north of Ekalaka on State 7

So named because Indians held medicine dances among its rocks, this park features huge sandstone formations eroded into striking shapes by centuries of wind and rain. These forms—spirals, arches, columns—look intensely white in the summer sun and like molten silver in the moonlight.

POMPEY'S PILLAR
28 miles east of Billings on U.S. 10

This massive natural block of sandstone on the **Yellowstone River** is 120 feet high and 350 feet across at its widest point. On July 25, 1806, on his return from the Pacific coast, Captain William Clark named it and carved his signature on its surface. Reputedly, Pompey's Pillar is the only extant landmark of the famous Lewis and Clark expedition. It also bears hundreds of other names. National Historic Landmark

Open June 1–Labor Day: daily 8–6. Admission: $1.00 per car

SELWAY–BITTERROOT WILDERNESS. *See* IDAHO

THREE FORKS OF THE MISSOURI
northwest of Three Forks on the Missouri River

Discovered by Lewis and Clark on July 27, 1805, the Three Forks is the point where the **Gallatin** joins the **Jefferson** and **Madison** rivers to form the **Missouri.** All 3 streams were named by the explorers. The Missouri River Headwaters State Monument features scenic vistas of the headwaters area. National Historic Landmark

NEBRASKA

AGATE FOSSIL BEDS NATIONAL MONUMENT
near village of Agate, 20 miles south of Harrison via State 29

This recently established monument contains numerous concentrations of well-preserved fossils of mammals that roamed the **Great Plains** between 13 and 25 million years ago. It takes its name from its proximity to beds that yield lovely blue agate, the state's official gemstone. The main fossil sites are grass-covered **Carnegie** and **University hills,** whose summits loom some 200 feet above the relatively flat valley of the **Niobrara River.** The monument also contains many "devil's corkscrews," casts of ancient beaver burrows. An estimated 75 per cent of the fossil-bearing section of the hills is still unexplored. At present, there are no exposed fossils to be seen in the quarry sites, but the National Park Service plans to uncover many..Roads, trails, bridges, and interpretive structures will also be built. The landscape is covered with grasses and colorful prairie flowers; willows and cottonwoods add to the charm of this natural museum.

For further information write: c/o Scotts Bluff National Monument, Box 427, Gering, Nebr. 69341

CHADRON STATE PARK
9 miles south of Chadron on U.S. 385

Located in rough, upland country, this park features ravines, rocky outcrops, and high buttes. It is heavily wooded with over 50 varieties of coniferous and deciduous trees. Graceful, wind-carved pines dot the walls of its canyons and ridges, and tall, dense groves and meadows fill the valley. The park is traversed by **Chadron Creek,** a

Left: Sandhills. Right: wind-etched pinnacle in North Platte River Valley

branch of the **White River,** and contains many hiking trails.

CHIMNEY ROCK NATIONAL HISTORIC SITE
3½ miles southwest of Bayard, on south side of North Platte River

Chimney Rock, an odd, eroded pinnacle rising 500 feet above the surrounding prairie and the nearby **North Platte River,** was one of the famous landmarks of the Oregon Trail. It was a welcome sight for the over 2 million 19th-century migrants who crossed the area in wagon trains on their way to the Far West. Even earlier, it was a guidepost for the "mountain men," the trappers and traders who journeyed between **Rocky Mountain** and **Missouri River** trading posts. Set on an eroded plateau of reddish sandstone, the rock consists of a conical mound with a spirelike formation rising from its summit. It is composed of clay, interlaid with volcanic ash and sandstone, and its resistance to erosion is probably due to the presence of hard sandstone in its upper strata. While the surrounding clay weathered away, the tower remained.

Open summer: daily 8–5. For further information write: c/o Scotts Bluff National Monument, Box 427, Gering, Nebr. 69341

COURTHOUSE AND JAIL ROCKS
several miles south of Bridgeport via State 88

Rising abruptly from the level plain, Courthouse and Jail rocks form the eastern limit of the **Wildcat Hills.** There are various stories concerning the origin of their names. According to one, Courthouse was named by St. Louis travelers who thought it resembled their county building. Nearby Jail Rock may have been so named because of the usual proximity of jail and courthouse. Their lower parts are made of Brule clay, and the upper parts are a banded formation of sandstone and clay cemented with lime.

FONTENELLE FOREST
1 mile south of Omaha on Bellevue Boulevard

The largest known remaining stand of virgin forest in the state, Fontenelle covers 1,500 acres. An interpretive program is offered. The area includes a high bluff and river flood plain just west and south of the **Missouri River.** Here one can see rich mixtures of oak, hickory, elm, walnut, locust, ash, and other species. Cottonwood, sycamore, boxelder, silver maple, red mulberry, and red cedar occur on the bottomlands. The tract also includes about 20 acres of true prairie, as well as a marsh, a swamp, and small lakes. Registered Natural Landmark

NIOBRARA STATE PARK
½ mile south and 1 mile west of Niobrara via State 12

Situated on a wooded island at the junction of the **Niobrara** and **Missouri rivers,** this park offers hiking and swimming. Nearby is **Maiden's Leap,** a 100-foot chalk rock from which a lovelorn Indian maiden is said to have jumped to her death.

PONCA STATE PARK
2 miles north of Ponca via State 9 or 12

Covering almost 500 wooded acres on the **Missouri River,** the state's eastern boundary, this park offers many trails and scenic views. Several miles north is **Ionia Volcano,** a steep bluff overlooking the river. It is composed of clays and shales containing iron sulphide, which produces heat when acted upon by water. This accounts for the smoking of the bluff and its name.

NEBRASKA

ROBIDOUX PASS
8 miles southwest of Scottsbluff
> A famed natural landmark on the Oregon Trail, this pass was used by the westbound travelers of the 1840s. They had their first look at Wyoming's Laramie Peak (*see*) from its crest. The pass is named for Joseph and Antoine Robidoux, who established a trading post at its western end in 1849. National Historic Landmark

SANDHILLS
most of west and northwest Nebraska
> Covering about 24,000 square miles, the Sandhills are Nebraska's most unusual and important natural feature. Originally created by glacial erosion, they were formerly barren, drifting dunes. Now, however, they are a wide expanse of gently rolling hills, largely stabilized by grass. In many places the terrain resembles a large emerald-green sea. Since the soil is almost pure sand, it soaks up rain, resulting in a vast, subterranean reservoir. In the many valleys between the hills, this water comes to the surface in the form of lakes. Today more than 6 million cattle graze in the region, thriving on the good forage and water supply. A marker on U.S. 83 just east of Thedford describes the Sandhills.

SCOTTS BLUFF NATIONAL MONUMENT
3 miles west of Gering via State 92
> This massive promontory, rising 800 feet above the **North Platte River Valley,** has been a landmark since ancient times. It is chiefly known for its association with the mass migrations westward across the **Great Plains** between 1843 and 1869, when the completion of the first transcontinental railroad marked the decline of the Oregon Trail. The bluff is named for Hiram Scott, a fur trapper who died nearby in 1828. In ancient times it was part of the High Plains. But

Scotts Bluff promontory

Chimney Rock pinnacle (see page 167)

through the ages erosion leveled the surrounding valleys to their present height, and Scotts Bluff and the adjoining hills remained as remnants of the unbroken plains that now exist farther to the west. The 3,084-acre monument contains a visitor center, featuring exhibits relating to the bluff's role as a landmark on the Mormon and Oregon trails. Other points of interest include the *Saddle Rock Self-Guiding Nature Trail*, devoted to a fuller understanding of the bluff's natural history. From the bluff's north promontory there is an observation point with a superb vista of the North Platte Valley, and other landmarks such as Chimney Rock and Laramie Peak, 100 miles to the west in Wyoming (*see both*). **Dome Rock**, a conspicuous outcrop, forms the monument's southeast boundary. **Mitchell Pass**, opened to covered-wagon traffic in 1850, supplanted Robidoux Pass (*see*).

For further information write: Box 427, Gering, Nebr. 69341

SIGNAL BUTTE
14 miles southwest of Scottsbluff

Another landmark on the Oregon Trail, this butte has great archaeological significance. Early Man spearpoints and the remnants of several prehistoric and historic cultures have been unearthed here. National Historic Landmark

TOADSTOOL PARK
16 miles north of Crawford on State 2, then 1 mile west

Located within the **Oglala National Grasslands**, a division of manmade **Nebraska National Forest**, this park preserves weird rock formations in a badlands area. These huge "toadstools" were produced by the erosion of soft clay from under a layer of sandstone and fine, silty soil which left bases of clay under wide stone caps. Fossils and rare agates are plentiful here.

NEVADA

BEAVER DAM STATE PARK
38 miles east of Caliente off U.S. 93

Located high in a scenic mountain wilderness, this park covers 1,716 acres. Camping and hiking are available against a backdrop of high cliffs and unspoiled pine forests.

BOUNDARY PEAK
about 12 miles south of Basalt off U.S. 6

This 13,145-foot mountain bears the distinction of being the highest point in Nevada. Located in the **White Mountains,** a rugged area well known to hunters, it is near the California border.

CARSON SINK
about 20 miles north of Fallon off U.S. 95

This dried-up lake bed is a remnant of Lake Lahontan, the prehistoric inland ocean that once covered northwestern Nevada (*see also Pyramid and Walker lakes*). A catch basin for the **Carson River,** the sink is 20 miles long and 15 miles wide and occupies a swampy area between the **Humboldt Range** and the **Stillwater Mountains.** **Carson Lake** (9 miles long and 6 miles wide) is to the south.

CATHEDRAL GORGE STATE PARK
16 miles north of Caliente on U.S. 93

This 1,578-acre park is notable for its steep bentonite clay walls of grayish-tan which have been eroded into many weird shapes. The fluted rocks, spires, and pinnacles here resemble cathedrals, skyscrapers, and a wedding cake.

DEATH VALLEY NATIONAL MONUMENT. *See* CALIFORNIA

HUMBOLDT NATIONAL FOREST
northeast Nevada, headquarters at Elko

Comprised of 9 different sections, this 2,523,000-acre forest is a scenic wonderland of desert (the **Great Basin**), sagebrush-covered hills, glacier-made lakes, and forested mountains. Among the many imposing ranges here are the **Ward Mountains,** featuring 3 limestone terraces which offer hikers magnificent views; the **White Pine Range,** with elevations varying from 5,000 feet to over 11,000 feet on **Duckwater Peak;** the **Grant Mountain Range,** highlighted by **Troy Peak** (11,263 feet); the **Santa Rosa Range** (a ride through these mountains along **Indian Creek** to **Hinkey** and **Buckskin summits** offers a fantastic view of lava domes, natural arches, and a 50-mile panorama of **Paradise Valley** and the **Quinn River Valley**); and the **Ruby Mountains.** A particularly beautiful section of this range is set aside in the **Ruby Mountains Scenic Area,** a 40,720-acre expanse which includes the headwaters of the **Humboldt River;** steepwalled, U-shaped canyons, such as **Lamoille Canyon;** countless clear waterfalls, streams, and lakes (a highlight is **Angel Lake**); and lofty peaks such as the 11,387-foot **Ruby Dome.**

One of the most interesting regions in the forest is the **Wheeler Peak Scenic Area,** a 28,000-acre stretch of the **Snake Range.** Dominated by 13,063-foot Wheeler Peak, the second highest mountain in Nevada, the scenic area was established to preserve a forest of ancient bristlecone pine. Also featured here are the *Asilo Verde Drive,* which offers an especially scenic route through these beau-

Top: Mohave yucca and Cathedral Rock in Toiyabe National Forest. Below: Jarbridge Wilderness in Humboldt National Forest

tiful mountains, and the Lehman Caves National Monument (*see*). To the north is **Mount Moriah,** a 12,049-foot peak in the Snake Range, that rises impressively above desert and canyons. Still another highlight in the vast and beautiful forest is the 64,830-acre **Jarbridge Wilderness,** one of the state's wildest and most remote areas. Bounded by the **Columbia River Plateau,** the Great Basin Desert, **Mary's River,** and the headwaters of the **Jarbridge River,** the wilderness includes 8 peaks over 10,000 feet. Among them are **Matterhorn** (10,839 feet), **Jarbridge Peak** (10,789 feet), and **Square Top** (10,687 feet). First established in 1908, and expanded in 1917 and 1957, the forest takes its name from the Humboldt River which John C. Frémont named for Prussian naturalist-explorer Baron Alexander von Humboldt.

For further information write: Superintendent, Elko, Nevada 89801

ICHTHYOSAUR PALEONTOLOGIC STATE MONUMENT
about 23 miles east of Gabbs via State 91

This 515-acre park contains the fossils of "fish-lizards," huge animals that once swam in a warm ocean (Lake Lahontan) that covered this area. It is believed that the ichthyosaurs, which ranged in size from 2 to 60 feet and resembled porpoises and whales in their body shape, came into existence in the Middle Triassic period and were extinct by the close of the Upper Cretaceous period, about 70 million years ago. Now dry, rugged terrain, this area was covered by a volcanic cap about 60 million years ago and finally eroded into canyons during the Pleistocene epoch.

KERSHAW-RYAN STATE RECREATION AREA
3 miles south of Caliente off U.S. 93

This 240-acre park is set in a small oak forest. Bordering the forest are grapevine-covered cliffs.

LAKE MEAD NATIONAL RECREATION AREA. See ARIZONA

LAKE TAHOE. See CALIFORNIA

LEHMAN CAVES NATIONAL MONUMENT
5 miles west of Baker, off U.S. 6 and 50, near the Utah boundary

Considered to be one of the most beautiful caves in the country, this underground fantasy is located on the eastern flank of **Wheeler Peak** in the Wheeler Peak Scenic Area in Humboldt National Forest

(*see*). Named for rancher Absalom S. Lehman, who popularized the caves, the national monument covers 640 acres in the forest's piñon pine-juniper belt; it is located 6,825 feet above sea level and is bounded by **Lehman** and **Baker creeks.** The caves were carved out by water charged with carbon dioxide which seeped into the cracks in the stone of the mountain. As the water wore away the softer underground rocks, the cracks were widened and enlarged into chambers. Soon passageways expanded until a maze of winding tunnels connecting huge vaulted rooms was created. With time the underground climate became less humid and the water receded beneath the cave floor, leaving dry, air-filled chambers. Now calcite-laden water began to drip through overhead rocks and developed the fantastic formations for which these caves are known. With the passage of perhaps 2 million years stalactites, stalagmites, and other formations—such as helictites, columns, draperies, and shields, or pallettes (round calcite disks)—developed giving these caverns their colorful decorations of white, buff, chocolate, orange, and red. In some places the dripping water accumulated, creating underground pools such as **Lake Como** and **Cypress Swamp.** Over 3,500 feet of lighted trails lead through the caverns, where a constant temperature of 50° is maintained. Since water continues to drip from overhead and add to the formations, the caverns have been designated living caves. A visitor center, open from April to October, is located near the tunnel entrance; about 1½ hours is required to cover the underground trails.

Open daily: summer 8–5; Sept–May 9–4. Write: Baker, Nev. 89311

PYRAMID LAKE
Pyramid Lake Indian Reservation, northeast of Reno

A remnant of the prehistoric inland sea (Lake Lahontan) that once covered northwest Nevada, Pyramid Lake is the largest natural body of water in the state. (It is 30 miles long and from 5 to 12 miles wide.) Named by John Charles Frémont in 1844, the lake is fed by the **Truckee River.** Surrounded by mountains and desert, it is located between the **Pyramid** and **Lake ranges** in the **Smoke Creek Desert,** a southwest extension of the **Black Rock Desert** that stretches for about 70 miles. Pyramid Lake is noted for its turquoise-blue waters where cutthroat trout abound and for the pyramid-shaped island that rises about 475 feet above its surface. Near the southeastern shore is **Anaho Island,** a federal bird refuge and home of a large rookery of rare, white pelicans.

Left: Lehman Caves. Below: looking across Nevada desert to White Mountains in Inyo National Forest (see California)

NEVADA

TOIYABE NATIONAL FOREST
south and central Nevada and west California, headquarters at Reno

Covering over 3 million acres, Toiyabe is the largest forest in the conterminous United States. It is located in 3 different sections with outstanding scenic attractions in each one. The central section includes the **Toiyabe** (black) **Range,** so named by the Shoshone Indians for the dark color of the dense stands of juniper and piñon trees that cover the mountain. Highlights here include **Antelope Peak** (10,207 feet), the **Toquema Range,** and **Austin Summit** (7,554 feet). The southern section, near Las Vegas, features 11,918-foot **Charleston Peak,** the highest peak in the **Spring Mountain Range** and the third highest in the state, located at the end of a 17-mile loop trail through **Kyle Canyon.** Other features here include **Cathedral Rock,** which provides a scenic overlook of Kyle Canyon; **Lee Canyon; Mummy Mountain** (11,532 feet); and *Spring Mountain Loop Drive,* a scenic route through mountains and forest affording outstanding views of the desert below. The section of the forest along the California-Nevada border lies on the eastern slopes of the **Sierra Nevada Range.** Highlights here are **Mount Rose** (10,778 feet) which offers a spectacular view of Lake Tahoe *(see Tahoe National Forest, California);* the scenic **Truckee River;** and **Dog Valley,** part of the 19th-century California Emigrant Trail. Perhaps the most outstanding attraction in the forest is the **Hoover Wilderness.** Covering 33,800 acres in Toiyabe and 9,000 acres in Inyo National Forest *(see California),* Hoover is an exceptionally rugged area, ranging in elevation from 8,000 to nearly 11,300 feet. Lying along the **Sawtooth Ridge** in the Sierra Nevada, the wilderness includes such fine fishing streams as the **Little Walker River,** and **Molybdenite, Buckeye, Virginia, Mill,** and **Green creeks.** The highest peak in the Inyo section is the 12,446-foot **Excelsior Mountain;** 12,347-foot **Dunderberg Peak** is highest in the Toiyabe section.
For further information write: Box 1331, Reno, Nev. 89504

VALLEY OF FIRE
35 miles northeast of Las Vegas off I-15 on State 40

Named for the blazing red, yellow, brown, and gray colors of its sandstone formations, this valley is located in a 30,000-acre state park of the same name. Here monoliths and boulders rising out of the desert, examples of geologic "overthrusting," have been carved into weird and intriguing formations with descriptive names such as **Elephant Rock, Beehives, Seven Sisters,** and **Donald Duck.** Other features include **Mouse's Tank,** a natural water basin, and the **White Domes Area,** a particularly scenic region of white sandstone formations. Archaeological investigations and petroglyphs have proved that the valley was occupied by various groups for about 2,000 years after 300 B.C. The park is crisscrossed by miles of trails which guide the visitor through this labyrinth of intricate outcroppings. Registered Natural Landmark

WALKER LAKE
Walker River Indian Reservation, U.S. 95

Like Pyramid Lake *(see),* this large lake is a remnant of a prehistoric inland sea (Lake Lahontan) that once covered northwestern Nevada. Fed by the **Walker River,** the lake is 24 miles long and from 2 to 6 miles wide. It is located in the **Wassuk Range,** just east of 11,303-foot **Mount Grant,** the highest point in these mountains. It was named for explorer Joseph Reddeford Walker, who crossed the **Great Basin** to California in 1833–34.

CARDIGAN STATE PARK
4½ miles east of Canaan, off U.S. 4 and State 118

This park features a mountain road leading to a recreation area on Mount Cardigan's western slope. From here several foot trails provide access to the mountain's 3,100-foot summit.
Open daily Memorial Day–Columbus Day

CRAWFORD NOTCH STATE PARK
12 miles north of Bartlett, on U.S. 302

Located in the center of White Mountain National Forest (*see*), this park features 10-mile-long scenic Crawford Notch. Formed when the continental ice sheet crashed through a narrow preglacial pass, the rugged notch extends from Crawford House southward to Bartlett. Its valley floor, which is bounded by the wooded slopes of **Mounts Webster** and **Willey,** is traversed by the **Saco River** and U.S. 302. Both mountains carry the markings of many landslides. At the northern end of the notch, near the highway, are **Silver** and **Flume cascades.** The park is crossed by many trails, including a section of the *Appalachian,* affording excellent views of the **Presidential Range** to the east. Another attraction is **Arethusa Falls,** at over 200 feet, one of the state's highest.
Open daily May 21–Columbus Day

DIXVILLE NOTCH
south of Lake Abeniki on State 26, between Colebrook and Errol

The **White Mountains'** northernmost and wildest pass, this 2-mile-long rocky gorge is enclosed by sheer mountain cliffs, sparkling brooks, and dark spruce and balsam trees. A favorite haunt of huntsmen and fishermen, the area is crossed by many hiking trails and Highway 26. Its scenic attractions include the beautiful man-made **Lake Gloriette,** waterfalls on **Cascade** and **Flume brooks, Table** and **Pulpit rocks,** and other interesting rock formations—some resembling cathedral spires.

Left: distant vista of Mount Chocorua. Right: Great Stone Face in Franconia Notch State Park

NEW HAMPSHIRE

ECHO LAKE STATE PARK
2 miles west of North Conway, off U.S. 302

This small mountain lake (not to be confused with its namesake in Franconia Notch State Park, *see*) lies in the shadow of spectacular **White Horse Ledge,** which rises almost directly above it. A scenic road leads from the lake to a vantage point near the top of **Cathedral Ledge,** a dramatic granite formation some 700 feet high, affording vistas of the **White Mountains,** the **Saco River Valley,** and the **Ossipee Mountains.**
Open daily mid-June–mid-October

FRANCONIA NOTCH STATE PARK
Franconia, on U.S. 3, via I-93

Surrounded by the White Mountain National Forest (*see*), this park features Franconia Notch, an 8-mile-long mountain pass between the **Kinsman** and **Franconia mountains.** It contains some of the state's most spectacular landmarks and scenery. Dominating the notch is the **Old Man of the Mountains,** New Hampshire's trademark, also called the **Profile** and the **Great Stone Face** (after Nathaniel Hawthorne's tale of the same name). The features are formed by 5 separate granite ledges protruding from sheer cliffs 1,200 feet above **Profile Lake.** The Old Man was formed some 200 million years ago when the cliff's granite crystallized, creating vertical cracks. Then, after glacial ice melted, frost action probably caused granite blocks to fall off the cliff, leaving the profile. From chin to forehead it measures about 40 feet, and it may best be seen from the lake's east shore. Another stunning attraction is **Flume Gorge,** a natural chasm extending 800 feet along the flank of 4,460-foot **Mount Liberty** and terminating at 25-foot **Avalanche Falls.** Its granite walls, between 60 and 70 feet high, are covered with luxuriant flowers, ferns, and mosses, which may be examined from the

Silver Cascades in Crawford Notch State Park (see page 175)

Sailboats on Lake Winnipesaukee

boardwalk that traverses the gorge. Among many other points of interest in the Flume is a 40-foot-deep pool and **Liberty Gorge** with its many cascades, formed as water rushes through a narrow defile. The park also offers a thrilling cable-car ride to the 4,200-foot summit of **Cannon Mountain.** Other attractions include **Echo Lake,** at the head of the notch; the **Basin,** a deep glacial pothole, 20 feet in diameter; and numerous hiking trails, including a segment of the *Appalachian National Scenic Trail.*

LAKE WINNIPESAUKEE
eastcentral New Hampshire, northeast of Laconia
Situated in the foothills of the **White Mountains,** this is one of the most enchanting as well as the largest of New Hampshire's lakes. It is some 20 miles long and has a 283-mile shoreline indented by bays and coves. The lake contains 365 islands, of which 274 are habitable, some rising at least 400 feet above the water's surface. Winnipesaukee is an Indian word meaning "smile of the great spirit." Ellacoya State Beach offers views of the **Sandwich** and **Ossippee mountains.**

MADISON BOULDER
3 miles north of Madison, off State 113
One of the largest erratic boulders in the United States, Madison is 83 feet long, 37 feet wide, and 23 feet high, and weighs an estimated 7,650 tons. Because of the rock texture, geologists believe that ice sheets brought it here from Albany, New Hampshire, 2 miles to the north. Registered Natural Landmark

MILAN HILL STATE PARK
2 miles west of Milan, off State 16, on State 110B
Situated high on the top of Milan Hill, this park offers superb views of southern Canada, the **White Mountains,** and the **Presidential Range.** A road leads almost to its 1,737-foot summit.
Open daily June 11–Sept 12

MILLER STATE PARK
3 miles east of Peterborough, off State 101
This 83-acre park features a road to the summit of 2,280-foot **Pack Monadnock Mountain.** It also has walking trails around the summit, affording fine views of Vermont and Massachusetts.
Open daily mid-June–mid-October

Flume Gorge in Franconia Notch State Park (see page 176)

MONADNOCK STATE PARK
4 miles northwest of Jaffrey, off State 124

Located on 3,165-foot **Mount Monadnock** (also called Grand Monadnock), this park covers nearly 700 acres. A haven for hikers, it has 30 miles of well-maintained trails leading to the summit, which offers views of all the New England states.
Open daily mid-May–Columbus Day

MOUNT KEARSARGE
southcentral New Hampshire, 7 miles southeast of New London

Mount Kearsarge affords superb views of the **White Mountains.** From Winslow State Park on its northern slope and Rollins State Park on its southern slope, there are many hiking trails to its 2,937-foot granite summit. Roads lead to scenic lookouts.
Parks open daily June–October

MOUNT SUNAPEE STATE PARK
just northwest of Newbury via State 103 and 103B

Covering over 2,000 acres on Mount Sunapee, this park overlooks **Sunapee Lake,** which takes its name from an Indian word meaning "wild goose." Nine miles long and at an altitude of 1,100 feet, it is the highest lake of its size in New England. It is noted for game fishing and its beautiful wooded shoreline. The park offers skiing and swimming, and 4-passenger gondola cars that ascend from a base elevation of 1,300 feet to the mountain's 2,700-foot summit. From here there are vistas of **Mounts Kearsarge, Chocorua, Washington, Ascutney,** among others. It also has trails to scenic views and to **Lake Solitude,** about 1 mile distant.

PRESIDENTIAL RANGE. *See* **WHITE MOUNTAIN NATIONAL FOREST**

SCULPTURED ROCKS
Groton, between State 118 and 3A on Cockermouth River

Here the **Cockermouth River** plunges some 30 feet through a cleft in the rocks. The gorge is filled with the so-called Sculptured Rocks, created by the great glaciers and water action. These are granite ledges eroded into potholes and other strange formations.

WHITE MOUNTAIN NATIONAL FOREST
northern New Hampshire and western Maine, headquarters at Laconia

Covering 1,100 square miles, this forest includes most of the White Mountains—the culminating peaks of the northeastern segment of the **Appalachian Range,** famed for its scenic passes or "notches." Its most notable feature is the **Presidential Range,** which covers an area about 8 miles long and 2 miles wide. Formed by mammoth continental ice sheets and glaciers that carved and eroded great beds of rock, the range includes **Mounts Adams** (5,798 feet), **Monroe** (5,385 feet), **Madison** (5,363 feet), **Franklin** (5,004 feet), **Pleasant** or **Eisenhower** (4,761 feet), **Pierce** or **Clinton** (4,310 feet), **Jackson** (4,052 feet), and **Webster** (3,910 feet). The summit of **Mount Washington** (6,288 feet), the highest peak in the state, may be reached by toll road, by cog railway, and by numerous hiking trails. Between it and Mount Monroe are the **2 Lakes of the Clouds.** Another important feature of this forest is 5,552-acre **Great Gulf Wilderness Area,** rimmed by the Presidential Range and the toll road. A glacial valley between 1,100 and 1,600 feet deep, this wilderness has many remarkable cascades, **Spaulding** and **Star** lakes, and a few scattered stands of virgin spruce. Its upper reaches are barren except for alpine flora, but the lower elevations are covered with spruce, fir, and northern hardwoods. South of here is **Pinkham Notch Scenic Area,** walled by the Presidential Range on the west and the **Carter-Moriah Range** on the east. Aside from the notch, points of interest here are **Glen Ellis Falls, Crystal Cascade,** and glacially formed **Tuckerman Ravine** with its **Snow Arch, Huntington Ravine,** and the **Alpine Garden,** with rare alpine flora. Also within the forest is picturesque **Kinsman Notch.** The **Lost River** frequently disappears underground, winds through glacial caverns and huge potholes, and emerges at the foot of this notch to form beautiful **Paradise Falls.** A scenic trail leads through or over some of the caverns. The forest boasts 31 recreation sites, including Passaconaway Information Station, and at least 1,000 miles of trails. *For further information write: Supervisor, Laconia, N.H. 03246*

Winter scene in White Mountain National Forest

NEW JERSEY

BASS RIVER STATE FOREST
6 miles west of Tuckerton off U.S. 9

This 9,100-acre forest features plants and animals typical of the **Pine Barrens**—the stretch of about 3,000 square miles of New Jersey's coast characterized by sandy soil, swamplands, and extensive pine stands. A self-guiding nature trail begins at **Lake Absegami** and passes through an unspoiled cedar swamp.

CAPE MAY

This 20-mile-long peninsula between **Delaware Bay** and the **Atlantic Ocean** is known for its island-dotted coastline. The salt marshes of the **Cape May Wetlands,** extending north from **Cape May Point** along the coast, and the **Brigantine Island** marshes near Atlantic City provide a resting place for migratory birds.

CHEESEQUAKE STATE PARK
5 miles south of Perth Amboy on the Garden State Parkway (exit 120)

This 990-acre park of open woodland and salt marshes surrounds the Cheesequake Creek, a tidal stream that empties into **Raritan Bay,** the western arm of **Lower New York Bay.** In the Nature Area, a scenic region with a variety of plants and birds, a trail leads from the marshes to higher ground with beech and oak forests.

DELAWARE WATER GAP. *See* PENNSYLVANIA

GREAT FALLS OF PATERSON

The 70-foot falls over basalt cliffs in the **Passaic River** are the result of various geological processes during the Triassic period. Because of their great geological importance, the falls and portions of the river immediately above and below them have been designated

Left: Palisades of the Hudson River. Right: Pine Barrens landscape

Registered Natural Landmarks. In 1791 Alexander Hamilton saw the falls as an excellent source of power and established an industrial community around them which developed into the city of Paterson. The falls provided the city with an invaluable source of power well into the 19th century. The district surrounding this site is now a National Historic Landmark.

GREAT SWAMP
7 miles south of Morristown

A rare combination of forest, swamp, and marsh, the Great Swamp was created about 15,000 years ago when the Wisconsin Ice Sheet moved into a deep basin (now known as the **Passaic Valley**) and formed Lake Passaic. As this extinct lake drained, it left behind the **Passaic River** and the Great Swamp. This 2,000-acre site is now the home of a wide variety of wildlife. Registered Natural Landmark

HACKLEBARNEY STATE PARK
2½ miles southwest of Chester, off U.S. 206

Situated in a lovely gorge of the scenic **Black River,** this park covers 569 acres of picturesque countryside. The park is also crossed by 2 tributary streams—**Trout** and **Rinehart brooks.**

HIGH POINT STATE PARK
north of Sussex on State 23

Extending for 8 miles along the crest of **Kittatinny Mountain,** a ridge in the Appalachian chain, this 12,372-acre scenic park includes the highest point in the state. At 1,803 feet above sea level, High Point affords a commanding view of the surrounding New Jersey, New York, and Pennsylvania countryside. From a 220-foot monument atop the ridge one can see the valley of the **Delaware River,** the Delaware Water Gap (*see Pennsylvania*), the **Pocono** and **Catskill mountains.** The 220-acre **Dryden Kuser Natural Area,** site of **Cedar Swamp,** is a virgin woodland of hemlock, white pine, black spruce, and southern white cedar. It is skirted by a 1,700-foot-high ridge crossed by a trail and supports a wide variety of wildlife. A section of the *Appalachian Trail* traverses the park.

ISLAND BEACH STATE PARK
east of Toms River on State 37

This 2,694-acre park is located on a 10-mile-long barrier beach—one of the few remaining natural areas of its kind on the East Coast. Bounded on the west by **Barnegat Bay** and on the east by the **Atlantic Ocean,** the island is constantly being reshaped by huge breakers. High sand dunes on the ocean side are backed by lower dunes covered with indigenous vegetation; on the bay side the island has occasional salt marshes. The park is divided into a botanical zone, a recreational zone, and a wildlife sanctuary in order to preserve its beautiful natural areas. The Barnegat Lighthouse State Park is directly south of Island Beach, across Barnegat Inlet, on **Long Beach Island.** From the top of the 172-foot lighthouse built in 1855, there is an awesome view of the bay and ocean.

JENNY JUMP STATE FOREST
12 miles southeast of the Delaware Water Gap, off I-80

Located on Jenny Jump Mountain, a ridge in the Appalachian chain, this forest varies in elevation from 399 feet above sea level at **Mountain Lake** to about 1,100 feet at forest headquarters. This lovely 967-acre preserve offers, from its nature trails, fine views

Bird watching in the Great Swamp (see page 181)

of **Kittatinny Mountain** and valley, the Delaware Water Gap (*see Pennsylvania*), and the **Great Meadows**, a 6,000-acre area of rich black soil dotted with farms.

MOGGY HOLLOW NATURAL AREA
2 miles east of Far Hills

This area was once the drainage point for ancient, glacial Lake Passaic. A combination of gorge, woodland, and bog, Moggy Hollow is of great ecological and geological importance. The woodlands on the steep, rock-strewn walls of the gorge were probably never logged, and the bog at the ravine bottom contains a wide variety of interesting plant life. Registered Natural Landmark

PALISADES INTERSTATE PARK

Established to protect the beautiful **Palisades of the Hudson River,** this park is located in New Jersey and New York State. (The New Jersey section extends for 13 miles from Fort Lee to the New York State line. The New York section (*see*) is made up of a number of separate state parks.) Rising from 350 feet to 550 feet above the Hudson, the Palisades are striking basalt bluffs. From various lookouts and from hiking trails that cross heavily wooded areas, there are lovely views, including the New York City skyline.

PENN STATE FOREST
5 miles southeast of Chatsworth, off County 563

Located in the coastal plain region of southern New Jersey, this 3,666-acre forest features sprout pitch pine and scrub oak, trees that seldom grow higher than 4 to 6 feet. A lovely scenic attraction here is the view of miles of unbroken wilderness from the observation tower atop 165-foot **Bear Swamp Hill.**

SANDY HOOK STATE PARK
on Sandy Hook on State 36

This narrow barrier peninsula between **Sandy Hook Bay** and the **Atlantic Ocean** extends for about 5 miles and marks the southern entrance to **Lower New York Bay.** Constant battering from ocean waves has changed its coastline and altered its proportions. It is estimated that the peninsula has grown about 35 feet per year in the past 2 centuries; a lighthouse built at the point of the peninsula in 1764 now stands about 1½ miles inland. A sea wall built in 1920–21 has prevented the ocean from cutting through the neck of the hook and separating it from the mainland, as has happened twice since 1778. The fine, natural wonders of Sandy Hook can best be seen in the Nature Area set aside to protect this unusual blend of wetland terrain—sandy upland thickets, tidal marshes, and open ocean waters. Covering the entire bay side of the peninsula and extending to **South Island** and **Spermaceti Cove,** the area features an exceptional waterfowl population and a rare holly forest. Self-guided trails lead to major points of interest. The remainder of the 470-acre park is devoted to recreational facilities.

STOKES STATE FOREST
north of Augusta off U.S. 206
This 13,544-acre forest adjacent to High Point State Park (*see*) is located along **Kittatinny Mountain,** a scenic ridge crossed by 75 miles of hiking trails (including the *Appalachian Trail*). The forest ranges in elevation from 420 feet to 1,653 feet atop **Sunrise Mountain;** a trail leading to the mountaintop affords a lovely view of the surrounding countryside. **Tillman Ravine** features steep rhododendron-covered banks worn down by **Tillman Brook,** a cascading stream tumbling down deep channels and over huge boulders.

TROY MEADOWS
near Troy Hills, via I-80
This 1,400-acre area contains the last sizable unspoiled freshwater swamp in New Jersey. A relic of ancient Lake Passaic, the marsh supports a wide variety of birds and mammals. Eligible Registered Natural Landmark

WASHINGTON ROCK STATE PARK
off U.S. 22 at Plainfield
This 36-acre park in the **Watchung Mountains**—2 low volcanic ridges of 400 to 500 feet—contains a natural lookout from which George Washington is said to have watched the movement of British troops. The vantage point offers today's visitor a lovely panoramic view of the surrounding countryside.

WHARTON STATE FOREST
20 miles from Atlantic City, off U.S. 206 at Atsion
This 97,578-acre forest in the **Pine Barrens** features historic sites, scenic areas, hiking and saddle trails, and many recreational facilities. Many natural areas have been set aside among woodlands, ponds, and bogs, where indigenous plants abound along with a wide variety of birds and animals. Miles of streams, offering quiet canoe trips, wind through this scenic forest.

WORTHINGTON STATE FOREST
north of U.S. 611, at the Delaware Water Gap
The beautiful forest extends for 6 miles along the crest of **Kittatinny Mountain** and features 5,747 acres of picturesque woodland adjacent to the **Delaware River.** A highlight here is the **Dunnfield Creek Nature Area,** centered around a lovely creek that gently falls 1,000 feet from **Mount Tammany** to the Delaware. A picturesque trail follows the creek for ⅔ of a mile. The *Appalachian Trail* passes through the forest along the crest of the ridge and provides access to **Sunfish Pond,** a beautiful glacial lake that has been designated an Eligible Registered Natural Landmark.

NEW MEXICO

APACHE NATIONAL FOREST. *See* ARIZONA

BANDELIER NATIONAL MONUMENT
46 miles northwest of Santa Fe via U.S. 285; visitor center off State 4

The site of a late flowering of the Pueblo Indian culture, this 46-square-mile national monument is situated on the **Pajarito Plateau**—an area composed of volcanic lava and ash deposited by an ancient volcano. The main ruins are located in **Frijoles Canyon,** a deep, forested gorge cut by a mountain stream. Occupied until about 1600, the canyon includes such features as circular Tyuonyi Ruin, the outline of the walls of a 400-room pueblo, and a series of 3-story dwellings with cave rooms gouged into the north wall of the canyon. Frijoles Canyon is accessible by a road that offers spectacular scenic views; other features (**Alamo Canyon, Painted Cave, White Rock Canyon**) can be reached by more than 60 miles of trails across rugged and dangerous mountain terrain. The Tsankawi section, 11 miles north of Frijoles Canyon on State 4, is located on a high mesa offering an outstanding panorama of the **Rio Grande Valley,** the **Sangre de Cristo Mountains,** and the **Jemez Mountains.**

For further information: Superintendent, Los Alamos, N. Mex. 87544

BOTTOMLESS LAKES STATE PARK
10 miles east of Roswell on U.S. 380 and then 7 miles south

This 581-acre park is famous for its picturesque chain of lakes encircled by scenic bluffs, which vary in depth from 45 to 600 feet.

CAPULIN MOUNTAIN NATIONAL MONUMENT
30 miles east of Raton and 3 miles north of Capulin on State 325

Rising 1,000 feet above the level plains, this once violent volcano is now a conical-shaped mountain of ash and cinder covered with plants and dense forests. From the highest point on its rim, 8,215 feet above sea level, the visitor is offered a striking panorama of parts of 5 states (New Mexico, Texas, Oklahoma, Kansas, and Colorado) against a backdrop of snow-capped mountains (the **Sangre de Cristos**), older extinct volcanoes (**Sierra Grande**), and large mesas topped with black lava (**Barella, Raton,** and **Johnson**). This area was once the hunting ground of Kiowa and Comanche Indians, and the mountain was a landmark to pioneers traveling the Cimarron Cutoff of the Santa Fe Trail. A young volcano (the last eruption was about 7,000 years ago), Capulin has beautiful contrasts of loose cinders and ash, rugged rocks, and trees, shrubs, and grasses. The lower slopes of the mountain feature ponderosa pine and juniper with mountain-mahogany and chokecherry at the higher reaches. Deer, porcupine, a wide variety of birds and many other animals can be found within the monument, along with thousands of ladybugs that come here every summer. A road leads from the visitor center, where descriptive exhibits are offered, to the mountain's summit.

For further information: Superintendent, Capulin, N. Mex. 88414

CARLSBAD CAVERNS NATIONAL PARK
27 miles southwest of Carlsbad on U.S. 62–180

Located in the **Chihuahuan Desert** in the foothills of the **Guadalupe**

Top: El Morro. Center. Chaco Canyon. Right: White Sands. Below: the Rio Grande in Sante Fe National Forest

Formations in the Big Room in Carlsbad Caverns

Mountains, this national park features one of the country's most out-standing underground wonders. The cave is made up of large rooms filled with fantastic and intricate decorations formed over millions of years. These caves began as a limestone barrier reef at the edge of an inland sea during the Permian Period. After having been buried under layers of sediment, the rock was raised during a period of mountain building, causing the reef to crack. Water that had absorbed small amounts of carbon dioxide seeped into the cracks and dissolved the limestone. The process continued over millions of years until chambers were formed, some 1,013 feet deep. Eventually the water table within the cavern lowered, leaving large air-filled rooms. Soon water diluted with minerals began to seep into the chambers, creating colorful stalagmites, stalactites, draperies and other formations for which Carlsbad Caverns are famous.

No one knows exactly how extensive the caverns are—only 3 miles of the 8 explored miles are open to the public. Among the fantastic chambers that can be seen during 2 supervised tours are the **Green Lake Room,** featuring a pool of water surrounded by sta-lagmites; the **King's Palace;** the **Papoose Room,** known for its stone draperies; and the **Queen's Chamber,** a small chamber 829 feet below the surface. But the most spectacular sights within the cavern can be seen in the **Big Room**—a massive chamber covering 14 acres. Dominating the 2,000-foot-long and 200-foot-high room is the **Giant Dome,** a massive and beautiful column 62 feet high and nearly 20 feet in diameter. Other awesome formations within the Big Room include **Twin Domes, Rock of Ages,** and **Totem Pole.** Visitors may walk down into the 56°caverns or descend by high-speed elevators from the visitor center; elevators return all visitors to the surface.

Perhaps even more unusual than the caves themselves is the un-paralleled spectacle that takes place nightly from April to October when hundreds of thousands of bats swarm out of the natural en-trance to the cave. Mainly Mexican freetail bats, the creatures fly all night to the valley of the **Pecos** and **Black rivers** where they feed on night-flying insects. The bats, who may have covered 150 miles in their nocturnal journey, return at sunrise to the caves to sleep all day. A park naturalist explains this not-to-be-missed demonstration during summer evenings. The stark beauty of the Chihuahuan Desert can be explored on a self-guided nature trail beginning near the natural entrance to the cave.

For further information write: Box 1598, Carlsbad, N. Mex. 88220

CARSON NATIONAL FOREST
northcentral New Mexico, headquarters at Taos

Located in the southern **Sangre de Cristo Mountains,** Carson is famous as the site of 13,160-foot **Wheeler Peak,** the highest point in New Mexico. Protected in the **Wheeler Peak Wilderness,** a small unspoiled region, the mountain features alpine tundra rarely found in the Southwest. The 1,411,113-acre forest straddles the upper **Rio Grande Valley** and the magnificent Rio Grande Gorge *(see)*; it includes the north portion of the beautiful Pecos Wilderness Area *(see Santa National Forest).* Many scenic drives lead throughout the forest and take the visitor past picturesque Spanish villages, well-stocked lakes and streams, and fine winter sports areas.

For further information write: Box 587, Taos, N. Mex. 87571

CHACO CANYON NATIONAL MONUMENT
23 miles southwest of Blanco Trading Post on State 56

Established to protect hundreds of fine Indian ruins, this national monument is located in a remote, semiarid region of Chaco Canyon, a sandstone gorge about 10 miles long and 1 mile wide. These ruins represent a major center of the Pueblo Indian culture that reached its peak between A.D. 1000 and 1100. The monument contains 12 large ruins and more than 400 smaller ones. The largest, Pueblo Bonito—4 or 5 stories high, in a floor plan exceeding 3 acres, and able to house about 1,000 people in its 800 rooms—is located at the base of the sandstone cliff that makes up the north wall of the canyon. Descriptive exhibits about the many archaeological sites in the monument are offered at the visitor center.

For further information write: Star Route, Bloomfield, N. Mex. 87413

Mountain landscape in Cibola National Forest (see page 188)

NEW MEXICO

CIBOLA NATIONAL FOREST
central New Mexico, headquarters at Albuquerque

This 1,660,631-acre forest located in numerous sections around Albuquerque includes parts of the **Datil, Gallina, Magdalena, Manzano, Sandia, San Mateo, Cebolleta,** and **Zuni mountains.** Because elevations range throughout the forest from 5,000 feet to 11,389 feet atop **Mount Taylor,** a variety of trees and other plant life can be found. Highlights of the forest include **Capillo Peak,** a 9,375-foot mountain accessible by car, **Bluewater** and **McGaffey lakes,** where fine fishing is available, and Sandia Ski Area. Accessible by an all-weather road and an aerial tramway, 10,678-foot **Sandia Crest** offers a spectacular panorama of Albuquerque, the **Rio Grande Valley,** and the many surrounding mountains. Also here is **Sandia Man Cave,** the home of hunters dating back 20,000 to 30,000 years.
For further information: Box 1826, Albuquerque, N. Mex. 87103

CITY OF ROCKS STATE PARK
22 miles northwest of Deming on U.S. 180 and 5 miles east on State 61

Located at an altitude of 5,000 feet above sea level in the desert of southwestern New Mexico, this 680-acre park is known for its unusual rock formations. Because of the way the rocks have eroded they appear to be metropolitan skyscrapers.

EL MORRO NATIONAL MONUMENT
43 miles west of Grant via State 53

Established in 1906, this 1,278-acre national monument protects an area of natural beauty and historical significance. This huge sandstone mesa, rising 200 feet above the surrounding valley, has served as a register of the desert. Through the centuries hundreds of travelers passed through the area and left inscriptions in the soft sandstone. El Morro, meaning "headland" or "bluff," was named by Spanish explorers—Don Juan de Oñate left the first Spanish inscription on April 16, 1605. The conquistadors were not here first, however, for ruins of Zuñi Indian pueblos have been found atop the bluff and prehistoric Indian petroglyphs are carved into the rock. After the United States occupation of Santa Fe in 1846, American army officers left their mark, as did the traders and settlers to follow. A self-guiding trail leads from the base of El Morro to the partially excavated ruins; a visitor center is at the start.
For further information: Superintendent, Ramah, N. Mex. 87321

Panoramic vista of the Enchanted Mesa

ENCHANTED MESA
3 miles northeast of Acoma on State 23

This stark, sandstone butte with rocky walls and sharp, jagged pinnacles rises 430 feet above the surrounding plains. According to Indian legend, ancestors of the Acomas lived on the top of the mesa, but the path down was closed either by a storm or an angry god, leaving the stranded people to die of starvation.

GILA NATIONAL FOREST
southwest New Mexico, headquarters at Silver City

Covering 2,694,471 acres in rugged mountain terrain, this forest features ocotillo and cactus at its lower elevations and juniper, pine, aspen, and spruce-fir forests at its higher regions. Special highlights here include the **Gila Wilderness**, a primitive area of steep canyons and timbered mesas in the **Mogollon Mountains**. The wilderness contains the site of the **Gila Cliff Dwellings National Monument**, where well-preserved prehistoric Indian ruins built into the natural cavities in a cliff can be seen. The **Gila** and **Black Range primitive areas**, 2 unspoiled mountain regions located in the Mogollon Mountains and the Black Range, feature rocky canyons and wild scenery in a land that once belonged to the Apaches. A 75-mile loop road beginning at Silver City offers the tourist a glimpse at the unusual desert-mountain terrain of the Southwest. A visitor center is located 43 miles north of Silver City on State 25 and 527.
Visitor center open daily June 15–Aug: 8–7; Sept–June 14: 8–5.
For further information write: 301 W College Ave, Silver City, N. Mex. 88061

HYDE MEMORIAL STATE PARK
8 miles northeast of Santa Fe on Hyde Park Road

This 350-acre park is located in the southern **Sangre de Cristo Mountains** at an elevation of 9,000 feet above sea level. From observation points on scenic drives that lead through the mountains, there are magnificent views of the **Rio Grande Valley**.

LAVA BEDS AND PERPETUAL ICE CAVES
25 miles southwest of Grant on State 53

Extending southwest through the valley between the **Oso** and **Zuni mountains**, these lava beds are among the largest in North America. Called "mal pais" by the Spanish, this fantastic landscape is considered to be one of the most formidable badlands in the country.

Within the lava beds are the Perpetual Ice Caves, located almost on top of the **Continental Divide** at 8,000 feet. The caves, lying in a volcanic sinkhole, are filled with aquamarine colored ice marked with dark horizontal stripes. The ice is formed by melting snow and rain and is insulated by air passing through underground channels. Nearby is **Bandera Crater,** a large inactive volcano that rises 500 feet above the surrounding valley. The lava beds are a Registered Natural Landmark.

Caves open daily. Admission: adults 85¢, children (6–11) 35¢

LINCOLN NATIONAL FOREST
southcentral New Mexico, headquarters at Alamogordo

Located in 3 sections, this 1,086,296-acre forest features dense stands of pine and fir in the **Jicarilla, Capitan,** and **Sacramento mountains.** The main attraction here is **White Mountain** (Sierra Blanca), an imposing peak whose 12,000-foot summit is located inside the Mescalero Apache Indian Reservation. Most of the mountain is preserved in the 31,171-acre **White Mountain Wilderness.** Here the mountain climbs from 6,000 feet above sea level to 11,400 feet—in this climb across 5 biological zones vegetation changes from desert grassland to subalpine terrain. A paved road and an enclosed gondola ride lead to the highest point in the wilderness and offer magnificent views of the surrounding scenic wonders. The wilderness also contains one of the largest deposits of molybdenum in the western hemisphere. The southern section of the forest is located in the scenic **Guadalupe Mountains.**

For further information write: Federal Building, Alamogordo, N. Mex. 88310

RIO GRANDE GORGE

For 70 miles of its 2,200-mile course—from just above the Colorado border south through New Mexico—the turbulent Rio Grande cuts a scenic gorge through layers of volcanic rock. As it passes into New Mexico the canyon is 1,300 feet wide and 200 feet deep. The next 48 miles of the river's course through its wildest section plus 4 miles of the tributary **Red River** have been set aside in the **Rio Grande Wild River**—the first such federally designated waterway in the country. In these 48 awesome and sometimes dangerous miles the river travels through unspoiled back country rich in wildlife and breathtaking, primitive beauty. Descending about 1,500 feet in its north-south journey, the Rio Grande is fed by many creeks on the east; however, no permanent streams enter from the west. Among the many scenic attractions to be seen along the river and from the trails along its banks (the Wild River also includes a fourth of a mile on either side of the river) are 10,093-foot **Ute Mountain,** 8,722-foot **Guadalupe Mountain, Cebolla Mesa, Big Arsenic Spring** (a cool spring gushing clear water at the astounding rate of 5,400 gallons per minute), and **Little Arsenic Spring.**

The gorge is about 4,000 feet from rim to rim and 800 feet deep when it is joined by the Red River. (The Red River enters through its own scenic gorge—1,300 feet wide and 800 feet deep.) A few miles below this confluence at **Manby Springs** is the Rio Grande Gorge High Bridge, a beautiful span 600 feet above the river and the only rim-level crossing. The Wild River segment continues until the spot where **Taos Creek** flows into the gorge through a picturesque chasm. From here the canyon, designated Rio Grande Gorge State Park, continues to its end at Velarde. Originally established in 1959 to protect the entire 70-mile stretch of the canyon, the state park now only includes that area not within federal jurisdiction.

SANTA FE NATIONAL FOREST
northcentral New Mexico, headquarters at Santa Fe

This 1,441,569-acre forest is divided into 2 sections by the **Rio Grande**. Dominating the eastern section is the southern **Sangre de Cristo Mountains**, where the major attraction is the **Pecos Wilderness**. Also located in Carson National Forest (*see*), this 167,416-acre wild area features **Truchas Peak** (13,102 feet), the second highest mountain in the state; the headwaters of the **Pecos River**; a 100-foot waterfall; countless lakes and over 150 miles of streams. The western section of the forest includes the **Jemez** and **San Pedro ranges** where elevations range from 10,000 to 12,000 feet. The **San Pedro Parks Wilderness** is on a 41,132-acre plateau of rolling mountaintops featuring open meadows and dense stands of spruce trees.

For further information write: Box 1689, Santa Fe, N. Mex. 87501

SHIPROCK PEAK
Navajo Indian Reservation, southwest of Shiprock off U.S. 666

Important in Navajo mythology (the Navajo called it "Sa-Bit-tai," or winged rock), this impressive peak stands 1,865 feet above the surrounding desert and dominates the landscape for miles. The rock (7,178 feet above sea level) is a huge volcanic plug pushed up through the earth's crust by internal pressure and eroded into its present shape after it cooled. Early pioneers probably named the peak for its resemblance to a ship under sail.

VALLE GRANDE
12 miles west of Los Alamos on State 4

Said to be the largest measured crater in the world, Valle Grande covers 176 square miles and rises 500 feet from floor to rim. Long believed to be a valley because of its tremendous size, the crater features tree-covered mountains on its slopes and grassy, grazing fields at its bottom.

VALLEY OF FIRES STATE PARK
3 miles west of Carrizozo on U.S. 380

Located in the volcano-created terrain called "mal pais," or badlands, by the Spanish, this park features many interesting lava formations. Geologists believe that this is the most recent flow in the United States (2,000 to 5,000 years ago)—much newer than the one at Grants (*see Lava Beds and Perpetual Ice Caves*).

WHITE SANDS NATIONAL MONUMENT
15 miles southwest of Alamogordo on U.S. 70 and 82

Located in the **Tularosa Basin**, a 100-mile-long area lying between the **Sacramento Mountains** on the east and the **San Andres Mountains** on the west, this national monument is a part of the largest known gypsum desert in the world. Once a plateau, the basin was created hundreds of centuries ago when the earth's crust settled by a geological process called graben faulting. From the air, these everchanging dunes that have accumulated over centuries appear to be a huge, rippling ocean. Because it is composed of gypsum, instead of the usual particles of gray, tan, and buff rock, the sand here is white. A visitor center offers exhibits explaining how this basin was formed and how the gypsum from the surrounding mountains reached the desert. A region of exquisite and unusual beauty, White Sands is best seen from the loop road that leads from the visitor center past some of the most interesting spots. Of particular note are the plants that have adapted to their environment.

For further information write: Box 458, Alamogorda, N. Mex. 88310

NEW YORK

ADIRONDACK MOUNTAINS

This famous resort region is a vast expanse of windswept peaks complemented by numerous lake-studded valleys. The range is bounded on the east by the **Lake Champlain** (*see also* Vermont) and **Lake George** regions. From here the mountains descend gradually to the **Saint Lawrence Valley** in the northwest and the **Black River Valley** in the southwest. Their southward extension stretches from foothills near the Quebec border to the **Mohawk River Valley**. Most of it falls within the **Adirondack Forest Preserve**, a National Historic Landmark—the first state preserve established in 1885—covering 3 million acres. **Mount Marcy**, rising 5,344 feet near Lake Placid Village, is New York's highest peak. It heads the list of the 46 Adirondack peaks that are 4,000 or more feet above sea level. Other high peaks are 5,112-foot **Mount MacIntyre**, 4,918-foot **Mount Haystack**, 4,920-foot **Mount Skylight**, 4,872-foot **Whiteface Mountain**, 4,185-foot **Wolf Jaw Mountain**, and **Blue Mount** which rises 3,759 feet above **Blue Mountain Lake**. Sparkling 32-mile-long Lake George, dotted with some 200 islands, most in the **Narrows**, is a top tourist attraction. It is connected to Lake Champlain by a 3-mile-long stream called **La Chute River**. A magnificent view of Champlain, the valley, and the Green Mountains of Vermont (*see*) may be admired from **Mount Defiance**. Other noted lakes in the region include **Lake Placid** and **Indian, Schroon, Cranberry, Big** and **Little Tupper, Big Moose, Long, Upper** and **Lower Saranac,** and **Raquette** lakes, as well as the **Fulton** chain. Another scenic Adirondack area is **Wilmington Notch** between Wilmington and Lake Placid. Nearby is **High Falls Gorge**, a great ravine cut deep into the base of Whiteface Mountain by the **Ausable River**. A network of bridges and paths permits one to admire the gorge, with its rapids, falls, potholes, and variegated rock strata. The Adirondacks contain the sources of several rivers: the mighty **Hudson** which rises here as **Opalescent River** in tiny **Lake Tear of the Clouds** near Mount Marcy; the Ausable River, which flows to Lake Champlain; the Black River which flows to **Lake Ontario;** and various tributaries of the Saint Lawrence. The reservation has 37 campsites and hundreds of miles of well-marked trails, many leading to mountain tops.

ALLEGENY STATE PARK
from Salamanca south to Pennsylvania border, access from State 17

Covering 60,480 acres of Appalachian highland within the bend of the **Allegheny River,** this is the state's largest park. It has some 70 miles of spring-fed mountain streams and a dozen miles of woodland routes. Wildlife is plentiful, an interesting example being the giant hellbender—a nocturnal, aquatic salamander.

AUSABLE CHASM
at Ausable Chasm, on U.S. 9 from exit 34 or 35 of I-87

The mighty sandstone cliffs, rising as high as 200 feet, of this 1½-mile-long chasm were formed an estimated 500 million years ago. The **Ausable River,** created by melting glacial ice, roars and plunges 50 miles from its headwaters at **Mount Marcy** to **Lake Champlain.** Part of its course flowed over a fault in the bedrock, and over the centuries the original fracture was carved deeper and deeper, eventually creating Ausable Chasm. On foot, one can admire **Rainbow** and **Horseshoe falls** and interesting stone formations such as

Left: Niagara Falls. Right: Elephant's Head in Ausable Chasm. Below: Whiteface Mountain in the Adirondack Forest Preserve

193

Pulpit Rock, Elephant's Head, Jacob's Ladder, Jacob's Well, the Cathedral, and Table Rock. The rest of the trip is made by boat through the Grand Flume, past the Sentry Box and the Broken Needle, and then through rapids, a whirlpool basin, and more rapids. *Open May–Oct: daily 8:30–6. Boat trip: adults $2.65, children (6–12) $1.15*

CATSKILL MOUNTAINS
southeast New York, about 10 miles west of the Hudson River

The Catskills, a part of the Appalachians, occupy a region of rolling, wooded hills and deep gorges known locally as "cloves." The range descends abruptly to the **Hudson River** on the east and extends north to the **Mohawk River Valley**, where the fossil-rich **Helderberg Mountains** form the northern escarpment of the plateau. Its rounded ridges, which rise over 4,000 feet, were once sedimentary rock covering an ancient ocean bottom. This floor was lifted up as a vast plateau and was eventually carved into valleys and peaks by erosion and stream action. Glaciers did the rest, gouging out clefts, leveling some ridges, and making others razor-sharp. The highest points in the Catskills are 4,204-foot **Slide Mountain**, west of Kingston, and 4,025-foot **Hunter Mountain**, west of Catskill. Two of the most scenic mountain passes are **Kaaterskill Clove**, adjoining the village of Haines Falls, and narrow, wild **Stony Clove**, which leads north from Phoenicia. The range is drained by headstreams of the **Delaware River** and by **Esopus, Schoharie, Roundout,** and **Catskill creeks**, whose waters play a vital role in New York City's water supply. Much of the region falls within the **Catskill Forest Preserve**, which covers almost 250,000 acres and offers many hiking trails. Some of the state's best fishing is available in **Beaverkill, Neversink,** and **Willowemoc streams**. This very popular resort region is the locale of the Rip Van Winkle legend.

ELLENVILLE FAULT-ICE CAVES
Ice Caves Mountain, 6 miles east of Ellenville off State 52

The area in which these caves lie is composed of thick beds of shale overlaid with quartz conglomerate. Ancient undercutting by **Roundout Creek** probably caused the quartz to slip and resulted in large, exposed faults, and ice caves developed where the fault crevices were coated with talus and glacial till. Nature trails lead to these snow- and ice-filled caves, past interesting rock formations to a mountain lookout. Registered Natural Landmark
Open Apr–Oct: daily 8–8. Admission: adults $1.85, children 75¢

Fishing on the Upper Hudson River in the Catskill region

Sand dunes on Fire Island National Seashore

FINGER LAKES
westcentral New York, roughly between Genesco and Syracuse

The 6 most important of these long, narrow, glacially formed lakes from west to east are, **Canandaigua, Keuka, Seneca, Cayuga, Owasco,** and **Skaneateles.** Seneca, covering about 67 square miles, is the largest, and Cayuga, stretching 38 miles, is the longest. They are situated in a scenic, valley-filled region with deep gorges, attractive native vegetation, rugged rock formations, grottoes, waterfalls, and many vineyards. It also has 13 state parks. **Taughannock Falls** park, on the western shore of Cayuga Lake, features the highest waterfall east of the Rockies. It cascades 215 feet in a secluded, mile-long glen with sides rising 350 to 400 feet. **Watkins Glen** park, at the head of Seneca Lake, has one of America's most impressive wonders—a valley, which has drops of some 700 feet within 2 miles. There are also 18 waterfalls (the loveliest is **Rainbow Falls**) and cliffs rising 200 feet. **Chimney Bluffs** park features unusual glacially formed bluffs along **Lake Ontario.** In **Buttermilk Falls** park, near Ithaca, **Buttermilk Creek** drops over 500 feet in a series of rapids and cascades. Nearby is Robert H. Treman State Park, which has glacial potholes, a deep gorge boring 2.5 miles into a hillside, and **Enfield Glen** with 12 picturesque falls, especially **Lucifer Falls.** **Fillmore Glen** park, near Moravia, has forested slopes dotted with waterfalls and ravines.

FIRE ISLAND NATIONAL SEASHORE
off south shore of Long Island, accessible by ferry from Bay Shore, Sayville, and Patchogue

Of all the coastline regions in the environs of New York City, Fire Island alone remains comparatively unspoiled and roadless. The largest remaining reach of barrier beach in the area, it extends 32 miles from Robert Moses State Park on the west to **Moriches Inlet** on the east and is ½-mile to less than 200 yards wide. Most of it is included in the national seashore, but private property, established communities, and the parks on either end (both accessible by parkway from Long Island) are excluded. Its Atlantic coastline, a huge expanse of dunes and the wide **Great South Beach,** has fine quartz sand highlighted by swirls of dark red sand and black magnetite. The plant communities spread over the marshy tracts and knolls of the interdune lands are particularly important since they alone hold

Genesee River Gorge

the sand in place against wind and moving water. The most common are poison ivy, wild rose, and beach plum. The western part of the island contains the finest thickets and forests—the best woodland is in the **Sunken Forest,** just east of Point O' Woods community. It is thickly vegetated with large serviceberry, black gum, and gnarled holly. The national seashore is rich in wildlife. It has grassy wetlands where long-legged herons stalk, tangled thickets filled with deer, salt marshes that are havens to wild geese, and the dunes, where red foxes sometimes forage. On **Great South Bay** side, striking marsh and bay vegetation serves as a valuable habitat for all sorts of mammals and birds. Terns nest on the bay islands and blackcrowned night herons nest in the pitch pine and other bayside forests. The waters surrounding the island are rich in fish and shellfish. The seashore is still under development, but ranger services are available at various points along the island—Smith Point West, the Sunken Forest, Sailor's Haven, and Watch Hill.

For further information write: Box 229, Patchogue, LI, N.Y. 11772

GENESEE RIVER GORGE
Portageville, on the Genesee River, in Letchworth State Park
The showpiece of this park is winding, 17-mile long **Genesee River Gorge,** sometimes called the Grand Canyon of the East, with precipitous walls rising as high as 600 feet. With the plunge and spray of its 3 falls—one 107 feet high—and the forest cover of its brink and sides, it is a scenic delight. It was created by the erosive action of the river upon strata of horizontally bedded Devonian rock. From *Inspiration Point* overlook there is a stunning view of the gorge and the **Upper** and **Middle Falls.**

GILBOA FOSSIL TREE STUMPS
In the village of Gilboa, just west of the bridge over **Schoharie Creek,** is a group of fossil tree stumps representing the oldest known

trees on earth. They were seed-bearing tree ferns that grew in the shoreline mud of the ancient Devonian Sea, which covered a huge area west of the present Catskill Mountains (see).

HOWE CAVERNS
at Howes Caves, 1¾ miles northwest of State 7, then 2 miles north
Visitors descend by elevators to these caves, which are between 160 and 200 feet below ground, and which contain an underground lake and a prehistoric ocean bed. The **Styx**, a subterranean river, winds through them. The caverns have many strange rock formations, such as **Titan's Temple**, a pagodalike stalagmite.
Open May 31–Sept. 6: daily 8–8; rest of year 9–6, closed holidays in winter. Boat trips: $2.50–3, children (4–10) half fare

LAKES CHAMPLAIN, GEORGE, AND PLACID. *See* ADIRONDACK MOUNTAINS

LONG ISLAND
Running parallel to the New York and Connecticut coastlines, this island is the site of many well-known resorts, historic communities, and some of the world's most beautiful beaches. It is bounded on the east by **Peconic** and **Gardiners bays**, on the south by the **Atlantic Ocean**, on the west by the **East River** and the **Narrows** of **New York Bay**, and on the north by **Long Island Sound**, a famous yachting center. There is a dramatic difference between the topography of its north and south shores. Its indented north shore has many bays and harbors, especially in the western section, separated from one another by moderately wooded peninsulas, known locally as "necks." The north shore, characterized also by many small irregular hills with swamp- and pond-filled areas between them, marks the southernmost limit of the area reached by the ice sheet. The land south of this moraine, a flat outwash plain, was never covered with ice. It is composed mainly of sand and gravel, sloping gradually to the sea; its sand bars and spits extend nearly all the way along the south shore from Rockaway to **Montauk Point**. About 75 miles of it is a barrier beach dotted by several inlets and sheltering large, shallow, constantly shifting bays, notably **Jamaica, Great South, Moriches**, and **Shinnecock**. This coast is also lined with resort centers such as Fire Island with its national seashore (see). Long Island also has many state parks including one at famous **Jones Beach** with its magnificent white sand. **Orient Point** park, on the northerly fluke of eastern Long Island, contains a bird sanctuary frequented by thousands of terns, gulls, and shorebirds. Montauk Point State Park is on the island's most easterly tip, famous for deep-sea fishing. A scenic highway connects this park with **Hither Hills** park, about 8 miles to the west, featuring acres of woodlands, high sand dunes, and ocean beach. Among this region's many other parks is Wildwood, situated on the high bluffs of the north shore.

MENDON PONDS PARK
11 miles south of Rochester
The terrain of this entire park is the product of the Wisconsin Ice Age. Here, the Mendon Ponds form a chain of 5 small lakes in what was once a drainage basin for glacial waters. In places the land has been modified by erosion and human activity, but kames, eskers, kettleholes, and other glacial formations are still clearly identifiable. There are also examples of bogs, ponds, swamps, and upland forest.
Registered Natural Landmark

NEW YORK

MIANUS RIVER GORGE
Bedford vicinity, from Merritt Parkway, 8 miles north on Long Ridge Road
This 207-acre tract includes the most rugged portion of Mianus River Gorge. It features a superb forest of hemlock, some of which are 300 years old, as well as 500 species of trees, shrubs, and smaller plants. The gorge is unsurpassed in the East as an area in which natural conditions have been relatively untouched by man. Registered Natural Landmark

NATURAL BRIDGE AND CAVERNS
town of Natural Bridge, on State 3
These amazing caverns, formed by water erosion, may be viewed on a ½-mile boat tour on the underground **Indian River.**
Open June–Oct: daily 8:30–5:30. Admission: adults $1.50, children (5–11) 75¢

NATURAL STONE BRIDGE AND CAVES
2½ miles north of Pottersville off U.S. 9; from I-87, take exit 26
A well-marked nature trail leads through and past a series of waterfalls, underground waterways, and interesting rock formations. These include lighted caves, grottoes, potholes, and a natural arch called "The Bridge of God."
Open daily: May–Oct. 15, 9–6; July–Aug. 8–dark. Admission: $1.85, children (6–12), 85¢

NIAGARA FALLS REGION
This scenic area is bordered on 3 sides by the waters of **Lake Erie,** the **Niagara River,** and **Lake Ontario.** Among its several major parks is **Niagara Reservation,** a National Historic Landmark covering 430 acres. Here the Niagara River, actually an inland strait running for some 36 miles between Lake Ontario and Lake Erie, forms the boundary between the United States and Canada. Since Lake Ontario is 326 feet lower than Erie, the river drops this distance between the lakes. Centuries of erosive action have formed the gorge through which it plummets. Constant undercutting has caused Niagara Falls to move 7 miles upstream from Lake Ontario since it came into existence an estimated 10,000 years ago. The falls are still moving at the rate of about 4 feet a year, and the deep gorge marks Niagara's successive retreats. There are actually 2 main cataracts: 182-foot **American Falls** and 176-foot **Canadian** or **Horseshoe Falls,** respectively some 1,000 and 2,500 feet wide. (Since the opening of hydroelectric stations on both sides of the river, the height of the falls is constantly changing. As the stations use water, the level of the pools below the waterfalls varies as much as 30 feet.) American Falls gets only about 10 per cent of the flow, which plunges into **Maid of the Mist Pool;** the other 90 per cent roars over Horseshoe. The volume is impressive, about 4 million gallons per minute. Lovely, wooded **Goat Island,** connected by bridges with smaller islands, notably the **Three Sisters,** divides the falls and offers vistas of both. **Bridal Veil Falls** is separated from the main falls by **Luna Island.** Another scenic attraction is **Cave of the Winds,** a natural water-carved chamber behind American Falls. Recently built Horseshoe Falls Gorge Walkway leads from Cave of the Winds to **Terrapin Point** below Horseshoe Falls and offers a spectacular view. Other state parks in the Niagara region include Beaver Island and Buckhorn, both on **Grand Island** in the Niagara River. Whirlpool State Park is in the northwestern section of the city of Niagara Falls. It features raging **Whirlpool Rapids** and the swirling **Whirl-**

pool, both about 3 miles north of the Falls. Here, relentless erosion by the turbulent waters has cut 300 feet into the rock. As water emerges from the narrow gorge it makes a complete turn on itself before it roars on to Lake Ontario. The Grand Island Parkways and Robert Moses State Parkway serve the region.

OTSEGO LAKE
28 miles southeast of Utica

The Glimmerglass Lake of James Fenimore Cooper's stories, Otsego lies in a beautiful hill and forest setting. Glimmerglass State Park is on its north end in the **Hyde Bay** area.

PALISADES INTERSTATE PARK

The New York section of this park (*see also* New Jersey) comprises a chain of parks along the west shore of the **Hudson River Valley** between the New Jersey line and **Bear Mountain.** Bear Mountain State Park, 5 miles south of West Point, features 1,314-foot Bear Mountain, whose summit is accessible by trail or by the *George W. Perkins Memorial Drive.* It is traversed by a portion of the *Appalachian Trail,* as are several other parks in the Interstate group. These include Harriman and Tallman Mountain state parks. The Palisades Interstate Highway, which runs 38 scenic miles between George Washington Bridge and Bear Mountain, links the parks.

PETRIFIED GARDENS
3 miles west of Saratoga Springs, via State 29

This site features a fossil reef preserving the first plants that grew under the Cambrian Sea, which in prehistoric times covered most of New York State. Existing 500 million years ago, this calcareous algae called cryptozoon represents an important event in the evolution of plantlife. Because of the concentric structure of the individual plants, the exposure is impressive even to the lay observer. A circular, self-guided tour leads over this reef with its deep glacially carved crevices and potholes. Registered Natural Landmark *Open June–Sept: daily 9–6. Admission: adults $1.50, children 50¢*

TACONIC STATE PARK
east of State 22 between Millerton and Hillsdale

One of the many parks preserving the natural beauty of the **Hudson River Valley,** Taconic is divided into 2 main divisions located on the side of the **Taconic Mountain Range.** The **Copake Falls** area, with its pine-tree forest, is a hiker's paradise. One of its many trails leads to Bash Bish Falls in Massachusetts (*see*).

THOUSAND ISLANDS
northern New York and southern Canada, in the Saint Lawrence River

This group of over 1,700 small islands is situated in the upper reaches of the **Saint Lawrence** between Cape Vincent and Ogdensburg. Some islands belong to Canada, some to the United States, and others to individuals. The group is actually formed by a very low ridge of the **Adirondack Mountains** that cuts through northern Jefferson County and crosses the Saint Lawrence River. Some are merely projecting rocks topped by a single tree, others are forested tufts, and several are large enough to support entire villages. The region, noted as a recreational center, contains 26 state parks. These include Robert Moses on **Barnhart Island** in the Saint Lawrence, Jacques Cartier and Keewaydin, both on the shore of the river, and **Mary Island** and **Wellesley Island** parks.

NORTH CAROLINA

BLOWING ROCK
2 miles south of Blowing Rock on U.S. 321

This large stone cliff, which overhangs **John's River Gorge,** is so named because light objects thrown over it return to the sender when upsurging air currents are present in the gorge.
Open daily: 7-7. Admission: 60¢, children (under 12) 25¢

BLUE RIDGE PARKWAY. *See* VIRGINIA

CAPE HATTERAS NATIONAL SEASHORE
Outer Banks, headquarters at Manteo, Roanoke Island

Extending from Whalebone Junction south and southwest to **Ocracoke Inlet,** this national seashore preserves 45 square miles of Outer Banks *(see)* beach land. It is divided into 4 sections: **Bodie, Hatteras,** and **Ocracoke** (where the notorious Blackbeard was killed in 1718) islands, each with a visitor center, and the **Pea Island National Wildlife Refuge.** Formerly separated from Hatteras Island by New Inlet, Pea Island is now part of Hatteras. Over 300 species of birds have been recorded within the seashore, including snow geese, Canada geese, whistling swans, and all the many species of duck found on the Carolina coast. The landscape is varied, with wildflowers, shrubbery, marsh grasses, and beach grasses stabilizing the dunes; live oak and loblolly pine are found in the **Buxton Woods** on Hatteras Island. A paved road runs the length of the seashore, except at **Hatteras Inlet** where there is a free ferry. A toll ferry runs between Ocracoke and **Cedar Island,** where a road provides access to the mainland.
For further information write: Box 457, Manteo, N.C. 27954

CAPE LOOKOUT NATIONAL SEASHORE
Outer Banks, headquarters at Beaufort

Authorized in 1966, this national seashore consists of 3 undeveloped barrier islands on the lower Outer Banks *(see)*—**Portsmouth Island, Core Banks** terminating in **Cape Lookout,** and **Shackleford Banks.** They extend for 58 miles from **Ocracoke Inlet** on the north to **Beaufort Inlet** on the south. They feature long, lonely stretches of ocean beach, dunes, maritime forestland, and extensive salt marshes— all showing little influence of man. No federal facilities are available yet, but there is summer ferry service from Harker's Island.
For further information write: Box 177, Beaufort, N.C. 28516

CHIMNEY ROCK PARK
25 miles southeast of Asheville, via U.S. 74 and 64 and Route 9

A giant granite column, used as a landmark by the Indians, Chimney Rock rises sharply 315 feet above its base and towers above the emerald waters of **Lake Lure.** It stands at the end of **Hickory Nut Gorge,** carved by the **Rocky Broad River,** and its summit may be reached via a 500-foot trail or by a remarkable elevator built inside the column. Other natural attractions located nearby are **Moonshiner's Cave, Needle's Eye,** the **Subway Grotto,** and **Pulpit Rock.** Above Chimney Rock are the **Opera Box,** a natural observation ledge, and **Devil's Head,** a rocky outcrop. From the top there is a breathtaking 75-mile vista of rolling, forest-clad mountains blending into the Piedmont. Three trails lead to **Hickory Nut Falls,** one of the highest waterfalls in the East, dropping some 400 feet.
Open daily: 8-sundown. Admission: adults $1.50, children (6-11) 75¢

Left: sanderlings on Cape Hatteras National Seashore. Right: Whitewater Falls in Nantahala National Forest. Below: Looking Glass Rock in Pisgah N.F.

NORTH CAROLINA

CLIFFS OF THE NEUSE STATE PARK
14 miles southeast of Goldsboro on State 111

Located on the banks of the Neuse River, this park features a 90-foot cliff filled with fossils dating back millions of years. It also contains a mixture of herbaceous plants, trees, and shrubs.

CROATAN NATIONAL FOREST
east North Carolina, headquarters at New Bern

Situated between **Neuse** and **White Oak rivers** in the heart of North Carolina's Coastal Plain, this 156,000-acre forest is particularly interesting from an ecological point of view. Approximately half of it is covered by loblolly and longleaf pine. The other half is pocosin (from an Indian word meaning "swamp on a hill")—a large flat swamp on a slightly higher elevation than the surrounding area. It is composed of organic soil ranging from a few inches to several feet thick. This organic layer holds water like a giant sponge, and it keeps accumulating because leaves, grass, and other plant litter do not decompose completely. Due to the peculiar soil-moisture-mineral relationship, plant growth is stunted in pocosin areas, which are covered with low brush and dwarfed trees. The forest also supports picturesque bald cypress trees and rare plants such as the venus flytrap and pitcher plant.

For further information write: Box 3355, New Bern, N.C. 28561

DISMAL SWAMP. *See* **VIRGINIA**

GRANDFATHER MOUNTAIN
about 2 miles east of Linville via U.S. 221, then toll road

Named because of its profile as seen from a distance, this 5,964-foot peak is the highest in the **Blue Ridge Mountains**. A famous mile-high pedestrian suspension bridge leads from the toll road to its summit. According to the U.S. Geological Survey, the mountain has rock formations that are at least a billion years old (among the oldest in the world) as well as gold deposits in 4 places on its slopes. The *Yonahlossee Trail* (U.S. 221), lined with a profusion of purple rhododendron, passes under the mountain on its way to Blowing Rock (*see*) 21 miles away.

Open Apr–Nov 15: daily 8–6. Admission: adults $2, children (6–12) $1

GREAT SMOKY MOUNTAINS NATIONAL PARK. *See* **TENNESSEE**

HAMMOCKS BEACH STATE PARK
4 miles south of Swansboro via State 24 to ferry landing

One of the most beautiful seashore areas in the state, this park features an unmarred beach and unusually high sand dunes. The great **Atlantic Ocean** sweeping out to the horizon and the marshes lying between the island and the mainland add to its majesty.

Free ferry operates June 1–Labor Day

HANGING ROCK STATE PARK
4 miles northwest of Danbury via local paved roads

Nestled in the **Sauratown Mountains,** this park offers rugged mountain terrain, sparkling streams, waterfalls, and a profusion of flowering shrubs, notably laurel, rhododendron, and stewartia. It encompasses Hanging Rock and **Moore's Knob,** from whose summits one can look across the **Dan River Valley** to the **Blue Ridge Mountains** of North Carolina and Virginia.

Linville Gorge

JONES LAKE STATE PARK
4 miles north of Elizabethtown via State 242

Like several others in the vicinity, 224-acre Jones Lake is said to have been formed by the impact of meteorites on the earth's surface. The park also features a Coastal Plain forest harboring good examples of upland shrub bogs, or pocosins.

JUMP-OFF ROCK
5 miles west of Hendersonville via 5th Avenue

Long used as a lookout point by the Indians, this rock is on the summit of **Jump-Off Mountain.** Accessible by trail and road, its view includes much of Pisgah National Forest *(see).*

LINVILLE CAVERNS
18 miles north of Marion, 4 miles south of Blue Ridge Parkway on U.S. 221

These caverns, lying deep under **Humpback Mountain** at the head of **Linville Valley,** served as a hiding place for deserters during the Civil War. They feature interesting stalactite and stalagmite formations, notably the **Frozen Waterfall** and **Natural Bridge.** A path leads along a subterranean, trout-filled stream.
Open daily: 7–sundown. Admission: $1

MORROW MOUNTAIN STATE PARK
7 miles east of Albemarle via State 27 and 740

Situated on the west bank of the **Pee Dee River,** this park covers 4,135 acres in the **Uwharrie Mountains,** part of what remains of the **Ocoee Mountains,** one of the oldest mountain ranges in America. It is bordered on 2 sides by **Lake Tillery,** and its lush green farmlands and heavy natural growth of pines and hardwoods make it an especially scenic spot in the Piedmont. The summits of **Morrow, Tater Top,** and **Sugar Loaf mountains** afford magnificent views.

MOUNT MITCHELL STATE PARK
33 miles northeast of Asheville via the Blue Ridge Parkway

Rising to an altitude of 6,694 feet, Mount Mitchell in the **Black Mountains** is the highest peak east of the Mississippi. Its slopes contain excellent stands of Frazer's fir and red spruce; black bear, deer, and wildcat frequent the area.

NAGS HEAD
just east of Roanoke Island on Outer Banks

This popular ocean-front resort was probably named after the highest point on the Scilly Islands—the last sight early voyagers had of their native England. According to legend, however, it acquired its name from an unscrupulous practice of its early inhabitants. They used to attach lanterns to the necks of ponies and march the animals along the high dunes. The swinging lights simulated boat lights, and captains were deceived into running aground on the shoals, where their cargoes would be commandeered. Nags Head is the site of **Jockey Ridge**, the loftiest sand dune on the Atlantic coast, towering 138 feet above the sea. Nearby are many other constantly shifting dunes such as **Engagement Hill**, all exceeding 100 feet in height.

NANTAHALA NATIONAL FOREST
southwest North Carolina, headquarters at Asheville

This 420,000-acre region of mountainous forestland and rushing streams gives rise to 10 rivers that feed the **Tennessee** and **Savannah rivers** among others. Its name—a Cherokee word meaning "Land of the Noonday Sun"—aptly describes its many deep, narrow valleys that receive the sun's direct rays only at noon. The forest is traversed by some 80 miles of the *Appalachian Trail.* Among its many points of interest are scenic waterfalls, notably **Glen** and **Whitewater falls**, where the **Whitewater River** plunges 400 feet in a series of spectacular falls and cascades, as well as **Cullasaja, Bridal Veil**, and **Dry falls** in **Cullasaja River Gorge**. **Nantahala Gorge** is 8 miles long with sides rising as high as 2,000 feet. The forest's many lakes include **Cliffside, Fontana, Santeetlah, Nantahala, Hiwassee, Cherokee**, and **Chatuge**, some created by the TVA dams. The area also embraces many mountains, including the **Cowee, Nantahala, Snowbird, Tusquitee**, and **Valley River ranges,** 5,498-foot **Standing Indian Mountain, Jackrabbit Mountain**, and **Wayah Bald**, whose panorama includes the **Blue Ridge** and the **Great Smoky mountains.** The forest contains (across

Left to right: dogwood blossoms; Cape Lookout National Seashore; Nantahala Lake

the Snowbirds from Andrews to Robbinsville) a segment of the "Trail of Tears," the route followed in 1838 by members of the Cherokee Nation when the United States government forcibly relocated them to Oklahoma, nearly 1,000 miles away. There are about 600 miles of roads and trails and 17 recreation areas, including **Joyce Kilmer Memorial Forest**, a 3,800-acre virgin wilderness. *For further information write: Box 2750. Asheville, N.C. 2880*

OUTER BANKS, CAROLINA BANKS, OR THE BANKS

Stretching along the coast for about 120 miles, the Outer Banks are a chain of sandy barrier islands separating the various sounds (notably **Currituck, Albemarle, Roanoke, Croatan,** and **Pamlico**) from the **Atlantic Ocean.** They vary in width from a few hundred yards to a few miles, and are noted for their resorts, such as Nags Head, and for dangerous capes, such as **Fear, Lookout,** and **Hatteras** (*see Cape Hatteras and Cape Lookout National Seashores*). The area has long been known as the Graveyard of the Atlantic because of the numerous vessels that have been wrecked on the seaward shoals, built up by the violent offshore meeting of opposite-moving air currents. The landscape of the banks is constantly undergoing changes because of wind and wave action. For instance, inlets connecting the ocean and the sounds are always appearing and disappearing—some existing for less than 100 years. The Outer Banks are also extremely rich in history. The **Fort Raleigh National Historic Site** at Manteo on Roanoke Island commemorates the short-lived, first English colony in the New World, established in 1585. The **Wright Brothers National Memorial** at Kill Devel Hills near Kitty Hawk on Bodie Island marks the spot where in 1903 Wilbur and Orville Wright made their first flight in a power-driven plane.

PETTIGREW STATE PARK
9 miles south of Creswell via U.S. 64 and state road

This park is on the shore of 16,000-acre **Lake Phelps,** a wildlife sanctuary surrounded by a magnificent growth of cypress.

PILOT MOUNTAIN STATE PARK
24 miles north of Winston-Salem via U.S. 52

Located in the Piedmont Plateau, Pilot Mountain rises some 1,500 feet above the surrounding countryside. This large quartzite monadnock was called the "Great Guide" by the Indians, who used it as a landmark. The view from its summit extends over 3,000 square miles.

NORTH CAROLINA

PISGAH NATIONAL FOREST
west North Carolina, headquarters at Asheville

Situated in the **Southern Appalachian Mountains**, 478,000-acre Pisgah is primarily a hardwood forest. It contains some 60 miles of the *Appalachian Trail* and a segment of the Blue Ridge Parkway (*see Virginia*). Among its many attractions are the **Craggy Mountain Scenic Area**, a rugged tract with waterfalls and virgin stands of eastern hemlock; and **Linville Gorge Wilderness**, which surrounds one of the wildest gorges in the east. Its steep walls enclose the **Linville River** for 12 miles, and from a shelf of rock called **Wiseman's View**, one can see the spectacular horizon of its eastern rim. The gorge, which is just below **Linville Falls**, is formed by **Linville Mountain** and **Jonas Ridge**, noted for odd rock formations such as **Sitting Bear, Hawksbill,** and **Table Rock mountains**, and the **Chimneys. Looking Glass Falls**, an unbroken rush of white water some 30 feet wide, crash 60 feet down a sheer rock face into a pool below. Nearby is **Looking Glass Rock**, a granite monolith so named because its sides glisten with water that seeps down from its forested, 3,967-foot top. A 3-mile foot trail leads from Davidson River Road up the rock's south side; its nearly vertical north flank has a sheer drop of some 400 feet. Another attraction is smooth-surfaced **Sliding Rock**, which is about 60 feet long and is always covered with water. With the pool below it, the rock is an ideal natural slide. **Roan Mountain Recreation Area** boasts 6,286-foot Roan Mountain, famed for its outstanding summer cover of purple rhododendron. **Shining Rock Wilderness**, high in the **Balsam Mountains** and accessible only by trail, features **Shining Rock Mountain**, an outcrop of white quartz. Other popular spots include **Bald** and **Black mountains, Coontree Creek, Lake Powhatan,** and **Sycamore Flats.** The **Pine Beds Area** has a visitor center commemorating America's first school of forestry, founded in 1898.

For further information write: Box 2750, Asheville, N.C. 28802

STONE MOUNTAIN STATE PARK
5 miles west of Roaring Gap via U.S. 21

This undeveloped park has several streams and hiking trails. It features unique Stone Mountain, an oval-shaped granite pluton, over 500 feet high and 3 miles in circumference at its base.

WEYMOUTH WOODS–SANDHILLS NATURE PRESERVE
1 mile southeast of Southern Pines via U.S. 1 and 501

This 403-acre wooded tract is situated in the heart of the famous **Sandhills** region of North Carolina. This area occupies nearly 1 million acres on part of the western boundary of the Coastal Plain. It consists of a series of alternating flat-topped, sandy ridges and relatively broad, flat valleys. Recent studies indicate that the Sandhills were formed from sediments of clay, sand, and gravel that were carried by streams and rivers from the Piedmont section and deposited at the edge or inland vicinity of the ancient sea that covered the Coastal Plain millions of years ago. Since then, exposure, weathering, and erosion have formed the ridges. The landscape of Weymouth Woods is characteristic of the Sandhills region. The ridges, covered with longleaf pine and turkey oak, drop into hardwood swamps in the valleys. Moist, narrow thickets, known locally as branchheads, are found on parts of the hillsides. The preserve, traversed by **James Creek**, has almost 400 varieties of plants.

NORTH DAKOTA

BADLANDS. *See* **THEODORE ROOSEVELT NATIONAL MEMORIAL PARK**

BURNING VEIN OF COAL
15 miles northwest of Amidon off U.S. 85

The burning vein of coal is a natural phenomenon caused when impure lignite coal is ignited by lightening or some other natural cause. The lignite is made up of layers of sedimentary rock deposited in streams and lakes and the vegetation that later grew over it. How long this particular vein, which lies some 30 feet below the surface, has been burning is unknown, but it was ignited before settlers came to the Dakotas. On the bottom of the valley in which the vein lies and on its western slope is a stand of columnar junipers —15-foot, bright-green trees found nowhere else in the state.

CUSTER NATIONAL FOREST. *See* MONTANA

LAKE METIGOSHE STATE PARK
10 miles north of Bottineau off State 14

This 700-acre park, inhabited by white-tailed deer, is located in the scenic **Turtle Mountains,** on a large plateau known for its dense stands of deciduous trees, rolling hills, and picturesque lakes. The plateau, which extends into southern Manitoba, is 2,000 feet above sea level and varies from 3 to 400 feet above the surrounding plains. Lake Metigoshe, one of the largest and most scenic of the Turtle Mountain lakes, features a 70-mile shoreline that reaches across the border to Canada.

Left: Little Missouri River. Right: columnar junipers growing near Amidon

NORTH DAKOTA

LONG LAKE NATIONAL WILDLIFE REFUGE
4 miles east of Moffit off U.S. 83

Located on a lake 20 miles long, this refuge covers over 22,000 acres on the Central flyway. Migratory waterfowl and other wildlife can best be seen here in early spring and late autumn.

LOSTWOOD NATIONAL WILDLIFE REFUGE
18 miles west of Kenmare off State 8

This large refuge covers 26,750 acres in an area dotted with prairie potholes. The hundreds of ponds thus created provide an excellent habitat for waterfowl; this region of the state annually produces close to 80 per cent of the nation's wild ducks.

PEMBINA VALLEY SCENIC DRIVE
from Walhalla on State 32

This 30-mile drive follows the **Pembina River** through a beautiful, heavily wooded gorge. The 275-mile river rises in the **Turtle Mountains** and flows into the **Red River of the North** at Pembina City.

RED RIVER VALLEY

This valley, once the bed of Lake Agassiz, contains some of the world's richest farming soil. An ancient glacial lake, Lake Agassiz covered an area larger than all of the Great Lakes. Forming the boundary between North Dakota and Minnesota, the **Red River of the North** begins at the confluence of the **Bois de Sioux** and **Otter Tail rivers** just above the South Dakota border; it flows north for 533 miles until it empties into **Lake Winnipeg** in Manitoba.

SHEYENNE RIVER SCENIC DRIVE
from Valley City to Lisbon

This lovely drive follows the course of the scenic Sheyenne River through its beautiful wooded glacial valley. Rising in central North Dakota, the river flows east and south for 325 miles; at Lisbon it turns northeast and flows into the **Red River of the North** 10 miles north of Fargo. Little Yellowstone Park and Fort Ransom Historic Site are located along the route south of Kathryn.

SLADE NATIONAL WILDLIFE REFUGE
2 miles south of Dawson on State 3

In an area of rolling prairie and glacier-made lakes and marshes, this 3,000-acre refuge provides a habitat for many kinds of waterfowl, shorebirds, and small mammals.

Prairie dog and Badlands landscape in Theodore Roosevelt National Memorial Park

THEODORE ROOSEVELT NATIONAL MEMORIAL PARK
headquarters at Medora on I-94

This park, named in honor of the state's most prominent publicist, covers 70,436 acres in the exotic **Badlands** along the **Little Missouri River.** A rough, barren region of creeks, streams, gullies, gorges, and ravines, set against multicolored buttes and ridges eroded by wind and water, these badlands are considered to be the most varied and spectacular in the country. The park is divided into north and south units, each featuring unusual scenic wonders. Midway between the 2 units, on the Little Missouri, is TR's Elkhorn Ranch, where he lived in the 1880s. (His first cabin from the Maltese Cross Ranch is also in the park.) Among the most outstanding sites in the south unit in the Medora area are: **Buck Hill** in the **Painted Canyon,** the highest and most important formation here, offering an excellent panorama of the Badlands; **Wind Canyon,** considered to be the best example in the park of a wind-eroded formation; and the petrified forests, remnants of the great forests that once covered the West. Scattered about the park, the petrified forests range from isolated trees to groups with stumps about 3 feet in diameter and logs about 5 feet long. Another intriguing feature of the south unit is a burning vein of coal. The lignite was formed millions of years ago; once ignited, by lightening or another natural cause, it will burn for years. The burning lignite usually bakes the clay surrounding it into red, bricklike rock, called scoria, or clinker. The burning vein here is believed to have been ignited in 1951; scoria can be seen around it. Nature trails, drives, and observation points (such as *Painted Canyon Overlook* on I-94) offer fine views of the region. The north unit (on U.S. 85 south of Watford City) features huge masses of blue bentonitic clay and impressive tilted slump blocks—cliffs whose bases have eroded. A 13-mile drive along the northern boundary of this section offers a spectacular view of the Badlands marvels.

The most conspicuous animal in the park is the black-tailed prairie dog—a rodent found in colonies called "towns." Other animals include bison, mountain sheep, raccoon, porcupine, jackrabbit, and 116 species of birds. In addition, a few of the remaining wild horses in the country roam the Badlands and the park. The park is a National Historic Landmark.

Open daily: summer 8–8; winter 8–5. For further information write: Medora, N.D. 58645

TWO–TOP MESA AND BIG–TOP MESA
14 miles northwest of Fairfield off U.S. 85

Located in the badlands terrain of western North Dakota, these mesas—standing 400 feet above the valley floor—are composed of sandstone, siltstone, and clay, all highly erodible substances. The area surrounding the mesas is included in the **Little Missouri National Grasslands** (a part of Custer National Forest—*see Montana*), a large region of grassy plains on the fringes of the **Badlands.** Because few, if any, grazing animals can reach the mesa tops, the vegetation here is quite different from that on the plains where the same soil and climate exist. Ecologists find here an excellent opportunity to study an unaltered grassland. Eligible Registered Natural Landmark

WHITE BUTTE
southeast of Amidon off U.S. 85

Rising above the level plains of southwestern North Dakota, this 3,506-foot butte is the state's highest point.

OHIO

BLUE HOLE
502 North Washington Street, Castalia

This natural phenomenon is an artesian spring of azure water. Its depth is unknown, but it appears to be about 50 or 60 feet where the water flows from the spring. It flows at the rate of 7 million gallons per day and maintains a constant temperature of 48°. The spring's water is dead (devoid of air), and until it is aerated by passing over small waterfalls and water wheels, fish are unable to live in it. After it is aerated it flows through springs, where rainbow, brook, and brown trout thrive.

Open Apr–May and Labor Day–Oct: daily 9–6; summer 9 A.M.– 10 P.M. Admission: adults 75¢, children under 12 free

CASCADE PARK
North Broad Street, Elyria

Lying in a deep, craggy gorge of the **Black River,** this park is famous for its natural beauty, caves, waterfalls, and lush forest. Some interesting erosion-created configurations include **Robber's Den** and **Natural Bridge.** The park has many foot and riding trails.

CEDAR BOG
7 miles north of Springfield

Located on the flood plain of the **Mad River,** this bog is a result of glaciation, which destroyed existing vegetation and brought from the north plants that are rare in Ohio today. As the ice receded it left many lakes in the till plains; through normal ecological succession, bogs with relict plants of the ice age developed in the lake beds. Here the progress has been from bog to the only stand of northern white cedar in the state. The bog also possessed various types of vegetation growing on mats of sphagnum, which in turn rests on marl. Registered Natural Landmark

Left: Nelson-Kennedy Ledges State Park. Right: Lake Erie

CLEAR FORK GORGE
in Mohican State Park, southwest of Loudonville along State 97

Located in the valley of the **Clear Fork of the Mohican River,** the gorge is 1,000 feet wide at the top, 200 to 300 feet wide at the bottom, and over 300 feet deep. It illustrates a fascinating glacial-geological story—the reversal of a stream's course. There is evidence here that the Wisconsin Ice Sheet damned a westward-flowing river. Eventually, the great pool formed broke through the sandstone shale wall to create an eastward-flowing river. The gorge also preserves a botanical oddity. The trees and other vegetation on its shady side are analogous to those of southern Alaska, and those on the sunny slopes resemble the vegetation on a Tennessee hillside. In the gorge there is an 8-acre forest of virgin white pine and hemlock. Registered Natural Landmark

CRANBERRY BOG
22 miles east of Columbus, northeast portion of Buckeye Lake

This bog is a relict of the ice age, having been left behind 17,000 years ago when Ohio's last glacier receded. It is the only known sphagnum bog that is floating in a lake surrounded by water. Thus it represents a reversal of the usual succession when bog vegetation encroaches from the shores to the center of a pond. It is covered with creeping vines of cranberry and unusual northern plants, such as poison sumac, alder bush, pitcher plants, and sundew. However, this "floating island" is disappearing because the bog species are gradually being eliminated around its edges and trees fall as they lose their supporting bog material. Registered Natural Landmark

CRYSTAL LAKE
Put-in-Bay, South Bass Island, Lake Erie

Discovered in 1897, this cave contains the largest deposit of strontium sulphate in the United States. (Strontia is a heavy mineral whose nitrate gives a vivid crimson color to flame and which is often used in the manufacture of fireworks.) Its side walls are made of solid strontium; its arch-shaped ceilings are hung with crystals that emit brilliant prismatic colors. The blue-white strontium crystals have 10 faces; the examples here are the largest found anywhere in the world—up to 18 inches long.
Open summer: daily 10–5:30. Operated by Heineman Winery and Vineyards

GLACIAL GROOVES STATE MEMORIAL
within Kelleys Island State Park, Kelleys Island in Lake Erie

Considered to be the finest glacial carvings in America, these grooves were gouged out of hard-rock formations because of tremendous pressures exerted by glaciers thousands of years ago. Although there are similar grooves throughout the whole general area, these are especially large, measuring several feet in depth and about 25 feet in length. Registered Natural Landmark

GLEN HELEN NATURAL AREA
Yellow Springs, on campus of Antioch College

A veritable outdoor laboratory at Antioch's doorstep, this natural area offers a fascinating interpretive program. At its upper end **Yellow Spring** has formed a mound of travertine extending into the valley below. The travertine has been tinted yellow by remains of the iron-fixing bacteria that lived in the spring's carbonate-loaded water. Yellow Spring Creek has cut deep into the dolomitic base

Carvings made by glacial actions (see page 211)

rock to form a steep-walled valley, sided with limestone ledges. These are filled with many small springs surrounded by ferns and other moisture-loving plants. The valley's rocks are rich in fossils, and the soil mantle supports an excellent stand of old-growth hardwoods. Registered Natural Landmark

HOCKING HILLS STATE PARK
southwest of Logan, access via State 56 and 374

This park covers over 9,000 acres within Hocking State Forest and is notable for the widest variety of trees on any Ohio landscape. It features extraordinary formations in Black Hand sandstone, and many scenic marvels are due to the particular qualities of this rock. Hocking Hills is divided into 6 separate units, each named for its major natural wonder. **Ash Cave**, a horseshoe-shaped recess in a great rock approached through a narrow, densely forested gorge, has an arc of 700 feet and is nearly 100 feet high. A little cataract comes streaming down into a pool below; the spray eats away at the sandstone's softer zones. **Cantwell Cliffs** are a stunning example of how the undermining of Black Hand sandstone creates one escarpment after another, because the resistant cap rock collapses when the middle zone is eroded. **Cedar Falls**, surrounded by a fern-covered glen and great, sleek beeches, are at the head of **Queer Creek Gorge**. A 3-mile trail connects this unit of the park with **Old Man's Cave**. This area features 2 miles of densely wooded, winding ravine, picturesque waterfalls, and 2 caves. **Conkles Hollow** is an untouched wilderness area featuring a trail leading up one of the state's steepest gorges. At the upper end of the hollow the cliffs are almost vertical and at the gorge's back end, a series of waterfalls cascades into a small pool. **Rock House** is a 200-foot tunnel-like passageway open at both ends, in the face of a perpendicular cliff.

HOLDEN ARBORETUM
about 25 miles east of Cleveland via I-90 at 9500 Sperry Road, Mentor

One of the world's largest museums of woody plants, Holden covers over 2,200 acres. Its more than 6,000 trees, shrubs, and woody vines have been collected from all over the world. Within the arboretum are 3 sections that comprise **Holden Natural Areas**, a 1,070-acre Registered Natural Landmark. The walls of **Stebbins Gulch**, a 600-acre tract, record 100 million years of geological history; its deep gorges still house subarctic plant life left by retreating glaciers. The gulch is covered with a mixed hardwood forest that has largely escaped cutting. **Bole Forest** is a 40-acre virgin forest with splendid specimens of northern hardwoods. In addition, there is a 30-acre buffer zone of excellent second-growth trees. **Hanging Rock Farm,** covering 400 acres, is a stand of mature northern hardwood. *Open Apr–Oct: Tues–Sun 10–7; Nov–Mar 10–4. Admission: adults 75¢, children (6–15) 25¢*

HUESTON WOODS
4½ miles north of Oxford, off State 732, in Hueston Woods State Park
A 100-acre tract of virgin maple-beech forest, on the east bank of **Four Mile Creek,** is the outstanding feature of this magnificent park. These woods are the most noteworthy example of this type of forest so far south as well as an awe-inspiring remnant of the pristine Midwest. Penetrable by a winding trail, the woods contain Ordovician limestone that are among the world's richest fossil-bearing deposits. Registered Natural Landmark

MOUNT PLEASANT
in Rising Park Lancaster
This 250-foot-high sandstone rock has a 2-acre flat top. The Wyandot Indians, who called it Standing Stone, used it as an observation point and defense fortress, as did early settlers. The rock commands an excellent view of the surrounding country; from its south side it resembles an Indian's profile.

NELSON–KENNEDY LEDGES STATE PARK
several miles southeast of Parkman on State 282
This park features unusual rock formations and rare ferns. Its huge rocks and caves and constantly flowing streams are the result of the great ice sheet that engulfed Ohio many thousands of years ago. As it moved, the glacier carved deep river passages and created the interesting formations.

The Rock House in Hocking Hills State Park

OHIO

OHIO CAVERNS
3 miles east of West Liberty on State 247
> Maintaining a constant temperature of 54°, these illuminated caverns are noted for their colored walls and striking formations. The stalactites and stalagmites are composed of pure white calcium carbonate and varicolored crystals.
> *Open daily 8–5. Admission: adults $2, children (8–14) $1*

OLENTANGY INDIAN CAVERNS
10 miles north of Columbus off U.S. 23
> Ohio's only 3-level cavern, Olentangy is also one of the oldest in the nation. It has a series of interconnected limestone caves, 55 to 105 feet below the ground, and is rich in historical lore. Its rooms and winding passageways were used by the Wyandot Indians for refuge from their enemies, the Delawares.
> *Open spring and fall: weekends; June–Aug: daily 9–6; holidays and Sun: 10–8. Admission: adults $1.25, children (7–12) 75¢*

PERRY'S CAVE
Put-in-Bay on South Bass Island in Lake Erie
> Discovered in 1813 by Commodore Oliver Hazard Perry, the hero of the Battle of Lake Erie, this cave is 52 feet under the ground, 208 feet long, and 165 feet wide. It maintains a constant temperature of 42°; its most interesting feature is the so-called **Wishing Well.** Over 60 feet deep, its water is so clear that a tiny pebble may be seen 50 feet down. The well rises and falls with Lake Erie, and so there must be a subterranean connection. In a side chamber, known as **Perry's Bedroom,** there are some fine stalagmites.
> *Tours May 30–Labor Day: daily 11–5. Admission charged*

SENECA CAVERNS
about 4 miles south of Bellevue, off State 18 and 269
> Among Ohio's major geological wonders, these 8 caves were created by an earthquake and remain in their natural state. Maintaining a constant temperature of 54°, the caverns are on different levels; at the lowest, 147 feet, is **Old Mist'ry,** a subterranean river that feeds the Blue Hole (*see*), 14 miles to the north.
> *Open May 30–Labor Day: daily 8–5; May–Oct: Sun only. Admission: adults $1.75, children 75¢*

SEVEN CAVES
4 miles west of Bainbridge, and 1 mile south of U.S. 50
> Located within a rugged, 100-acre park noted for deep gorges and waterfalls, these caves may be entered at intervals along 3 different foot trails that traverse the park. The caves are electrically lighted and may be explored without a guide.
> *Open March 15–Nov 15: daily 8–5. Admission: adults $1.50, children (6–12) 75¢*

STARK WILDERNESS CENTER
on U.S. 250 near village of Wilmot
> In this 409-acre natural preserve one can enjoy a hike through **Sigrest Woods,** which features trees over 300 years old. There are also interesting outcrops of Pennsylvania-age bedrock, deposits of glacial boulders and gravel, as well as ridges up to 200 feet high affording wonderful views of rolling countryside. A nature center is open on weekend afternoons.
> *Open daily during daylight hours*

TINKERS CREEK GORGE
within Bedford Reservation, Cleveland
> This lovely gorge displays 2 types of virgin forest: its steep slopes provide a cool, shaded environment near the bottom where a beech-maple-hemlock forest thrives. The added light and warmth near the top favors an oak-hickory forest. The in-between zone shows transitional cover, and thus the gorge is an excellent relict of the original forest cover. Registered Natural Landmark

WAYNE NATIONAL FOREST
southeast corner of Ohio, headquarters at Bedford, Indiana
> Sister to Indiana's Hoosier National Forest (*see*), Wayne covers some 137,000 acres of rolling, timbered hills and gentle streams. It boasts huge rock outcroppings of sandstone and shale, as well as several recreation areas. One of its most interesting sections is the **Hanging Rock Region.** During the Civil War this was one of only 3 places in the world capable of producing the high-grade iron needed for heavy cannon. The forest also has a variety of wildlife, hiking trails, and a division abutting the **Ohio River.**
> *For further information write: Wayne-Hoosier National Forest, 1615 J Street, Bedford, Ind. 47421*

ZANE CAVERNS
7 miles north of Bellefontaine via State 540
> These spectacular 2-level caves feature stalactites and stalagmites that are still growing, and thus are among the few caves that are "active." They maintain a constant temperature of 54° and are illuminated by floodlights. Zane Caverns are in a 100-acre tract containing beautiful forest and scenic canyons.
> *Open daily Apr 15–Nov 15. Admission: adults $1.50, children 75¢*

Water scene in Wayne National Forest

OKLAHOMA

ALABASTER CAVERNS STATE PARK
6 miles south of Freedom on State 58

This 200-acre park includes one of the world's largest gypsum caves—a huge cavern that began forming over 200 million years ago when this area was covered by an inland sea. From the entrance in an opening in a huge rock cliff, a lighted 2,300-foot-long trail leads through the cavern. The principal rock formations in the cave are of alabaster—a fine-grained, transluscent gypsum. In a large chamber (400 feet long, 200 feet wide, and 70 to 80 feet high) near the entrance, one can see glistening alabaster and white gypsum formations, including massive gray, rust, and pink alabaster boulders and chunks of selenite, a crystalline form of gypsum. The cave maintains an average temperature of 55° and is inhabited by 8 species of bats. At the exit of the cavern a plateau offers a sweeping view of a rugged 2-mile-long gorge, **Cedar Canyon.** Rising 150 feet above the floor of the canyon (northwest of the entrance) is **Natural Bridge.** Formed by stream erosion undercutting the gypsum, the bridge can be reached by a trail that leads down into Cedar Canyon and up to the bridge.
Guided tours are conducted hourly: 8–5

ANTELOPE HILLS
south of Arnett off U.S. 283

These 6 peaks rising above the **Plains** were a landmark to pioneers going West. From the top there is a scenic view of the surrounding countryside and the **South Canadian River** to the north.

ARBUCKLE RECREATION AREA. See PLATT NATIONAL PARK

Left: typical grassland in the Panhandle. Right: Turner Falls

BEAVERS BEND STATE PARK
7 miles north of Broken Bow on State 259 and 3 miles east on State 259A

In a region of tall trees and impressive mountains, this 5,135-acre park is crossed by the **Mountain Fork River**, a clear stream flowing through scenic rock-strewn canyons. A dam in the river has created a 14,240-acre lake offering a variety of water sports; hiking trails lead throughout the park.

BLACK MESA STATE PARK
30 miles northwest of Boise City

This 296-acre park is located on the Black Mesa, a volcanic plateau at the western tip of the **Panhandle**. It is famous for its lava formations, petrified wood, dinosaur pits, and Indian pictographs; artifacts dating back 10,000 to 12,000 years have been unearthed here. About 12 miles northwest of the park the Black Mesa reaches an altitude of 4,978 feet—the highest point in the state. Farther northwest is the common point where the borders of Oklahoma, New Mexico, and Colorado meet.

BOILING SPRINGS STATE PARK
8 miles northeast of Woodward on State 34 and 34C

This 820-acre park is named for the unusual cold-water springs that "boil up" through the white sand of the **Plains** here. Located on the tree-shaded north bank of the **North Canadian River**, the springs were a popular watering place in pioneer days. A 7-acre lake is fed by water from the springs; hiking trails wind through this scenic area where wild turkeys abound.

CHIMNEY ROCK
about 8½ miles southeast of Freedom

This sandstone pinnacle was carved by erosion into its unusual chimneylike shape. A famous Oklahoma landmark, the rock is located in the scenic valley of the **Cimarron River**.

GLASS MOUNTAIN
northwest of Fairview off U.S. 60

Named for the millions of glassy, selenite crystals covering its surface, this series of buttes range in elevation from a few feet to 300 feet above the valley of the **Cimarron River**. It is a part of the **Blaine Escarpement**—a great gypsum formation extending across western Oklahoma. This mountain has been eroded into strange formations topped by a gypsum cap 4 to 5 feet thick; bands of satin spar, another variety of gypsum, also cover these hills.

GREAT SALT PLAINS
east of Cherokee off State 11

Covering an area 7 miles long and about 3 miles wide, the Salt Plains are a flat expanse of sand covered with a thin layer of white salt. Included in this vast, plantless flatland are the **Salt Plains National Wildlife Refuge** and Great Salt Plains State Park. The 32,000-acre refuge is an important habitat for many species of wildlife, including migratory waterfowl—it is one of the main stops for geese on the Central flyway—and over 250 species of birds. In addition, visitors are permitted to dig for selenite, a crystallized form of gypsum formed beneath the salt-encrusted surface of the Plains. An observation tower near the refuge entrance provides a panoramic view of this flat, treeless region. The 840-acre state park offers recreation facilities on a part of the Great Salt Plains Reservoir, created

OKLAHOMA

by a dam in the **Salt Fork of the Arkansas River.**
Digging in designated areas only Apr–Oct 15: Sat, Sun, holidays 8–5

LITTLE SAHARA RECREATION AREA
3 miles south of Waynoka on U.S. 281

Located on the **Cimarron River,** this 339-acre park features beautiful sand dunes (buggy rides over the dunes are available). A lookout tower provides a scenic view of the area. Also found here are camels, goats, and Indian and longhorn cattle.

OSAGE HILLS STATE PARK
northeast of Pawhuska off State 35, via State 99 and U.S. 60

Located in the rugged terrain of the Osage Indian Reservation, this 1,199-acre park includes deep, forested gorges and scenic bluffs. **Sand Creek,** a beautiful clear stream, crosses the park and empties into **Lake Lookout,** a well-stocked 18-acre lake.

OUACHITA NATIONAL FOREST. *See* ARKANSAS

PLATT NATIONAL PARK AND ARBUCKLE RECREATION AREA
southeast of Sulphur, off U.S. 177 and State 7

Called an "oasis of woodlands in the prairie," this national park is located in the foothills of the **Arbuckle Mountains.** Here, where the eastern hardwood forest meets the western prairie, one can see a scenic blend of wooded valleys, gently rolling hills, clear streams, and many mineral and freshwater springs. Platt is the smallest national park in the country with just over 900 acres. Of the 31 large springs found here 18 are sulphur, 4 are iron, 3 are bromide, and 6 are freshwater. **Antelope** and **Buffalo,** 2 large freshwater springs, have a combined flow of more than 5 million gallons daily; accessible by a self-guided trail, these springs feed **Travertine Creek.** **Bromide Spring** and **Medicine Spring** emerge from the base of **Bromide Hill;** a walk to the top of this 140-foot-high wooded hill offers a beautiful view of the surrounding countryside. Many other trails wind throughout the park and a 6-mile loop road provides a picturesque tour. Of the many animals found in the park, the most popular is the small herd of bison that roams certain areas; others include the opossum, armadillo, southern flying squirrel, and gray fox. Nearly 150 species of birds have been sighted here, including the brown-headed cowbird, southern yellow-shafted flicker, and orchard oriole. Vividly colored wildflowers flourish along with cottonwood, redbud, and a wide variety of trees. A museum and nature center provide exhibits of the park's many natural wonders.

About 8 miles southwest of Platt is the **Arbuckle Recreation Area,** an 8,851-acre complex created by the construction of Arbuckle Dam. Built at the confluence of **Buckhorn, Guy Sandy,** and **Rock creeks,** the dam provides facilities for a variety of water sports. Surrounding the recreation area are springs, streams, bluffs, and wooded hills in the Arbuckle Mountains. Elevations reach 1,450 feet above sea level, about 500 to 700 feet above the prairies.

For further information on both write: Box 201, Sulphur, Okla. 73086

QUARTZ MOUNTAIN STATE PARK
7 miles south of Lone Wolf on State 44

Set in beautiful granite mountains, this 4,284-acre park features rugged terrain and many charming lakes. Recreational facilities are offered on **Lake Altus,** a huge reservoir created by the damming of the **North Fork of the Red River.**

RED ROCK CANYON STATE PARK
½ mile south of Hinton on State 8 and U.S. 281

This 211-acre park is located in a beautiful canyon named for its colorful red walls. The canyon is crossed by scenic trails; recreational facilities are provided on a small, man-made lake.

ROBBERS CAVE STATE PARK
6 miles north of Wilburton on State 2

Named for the cave which legend says was used as a hide-out by outlaws (Belle Starr's gang) and deserters from the Union and Confederate armies, this 8,246-acre park is located in the rugged **Sansbois Mountains** of southeast Oklahoma.

TURNER FALLS
southwest of Davis off I-35

Situated in the picturesque **Arbuckle Mountains,** this is the most famous waterfall in Oklahoma. Here **Honey Creek,** a clear sparkling stream fed by pure mountain springs, rushes downhill through a rock-strewn gorge until it tumbles 77 feet over the falls.

WICHITA MOUNTAINS WILDLIFE REFUGE
north of Cache on State 115

Established in 1905 to protect the dwindling wildlife of the **Plains,** this 59,020-acre preserve features one of the world's largest herds of buffalo. Here, too, wild turkeys, wild longhorn cattle, and elk can be found in the rugged terrain of the Wichita Mountains. A low, granite chain (the maximum altitude is 2,464 feet above sea level), these mountains cover an area about 60 miles long and 25 miles wide. Special features include grassy plains, wooded peaks, and over 15 lakes and streams—a welcome contrast to the dry, flat Plains. A paved road leads to the top of **Mount Scott** from which there is a fine panorama of the surrounding country.

Scattered stand of live oak on slope of granite outcropping

OREGON

AINSWORTH STATE PARK
37 miles east of Portland on U.S. 30

The main attractions in this 156-acre park in the scenic **Columbia Gorge** are a beautiful fir and hemlock forest and a 2,000-foot basalt pinnacle, **Saint Peter's Dome.**

CROOKED RIVER NATIONAL GRASSLAND. *See* OCHOCO NATIONAL FOREST

CRATER LAKE NATIONAL PARK
south entrance 46 miles north of Klamath Falls on State 62; west entrance 9 miles east of Medford

The setting of this national park has been described as "one of the most peaceful and beautiful scenes in the world." Its main feature is Crater Lake, which is 1,932 feet at its deepest point and is the deepest lake in the United States and the second deepest one in the Western Hemisphere—it is exceeded only by Canada's Great Slave Lake. Six miles wide and 20 miles in circumference, the lake was created about 7,000 years ago when massive and violent volcanic activity caused the collapse of the summit of Mount Mazama, once a mighty peak in the **Cascade Range.** Because so much volcanic material was spewed out of or drained through cracks beneath the mountain during eruptions, leaving no foundation or support, its summit literally collapsed, and a "caldera"—a nearly circular basin-shaped depression—was formed. When the caldera filled with rain and snow Crater Lake was formed. Volcanic activity continued from vents at the floor of the caldera and 3 small cinder cones were formed. Only one of these—the 2,600-foot **Wizard Island**—rises high enough above the lake to be visible; the other 2 remain below the water's surface. Since Crater Lake has no outlet or inlet it is filled only by rain and snow; evaporation and precipitation keep the water at a fairly constant level. Perhaps the most outstanding feature of Crater Lake is the almost unbelievable color of its crystal-clear, pure blue water. The water is said to be so clear that objects 75 feet below the surface appear to be near at hand. Aquatic moss has been found at a record depth of 425 feet. Surrounding the lake are magnificent multicolored cliffs that rise as high as 1,980 feet above the shore. The lake is circled by the 33-mile-long *Rim Drive,* which offers spectacular views of the caldera from numerous mountainous observation points. Outstanding lookouts along the route are the **Watchman,** an 8,025-foot peak accessible by a short trail and affording a fine view from 1,230 feet above the lake; **Hillman Peak,** at 8,156 feet the highest point on the rim; **Kerr Notch,** from which one can see the **Phantom Ship,** a mass of igneous rock and volcanic ash jutting 160 feet above the lake; and **Llao Rock,** a great lava flow that fills an earlier glacier valley. A short spur road leads from the drive to **Cloudcap** (8,070 feet), from which there is a marvelous view of the lake to the west and of 8,926-foot **Mount Scott** to the east, the highest point in the park; a 2.5-mile trail ascends the mountain and offers a view from almost 2,800 feet above the lake. Another spur road leads 6 miles from Kerr Notch to the **Pinnacles**—marvelously eroded spires of pumice that rise 200 feet out of **Wheeler Creek Canyon.** Among the fine trails in the park are *Garfield Peak Trail,* a 1.7-mile hike to a point 1,900 feet above the lake; *Discovery Point Trail,* a 1.5-mile trail leading to the spot where the lake was

Top left: Cape Perpetua in Siuslaw National Forest. Top right: Mount Hood and squaw grass in Mount Hood National Forest. Below: Crater Lake

OREGON

first seen by a white man in 1853, John Wesley Hillman; and the *Cleetwood Trail,* a mile-long descent from the northern rim to the lake and the only access to the water. Boat trips around the lake and to Wizard Island are available from here; a trail also leads to the 90-foot-wide, 300-foot-deep crater atop Wizard Island. The park is crossed by other trails beyond the lake, including the *Oregon Skyline Trail,* a section of the *Pacific Crest National Scenic Trail,* that traverses the **Pumice Desert**—a huge area covered with pumice deposits to a depth of 200 feet. One of the best views of the caldera is from the **Sinnott Memorial Overlook,** near the Exhibit Building, where there are fine displays of the natural features within the park. Nearby is the *Castle Crest Nature Trail,* a half-mile self-guided walk through a beautiful natural garden where some of the more than 570 species of plant life found within the park can be seen. Because of heavy snows the northern entrance road and Rim Drive are usually closed from about mid-October to early July.

For further information write: Box 7, Crater Lake, Oreg. 97604

DESCHUTES NATIONAL FOREST
central Oregon, headquarters at Bend

This lush forest covers about 1.5 million acres on the eastern slopes of the **Cascade Range**—a northern continuation of the **Sierra Nevada.** A small section of the forest is located on a high plateau surrounding **Newberry Crater;** 2 lakes (**Paulina** and **East**) are trapped at its summit. This section of the forest includes many other fascinating volcanic formations, such as **Lava Butte,** a 500-foot-high cinder cone; **Lava Cast Forest,** which features many trees buried by a volcanic lava flow; **Arnold Ice Cave;** and **Paulina Peak,** a 7,980-foot mountain offering a spectacular panorama of Newberry Crater and the surrounding countryside. Also located here is Lava River Caves State Park (12 miles south of Bend on U.S. 97), known for its lava tube caves. The principal feature of the 23-acre park is the **Lava River Tunnel,** which measures nearly a mile long, 50 feet wide, and 35 feet high.

Deschutes is known for its fine fishing; there are 150 lakes and reservoirs and 235 miles of streams and rivers, including the headwaters of the **Deschutes River.** In addition the visitor can see rivers that emerge from huge underground springs, such as the **Metolius River** that flows from the foot of **Black Butte.** Another outstanding site is **Tumalo Falls,** a 96-foot drop in scenic **Tumalo Creek.** Four wilderness areas are included in the forest—the **Mount Jefferson, Mount Washington, Diamond Peak,** and **Three Sisters areas.** Located mainly across the Cascades in Willamette National Forest (*see*), these wildernesses offer unspoiled scenic beauty and miles of hiking and saddle trails. About 250 species of mammals and birds have been spotted in the forest, including such endangered specimens as the American osprey, prairie falcon, and bald eagle. Several pairs of bald eagles can be seen along the *Cascade Lakes Highway*—a 71-mile road that crosses the beautiful lake area between the crest of the Cascades and the Oregon plains.

For further information write: 211 East Revere, Bend, Oreg. 97701

DEVIL'S PUNCH BOWL STATE PARK
8 miles north of Newport

This small park is famous for the bowl-shaped rock formation from which it takes its name. Far down within the bowl the **Pacific Ocean** swirls in through a cavern, filling the bowl at high tide. The park offers marine gardens, sandy beaches, and views of the ocean.

FREMONT NATIONAL FOREST
southcentral Oregon, headquarters at Lakeview

Named in honor of John C. Frémont, who in 1843 led one of the first exploring parties through the area, this 1,145,000-acre forest is located on the eastern slopes of the **Cascade Range**. A section in the **Warner Mountains** stretches from the California line to **Abert Rim**— the largest known exposed geologic fault in North America. The rim rises about 2,500 feet above the eastern shore of **Lake Abert**; there is a 640-foot cliff of lava strata at the top. Among the most spectacular regions in the forest is the **Gearhart Mountain Wilderness**, an unusually rugged area of canyons, ridges, and 500-foot cliffs; elevations range from 6,000 feet to 8,364 feet atop Gearhart Mountain. Composed mainly of volcanic rock, the mountain features a sheer cliff (**Gearhart Notch**) that rises 300 feet on its north side. Glaciation has carved out many interesting formations in the rock here. An extremely primitive area, the wilderness does not have many trails; the main route extends from **Lookout Rock** to a point near the summit of Gearhart Mountain, and it then continues on to **Blue Lake** and **Nottin Creek**.

For further information write: Box 551, Lakeview, Oreg. 97630

GOLDEN AND SILVER FALLS STATE PARK
24 miles northeast of Coos Bay

This lovely park, covering 157 acres in the scenic **Coast Range**, is noted for its 2 beautiful waterfalls, both about 200 feet wide.

GUY W. TALBOT STATE PARK
27 miles east of Portland on U.S. 30

Located in a particularly scenic area, this 236-acre park features **Latourell Falls**, where the **Columbia River** drops 250 feet over basaltic bluffs. There are hiking trails throughout the park.

MALHEUR CAVE
55 miles southeast of Burns, off State 78

This lava-tube cave on **Indian Creek** is about a mile long, 50 feet wide, and from 10 to 25 feet high. It has unusual glazed walls and contains at its far end an especially beautiful lake that has no inlet or outlet.

Left: deer in Deschutes National Forest. Right: Devil's Punch Bowl

OREGON

MALHEUR NATIONAL FOREST
eastcentral Oregon, headquarters at John Day

This majestic, 1,470,000-acre forest in the **Blue Mountains** contains 3,200 miles of roads and 527 miles of trails. Among the prime attractions are **Strawberry Mountain Wilderness**, a 33,003-acre preserve dominated by the 9,044-foot Strawberry Mountain and featuring 5 glacial lakes; the 4,000-acre **Vinegar Hill–Indian Rock Area,** in the **Greenhorn Mountains,** noted for its spectacular scenery above the timber line; and **Magone Lake,** which was formed by a landslide early in the 1800s. The lake is reached by a rough trail marked by trees that were twisted by the landslide. Other attractions in the forest include **Cedar Grove,** a 60-acre tract of Alaska cedar that is hundreds of miles away from any similar stand; **Rosebud Geological Area,** featuring many unusual fossils and rock formations; and the high mountain areas around **Baldy** and **Sheep mountains, Coal Pit Mountain,** and **Fields Peak.** The forest also contains miles of fishing streams, as well as the headwaters of the **Malheur** and **Silvies rivers** and a major portion of the headwaters of the **John Day River.**

For further information: Superintendent, John Day, Oreg. 97845

MARY'S PEAK
16 miles west of Corvallis on State 34

The highest point in the **Coast Range,** the summit of this 4,097-foot peak is reached by a 9-mile gravel road. There is a magnificent panoramic view from the **Pacific Ocean** on the west to the **Cascade Mountains** on the east.

MOUNT HOOD NATIONAL FOREST
north Oregon, headquarters at Portland

Stretching south from the **Columbia River** to **Mount Jefferson,** this forest encompasses 1,115,327 acres rich in scenic wonders. Its outstanding attraction is the highest point in Oregon, Mount Hood, an 11,245-foot, perpetually snow-capped peak. An ancient, but not yet extinct volcano, the mountain stands in the center of the **Mount Hood Wilderness**—a beautiful alpine preserve enjoyed by hikers, skiers, and mountain climbers. *Mount Hood Loop Highway*—a one-day drive from the mountain to the Columbia River—passes by cascading waterfalls and mountain meadows along the **East Fork of the Hood River** to the imposing basalt cliffs of the **Columbia Gorge.** A land of hot springs (**Austin Hot Springs**), alpine meadows, tumbling waterfalls (**Punchbowl Falls**), clear lakes (**Lost Lake**), and rushing rivers (**Clackamas River**), the forest is crossed by miles of trails. The major trails closed to vehicular traffic are those in the **Columbia Gorge Area;** the *Timberline Trail* in the Mount Hood Wilderness, which circles the mountain; trails in the **Bull-of-the-Woods Area,** a region of lakes and towering old trees; and the *Oregon Skyline Trail,* a section of the *Pacific Crest National Scenic Trail,* which, as it winds south passes such sites as **Wahtum Lake, Lolo Pass,** the west side of Mount Hood, the high lake country, and enters the Mount Jefferson Wilderness Area (*see also Deschutes and Willamette national forests*). Other outstanding attractions in this spectacular forest include **Larch Mountain,** accessible by car and offering beautiful views; the **Olallie Lakes Area,** where fine fishing for rainbow, cutthroat, steelhead, and Eastern brook trout is available; and **Multnomah Falls,** where a visitor information center offers exhibits about the Columbia Gorge area.

For further information write: Box 16040, Portland, Oreg. 97216

NEPTUNE STATE PARK
3 miles south of Yachats on U.S. 101

Bordering the rocky shore of the **Pacific Ocean** for 3 miles, this 296-acre park also includes forested areas and huckleberry-covered slopes. The most unusual site here is **Cook's Chasm**, where the ocean furiously swirls into a long, deep fissure in the rocks.

OCHOCO NATIONAL FOREST
central Oregon, headquarters at Prineville

Set aside as a national forest in 1911, this 845,855-acre region at the western end of the **Blue Mountains** lies in the geographic center of Oregon. The forest also administers the 106,000-acre **Crooked River National Grassland,** land originally homesteaded around the turn of the century and returned to the government in the 1930s. The **Steelhead Falls Unusual Interest Area** on the Grassland is a scenic canyon of the **Deschutes River,** with multicolored rock walls and jutting rock pillars. Another fascinating spot is the **Steins Pillar Unusual Interest Area** in the forest which features 3 rock spires—the largest rises 350 feet and is 120 feet in diameter at the base. Other scenic areas include **Squaw Creek, Alder Springs Canyon,** and **Sherwood Canyon.** Known as one of the outstanding "rockhound" areas in the country, Ochoco attracts thousands of visitors who search over designated areas for such interesting rocks as thunder egg, agatized wood, amygdules, and banded rhyolite. Many animals can be seen roaming the forest and grassland; among the most intriguing are the pronghorn antelope, which can be found in summer, spring, and fall near the **Big Summit Prairie,** and the Rocky Mountain elk, which are especially visible in the **Battle Mountain–Black Canyon Creek Area.**

For further information write: Box 490, Prineville, Oreg. 97754

OREGON CAVES NATIONAL MONUMENT
20 miles from Cave Junction on State 46

First discovered in 1874, this cavern (the word "caves" is a misnomer) in the **Siskiyou Mountains** contains intricate and beautiful marble formations. Millions of years ago, when an ancient ocean covered the area, calcium carbonate deposits hardened into limestone; when the limestone was uplifted to form mountains, it was changed into marble by heat and pressure. Further mountain building caused small cracks in the marble which were slowly enlarged by water. Eventually the water, charged with minerals, so eroded

Unusual rock formations in Ochoco National Forest

the fissures that this cave was formed. The decorations found throughout the cavern, where the temperature remains about 48°, have many unusual shapes; of particular interest are the miniature waterfalls of stone. Highlights include **Paradise Lost, Ghost's Chamber, Neptune's Grotto,** and **Joaquin Miller's Chapel,** named for the "poet of the Sierra" who wrote about the cave. Located at an altitude of 4,000 feet, the monument is surrounded by Siskiyou National Forest (*see*) and boasts beautiful stands of Douglas fir, western hemlock, and Port Orford cedar. Black bear, mule deer, and bobcat are among the mammals that inhabit the monument.

For further information write: Box 377, Cave Junction, Oreg. 97323

OSWALD WEST STATE PARK
north of Manzanita on U.S. 101

This 2,500-acre park on the **Pacific Ocean** contains beaches, agate caves, creeks, and most of **Neahkahnie Mountain.** A portion of the scenic *Oregon Coast Highway* crosses an almost perpendicular rock face 700 feet above the sea.

OREGON DUNES. *See* SIUSLAW NATIONAL FOREST

PETER SKENE OGDEN SCENIC WAYSIDE
9 miles north of Redmond on U.S. 97

This 98-acre park skirts the beautiful **Crooked River Gorge.** The canyon has vertical walls and is 400 feet wide and 304 feet deep. Fine views are available from an overlook along the south rim.

PILOT BUTTE STATE PARK
east of Bend on U.S. 20

The main feature in this 101-acre park is Pilot Butte, a lone cinder cone rising 511 feet. A road leads to the summit where there is a magnificent view of the **Cascade Range** and stately **Mount Hood.**

ROGUE RIVER NATIONAL FOREST
southwest Oregon, headquarters at Medford

This 620,592-acre forest has 2 sections—one along the western slopes of the **Cascade Range** and the other in the **Siskiyou Mountains** extending across the California border. The Cascade section, which skirts Crater Lake National Park (*see*), contains superb stands of ponderosa pine, sugar pine, and Douglas fir. Among the outstanding sites are the **Rogue River Gorge,** a deep, narrow canyon cut out of ancient lava; a natural bridge, where the river disappears into a lava tube to emerge 300 feet downstream; majestic **Mount McLoughlin,** a 9,495-foot peak; and the **Mammoth Sugar Pine,** a great fallen tree accessible by a short nature trail. This part of the forest also features a section of the famous *Oregon Skyline Trail* and the **Sky Lakes Area,** an unspoiled preserve noted for its fine fishing; it is partially located in Wimena National Forest (*see*). The main feature of the southern section of the Rogue River National Forest is **Mount Ashland,** an imposing 7,533-foot peak. A 75-mile loop road crosses the forest and the Siskiyou Mountains and passes within 12 miles of the summit of Mount Ashland, providing a magnificent view of rugged mountain peaks and green forests. From this vantage point one can see Mount McLoughlin to the north.

For further information write: Box 520, Medford, Oreg. 97501

ROGUE RIVER NATIONAL SCENIC RIVERWAY. *See* SISKIYOU NATIONAL FOREST

OREGON

SEA LION CAVES
11 miles north of Florence on U.S. 101
These huge caverns, cut out of rock by the **Pacific Ocean**, are the home of the only known mainland rookery of sea lions. Within the caves, which are reached by elevator, one can see interesting geological formations and the mummified remains of sea lions. *Open daily during daylight. Admission: adults $1.25; children 50¢*

SHEPPERD'S DELL STATE PARK
28 miles east of Portland on U.S. 30
Overlooking the mighty **Columbia River**, this 332-acre park features beautiful waterfalls and unusual rock formations.

SILVER FALLS STATE PARK
26 miles east of Salem on State 214
The largest in Oregon, this 8,337-acre park is noted for its spectacular waterfalls. Of the cascades here, 5 are over 100 feet high; the highest plunges 178 feet.

SISKIYOU NATIONAL FOREST
southwest Oregon, headquarters at Grants Pass
This beautiful forest, a botanist's paradise, covers 1,158,420 acres in the **Siskiyou Mountains** and includes a small section in California. Because the Siskiyou Mountains are a link between the **Coast** and the **Cascade ranges,** plant life indigenous to widely scattered zones is found here. Some plants that grow in the forest can be found nowhere else in a wild state. Among the rarest and most unusual plants is the kalmiopsis, a shrub resembling a miniature rhododendron dating back to the pre-ice age, which is preserved in the **Kalmiopsis Wilderness.** That beautiful 76,900-acre region of low, rocky canyons and rushing streams includes some of the most rugged terrain in Siskiyou. In addition to the kalmiopsis, the area features many rare orchids, lilies, and other plants, as well as 12 species of conifers and 9 species of hardwood trees. One of the most outstanding attractions in the forest is the 85-mile stretch of the **Rogue River** which has been designated a part of the National Wild and Scenic Rivers System. Extending downstream from the mouth of the **Applegate River,** the Rogue twists through rocky gorges and canyons, and rapids are frequent. A trail affording magnificent scenic views follows the north side of the river from the mouth of **Grave Creek** to Illshe; 1-day, 3-day, and 5-day mail boat trips are also available. Other rivers originating in the forest include the **Winchuck, Chetco, Pistol, South Fork of the Coquille,** and the **Illinois.**
For further information write: Box 440, Grants Pass, Oreg. 97526

SIUSLAW NATIONAL FOREST
western Oregon, headquarters at Corvallis
One of the most unusual forests in the country, this 622,180-acre forest of Sitka spruce, western hemlock, cedar, and Douglas fir is the only one in the 48 contiguous states with an appreciable amount of ocean shoreline. Named for a small tribe of Yakona Indians, Siuslaw stretches in scattered sections from **Coos Bay** north to Tillamook. Among the interesting attractions here are the **Neskowin Crest Natural Area,** a scientific preserve featuring a trail through a rain forest to Cascade Head and the **Cascade Head Scenic Area,** where there is a magnificent view of the **Pacific Ocean** from a high bluff; **Cape Cove Beach,** where during the spring and fall migrating blue whales weighing up to 115 tons can be seen; and the **Umpqua**

OREGON

Dunes Scenic Area. This 2,760-acre region of fantastic sand dunes is a section of the **Oregon Dunes,** a vast stretch of beach from **Heceta Beach** to Coos Bay, featuring shifting dunes as high as 200 feet. A visitor information center at **Cape Perpetua** offers exhibits on the natural phenomena along the coast and within the forest.
For further information write: Box 1148, Corvallis, Oreg. 97330

THOMAS CONDON–JOHN DAY FOSSIL BEDS STATE PARK
8 miles west of Dayville on State 19

This 4,345-acre park is famous as the site of fossil beds believed to be 30 million years old. Found in a deeply eroded ridge, the beds include the remains of such extinct animals as the sabertooth tiger and miniature horse, indicating that this area was once a low, tropical jungle. In addition to the fossil beds (a Registered Natural Landmark), the park also has many scenic attractions; highlights include **Sheep Rock, Turtle Cove,** and ancient Indian pictographs.

UMATILLA NATIONAL FOREST
northeastern Oregon, headquarters at Pendleton

Covering nearly 1,400,000 acres, this forest is divided into 2 separate sections and extends into Washington State. Situated partially in the **Blue Mountains,** the forest includes scenic rivers and streams, such as the **Grande Ronde, Umatilla, Walla Walla,** and **North Fork of the John Day rivers,** all popular for trout fishing. Although there are many lakes within the forest, only one natural lake—the 145-acre **Olive Lake**—is more than 3 acres in size. A beautiful region rich in wildlife, the forest boasts 1,400 miles of scenic roads, including the outstanding *Kendall-Skyline Forest Road* along the summit of the Blue Mountains and over 1,000 miles of trails. A 35-mile raft trip on the Grande Ronde River is offered. The most outstanding feature in the forest is the **Wenaha Backcountry Area.** This 111,200-acre preserve at the crest of the northern Blue Mountains is a rugged area of basaltic ridges, steep canyons, and rushing streams, crossed by more than 150 miles of trails. Rocky Mountain elk, mule deer, and white-tailed deer are found here, and fine fishing is available in the **Wenaha River, Crooked Creek,** and **Butte Creek.** There is a virgin stand of western white pine, far removed from its natural range; among the trees is a giant white pine—66 inches in diameter and 180 feet tall.
For further information write: Box 1208, Pendleton, Oreg. 97801

Left: Siskiyou National Forest. Right: Sheep Rock in John Day Fossil Beds

OREGON

UMPQUA LIGHTHOUSE STATE PARK
south of Winchester Bay off U.S. 101

This 2,715-acre park skirts the **Pacific Ocean** for 2.5 miles and is famous for its spectacular sand dunes. Among the highest in the country, the dunes rise in some places to 500 feet. The park, which abuts the mouth of the **Umpqua River**, has a delightful seasonal display of rhododendrons.

UMPQUA NATIONAL FOREST
southwest Oregon, headquarters at Roseburg

Named for the Indian tribe who once lived here, this forest of nearly 900,000 acres runs westward from the crest of the **Cascade Mountains**. Among the many outstanding attractions here are **Eagle Rock**, a towering pinnacle jutting above the trees; **Diamond Lake**, a 3,000-acre recreational lake located at 5,184 feet and dominated by **Mount Thielson**, a rugged 9,173-foot peak; and the **North Umpqua River**, a beautiful waterway boasting outstanding fishing in a magnificent mountain setting. One of the forest's most unusual sites is the **Colliding Rivers**, where the **North Umpqua** and the **Little River** crash head on; nearby are interesting marine fossil beds. The *Oregon Skyline Trail*—a section of the *Pacific Crest National Scenic Trail*—crosses the forest, and a new highway between Diamond Lake and the town of Roseburg offers an especially scenic drive.

For further information write: Box 1008, Roseburg, Oreg. 97470

UPPER KLAMATH LAKE
Klamath Falls, on U.S. 97

This 40-mile-long lake is the largest freshwater lake in Oregon. Surrounded by mountains and Winema National Forest (*see*), the lake is connected to the now-dry Lower Klamath Lake in California. U.S. 97 skirts this scenic area for 28 miles.

WALLOWA–WHITMAN NATIONAL FOREST
northeast Oregon, headquarters at Baker

Divided into 2 sections, this forest covers 2,490,892 acres in the **Blue Mountains**, the **Elkhorn Mountains**, and the **Wallowa Mountains** along the **Snake River**. Called a "land of contrasts," the forest features alpine peaks, forested slopes, clear mountain lakes, and grassy canyons. Among the major attractions here is the **Eagle Cap Wilderness**, a 220,416-acre preserve at the crest of the Wallowa Mountains. Boasting rugged granite peaks, glacier-formed canyons, and more than 60 well-stocked lakes—such as beautiful **Mirror Lake** —the area is closed to all vehicular traffic. The **Elkhorn Mountain Area**, a recreational area extending southeasterly from **Anthony Lake**, is a beautiful alpine region of snow-capped peaks crossed by the **North Powder River** and **Rock Creek**. The eastern border of the forest is included in the Hells Canyon–Seven Devils Scenic Area (*see Idaho*), which contains the spectacular gorge cut out by the Snake River. Also within the forest's boundary is Wallowa Lake State Park, a forested area covering 166 acres at the southern end of **Wallowa Lake**.

For further information write: Box 471, Baker, Oreg. 97814

WILLAMETTE NATIONAL FOREST
westcentral Oregon, headquarters at Eugene

This beautiful forest stretching for 110 miles along the western slopes of the **Cascade Mountains** is dominated by Douglas fir and is among the top timber producers of all the country's national forests.

229

More than 15 per cent of Willamette's 1,600,000 acres are included in 4 wilderness areas—the **Mount Jefferson, Mount Washington, Three Sisters,** and **Diamond Peak areas.** Extending into Deschutes National Forest (*see*) on the eastern slopes of the Cascades, these wildernesses are centered around imposing mountain peaks— Mount Jefferson, 10,497 feet; Mount Washington, 7,794 feet; Diamond Peak, 8,744 feet; and the Three Sisters, each over 10,000 feet. Set aside to insure their preservation, the wildernesses are accessible only by foot or horseback and are crossed by the *Oregon Skyline Trail,* a section of the *Pacific Crest National Scenic Trail.* In addition to their majestic mountains the wildernesses include many other natural attractions. These are, for instance, vast volcanic formations in the Diamond Peak Area, and in the Three Sisters are **Proxy Falls,** 2 beautiful waterfalls tumbling 200 feet over lava cliffs. A number of smaller natural areas have also been established within the forest; among these are **Lamb Butte Scenic Area, Gold Lake Bog Area,** and **Rebel Rock Geological Area.** The forest also includes **Waldo Lake,** the second largest natural lake in Oregon; found near the crest of the Cascades, this 6,000-acre lake offers a wide range of recreational facilities. Other attractions in Willamette include the Dee Wright Observatory near **McKenzie Pass,** offering magnificent panoramas of mountains and lava fields (the half-mile *Lava River Trail* is here); **Koosah** and **Sahalie falls,** 2 cascades in the **McKenzie River; Sawyer's Cave,** an area of small ice caves; and **Salt Creek Falls,** a lovely 286-foot drop. **Clear Lake** has an unusual feature, an underwater forest drowned 3,000 years ago when a lava flow damned a stream to form the lake.

For further information write: Box 1272, Eugene, Oreg. 97401

WINEMA NATIONAL FOREST
southcentral Oregon, headquarters at Klamath Falls

Officially proclaimed in 1969, this national forest of more than 900,000 acres is partially made up of former tribal lands of the Klamath Indians. Named for the heroine of the Modoc War of 1872, the forest stretches east from the **Cascade Range** and includes forested mountain slopes dotted with countless scenic lakes. Among the many attractions here are **Spring Creek,** an especially beautiful river that emerges from a water-bearing lava formation; **Miller Lake,** a 554-acre lake at 5,600 feet above sea level offering fine fishing in a mountain setting; **Fourmile Lake,** a 900-acre natural reservoir near **Mount McLoughlin;** and **Mares Egg Spring,** a scenic area boasting a colony of Nostoc algae—rare botanical forms resembling greenish "cobblestones" that are found at the bottom of the spring. One of the most scenic regions in the forest is the **Sky Lakes Area,** a 20,000-acre preserve on a high mountain plateau that includes 23 well-stocked lakes. This beautiful area, part of which is in Rogue River National Forest (*see*), is crossed by the *Oregon Skyline Trail*—a rugged saddle trail through unspoiled back country. **Mountain Lakes Wilderness,** another magnificent area, is made up of 23,071 acres of rugged terrain and beautiful mountain lakes. The area centers around a large glacial cirque, 4 smaller cirques, and includes such imposing peaks as **Aspen Butte** (8,208 feet), **Mount Harriman** (7,979 feet), **Crater Mountain** (7,785 feet) and **Greylock Mountain** (7,747 feet). Recreational facilities are available at **Lake of the Woods,** a beautiful mountain area that is situated at an altitude of 4,950 feet.

For further information: PO Building, Klamath Falls, Oreg. 97601

PENNSYLVANIA

ALLEGHENY NATIONAL FOREST
northwest Pennsylvania, headquarters at Warren

Situated on the rolling tableland of the **Allegheny Plateau,** this forest extends from the New York border some 40 miles into Pennsylvania. Coursing through it are many rushing trout streams, lakes, the **Clarion River, Tionesta** and **Kinzua creeks,** and the **Allegheny River** and its tributaries—all well stocked for fishermen. There are miles of woodland for hiking and 2 outstanding scenic areas. The **Hearts Content Scenic Area,** 15 miles south of Warren, is a 120-acre tract of pristine wilderness. In a mixed forest of virgin white pines that tower high above hemlocks and hardwoods, there are 2 self-guiding interpretive trails, *Jack's* and *Farm,* that meet near **Wheeler Spring.** The **Tionesta Scenic Area,** near the forest's center, is a 2,000-year-old remnant of the original forest that once covered 6 million acres on the Allegheny Plateau. A typical stream-dissected high plateau, it has huge 400-year-old hemlocks and 300-year-old beeches. On some 375 acres of this scenic area, a new forest of black cherry, birch, red maple, white ash, and beech thrives. Two interpretive trails lace this scenic area, which is also rich in wildlife. Some of the animals one might encounter are deer, black bear, wild turkey, red fox, porcupine, weasel, and opossum. There are 68 species of birds including the giant pileated woodpecker, the brilliant scarlet tanager and cardinal, and the yellow-billed cuckoo.

Left: Presque Isle in Lake Erie. Right: ancient stand of eastern hemlock

231

PENNSYLVANIA

The forest also contains an interesting outcrop, the **Boulders**.
For further information write: Supervisor, Warren, Pa. 16365

ARCHBALD POTHOLE STATE PARK
5 miles southwest of Carbondale off U.S. 6
This park features a glacial pothole 42 feet wide and 38 feet deep. It was hollowed out of solid rock by glacial waterfalls cascading down through crevices from the top of an ice sheet.

BEAR MEADOWS NATURAL AREA
6 miles southeast of State College off State 45
The main feature of this 550-acre tract is a peat bog significant for the vast accumulation of pollen embedded in the layers of peat. Studies of its contents have revealed information concerning vegetational and climatic changes in this region extending as far back as 10,000 years ago. The bog contains trees uncommon in this part of central Pennsylvania, such as black spruce and balsam fir. Registered Natural Landmark

BIG SPRING STATE PARK
5½ miles southwest of New Germantown on State 274
Located in Tuscarora State Forest, this park features Big Spring, which has a flow of some 20 million gallons per day.

BOX HUCKLEBERRY SITE
2 miles south of New Bloomfield
In 1918 it was discovered that this colony of box huckleberry consisted of a single plant that had spread over 8 acres by means of rootstocks. Since box huckleberry grows some 6 inches a year, it is estimated that the colony must have sprung from a seed germinated some 1,200 years earlier. Registered Natural Landmark

BUSHKILL FALLS
at Bushkill, 2 miles northwest of U.S. 209
Access to this 300-foot series of roaring waterfalls is over rustic bridges and paths that lead through a scenic gorge. The main drop is 100 feet; the mist at the base sometimes forms a rainbow.
Open Apr–Oct: daily 8–7. Admission: adults $1.50, children 50¢

COOK FOREST STATE PARK
headquarters at Cooksburg on the Clarion River
This 8,000-acre park is a wildlife sanctuary encompassing Cook Forest, which contains one of the largest remaining stands of virgin timber in the state. Eastern white pine dominates, but some hemlock and mixed hardwoods also occur. Many of these old-growth specimens are over 200 feet tall. Registered Natural Landmark

CONNEAUT LAKE
10 miles west of Meadville on U.S. 6 and 322
The largest natural lake wholly within the state, Conneaut covers 929 acres. It is 3 miles long and 1½ miles at its widest point.

CORAL CAVERNS
at Manns Choice, 300 yards east of State 31
This rare coral-reef type of cave features stalactites and stalagmites of unsurpassed color and configuration.
Open summer: daily 9:30–7. Admission: adults $1.50, children (8–12) $1.00

CRYSTAL CAVE
3 miles west of Kutztown via U.S. 222
> This cave contains stalactites and stalagmites that have a crystalline appearance. At every turn there are striking formations—graceful stone curtains, frozen rock fountains, and delicate flutings.
> *Open Feb 15–Nov: daily 9–5; summer 9–7. Admission: adults $2.00, children (6–14) $1.00*

DELAWARE WATER GAP NATIONAL RECREATIONAL AREA
3½ miles east of Stroudsberg via U.S. 611 and I-80
> The Delaware Water Gap is a picturesque gorge cut by the **Delaware River** through **Kittatinny Mountain**, an Appalachian ridge extending from **Shawangunk Mountain** in New York to **Blue Mountain** in Pennsylvania. Like all gaps, this one was formed as the river cut downward through the ridge. Scenic 1,463-foot **Mount Minsi** rises on its Pennsylvania side, and 1,549-foot **Mount Tammany** rises on its New Jersey side. The national recreation area, which was authorized in 1965, will ultimately comprise over 70,000 acres astride the river boundary of the 2 states. It will surround a 12,000-acre reservoir to be impounded by a proposed dam at **Tocks Island,** and it will be divided into 10 sections. Most of the land is still in private ownership, but parts are already open to the public. Like the reservoir, the national recreation area is scheduled to be in full operation by 1979. Its Delaware River Gap section extends for 6 miles downstream from the dam. Its many features include **Labar, De Pue, Shawnee, Schellenbergers,** and **Arrow islands** in the Delaware; parts of Kittatinny Mountain and the *Appalachian Trail;* and of course the famous river-cut gorge. The whole area will be laced with trails and overlooks.
> *For further information write: Interstate 80, Columbia, N.J. 07832*

Delaware Water Gap

Boulder Field in Hickory Run State Park

FAIRMOUNT PARK
northwest Philadelphia, reached by Benjamin Franklin Parkway

This beautiful, natural park covers over 4,000 acres along both banks of the **Schuylkill River** and **Wissahickon Creek.** It is criss-crossed by miles of scenic drives, trails, and bridal paths, and contains the Philadelphia Zoological Garden, America's oldest zoo. Most interesting of all is **Wissahickon Valley,** a Registered Natural Landmark. Most of its central portion, covering 1,250 acres, has been virtually untouched by modern civilization. Located beyond the southern limits of the continental glaciation of the Pleistocene period, this steep-walled valley represents a natural ecological environment. Heavily wooded with large hemlocks, it has an aura of solitude and primeval grandeur.

HAWK MOUNTAIN SANCTUARY
near Drehersville, about 30 miles north of Reading via State 61 and 895

Hawk Mountain is a promontory overlooking **Kittatinny Mountain,** Pennsylvania's easternmost Appalachian ridge. It is located along the ancestral migratory channel of hawks and eagles who ride air currents that take them southward from Canada and New England. Because of a narrowing of Kittatinny ridge, which is 1,200 to 2,000 feet high at this point near Hawk Mountain, certain updrafts are produced that are especially suited to the soaring habits of the raptors. The greatest value of this 2,050-acre sanctuary is the protection it gives to large numbers of hawks who migrate along Kittatinny each autumn. Here they are saved from gunners who formerly hunted in the area. Registered Natural Landmark

HICKORY RUN BOULDER FIELD
22 miles northeast of Hazleton via State 940 and State 534

Hickory Run State Park, which covers some 15,500 acres bordering the **Poconos,** features Boulder Field. The surface of this 30-acre tract is a boulder-strewn area with little vegetation. The huge stones, up to 20 or more feet in length, are unsorted and loosely packed. The field, which is still in its natural state, is the result of climatic conditions in an area that was near to but not covered by the Wisconsin Ice Sheet. Registered Natural Landmark

INDIAN CAVERNS
11 miles east of Tyrone on State 45 between Water Street and State College

Located in the heart of **Spruce Creek Valley,** these extensive caverns contain formations ranging from jewel-like grottoes to **Frozen Niagara,** an enormous sheet of flowstone larger than a 2-story build-

ing. Another unique feature is the **Star Room,** which reveals many starlike formations when darkened.
Open daily: 9–dusk. Admission: adults $2.50, children (6–12) $1.00

INDIAN ECHO CAVERNS
just south of Hummelstown off U.S. 322

These caverns are a wonderland of huge pillars and pipes set against a backdrop of sparkling flowstone that resembles curtains and cascades. Notable features include the **Ballroom Chamber,** with its 49-foot ceiling, and the towering **Rainbow Room.**
Open May–Labor Day: daily 9–8. Apr, Sept, Oct, weekends 10–5. Admission: adults $1.75, children (6–11) 90¢

LAUREL CAVERNS
8 miles east of Uniontown on U.S. 40

These "Caverns in the Clouds" are set in the magnificent Laurel Highlands (*see*). A progression of colored lights re-creates a western sunrise in the **Grand Canyon Passage.**
Open Apr–Nov 15: daily 10–dusk. Admission: adults $2.00, children (6–12) $1.00

LAUREL HIGHLANDS
southwest Pennsylvania

These forested highlands, covering over 2,000 square miles, are replete with brooks, streams, creeks, rivers, and waterfalls, including beautiful **Ohio–Pyle Falls. Chestnut Ridge** and **Laurel Hill,** ridges of the **Allegheny Mountains,** are located here, as is the state's highest point, 3,213-foot-high **Mount Davis** near Salisbury. The area abounds in historic sites and is famous for winter sports.

LINCOLN CAVERNS
3 miles west of Huntingdon, directly on U.S. 22

Maintaining a constant temperature of 52°, these limestone caverns contain abundant crystal formations. The lower cave features the **Giant Pagoda;** the upper one has the **Pipe Organ.**
Open Memorial Day–Labor Day: daily 9–7. Apr, May, Sept, Oct: daily 9–5. Admission: adults $2.50, children (6–12) $1.25

LOST RIVER CAVERNS
Hellertown, a half mile east of State 412

This limestone cave contains an underground river and various crystal formations in its 5 chambers. Highlights include the **Inverted Forest** and the **Long Bridge.**
Open daily 9–9. Admission: adults $1.95, children 95¢

PENN'S CAVE
5 miles east of Centre Hall on State 192

At this cave's entrance is a large spring of unknown origin that flows into and through the cave's passageways. A mile-long tour may therefore be made by boat.
Open May 30–Labor Day: daily 9–8; rest of year, daily 9–5. Admission: adults $2.50, children (6–12) $1.00

PINE CREEK GORGE
about 10 miles southwest of Wellsboro in Tioga State Forest

Pine Creek flows for much of its length through a glaciated gorge some 50 miles long and 1,000 feet deep, that is often called the Grand Canyon of Pennsylvania. With its 300,000 acres of forestland, its deep valleys, rushing creek, and waterfalls, the canyon

PENNSYLVANIA

affords awe-inspiring vistas—especially from Harrison State Park on its east rim and from Colton Point State Park on its west rim. Between the towns of Ansonia and Blackwell, Pine Creek flows through a nearly roadless, steep-walled gorge. This 12-mile stretch, a Registered Natural Landmark, is one of the finest examples of a deep-walled gorge in the eastern United States.

POCONO MOUNTAINS
northeast Pennsylvania

Comprising some 1,200 square miles of wooded hills, valleys, and gorgeous waterfalls, this mountain region contains many famous resorts. The average elevation is about 2,000 feet; the area is bounded on the south by **Kittatinny Mountain** and **Wind Gap,** on the west by **Lake Harmony,** on the east by the **Delaware River,** and on the north by **Lake Wallenpaupack** (the state's largest artificial lake). The Delaware Water Gap (*see*) is a picturesque gorge that serves as the natural gateway to the region.

PRESQUE ISLE
about 5 miles from Erie via Peninsula Drive (State 832)

Jutting out into **Lake Erie,** this 6-mile-long peninsula is the largest sand spit in the **Great Lakes** region. Since Erie's formation some 11,000 years ago, its eastward-moving currents and storm waves have sorted and transported glacial sands from its bed. These have accumulated to form this hook-shaped spit that encloses **Presque Isle Bay,** harbor for the city of Erie. The peninsula, which has been a state park since 1921, supports a climax forest and has about 6 miles of trails cutting through its wooded areas. Presque Isle has 450 species of plant life, 250 species of birds, several deer herds, and a wealth of small wildlife. Registered Natural Landmark

RICKETTS GLEN STATE PARK
25 miles east of Williamsport

This large park contains the **Glens Natural Area,** a 2,500-acre Registered Natural Landmark. The main feature is **Kitchen Creek,** formed by 3 streams that originate in glacially formed lakes. In its 3-mile course through the Glens, the creek falls nearly 1,000 feet; there are 28 waterfalls up to 100 feet high. The flumes, potholes, and ledges of the creek are excellent illustrations of land being shaped by stream erosion.

SNYDER–MIDDLESWARTH NATURAL AREA
5 miles west of Troxelville

This 245-acre virgin forest tract has been preserved with integrity, the only man-made addition being a meandering foot trail. It is an outstanding example of a white pine-hemlock forest which has reached its culminating stage in this region. These giant trees, some of which are over 4 feet in diameter and up to 200 feet high, form the forest canopy. Registered Natural Landmark

TINICUM WILDLIFE PRESERVE
Philadelphia, access from I–95 at International Airport via Tinicum Ave

This natural marshland refuge for wildfowl and game is a 205-acre remnant of the once extensive tidal marshes that covered south Philadelphia. It is no longer tidal, but contains representative flora and fauna. **Darby Creek** is the major stream flowing through the marshland; any pollutants in it are diverted from the preserve. Over 250 species of birds are here. Registered Natural Landmark

RHODE ISLAND

BLOCK ISLAND
about 10 miles offshore midway between Point Judith and Montauk Point, N.Y.

A noted resort and fisherman's paradise, Block Island is a largely treeless expanse of rolling moors, dotted with over 300 freshwater ponds and often obscured by fog. The **Great Salt Pond,** covering over 100 acres and almost bisecting the island, is its only salt pond. The island's most striking feature is its seaward face—a lofty, steep cliff of sand and rock that plummets downward to a boulder-strewn beach and submerged ledges. These ledges are one of the best known marine graveyards on the **Atlantic Coast;** it is said that early settlers lured ships onto these rocks and looted their cargoes. **Mohegan Bluffs,** towering some 200 feet above sea level, stretch for about 5 miles along the southeast coast and offer a spectacular marine vista. **Clay Head,** rising 110 feet at the island's northeast end, bears a strong resemblance to the famous White Cliffs of Dover, England. The Block Island State Beach is also on the eastern shore.

COLT STATE PARK, *Bristol*

Covering over 400 acres along scenic Narragansett Bay (*see*), this park features *Colt Drive,* which extends 2 miles along the shore.

Top: Mohegan Bluffs on Block Island. Below: sailboats in Narragansett Bay

RHODE ISLAND

DIAMOND HILL
in Diamond Hill State Park, at Diamond Hill on State 114

Rising abruptly to some 460 feet, this mile-long hill is heavily veined with quartz deposited millions of years ago by mineral-laden hot water flowing along a fracture in the earth's crust. The hill also contains red masses of jasper.

GREAT SWAMP MANAGEMENT AREA
southeast Rhode Island, access via State 2 and State 138

A state wildlife reservation adjacent to **Worden Pond,** the Great Swamp is haven to deer, Canada geese, foxes, woodchucks, pheasants, snakes, mute swans, and a variety of other wildlife. Its flora is astonishingly varied, ranging from arctic moss to semitropical orchids, and includes an estimated 4,000 different species. This bewitching swamp, which is traversed by many streams, contains countless islets, tussocks of waving grass, and the chalk-colored trunks of drowned trees. On December 19, 1675, during King Philip's War, it was the site of the Great Swamp Fight which nearly annihilated the Narraganset Indians.

INDIAN CEDAR SWAMP
off King's Factory Road, Charlestown

This 700-acre state-owned swamp was once part of a Narraganset Indian Reservation. It was partially drained in order to be used as farmland, but the project was terminated in the 1920s, and the swamp has now returned to its wild condition. It is an ideal habitat for a variety of wildlife, including snowshoe hare and deer. Indian Cedar Swamp is adjacent to Burlingame State Park, which offers boating and fishing in **Watchaug Pond.** Several outstanding Atlantic Ocean beaches are nearby.

LINCOLN WOODS STATE PARK
on State 146 in Lincoln

Situated in an attractive area of woodlands and rock formations, this park features **Olney** and **Barney ponds** as well as several smaller ponds. There is a beach area at Olney Pond, where there are also fishing and boating facilities. Hiking trails and bridal paths run through much of the park. The best known outcrops in the rock district are **Pulpit Rock, Goat Rock,** and **Tablerock Hill.**

NARRAGANSETT BAY

This inlet of the **Atlantic Ocean,** 30 miles long and between 3 and 12 miles wide, is the state's most notable feature. It is bounded on the south by **Rhode Island Sound; Mount Hope Bay** forms its northeast arm. The bay shelters many islands, the largest being **Rhode Island,** or Aquidneck, the site of Newport; **Sakonnet River** lies east of this island. The islands—including **Conanicut, Prudence, Patience,** and **Hope**—and the bay's many inlets were shipping centers in colonial times. Striped bass, bluefish, tautog, cod, flounder, and bluefin tuna are among the record-breaking fish caught in the bay, which also contains many types of shellfish.

POINT JUDITH
on the Atlantic Coast, 11 miles southwest of Newport

A spur of land jutting out into the ocean, this promontory has been the scene of countless marine disasters. It is often hit by violent storms; many vessels take refuge to the west in **Point Judith Pond,** a harbor with an inlet from the Atlantic.

SOUTH CAROLINA

AIKEN STATE PARK
16 miles east of Aiken between U.S. 78 and State 215
This picturesque park features 4 spring-fed lakes and the slow, meandering **South Edisto River**. Beautiful winding trails and drives weave through woodlands and over sand hills.

CAESARS HEAD MOUNTAIN
Caesars Head, in the Blue Ridge Mountains of northwest South Carolina
Caesars Head Mountain rises some 3,000 feet above the resort town of the same name. From the rock that actually forms the head (bearing a resemblance to the profile of Julius Caesar) to the **Saluda River Valley** below, there is a sheer drop of 1,200 feet. The observation tower on top affords a magnificent panorama.
Open daily: 8–dark. Admission: adults 75¢, children (under 12) 50¢

FRANCIS MARION NATIONAL FOREST
eastcentral South Carolina, headquarters at Columbia
Covering some 245,000 acres in the Coastal Plain, this forest is characterized by low flatlands, sandy areas, black swamp waters, huge pines, and moss-festooned oaks. In addition it features "Caro-

Left: Whitewater Falls in Sumter National Forest. Right: beach vista on Hilton Head in Sea Islands

lina bays," small lakes said to have been formed by meteors. The forest was named for General Francis Marion, a Revolutionary War hero known as "Swamp Fox" because he took refuge in the swamps here. Among the forest's major attractions are the fine stands of longleaf pine near **Lake Moultrie** and the **Guillard Lake Scenic Area,** featuring an oxbow-shaped lake formed by the **Santee River.** A strip of land separates the river and the lake, which is surrounded by large, old cypresses. Cypress "knees" up to 8 feet tall are common here. Also within this area is **Dutart Creek,** lined with unique, perforated limestone outcroppings. **Huger Creek,** part of a system that drains **Hell Hole Bay,** is a colorful waterway flanked by moss-covered gums and cypress, old rice fields, and tall loblolly pines. The inky waters of **Wambaw Creek,** which empties into the Santee River, are shaded by a heavy archway of cypress and gums. From the creek one can observe turkey, deer, waterfowl, and alligators. Its banks, particularly the lower reaches near the Echaw road, furnish nesting sites for the Eastern swallow-tailed kite. The **Buck Hall Recreation Area,** with its spreading, moss-draped live oaks and pines, overlooks the flats of the **Cape Romain National Wildlife Refuge.** This sanctuary for migratory birds is separated from the mainland and the forest by the Intracoastal Waterway. Its salt marshes, sandy beaches, and sea islands are havens to a large, wintering population of shore birds and waterfowl. The refuge, which is spread over several islands clustered around **Bull Bay,** includes **Cape Island** with **Cape Romain** at its tip, **Bull Island, Raccoon Key,** and **Lighthouse Island.**

For further information write: 1612 Marion St, Columbia, S.C. 29201

GIVHAN'S FERRY STATE PARK
16 miles west of Summerville on State 61
> Located on the high bluffs overlooking the **Edisto River,** this park features the moss-draped oaks characteristic of the region. It also contains a fair-size stand of large loblolly pines, which gives the area a cathedral-like appearance.

HUNTINGTON BEACH STATE PARK
3 miles south of Murrells Inlet on U.S. 17
> Situated on one of the East Coast's finest beaches, this park has a vast expanse of dunes, inlets, marshes, and freshwater ponds. The unspoiled barrier sand dunes and saltwater marsh at its north end are exceptionally beautiful.

LEE STATE PARK
3 miles northeast of Bishopville on U.S. 15, then 4 miles south at sign
> This park features flowing artesian wells, sand hills, and the **Lynches River Swamp** with its dark undergrowth.

LITTLE PEE DEE STATE PARK
11 miles southeast of Dillon off State 57
> This park is a top fishing spot on the **Little Pee Dee River.** Its scattered, pure white sand dunes are a reminder that a prehistoric ocean once covered the area.

PARIS MOUNTAIN STATE PARK
9 miles north of Greenville off U.S. 25
> High on 2,054-foot Paris Mountain, this park boasts a spectacular view of the **Piedmont Valley.** Its 3 lakes and several streams offer good fishing, and hiking trails wind through virgin forest.

POINSETT STATE PARK
18 miles southwest of Sumter off State 261

An exceptional area, geologically and botanically, this terrain was once covered by the ocean. Nature trails lead from hills to swamps, and dogwoods, yellow jasmine, and birds are everywhere.

SEA ISLANDS

The chain of "sea islands" that lie off the **Atlantic Coast** begins at the mouth of the **Santee River** in South Carolina and continues south off Georgia (*see*) to the mouth of the **Saint Johns River** in northern Florida. South Carolina's islands—including **Folly, Murphy, Wadamalaw, Edisto, Saint Helena, Ladies, Port Royal, Hunting, Parris,** and **Hilton Head**—comprise a vast, wide area of subtropical islands, channels, and beaches. On most, the inner shore is a broad marsh, supporting huge flocks of wintering fowl, as well as otter and other animals. The beaches on the outer shores are often used as nesting places by giant sea turtles. The islands are largely forested. Murphy, for instance, is characteristic with its inland ponds and alligator sloughs, its gums, live oaks, pines and yaupon, and its wild cattle. Edisto Beach State Park boasts over 2 miles of palm-lined beach, rich in seashells, fossils, and driftwood. Hunting Island also has a state park and it is a veritable subtropical coastal forest with palmettos and salt cedars.

SUMTER NATIONAL FOREST
northwest sector of South Carolina, headquarters at Columbia

This forest, comprising 3 separate divisions, covers some 341,000 varied acres. The foothills of the **Appalachians**, the rolling Piedmont, and the upper reaches of the **Savannah River** are some of its many attractions. The Enoree Division is bisected by the **Broad River**, shaded in places by large, bottomland hardwood trees. The Andrew Pickens Division, called gateway to the mountains, features 15 miles of hiking trails and over 80 miles of trout streams for fishing. There are also many waterfalls here because of the abrupt change from rolling country to mountainous terrain. Spectacular **Whitewater Falls**, which originate in North Carolina's Nantahala National Forest (*see*), plummet over 400 feet in a jumble of cascades along the **Whitewater River. Ellicott Rock Scenic Area,** which extends into North Carolina and Georgia, is in this unit. Its 3,584 acres are filled with rugged mountains, tumbling streams, and waterfalls, and it preserves the outdoors in almost pristine condition. Another attraction here is the **Chattooga River**, which forms the border between South Carolina and Georgia for some 40 miles. It begins as a small stream high in the mountains of North Carolina and before flowing into **Tugaloo Lake**, some 50 miles away, becomes a rough whitewater stream that is a real challenge to canoeists. In many places the river is wild and remote, accessible only by foot. Oconee State Park is entirely surrounded by this division. The Long Cane Division preserves samples of the cane brakes that once covered the Piedmont's stream banks.
For further information write: 1612 Marion St, Columbia, S.C. 29201

TABLE ROCK STATE PARK
16 miles north of Pickens between U.S. 178 and State 11

With high Appalachian peaks as its background, this scenic park has a variety of hill and valley trails and many refreshing mountain springs. Its major feature, 3,157-foot Table Rock, is an outlier of the **Blue Ridge.** Near it is 3,400-foot **Pinnacle Mountain.**

SOUTH DAKOTA

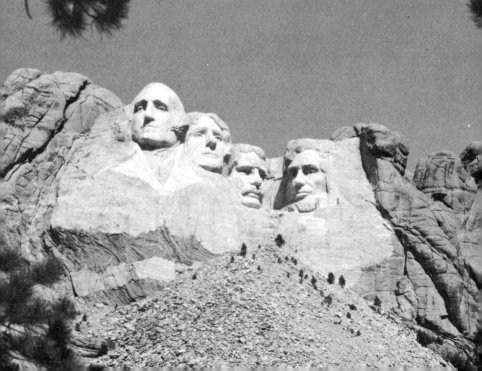

BADLANDS NATIONAL MONUMENT
southwest South Dakota, accessible from east-west I-90 and U.S. 16

Covering over 170 square miles, these are the most spectacular badlands in America. In places sharp-edged, pointed formations rise as high as 300 feet. At one time, during the Oligocene period between 40 to 25 million years ago, this area was a broad marshy plain crossed with sluggish streams trickling down from the highlands. A large number of reptiles, mammals, and birds lived here; their remains were often buried by river sediment or sunk into the marshes. (The monument is now extremely rich in fossils.) Gradually, highland streams deposited layers of sediment that eventually became shales, clays, and sandstones. Then volcanic activity to the west, possibly when the Black Hills (*see*) were being formed, hurled huge quantities of fine ash into the air. The wind bore some of this material eastward, depositing some 25 feet of it over the sedimentary beds that now comprise the Badlands. Much of this volcanic material has been washed away, but some can still be seen as a chalky substance in and near **Sheep Mountain,** on the monument's southwestern tip, and at **Cedar Pass** above the visitor center. Over succeeding millions of years the climate became dryer, rainfall diminished, and grasslands replaced the swamps and silted marshes. The **White River** and its many tributaries began carving the soft sedimentary layers into fins. These were exposed to rain action which helped sculpt the weird formations that characterize the Badlands—steep-walled canyons, sawtoothed ridges, cliffs, pinnacles, spires, knobs, ranging in color from snowy white to deep pinks and orange. Today the annual rainfall here is less than 16 inches. Water still drains from the highlands, but it now cuts into the terrain adding to the erosion, and the landscape is constantly changing. This raw, arid region supports little life. Swifts and cliff swallows nest in the cliff faces, rock wrens build in the crevasses, and golden eagles are sometimes seen atop high buttes. Prairie dogs, coyotes, and badgers and other small mammals as well as snakes live within the monument.

For further information write: Interior, S. Dak. 57750

BEAR BUTTE STATE PARK
5 miles north of Sturgis via State 34 and 79

Once a sacred Indian shrine and landmark for fur traders, pioneers, and gold seekers heading into the Black Hills (*see*), Bear Butte is a huge cone-shaped mass of igneous rock rising 1,400 feet above the surrounding prairie. It was formed millions of years ago when tremendous pressure from deep within the earth pushed molten lava up against overlying rock strata, arching the rock into a dome-shaped mountain. Gravel trails lead to its summit, and a small buffalo herd roams the range beneath it. The park also contains **Bear Butte Lake** and offers an interpretive program. Registered Natural Landmark

BLACK HILLS OF SOUTH DAKOTA
southwest South Dakota and east Wyoming

About 100 miles long and 60 miles wide, this forested mountain region is enclosed by the **Belle Fourche River** on the north and by the **Cheyenne River** on the south. It rises some 2,000 feet above the nearby plains, which are about 3,000 feet above sea level. The

Top left: Eye of the Needle in Custer State Park. Top right: Badlands. Center: bison in Custer State Park. Below: Mount Rushmore National Memorial

Black Hills are ancient; they were full-fledged mountains when the Alps were still a plain and the Himalayas a swamp. The terrain on which the range now stands was once covered by a prehistoric inland sea. Over millions of years a fault in the earth's surface was subjected to immense internal pressure. Eventually a great dome was pushed up that was about 60 miles wide, and 100 miles long, and reached an altitude of some 14,000 feet above sea level. Weathering during succeeding ages gradually withered away the top half of the dome, exposing its inner core of granite, shale, and sandstone. Natural forces also carved peaks, cathedral-like spires (called the **Needles**), ridges, humps, and hogbacks, all separated by winding gulches and canyons. Today the mountain tops are covered with spruce and ponderosa pine, the many creeks are lined with birch, and the floors of canyons and gulches are carpeted with emerald grasses. Because they stand close together the Black Hills look, at close range, like a dark green blanket; at a distance of about 30 miles they seem black, and at 50 miles they appear blue. The area also contains about 12 known natural caves and probably many more unknown ones. All are lined with varicolored calcite crystal, usually in dogtooth and boxwood formations. The Sioux Indians venerated the hills, calling them Paha Sapa, or the sacred grounds. In 1874, spurred by rumors of gold, Lieutenant Colonel George A. Custer invaded the region with 1,200 men. His triumphant reports of gold provoked a stampede of prospectors and such notorious personalities as Wild Bill Hickok, Calamity Jane, and the legendary Deadwood Dick. Eventually the land was wrested from the Indians; the area still yields millions of dollars worth of gold each year. Most of the region falls within Black Hills National Forest, Wind Cave National Monument, and Custer State Park.

BLACK HILLS NATIONAL FOREST
southwest South Dakota and eastern Wyoming, headquarters at Custer
Comprising some 1,500,000 acres in the Black Hills (*see*), this forest boasts a mountainous terrain filled with numerous lakes and creeks. Heavily forested, 7,071-foot **Terry Peak,** the second highest in the state, lies about 4 miles west of Lead, the site of the famous Homestake Mine. From the peak's crest there is a panoramic view of Montana, Wyoming, and North Dakota. **Pactola Lake,** just west of Silver City, is the largest in the forest. Other attractions include **Bridal Veil Falls** on **Spearfish Creek, Roughlock Falls** on **Little Spearfish Creek,** and **Little Spearfish Canyon.**
For further information write: Custer, S. Dak. 57730

CUSTER NATIONAL FOREST
northeast South Dakota, headquarters at Deadwood
Some 200,000 acres of this forest are in 4 areas of Harding County, South Dakota, the main part is in Montana (*see*), and there is a small portion in North Dakota. The **Slim Buttes** are a long range of pine-topped hills with limestone cliffs facing west and ridges and valleys sloping to the east. The **East and West Short Pine Hills** are limestone-capped ridges covered with ponderosa pine. **Cave Hills** lost their limestone caps and have rounded tops sprinkled with pine.
For further information write: Deadwood, S. Dak. 57732

CUSTER STATE PARK
6 miles east of Custer on U.S. 16 Alt.
Nestled amongst the towering peaks and deep valleys of the Black

Hills (*see*), this 72,000-acre park is sanctuary for 1,450 bison, one of the world's largest herds, as well as for deer, antelope, turkeys, elk, and Rocky Mountain sheep. There is fine trout fishing in **Stockade, Sylvan, Legion,** and **Center lakes,** as well as in the miles of streams that course through the park. Trails lead to lookouts atop 6,400-foot **Mount Coolidge** (formerly Sheep Mountain) and 7,242-foot **Harney Peak,** the highest point east of the Rockies. Other features include the **French Creek Gorge Wilderness** area and hiking trails. There are several excellent, scenic roads such as *Wildlife Loop Road* and famous *Needles Highway* (State 87), which goes through the **Needles,** spirelike granite peaks near Sylvan Lake.

DELLS OF THE SIOUX
north of Sioux Falls on U.S. 77, near Dell Rapids

The rapids of the **Big Sioux River** have cut a gorge through red quartzite to form these beautiful, craggy rock formations. One can drive along the picturesque dells on U.S. 77, but a walk along the clifftops affords a more spectacular view.

DEVIL'S GULCH
slightly southwest of Garretson near the Minnesota–Iowa border

This deep chasm through solid rock features creviced walls of pink and purple quartzite. Cedars grow on the tops of the cliffs, clinging mysteriously to the bare rock, and bushes and ferns grow where small clumps of earth are lodged in the narrow ledges. At the head of the gulch is famous **Devil's Staircase,** a hazardous rocky descent leading to the dark green waters at the chasm's bottom.

JEWEL CAVE NATIONAL MONUMENT
about 14 miles west of Custer via U.S. 16

Surrounded by Black Hills National Forest (*see*), this national monument covers 1,275 acres on a high, rolling plateau broken by many gulches and ravines. It is traversed by **Teepee Canyon** on the west and by **Hell Canyon** on the east. This small but beautiful cave is set in the limestone cliffs on the east side of Hell Canyon. Its main passages are supplemented by side galleries and chambers of various sizes. Many of these underground chambers are lined with a solid coating of pyramid-shaped calcite crystals, called dogtooth, which glitter like gems in the light. These range in color from a light green to a darker green and bronze. Some walls and ceilings are lined with boxlike cavities filled with tiny crystals that range in color from light brown to deep chocolate. Bats, whitefooted mice, and bushy-tailed wood rats inhabit the cave.
Cave tours available June 1–Labor Day: daily 8–5. For further information write: Hot Springs, S. Dak. 57747

MOUNT RUSHMORE NATIONAL MEMORIAL
17 miles southwest of Rapid City off U.S. 16

On a 6,000-foot mountain in the central **Black Hills,** the heads of 4 American presidents—George Washington, Thomas Jefferson, Abraham Lincoln, and Theodore Roosevelt—have been carved into the solid granite by sculptor Gutzon Borglum. Begun in 1927 and finished in 1941, the memorial is a masterpiece of engineering and boldly symbolizes the ideals of the young nation through its great leaders. Each head is approximately 60 feet high and is best viewed under morning light. Floodlights illuminate the faces at night from June 1 to Labor Day.
For further information write: Keystone, S. Dak. 57751

SOUTH DAKOTA

PALISADES STATE RECREATION AREA
8 miles north of Beaver Valley on State 11

This scenic 102-acre area features the Palisades, mammoth pillars of red, gray, and purple quartzite, which tower above the trees like ancient ruins. This striking illusion is created by the stone which seems to be divided into regular blocks by lines and surface fissures. Dark cedars dot the bare rock. **Split Rock River** traverses the park and has trails leading to unexpected crevices and strangely shaped rocks on both sides.

RUSHMORE CAVE
near Keystone, 6 miles east of U.S. 16A

This multichambered underground cavern features stalagmites, stalactites, helictites, and unusual flowerlike formations.

Open summer: daily 7–10; May, Sept, Oct: daily 8–6. Admission: adults $1.50, children (7–13) 50¢

SIECHE HOLLOW STATE PARK
15 miles northwest of Sisseton off State 10

Located on the east escarpment of **Coteau des Prairie,** a plateau in northeast South Dakota and west Minnesota, this park covers 887 wooded acres overlooking the **Minnesota River Valley.** It has a rough glaciated terrain with a continuously flowing cold, spring-fed stream that encourages vegetation rarely seen in the surrounding prairie country. Registered Natural Landmark

SITTING BULL CRYSTAL CAVERNS
9 miles south of Rapid City on Rushmore Road (Highway 16)

Featuring rare dogtooth spar formations, a form of calcite in acute crystals, this cave has been recognized by the United States Geological Society as an outstanding crystal cave. Petrified sea life is embedded in its walls and there are scenic tours of its caverns.

SPEARFISH VALLEY

One of the most popular fishing and scenic retreats in the northern end of the Black Hills (*see*), this fertile valley lies at the head of beautiful **Spearfish Canyon.** The cliffs on both sides of the canyon are made of rimrock, called Deadwood formation, composed of gray and red sandstone, greenish shales, and limestone; the cliffs constantly change color in the sunlight. The flora includes green pine, birch, poplar, and quaking aspen. *Spearfish Canyon Drive* is a 17-mile segment of U.S. 14A that follows **Spearfish Creek.**

TIMBER OF AGES BLACK HILLS PETRIFIED FOREST
about a half mile south of Piedmont, a mile off I-90

This 2-acre tract features an outstanding collection of the broken remains of petrified trees, some as large as 80 feet long and 3 feet thick. There are frequent lecture tours through the area. The museum exhibits cut and polished petrified wood, minerals, rocks, and fossils from the Black Hills and Badlands (*see both*).

Open May–Sept: daily 7–7. Admission: adults $1.25, children 75¢

WILDCAT CAVE
about 7 miles southwest of Rapid City on State 40, then a half mile west at sign

This cave features limestone chambers connected by a fissure that is 160 feet high in some places. There are fine examples of flowstone and various crystal formations, notably rare frostwork.

Open daily: Apr–Oct. Admission: adults $1.25, children (6–11) 45¢

Left: rock formations in Custer National Forest. Right: prong-horn antelope

WIND CAVE NATIONAL PARK
about 10 miles north of Hot Springs via U.S. 285

Lying on the southeastern flank of South Dakota's **Black Hills**, this park preserves a relatively unspoiled section of the original prairie grasslands. It is a region of rolling wooded plains covered with rippling seas of wild grasses and bright splashes of wild-flowers, as well as eastern bur oak and ponderosa pine. The outstanding feature is an unusual type of limestone cavern containing numerous subterranean passages and rooms, some of which are lined with colorful calcite crystal formations. The air currents that blow in and out of the cave, a phenomenon probably caused by changes in atmospheric pressure, suggested the park's name. The limestone bed in which Wind Cave was formed is between 300 and 630 feet thick. Known as Pahasapa limestone, it was deposited in a huge inland sea some 300 million years ago. Subsequently, several periods of elevation and subsidence occurred. Geologists believe that the final uplift of this land from beneath the sea occurred about 60 million years ago, and that the cave began at this time. The ceilings and walls of some of the caverns are covered with boxwork, delicately colored calcite fins arranged in a honeycomb pattern. There are also displays of rare "frostwork" and "popcorn." With guides, visitors can follow over a mile of the explored passages; most of the chambers are still unexplored. The trails descend some 326 feet to the lowest point, and cave trips are conducted daily from April 1 to October 31.

The park is also a wildlife sanctuary for many species that were characteristic of the **Great Plains** and **Rocky Mountains** before the arrival of the white man. These include a bison herd, black-tailed prairie dogs, and graceful pronghorn antelopes, the swiftest North American mammal.

For further information write: Hot Springs, S. Dak. 57747

WONDERLAND CAVE
between Rapid City and Sturgis, off I-90 and Hwy 14, up Little Elk Canyon Rd

This 2-level living cavern extends under the mountain for many miles, radiating out in every direction. It features a large variety of crystal formations—stalactites, stalagmites, helictites, and glittering dogtooth spar formations about 60 million years old.

Open daily May 15–Sept. Admission: adults $1.50, children 60¢

TENNESSEE

BRISTOL CAVERNS
5 miles southeast of Bristol on U.S. 421

These caverns contain interesting stalagmites and stalactites. A well-lit trail leads through their several levels and along the banks of an underground river.

Open: Mon–Sat 8:30–6, Sun 12–6, also evenings June 15–Labor Day. Admission: adults $1.50, children (7–12) 90¢

CEDARS OF LEBANON STATE PARK
about 8 miles south of Lebanon, on U.S. 231 and State 10

Named after the dense cedar forest that covered much of Biblical Lebanon, this area is divided into 2 sections. About 500 acres are reserved for recreation, and 8,519 acres comprise a state forest protecting one of the largest stands of red cedar remaining in the United States. There are many open limestone glades—peculiar to this region—which contain fossils, rare orchids, and native plants. Limestone caverns and "sinks" are also of interest.

CHEROKEE NATIONAL FOREST
east Tennessee, headquarters at Cleveland

Named for the Indian tribe that once occupied the **Tennessee River Valley,** this national forest covers some 610,000 acres in a long, narrow strip of rugged **Appalachian Mountain** terrain on the Tennessee-North Carolina border. Its 2 divisions are separated by Great Smoky Mountains National Park (*see*). Dominant tree species here are pine, hemlock, oak, and poplar. The forest is also rich in wildlife, beautiful lakes, and scenic splendor. There are over 500 miles of hiking trails, including many self-guiding nature walks and a section of the famous *Appalachian Trail*. The Appalachians are among the oldest mountains in the world, and the mountains of the Cherokee are outstanding attractions. **Roan Mountain,** about 10 miles southeast of Johnson City on the state line, extends into North Carolina's Pisgah National Forest (*see*). There is a 600-acre rhododendron garden on the mountain; a highway leads to **Roan High Knob,** its 6,313-foot summit. **Unaka Mountain,** about 5 miles east of Erwin, is another popular landmark on the state boundary. It is famous for its virgin spruce forest. Cherokee National Forest contains many other mountains and ranges, including **Greene, Stone, Meadow Creek, Sampson, Buffalo, Holston, Forge,** and **Chilhowee mountains,** and the **Bald, Iron, Unaka,** and **Unicoi ranges.** More than 100 waterfalls grace the Cherokee, notably **Bald River Falls,** near Tellico Plains, and **Benton Falls,** a unique umbrella-type falls near the **Chilhowee Recreation Area.** The fauna is varied, including black bear, Virginia white-tailed deer, ruffed grouse, Eastern wild turkey, squirrel, fox, raccoon, and cottontail rabbit; European wild boar are found in the Tellico Ranger District. Fishing is excellent in the forest's 17,000 acres of lake water and over 300 miles of trout streams. There are also more than 50 recreational areas.

For further information write: Box 400, Cleveland, Tenn. 37311

CHICKASAW STATE PARK
18 miles south of Jackson and near Henderson, access from U.S. 64 and 45 and State 100

This park, which covers 11,315 acres of magnificent west Tennessee timberland, was begun in 1934 by the Works Progress Administration (WPA) and the Civilian Conservation Corps (CCC) to reclaim submarginal land and to preserve trees and game. Its heavily wooded terrain is cut with many precipitous ravines. The first construction was 54-acre **Lake Placid,** located in a low valley on **Piney Creek.** It is surrounded by stands of oak, hickory, elm, and pine. Later, 50-acre **Lac La Joie** was built on **Gray's Creek.** Its irregular shoreline is lined with trees. The fishing at Chickasaw is excellent, especially for bass and bluegill. The park is rich in wildlife, notably quail, turkey, as well as squirrel, rabbit, raccoon, opossum, and red fox. There are also many good hiking trails.

CUMBERLAND CAVERNS
7 miles southeast of McMinnville on Highway 8, reached by U.S. 70S

These caverns at the western edge of the **Cumberland Mountains** contain many enormous galleries. The **Hall of the Mountain King** is reputed to be the largest cave room in eastern America. Other attractions include waterfalls, tapering stalactites and stalagmites, stone draperies, and a saltpeter mine.

Open: daily June–Aug; weekends only in May, Sept, Oct

CUMBERLAND GAP NATIONAL HISTORICAL PARK. *See* KENTUCKY

DAVID CROCKETT STATE PARK
a half mile west of Lawrenceburg on U.S. 64

This 1,000-acre park was dedicated in 1957 to honor one of Ten-

Left: scenic vista in Cherokee National Forest. Top right: Reelfoot Lake. Below: rhododendron in full bloom in Great Smoky Mountains National Park

nessee's most famous sons. It is located on the banks of **Shoal Creek,** where Davy Crockett once operated a powder mill, gristmill, and distillery. There is year-round fishing in picturesque 40-acre **Crockett Lake** and hiking on superb trails.

FALL CREEK FALLS STATE PARK
12 miles west of Pikeville on State 30, then 4 miles south
Waterfalls, deep chasms, gorges, and virgin timber are to be seen in this spectacular 16,000-acre park. Fall Creek Falls plunge 256 feet into a shaded pool. Other equally impressive waterfalls include **Piney, Cane Creek, Cane Creek Cascades,** and **Rock House Creek falls.** A picturesque swimming beach is located on Cane Creek, with its rocky cliffs and tall pines.

GREAT SMOKY MOUNTAINS NATIONAL PARK
east Tennessee and west North Carolina, headquarters 2 miles south of Gatlinburg, Tenn.
Split by the *Appalachian Trail,* which forms part of the border between North Carolina and Tennessee, this park covers 800 square miles and is about equally divided between the 2 states. The primeval, time-worn **Smokies,** a segment of the **Appalachians,** take their name from the bluish haze, sometimes as dense as smoke, that hangs over them. With 12 summits over 6,000 feet high and the main ridge more than 5,000 feet high for its length of 36 miles, they are among the highest peaks in the eastern United States.

The main feature of this park is its dense vegetation—over 95 per cent of the area is dominated by forest, and 40 per cent is essentially unaltered, making the park one of America's great wilderness regions. Fertile soils and heavy rains over a long period have permitted a variety of flora to develop—there are some 1,400 types of flowering plants, almost 300 mosses and liverworts, 230 lichens, over 2,000 fungi, and an inestimable variety of trees. Broadleaf trees predominate in the park's many coves, and the ridge crest above 6,000 feet is covered with conifer forest similar to those of central Canada. Here red spruce and Fraser fir represent the southernmost limit of the Canadian zone in eastern America. Hemlock forests are common between about 3,500 feet and 5,000 feet, and cove hardwoods occur in sheltered situations below 4,500 feet. Northern hardwoods, predominantly yellow birch and American beech, occur about 4,500 feet. There are many other types of trees, notably oaks and pines. The Smokies are also famous for their balds, or treeless areas on mountain tops, and ridges that are thickly carpeted with plants. If plants of the heath family predominate, they are called heath balds. Known locally as slicks, heath balds here consist mainly of catawba rhododendron and mountain laurel. Balds on which grasses and sedges predominate are termed grass balds. Each spring the whole park is blanketed with a magnificent profusion of wildflowers.

Great Smoky's major attractions include 6,643-foot **Clingman's Dome,** the highest mountain in the range and the highest point traversed by the Appalachian Trail. (In all, the park has some 600 miles of hiking and horse trails, including several self-guiding ones.) Its second highest peak is 6,621-foot **Mount Guyot,** and its third highest, 6,593-foot **Mount Le Conte.** These peaks are covered with spruce-fir stands. Other natural wonders include the **Chimney Tops,** which tower at the head of **Sugarlands Valley; Alum Cave Bluffs;** 5,048-foot **Newfound Gap;** and **Caves Cove,** traversed by an 11-mile loop road. Wildlife is abundant and includes bears, bob-

Mount Le Conte and bear cub in Great Smoky Mountains Park

cats, and great horned owls. There are over 600 miles of fast-flowing boulder-strewn streams, such as **Little River,** in which 70 types of fish are found. Great Smoky is accessible via the transmountain highway (U.S. 441), which crosses it through Newfound Gap; by Tennessee State 73 and 32; and by North Carolina State 284. The park lies at the southern end of the famous Blue Ridge Parkway (*see Virginia*).

For further information: Superintendent, Gatlinburg, Tenn. 37739

JEWEL CAVE
15 miles northwest of I-40 via Dickson exit of 46A

This cave features pillars, flowstones, and unusual onyx formations. There are exhibits of fossils and prehistoric bones.

Open May–Sept: daily 9–7; rest of year by advance request. Admission: adults $2.00, children (6–16) $1.00

KENTUCKY LAKE

Kentucky Lake, on the **Tennessee River,** is the largest man-made lake in the world. It is formed by Kentucky Dam, just southeast of Paducah, Kentucky. The lake extends south from the dam; about 40 miles are in Kentucky, and the other 184 miles stretch through the heart of western Tennessee. It covers about 160,300 acres and has over 2,300 miles of wooded shoreline, which is dotted with state parks and resorts. Kentucky Dam is the largest in the famous Tennessee Valley Authority (TVA) system, a vast network of dams on the Tennessee River in Tennessee (especially the eastern part of the state), Alabama, and North Carolina. TVA dams and reservoirs made possible rural electrification and important flood control, navigational, and recreational projects in the Tennessee River drainage basin.

LOOKOUT MOUNTAIN
Chattanooga vicinity

This famous mountain is actually a narrow ridge, about 2,000 feet high, of the **Cumberland Plateau,** which extends into Tennessee, Georgia, and Alabama. It begins near the famous **Moccasin Bend of the Tennessee River** near Chattanooga. The northern part of Lookout Mountain may be reached by Lookout Mountain Road, by Ochs Highway, or by Lookout Mountain Incline Railway. One of the steepest such railways in the world, the Incline Railway starts

251

from Saint Elmo Avenue in Chattanooga and runs to the mountain's 2,392-foot northeast end. **Point Park,** a federal area on top of the mountain, offers a fantastic view of Moccasin Bend below and the famous, balanced **Umbrella Rock.** This portion of the ridge was also the site of the Civil War "Battle Above the Clouds." Also atop Lookout Mountain is **Rock City Garden,** a natural city of rock featuring some 10 acres of lichen-coated sandstone formations. The *Enchanted Trail* goes through narrow crevices, some as deep as 100 feet, and a thrilling suspension bridge carries the trail between 2 high bluffs. From **Lover's Leap,** a rocky promontory named after an old Cherokee legend, there is a panoramic view of the **Tennessee Valley** and 7 states beyond.

LOST SEA
off State 68 between Sweetwater and Madisonville
This gigantic underground lake, which may be toured on glass-bottomed boats, is well stocked with rainbow trout. The caverns leading to it are filled with rock and mineral deposits and rare cave flowers.
Open June–Labor Day: 8–sundown; rest of year: 9–sundown. Admission: adults $2.95, children (6–12) $1.50

MEEMAN–SHELBY FOREST STATE PARK
13 miles north of Memphis, off U.S. 51
The mighty **Mississippi River** forms the western boundary of this 12,500-acre park, which is one of the most beautiful in the state. It is filled with wildlife and natural areas, which may be reached by miles of outstanding hiking trails. There is good year-round fishing in 125-acre **Poplar Tree Lake,** and the Meeman Museum and Nature Center is open daily from May through Labor Day. A stable of horses and many miles of wooded trails are available for the enjoyment of horseback riders.

NATCHEZ TRACE PARKWAY. *See* MISSISSIPPI

PICKETT STATE PARK
12 miles north of Jamestown via U.S. 27 and State 154
A lovely, remote wilderness park, Pickett covers some 14,000 acres. It is distinctive for its unusual rock formations and its many scenic points of interest. It encompasses an extremely wide range of vegetation, and wildlife is abundant. The park also contains 45-acre **Arch Lake** with its beautiful, cliff-lined, sandy beach. Some 50 miles of rhododendron-lined trails lead through primitive forests to caves, waterfalls, and natural bridges.

REELFOOT LAKE
northwest Tennessee, just east of Tiptonville
This lake was formed during the winter of 1811–12, when a series of shocks, known as the New Madrid earthquake, caused upheavals from Boston to New Orleans. Scientists consider it the most severe quake ever recorded in the United States. The most serious shocks occurred in this corner of Tennessee, where the land sank 8 to 25 feet. The waters of the **Mississippi River** seeped into the depression to form this 14,500-acre lake. Its surface is covered with tree stumps, other weird remains of a once-dense forest, and floating lotus beds. Giant cypress covered with wild grape and muscadine line its shores. The environment provides sanctuary for 250 species of birds, some of which nest on its islands. It is unexcelled as a potential study area for marsh-plant succession. Reelfoot State Park is on its southwest shore. Registered Natural Landmark

RUBY FALLS
3 miles from center of Chattanooga, on Lookout Mountain Scenic Hwy (State 148)

These falls, inside **Lookout Mountain Caves**, occur when a stream, 1,120-feet below the earth's surface, drops a sheer 145 feet. They may be reached by an elevator that descends through 260 feet of solid rock. Other features of these subterranean caves are curtains and draperies of varicolored stone. The passages and chambers are filled with rock formations with descriptive names such as **Onyx Jungle,** the **Cactus and the Candle, Elephant's Foot, Beehives,** and **Steak and Potatoes.** The fantastic **Hall of Dreams** contains hundreds of crystal-like "capillary tubes" and helictites millions of years old and still in the process of formation.
Open May–Oct: daily 7–11; Nov–Apr: 7:30–9:30. Admission: adults $2.00, children (6–12) 75¢

SIGNAL MOUNTAIN
9 miles north of Chattanooga, off Cherokee Boulevard

This is a southern spur of **Walden Ridge,** a portion of the **Cumberland Plateau.** Signal Mountain extends about 60 miles between **Sand Mountain** on the south and **Crab Mountain** on the north, and parallels the **Sequatchie River.** It acquired its name during the Civil War, when southern armies used it as a communication point. **Signal Point** and **James Point** afford splendid views of the **Tennessee River** as it passes through **Raccoon Mountain, North Chickamauga Gorge,** and the **Grand Canyon of the Tennessee.**

TUCKALEECHEE CAVERNS
3 miles south of southern edge of Townsend via paved road off State 73

Surrounded by Great Smoky Mountains National Park (*see*), this cave is noted for its onyx formations. It has an unusually large chamber.
Open Apr–Oct: daily 9–6. Admission: adults $2, children (6–12) $1

WONDER CAVE
4 miles north of Monteagle and a half mile off U.S. 41

This cave, which contains unusual onyx formations, features an underground stream near its mouth. The main stalactite room is some 400 yards long, 100 yards wide, and 8 feet high.
Open daily: 7–sunset. Admission: adults $2, children (6–12) 85¢

View of Lower Sequatchie Valley from Signal Mountain

TEXAS

AMISTAD RECREATION AREA
south Texas, on Rio Grande between Langtry and Del Rio

This is an international recreation area centered around Amistad Reservoir, created by Amistad Dam on the **Rio Grande**. The dam— 12 miles upstream from Del Rio, Texas, and Ciudad Acuna, Mexico —was a cooperative Mexican-American undertaking. The reservoir offers boating, water skiing, and fishing. Within the recreation area there is also limited hunting for doves, quails, and waterfowl, as well as for small animals such as raccoons, rabbits, and squirrels. The flora and fauna here are mostly those found on the **Edwards Plateau** of southwest Texas, but there are also many species of plants and animals from the **Chihuahuan Desert**. The most common plants are blackbrush, guajillo, cenizo, yucca, sotol, mesquite, creosote bush, leatherplant, and various cacti.

For further information write: Box 1473, Del Rio, Texas

ANGELINA NATIONAL FOREST
eastcentral Texas, headquarters at Lufkin

This small forest covers 154,389 acres on the **Angelina** and **Neches rivers**. It includes **Bouton Lake**, bordered by river-bottom hardwoods; **Boykin Springs**, a 10-acre spring-fed lake surrounded by longleaf pine and a scenic foot trail; and Sam Rayburn Reservoir, offering recreational facilities in an attractive setting.

For further information write: Box 969, Lufkin, Texas 75901

BENTSEN–RIO GRANDE SCENIC PARK
about 6 miles southwest of Mission, via U.S. 83, Farm Rd 2062, and Park Rd 43

Bordered by the Rio Grande, this park preserves the flora and fauna of the **Lower Rio Grande Valley**. It is a favorite spot for bird watchers who have sighted 200 species, including rare specimens— the zone-tailed hawk, groove-billed ani, and red-eyed cowbird.

BIG BEND NATIONAL PARK
southwest tip of Texas, headquarters in the park at Panther Junction

Bounded on 3 sides by the U-shaped "Big Bend" of the **Rio Grande** (which forms the boundary between the United States and Mexico), this park covers 708,221 spectacular acres. It is a region of wild, stark expanses of desert; colorful, deep canyons; and rugged mountains that rise abruptly from arid plateaus. The winding Rio Grande flows for 107 miles in its bend around the southern side of the park, where it has carved several canyons through mountains and mesas. The longest (25 miles) and most colorful of these gorges is **Boquillas**, cut through the **Sierra del Carmen**. Others include **Santa Elena** (1,500 feet deep and 18 miles long) cut through the **Mesa de Anguilla**, as well as **Mariscal Canyon**, cut through **Mariscal Mountain**. Big Bend also includes the entire range of the **Chisos Mountains**, which rise to 7,777 feet at **Emory Peak**, highest in the park. Several roads and trails begin at the **Basin** of these mountains and lead to the various natural wonders. One of the most rewarding drives is to Santa Elena Canyon, which can be explored on foot. Here one has a magnificent view of the Rio Grande as it is joined by **Terlingua Creek** at the gorge's mouth. The Chisos Mountains are the central feature of the park; as the surrounding desert slopes downward from their bases, it is broken by a series of hills and

Top left: windswept dunes on Padre Island. Top right: El Capitan in Guadaloupe Mountains National Park. Center: cattle grazing in Panhandle region. Bottom: landscape in Big Bend National Park

mesas. These include the **Grapevine Hills** with their sawtooth ridges, and **Dagger Flat,** covered with yucca. There are several self-guiding trails, including *Lost Mine,* which begins at the Basin and goes to **Lost Mine Ridge** offering a vista of the whole park. This trail also includes an overlook at the head of **Juniper Canyon,** from where one can see many miles into Mexico.

Big Bend features over 1,000 species of plants. The lowland river valleys are covered with cottonwoods and willows; the desert floor is the habitat of tenacious creosote bushes and flowering cacti; and the rugged mountain slopes are dotted with piñon, juniper, Douglas fir, and Arizona cypress. Wildlife is plentiful, including more than 200 species of birds, deer, coyotes, foxes, collared peccaries (piglike mammals), and mountain lions.

For further information write: Big Bend National Park, Tex. 79834

CADDO LAKE

northeast Texas and northwest Louisiana, west of Jefferson, Texas

Legend says that this 32,700-acre lake was formed in the dark of the moon by shaking earth spirits who had been angered by a Caddo Indian chief. Scientists, however, tell us that it may have been created by the great New Madrid earthquake in 1811. The huge lake has a primeval, swamplike atmosphere due to the moss-draped trees and dense forests on its banks. Covered by a lush aquatic growth, it is fed from the west by waters of **Big Cypress Bayou** and other streams. Its 42 miles of channels function as boat roads; Caddo Lake Scenic Park is on its southern shore.

CAVERNS OF SONORA

about 15 miles southwest of Sonora via U.S. 290 and Farm Road 1989

In these fantastically beautiful caverns, situated at a shallow depth in Cretaceous limestone, every hue of the rainbow shimmers from an intricate network of cave growth. They can be observed from a 1-mile trail. In addition to all the usual formations, this cave contains a rare, complex type of helictite that is often clear or transparent and bladed instead of cylindrical. Many walls are covered with a coral-like growth that has a feathery appearance. The cave is generally quite active (wet), especially in its lower regions. Registered Natural Landmark

Open daily: 8–6. Admission: adults $2.00, children $1.00

DAVIS MOUNTAINS STATE SCENIC PARK

1 mile north of Fort Davis on State 17, then west on State 118 for 3 miles

This 1,869-acre park is set in a sloping basin in the Davis Mountains in the midst of many peaks, canyons, and sunny upland pastures. A highly scenic loop drive (State 17, 118, 166) through the mountains traverses the park and goes past Fort Davis National Historic Site, **Madera Canyon,** and **Skillmans Grove.** It skirts **Mount Locke,** upon whose 6,791-foot peak stands the University of Texas McDonald Observatory.

DAVY CROCKETT NATIONAL FOREST

eastcentral Texas, headquarters at Lufkin

Covering 161,556 acres of pine woods, Davy Crockett extends west from the banks of the **Neches River.** From **Neches Bluff,** there is a fine view of the river bottom. The 6-acre spring-fed **Ratcliff Lake** has a winding footpath, which leads along its shore and through an adjacent forest zone.

For further information write: Box 969, Lufkin, Texas 75901

DINOSAUR VALLEY STATE SCENIC PARK
1 mile west of Glen Rose on Farm Road 205, then 1 mile west on gravel road

The fossil footprints found here preserved in limestone have been exposed in the bed of the **Paluxey River** and tributary creeks by stream erosion. These are extremely well preserved and provide insight into the habits of large dinosaurs. The tracks represent 3 types of dinosaur: sauropods, huge plant-eating reptiles whose footprints are 38 inches long from heel to toe; theropods, 12-foot-tall meat eaters, who walked on their hind legs; and ornithods, or "duckbilled" dinosaurs, about 30 feet long, 16 feet tall, and primarily vegetarians, having 2,000 tiny teeth in their duckbill snouts. Registered Natural Landmark

GUADALOUPE MOUNTAINS NATIONAL PARK
110 miles east of El Paso, adjacent to U.S. 62–180

This recently-established 77,518-acre park is situated in the Guadaloupe Mountains, a V-shaped range, whose northwestern and northeastern arms extend into New Mexico. **Guadaloupe Peak,** at 8,751 feet, is the highest point in Texas. Other peaks in the Texas portion of the range include 8,087-foot **El Capitan** and 8,676-foot **Bush Mountain.** The mountains are composed of Permian marine limestone and contain one of the most extensive and significant fossil reefs in the world.

The park includes both desert lowlands and forested mountains and canyons, and its vegetation is extremely varied. Typical **Chihuahuan Desert** plants are found at low elevations, hardwoods in the canyons, and evergreen forests of Ponderosa pine and Douglas fir in the highlands. Some of the deep canyons, cut by highland waters, contain unique groups of plant and animal life that are relict associations of the Pleistocene epoch. The animal life includes the Wapiti or American elk, mule deer, coyote, and bobcat; black bear and mountain lion are sometimes seen. Public facilities and staffing are limited and extensive visitor use is not encouraged at this time. There are some 55 miles of rough mountain trails, and good views of the peaks may be had from U.S. 62–180, which crosses the park's southeast edge.

For further information: Box 1598, Carlsbad, New Mexico 88220

HUECO TANKS STATE PARK
22 miles northeast of El Paso, off U.S. 62

This park features unique natural cisterns formed by depressions in limestone. These tanks store water during infrequent rains and provide the only water for many miles. In prehistoric times Indians camped here and left behind cave drawings. The site also served as a watering place for the Butterfield Overland Mail route.

INNER SPACE CAVERNS
1 mile south of Georgetown, on I-35

Discovered in 1963 by the constructors of Interstate 35, this subterranean cave is filled with stalagmites, stalactites, and flowstone. The main chamber, reached by cable car, is where the remains of prehistoric mastodons and wolves and Ice Age animals are on display. The caves maintain an average temperature of 72°.

Open summer: daily 9–7; after Labor Day 10–5. Admission: adults $2.00, children (6–12) $1.00

LLANO ESTACADO, or STAKED PLAIN

This vast, semiarid treeless segment of the southern **Great Plains** extends over most of the Texas **Panhandle** south of the **Canadian River** and into a portion of New Mexico east of the **Pecos River.** The area, characterized by almost level, wind-swept grasslands, is broken only by canyons formed by streams that eventually contribute to major Texas waterways—the Canadian, **Red, Brazos,** and **Colorado rivers.** It is sometimes divided into the **High** (or Panhandle) **Plains** centered around Amarillo, and the **South Plains** in the vicinity of Lubbock. The Llano Estacado is bordered on the east by the irregular **Cap Rock** escarpment, which marks the transition to prairie country. On the southeast, rugged **Edwards Plateau,** known locally as the Hill Country, forms an extension.

LONGHORN CAVERN STATE SCENIC PARK
5 miles south of Burnet on U.S. 281 to Park Road 4, then 5.5 miles west
Located in one of the world's oldest geological areas, this 708-acre park features what is reputedly the third largest cavern in the world. The cave was the home of prehistoric cavemen; in the 19th century it was used by the Confederate Army and was later a hideout for outlaws. Its 2 miles of lighted passageway lead to 5 chambers formed of transparent crystal.
Open June–Labor Day: daily 8:30–5:30

MACKENZIE STATE RECREATION PARK
4 miles east of downtown Lubbock, entrance at Park Road 18
This park has one of the few remaining prairie-dog towns in the state. It also includes a segment of **Yellow House Canyon,** where **Double Mountain** and **Yellow house forks of the Brazos River** meet.

MONAHANS SANDHILLS SCENIC PARK
south of Odessa, five miles off I-20/U.S. 80
This unusual park covers 3,840 acres of wind-sculptured sand dunes, only a small portion of the huge, 40,000-acre **Texas Sandhills** region. This area was a severe obstacle to pioneers in their wagon trains. Indians who were familiar with it, however, often camped in the region; by digging a trench they could scoop up fresh water from between the dunes. The Texas Sandhills also contain one of the nation's largest oak forests, a portion of which is also in this park. The forest is not readily apparent because the mature Har-

Left: limestone formations in Natural Bridge Caverns. Right: white pelicans resting on Padre Island National Seashore

vard oaks are rarely over 3 feet tall. To compensate for this miniature surface growth, their roots descend as far as 90 feet into the
ground. The park offers sand buggy rides over the rolling dunes.

NATURAL BRIDGE CAVERNS
between San Antonio and New Braunfels, about 6 miles from I-35
The gigantic rooms and colorful limestone formations of this living
cave stretch for more than one mile underground. Some of the rooms
are 300 feet long and 5 stories high. Registered Natural Landmark
*Open Sept–May: daily 9–6; June–Aug daily 9–6:30. Admission:
adults $2.50, children $1.50*

ODESSA METEOR CRATER
about 10 miles southwest of Odessa via U.S. 80
The second largest meteor crater site in the United States (the largest is Barringer in Arizona), the 40-acre tract contains 2 meteorite
impact craters. The largest, **Main Crater,** is about 550 feet wide
and drilling has revealed its depth to be about 100 feet. It is now
silted almost level with the surrounding plain. Excavation of **Crater
Number 2** has shown it to be 70 feet wide and 17 feet deep. Meteorites of nickel-iron have been found in the craters and their environs.
Registered Natural Landmark
Open June–Aug: Thurs–Mon 11–6; Sept–May: Sat and Sun 11–5

PADRE ISLAND NATIONAL SEASHORE
*parallel to Gulf Coast between Corpus Christi and Port Isabel, headquarters at
Corpus Christi*
Padre Island, which stretches over 100 miles along the Texas **Gulf
Coast** from Corpus Christi on the north almost to the **Rio Grande**
on the south, ranges in width between a few hundred feet to about
3 miles. It is an excellent example of a barrier island, having been
built up by wave action and crowned by wind-formed dunes. It is
separated from the mainland by the shallow **Laguna Madre,** which
is part of the Intracoastal Waterway and is nowhere wider than 10
miles. Both ends of this long, narrow island have been developed
and have parks and palm-fringed resorts. The central portion, about
80 miles long and comprising the longest national seashore in the
United States, is in its natural state.

From the Gulf of Mexico to the lagoon side, Padre Island consists
of a wide clean beach of sand and tiny shells, dunes, grassy flats
interrupted by smaller dunes, and finally an area of sand dunes and
mud flats that merge with the waters of the lagoon. The landscape
changes continually because of winds and strong tides. The dunes,
many 50 feet high, sometimes shift over to the grass-covered flatlands; some have become somewhat stabilized by the roots of
grasses and shrubs. Plants struggle for survival; on the outer dunes
these include senna, croton, railroad vine, and evening primrose.
Grasses are prevalent on the flats, and the area near the lagoon
features pure stands of sesuvium. Birds, mammals, reptiles (marine
loggerhead turtles), and marine creatures thrive here. Over 350
species of birds are seasonal (sandhill cranes) or year-round residents (great blue herons). Although the island was discovered in
1519, it was named for Padre Nicolas Balli, a Spanish priest who
arrived in 1800, and who with his nephew established the Santa
Cruz Ranch about 30 miles from the southern tip. Since then cattle
have always been raised on the island. Causeways at Corpus Christi
and Port Isabel connect it with the mainland.
For further information write: Box 8560, Corpus Christi, Tex. 78412

PALO DURO CANYON STATE SCENIC PARK
12 miles east of Canyon on State 217 to Park Road 5

Texas' largest state park, Palo Duro covers 15,104 scenic acres on the **High Plains** (*see Llano Estacado*). The **Prairie Dog Town Fork of the Red River** carved the incredible spires, pinnacles, and other formations of the canyon, whose brilliant, varicolored walls rise 1,000 feet above its floor. Palo Duro is 9 miles wide and 100 miles from northwest to southeast. It is 1 million years old, and exposes 90 million years of geological formations. State 207 plunges right through its scenic wonders. Other attractions in the park include hiking and riding trails, nature study, and a prairie-dog town.

SABINE NATIONAL FOREST
eastcentral Texas, headquarters at Lufkin

Covering 183,843 acres, this forest extends west from the **Sabine River,** which forms the border between Texas and Louisiana. There are recreational facilities in an attractive pine-hardwood forest along the shores of the Toledo Bend Reservoir, formed by the damming of the beautiful Sabine River. The fishing is superb—black bass is the favorite game fish.

For further information write: Box 969, Lufkin, Texas 75901

SANFORD NATIONAL RECREATION AREA
north Texas, southwest of Sanford, headquarters at Sanford

This recreation area is situated in the **High Plains** of the **Texas Panhandle.** It is centered around **Lake Meredith,** backed up by the Sanford Dam on the **Canadian River.** The lovely lake is surrounded by the breaks of the river, which are composed of 200-foot deep, steep-walled canyons and intervening grasslands. Meredith's waters are open to fishing, water skiing, and boating. The main bottomland tree species are cottonwoods, plums, hackberries, chinaberries, and tamarisks (salt cedars); in the upland, there are mixed grasses, mesquite, and yucca—characteristic High Plains flora. The wildlife of this Canadian River country includes deer, pronghorn antelope, coyote, turkey, quail, and dove. The nearby **Alibates Flint Quarries** and **Texas Panhandle Pueblo Culture National Monument** is only open to the public by prior arrangement on weekends, when there are guided tours.

For further information write: Box 326, Sanford, Texas 79078

Llano Estacado landscape (see pages 257–58)

PALMETTO STATE SCENIC PARK
7 miles south of Luling on U.S. 183, then southwest on Park Road 11 for 3 miles
Situated on the **San Marcos River,** this 178-acre park has a rare botanical garden with a mass of subtropical plants, some found nowhere else in the Southwest. The flora includes quaking bogs, wild orchids, water lilies, ferns, moss-draped trees, and a seasonal profusion of wildflowers. The park also has sulphur springs, artesian wells, and a natural spring.

SAM HOUSTON NATIONAL FOREST
eastcentral Texas, headquarters at Lufkin
This 158,235-acre forest offers excellent opportunities for swimming, fishing, and hunting. It includes **Walker Lake** and **Stubblefield Lake,** a narrow overflow of **West Fork of San Jacinto River** that is surrounded by moss-festooned cypress trees. A foot trail leads from 250-acre **Double Lake** to the **Big Thicket Scenic Area,** a 1,100-acre natural tract. Two miles of trails lead along running streams and through vegetation that includes yaupon, dogwood, and redbud. This scenic area is on the edge of the Big Thicket, a vast East Texas region of tangled, often impenetrable woods, streams, and marshes.
For further information write: Box 969, Lufkin, Texas 75901

SIERRA DE CRISTO REY, THE MOUNTAIN OF CHRIST THE KING
3 miles from El Paso on loop 16 west
This famous mountain looms above El Paso, at the point where Texas, New Mexico, and Mexico meet. Its 4,576-foot summit is crowned with a massive statue of Christ on the Cross. A 4-mile foot trail, with 14 Stations of the Cross, winds to the shrine, which is visited by thousands of pilgrims each year.

WONDER CAVE
San Marcos, just off I-35
The only fault, or dry-formed, natural cave in the state (most caves are formed by water erosion), Wonder Cave is 500 million years old. A trail leads through its subterranean depths, where there are unusual formations and growths.
Open May 15–Sept 15: daily 8–8; rest of year, 9–5. Admission: adults $2.80, children (6–12) $2.00

UTAH

ARCHES NATIONAL PARK
southeast Utah, about 6 miles northwest of Moab, headquarters at Moab

Situated in the heart of Utah's celebrated red-rock country, this park (which only recently was elevated from a national monument to national park status) covers 73,300 acres. It is bordered on the southeast by the **Colorado River** and contains more natural stone arches, windows, spires, and pinnacles than any other site in the United States. Nearly 90 arches have been counted, but others are probably hidden away in remote areas; they are the most majestic landforms in the park. The area is also dotted with other spectacular forms: some resembling people and animals; balanced rocks; and weird shapes—carved by the combined forces of running water, wind, rain, frost, and heat. The arches are formed out of a 300-foot layer of rock called Entrada sandstone. About 150 million years ago sand deposits, probably carried by the wind, accumulated into a huge desert, which was then covered by additional sand layers and hardened into rock. This rock was ultimately uplifted, twisted, and cracked several times, and later erosion stripped away the overlying layers, exposing the Entrada sandstone. Over thousands of years water has dissolved the sandstone, enlarging the joints and leaving huge fins, or fissures, between the slabs. Once these fins are perforated, their openings are enlarged by weathering and gravity to become arches. Arches in all stage of development are exhibited here. Much of the park may be viewed from a *Scenic Drive,* which begins near the visitor center and passes many wonders.

Many of the park's other attractions may be reached by foot trails and unpaved roads. One of the most scenic features is **Delicate Arch,** set in a fantastic array of cliffs and domes, with the gorge of the Colorado River beyond and the snow-capped peaks of the **La Sal Mountains** in the distance. The arch is reached by graded road and trail. The *Tower Arch Trail* winds through **Klondike Bluffs,** a striking formation at the upper end of **Salt Valley,** and ends at 5,560-foot **Tower Arch.**

For further information write: PO Building, Moab, Utah 84532

ASHLEY NATIONAL FOREST
northeast Utah, headquarters at Vernal

The **Uinta Mountains,** one of the few east-west mountain ranges in the United States, provide a unique setting for this 1,313,000-acre forest. The range includes 13,498-foot **Kings Peak,** the highest in the state, as well as several other peaks over 13,000 feet. These majestic mountains tower above basins and glades, dotted with sapphire-blue lakes. Some 7,000 feet below is a sagebrush-covered benchland, bisected by the **Green River.** Between the 2 elevations are huge timber areas, many of them virgin.

The **High Uintas Primitive Area** is situated on the main divide of the 150-mile-long range. About 63 per cent of its 244,000 acres lies within Ashley; the remainder is in Wasatch National Forest (*see*). The region is characterized by high rugged ridges looming above the timberline. Below are extensive stands of lodgepole pine and Engelmann spruce. Numerous glacially formed lakes fill the area and provide some of the best fishing in Utah.

The forest also encompasses part of 201,000-acre **Flaming Gorge National Recreation Area,** which extends northward into Wyoming. It includes **Flaming Gorge** and **Red Canyon,** carved by the Green

Left: pinnacle in Canyonlands National Park. Top right: erosion-carved rocks in Bryce Canyon National Park. Center: elk. Below: east entrance of Zion Canyon

River as it cuts through the Uintas. It surrounds Flaming Gorge Reservoir, created by Flaming Gorge Dam on the Green River. This lake, which provides many scenic boat trips, is bounded by Red, **Horseshoe**, and **Hideout canyons** on the south and abrupt cliffs on the north. Floating the Green River below the dam is a popular activity.

Sheep Creek Canyon Geological Area, west of Flaming Gorge Reservoir, is a 3,600-acre tract filled with sheer vertical walls and huge, colored rock pinnacles. It is traversed by the *Drive Through the Ages* (U.S. 44), one of the few routes in the world where a tourist can see geological formations representing millions of years of formation in only 15 minutes of driving.

For further information write: Supervisor, Vernal, Utah 84078

BRYCE CANYON NATIONAL PARK
7 miles south of Panguitch via U.S. 89, then east on State 12 to park

This canyon is actually a series of 12 natural horseshoe-shaped amphitheaters that were carved out of white and pink limestone, shale, and sand along a 20-mile rim of the **Paunsaugunt Plateau** by tributaries of the **Paria River**. They form a great depression, roughly 2 miles wide, 3 miles long, and several hundred feet deep. The spectacular eastward-facing escarpment that forms the plateau's rim is part of the **Pink Cliffs**. These are composed of countless structures resembling cathedrals, spires, arches, and many other shapes, all tinted in shades of pink, red, and orange, softened by touches of gray, white, cream, and some lavender. This stone wonderland was completely sculptured by the forces of erosion—notably rain, freezing, thawing, and wind. There are foot trails all along the canyon's rim, and strenuous paths lead to various levels below.

One of the best introductions to this spectacular 36,010-acre park is via the 1.5-mile *Navajo Loop Trail*, which begins at **Sunset Point** and descends 521 feet into the canyon. Highlights along the way include **Wall Street**, the **Temple of Osiris, Thor's Hammer**, the **Camel and Wise Man**. The self-guiding *Queen's Garden Trail*, the easiest one below the canyon rim, leads to interesting formations—**Gulliver's Castle, Queen's Castle, Queen's Garden**, the **Totem Poles**, and **Queen Victoria**. There are also several horseback trails, notably *Peekaboo Loop Trail* to **Peekaboo Canyon**, which affords views of the **Hindu Temple**. The best automobile road is *Rim Drive* (partially closed in winter). This road exposes the visitor to the park's general features, including a view of the **Silent City** from **Inspiration Point**.

For further information write: Superintendent, Bryce Canyon, Utah 84717

CACHE NATIONAL FOREST
northcentral Utah and southeast Idaho, headquarters at Logan, Utah

Extending from the **Weber River** in Utah to **Soda Springs** in Idaho, this 650,000-acre forest is situated in rugged and mountainous terrain, with several small mountain lakes and high basins, numerous springs, streams, and sinkholes. It includes the **Bear River Range** overlooking **Bear Lake** on the Idaho-Utah line; the northern end of the **Wasatch Mountains;** and **Wellsville Mountains**, on the western edge of fertile **Cache Valley**. One of its special attractions is **Logan Canyon**, between Logan and Bear Lake on U.S. 89. Carved by the relentless force of the **Logan River**, where fishing is excellent, it is nearly 1 mile deep and reveals 200 million years of geological history. **Tony Grove** and **White Pine lakes** are beautiful glacial lakes within the canyon. The *Jardine Juniper Trail* leads about 15 miles up canyon to the largest (44 feet tall, 27 feet in circumference, 8 feet in diameter) and oldest (over 3,000 years) tree of its kind. The self-guiding *Limber Pine Nature Trail* follows a moderate grade through fir, pine, and sage on the canyon's south ridge to the so-called **Mountain Monarch,** the largest known limber pine. It is probably over 2,000 years old, and it measures 24 feet in circumference and is still growing. Logan Canyon is most spectacular in the fall, when the coloring of its box elder, cottonwood, maple, and aspen is outstanding. Another natural wonder in Cache is the **Saint Charles Canyon,** about 8 miles west of Saint Charles, Idaho, which contains famous Minnetonka Cave (*see Idaho*). Geological faults in the terrain are responsible for several large springs. Most widely known are **Ricks** and **De Witt** in Logan Canyon; **Big Spring,** which gives rise to the left fork of **Cub River;** and **Paris Spring** in **Paris Canyon.**

For further information write: Federal Building, Logan, Utah 84321

CANYONLANDS NATIONAL PARK
west of U.S. 163 between Moab and Monticello, headquarters at Moab

The landscape of this 257,640-acre national park contains a fantastic diversity of brilliantly colored erosional features. Located on the wild, remote **Colorado Plateau,** it encompasses an immense array of chasms, fins, pinnacles, pillars, arches, crenelated mesas, and standing rocks. Natural forces have carved these formations during the last 300 million years from the layers of sandstone that comprise the plateau. Running water has been the master sculptor, aided by wind, rain, frost, and other weathering processes.

The **Colorado River** with its tributaries has been the greatest force here. Within the park it joins its largest tributary, the **Green River.** Together these 2 mighty rivers have slashed across the terrain, incising a fantastic succession of labyrinthine, down-plunging gorges. Both are entrenched in canyons and have cut their way across the plateau, carving up its surface and stripping off great sections of the relatively soft, sedimentary rocks to expose a cross section of the earth's crust. The Colorado River, whose narrow, steep-walled canyon is still being cut, enters the park from the northeast and flows southwest. The Green River enters at the northwest corner. It follows a meandering course into the heart of the Canyonlands, where it is captured by the Colorado, which then cuts through **Cataract Canyon** on its southwestward journey to the Grand Canyon (*see Arizona*). It is at this point that the Colorado becomes one of the continent's wildest, most turbulent rivers.

The Colorado, Green, and Cataract canyons divide the park into 3 major sections. The northern one is dominated by the **Island in the Sky,** a cliff-bordered upland some 6,000 feet above sea level. Its southernmost tip is 6,100-foot **Grandview Point,** accessible by dirt road, and it is joined to the grasslands of the north by **The Neck,** a precipitous, 40-foot-wide corridor of land with drop-offs on both sides. The Island is surrounded by 4,800-foot-high **White Rim,** which rises above **Standing Rock Basin,** some 500 feet below.

The park's southeast section, which lies east of Cataract Canyon, is the 55,000-acre **Needles Area** named for the dazzling display of erosion-formed pinnacles, spires, and delicately balanced rocks. These multicolored rock needles are well exhibited in **Virginia** and **Chesler Parks,** natural parks of flat grasslands, which can be reached by jeep, on horseback, or on foot.

The third section is adjacent to the park, just outside its southwest border. It is a wilderness area that must be entered by jeep, foot, or horseback. It is dominated by 2 features: the **Maze,** a wild erosion-carved wilderness of intricate, interlocking canyons; and the **Land of Standing Rocks,** a group of erosional remnants.

For further information write: PO Building, Moab, Utah 84532

CAPITOL REEF NATIONAL PARK
12 miles east of Torrey on State 24

This 61-square-mile tract protects Capitol Reef, a portion of **Water-pocket Fold,** a great doubling up of the earth's crust. The fold extends from Thousand Lake Mountain in Fishlake National Forest (*see*) southeastward about 100 miles to the Colorado River. This great tilt occurred millions of years ago, and since then erosion has carved the formation into highly colored towers, domes, and pinnacles that rise majestically from the surrounding desert floor. Capitol Reef is a high escarpment (about 20 miles long) of brilliantly hued layers of rock. It is named for the white, dome-shaped Navajo sandstone formations that cap its many strata. Near the visitor center, these cliffs rise over 1,000 feet above the **Fremont River.** This river and its tributaries, **Sulphur** and **Pleasant creeks,** are the only perennial streams in the area.

At the northern end of the monument is **Cathedral Valley,** where giant reddish-brown monoliths rise between 400 and 700 feet. Near its entrance are **Twin Rocks,** the **Motorman, Chimney Rock,** and **Sulphur Creek Gorge. Hickman Natural Bridge,** carved through the rock by flowing water and blowing sand, is 72 feet high and has a 133-foot-tall span. Other formations here, all accessible by road or trail, are **Cohab Canyon, Cassidy Arch,** and **Grand Wash,** where 1,000-foot walls are only 16 feet apart.

For further information write: Superintendent, Torrey, Utah 84775

CEDAR BREAKS NATIONAL MONUMENT
23 miles from Cedar City via State 14, or 27 miles from U.S. 89 at Long Valley

Completely surrounded by Dixie National Forest (*see*), this nearly 10-square-mile monument is located on the **Markagunt Plateau** at an altitude of 10,400 feet. It preserves a gigantic, coloseum-shaped amphitheater that has been scooped out by water and other forces to a depth of nearly 2,000 feet. It is composed of multicolored sandstone and limestone—white, cream, purple, yellow, brown, green, and red, all dominated by a bright orange-pink. These tints change

Sandstone cliffs in Capitol Reef National Park

constantly according to the quality of sunlight. The name, Cedar Breaks, is derived from the early settlers' use of the word "breaks" for badlands, coupled with their mistaken assumption that the junipers near the base of the cliffs were cedars.

The layers of rock comprising the amphitheater walls were deposited some 55 million years ago as a limy ooze on the bottoms of shallow freshwater lakes near sea level. During the last 13 million years the area slowly rose, the lakes disappeared, and finally the land was uplifted to its present elevation. This produced the steep, westward-facing limestone escarpment that has been subjected to erosion. Gradually water, wind, and frost wore away the softer parts, and the more resistant portions have remained as spires, ridges, and countless other shapes.

Although there are no trails or roads to the bottom of the amphitheater, there are several around or near its rim. The *Rim Drive* is a 5-mile road through forests and wildflower fields. It features many panoramas of the cliffs and surrounding high country, and adjacent to it are 4 major viewpoints: *Point Supreme, Sunset View, Chessmen Ridge Overlook,* and *North View.* The *Wasatch Ramparts Trail* starts at 10,350-foot Point Supreme and runs for 2 miles along the rim, leading through forests, open fields, and a stand of bristlecone pine on 10,285-foot **Spectra Point.**

For further information: Zion National Park, Springer, Utah 84767

CORAL PINK SAND DUNES STATE PARK
4 miles south of Mount Carmel on U.S. 89, then 7 miles south on paved road
These dunes—some as high as 25 feet—comprise a wonderland of shifting mounds of sand, shaped by wind. They are composed of material that has twice been reduced to sand in the course of millions of years. The towering mesas and buttes that surround this pocket-sized Sahara are made of Navaho sandstone formed about 100 or 150 million years ago. But this sandstone was itself created out of the residue of much more ancient mountains worn down yet millions of years earlier. The flora here is quite spectacular.

DINOSAUR NATIONAL MONUMENT. *See* COLORADO

DIXIE NATIONAL FOREST
southwest Utah, headquarters at Cedar City
Covering almost 2 million acres and stretching about 170 miles across southern Utah, this is the state's largest national forest. It is known as the "Land of Rainbow Canyons" because of its deep, vibrantly colored canyons and its scenic, high plateaus. The forest, which is divided into 4 separate units, straddles the divide between the **Great Basin** and the **Colorado River,** famous for thousands of miles of steep-walled gorges cut into brightly colored cliffs. Dixie also supports the state's largest timber stands, mainly ponderosa pine and spruce. It embraces many mountains and several plateaus including **Markagunt, Paunsaugunt, Sevier, Table Cliff, and Aquarius plateaus.** The latter is dotted with hundreds of small lakes, has sage-silvered deserts from which huge mesas, pinnacles, and spires rise, and is crisscrossed with canyons and creeks. Just east of Aquarius is **Hell's Backbone,** a knife-edged ridge with a bridge on top spanning a streamless crevice. On each side of the ridge precipitous walls drop hundreds of feet, one into **Sand Creek Canyon,** the other into **Death Hollow.** The **Escalante Mountains** are west of the plateau. The Markagunt Plateau, about 9 miles southeast of Cedar City via State 14, offers numerous recreational

facilities. Trails and roads lead to 11,307-foot **Brian Head Peak,
Strawberry Point, Panguitch Lake,** and **Navajo Lake.**

For further information write: 500 S Main, Cedar City, Utah 84720

FISHLAKE NATIONAL FOREST
southcentral Utah, headquarters at Richfield

Divided into 4 separate tracts, this forest covers 1.5 million mountainous acres near the southern end of **Great Salt Lake Basin.**
It straddles parts of the **Wasatch, Aquarius, Sevier,** and **Tushar
plateaus** as well as all of the **Fish Lake** and **Pahvant plateaus.**
The tops of these plateaus are relatively small areas, either flat
or with gently rolling hills. Their greatest expanses are between
their rims and the valleys below, regions covered with numerous
canyons radiating out from the rims.

The forest is named for aspen-bounded Fish Lake; about 6 miles
long and 1 mile wide, it is a popular fishing site, especially for huge
Mackinaw and rainbow trout. The lake occupies a depression
caused by geologic faulting, and glacial deposits dam its northern
end. South of Fish Lake is scenic 11,306-foot **Thousand Lake
Mountain,** and just outside the forest's boundary is lemon-colored
Big Rock Candy Mountain. It looms above the Sevier River and U.S.
89 several miles south of Sevier.

For further information write: 170 N Main, Richfield, Utah 84701

FLAMING GORGE NATIONAL RECREATION AREA. *See* ASHLEY NA-TIONAL FOREST

GLEN CANYON NATIONAL RECREATION AREA
south Utah and north Arizona, headquarters at Page, Arizona

Located mainly in Utah where it adjoins Canyonlands National
Park (*see*), this area boasts some 1,800 miles of shoreline around
186-mile-long **Lake Powell,** formed by Glen Canyon Dam. The
lake, which lies in the old **Colorado River** channel, winds through
numerous fiordlike side canyons as well as coves and inlets, all
cut out of red Navajo sandstone. Some of the cliffs rise 1,000 feet
above its blue waters. Boating, fishing, camping, and water skiing are the main activities here. Boat trips on the lake may be arranged with concessioners at Bullfrog, Halls Crossing, Hite,
Wahweap, and Lees Ferry. Desert flora and fauna line the waterway, and naturalist programs are held in the evening during the
summer months. The most outstanding natural feature is Rainbow
Bridge National Monument (*see*). Goosenecks of the San Juan
River State Park (*see*) also lie within the area.

For further information write: Box 1507, Page, Arizona 86040

GOBLIN VALLEY STATE PARK
13 miles north of Hanksville via State 24, then several miles on dirt road

This undeveloped park is in a mile-wide basin filled with weird,
chocolate-brown rocks, many of them suggesting goblins. Sculptured through the ages by erosion, the formations also include
spires, pedestals, and balanced rocks. Jeep tours into this fascinating
area may be arranged at Green River and Hanksville.

GOOSENECKS OF THE SAN JUAN RIVER STATE PARK
5 miles north of Mexican Hat via State 261, then 4 miles west on dirt road

This park features a cliff-top overlook onto the famous goosenecks
of the San Juan River—spectacular examples of an entrenched
meander. Here the San Juan makes a series of symmetrical bends

through a mud-gray canyon over 1,200 feet deep. It flows 6 miles in a series of close-cut curves to cover an air distance of 1 mile. Originally the river traveled over a level plain, but an uplift of the land in the area forced the stream to cut deeper and deeper into the plain. In millions of years the San Juan will probably cut through the walls of the goosenecks, creating a series of huge natural bridges like those in Natural Bridges National Monument (*see*).

GREAT SALT LAKE
northeast Utah

Next to the Dead Sea, Great Salt Lake is the world's saltiest body of water. Its saline content is greater than that of the ocean, averaging about 25 per cent salt, enough to support even the poorest swimmer. The lake is a remnant of an enormous prehistoric inland sea, known as Lake Bonneville, which once covered northwest Utah, eastern Nevada, and southern Idaho. Great Salt Lake is fed by the **Jordan, Bear,** and **Weber rivers,** but has no outlets and therefore fluctuates greatly in size. It is presently about 70 miles long and 50 miles wide. The lake contains 10 islands of varying sizes, notably **Antelope,** whose northern end is the site of Great Salt Lake State Park. The other islands are **Bird, Cub, Dolphin, Egg, Fremont, Gunnison, Carrington, Stansbury,** and **White Rock.** A few are privately owned, and all teem with bird life and are seasonal nesting grounds.

West of Salt Lake is **Great Salt Lake Desert,** part of Lake Bonneville's bed. For a long time this vast alkali desert was a formidable obstacle to westward migration. It is now traversed by highways and railways. An extremely level stretch near the Nevada line is used for automobile testing and racing. This area of tightly packed salt and sand is known as the **Bonneville Salt Flats.**

INDIAN CREEK STATE PARK
12 miles west of U.S. 163 between Monticello and Moab

Southern Utah, especially the Moab area, is known for its numerous ancient Indian petroglyphs, many carved 20 centuries ago. Some of the finest may be seen here, especially on famous **Newspaper Rock.** The park also contains a scenic canyon and Indian ruins.

JOSHUA TREE NATURAL AREA
10 miles southwest of Saint George

This 1,000-acre tract supports a fine stand of Joshua trees, which grow here near the northern limit of their range. It is a characteristic Joshua-tree forest, with flora and fauna predominantly of the Mojave Desert types. Registered Natural Landmark

MONUMENT VALLEY NAVAJO TRIBAL PARK. *See* ARIZONA

MANTI-LASAL NATIONAL FOREST
central and southeast Utah, west Colorado, headquarters at Price, Utah

Noted for its varied terrain, this forest covers over 1.3 million acres in 2 divisions, including green forests of aspen, ponderosa pine, spruce, and fir; beautifully colored sandstone cliffs and canyons; and cactus-filled deserts. The Manti division hugs a rugged, rambling strip of the **Wasatch Plateau** in the heart of central Utah. The LaSal division, near the Utah-Colorado border, is comprised of 2 sections: the Monticello section—dominated by the **Abajos Mountains;** and the Moab section—dominated by the **LaSal Mountains**—which includes a small area in Colorado.

The forest contains numerous roads and trails. The scenic *Sky-*

line Drive runs from north to south along the top of the Manti Division and offers superb views. On a clear day one can see westward to the mountains of Nevada and southeastward to the LaSal Range. The many streams, lakes, and reservoirs provide good fishing, and hunting is popular, especially for deer and elk.

For further information write: Superintendent, Price, Utah 84501

NATURAL BRIDGES NATIONAL MONUMENT
4 miles south of Blanding via U.S. 163, then 40 miles west on State 95

This 7,600-acre monument protects 3 canyons—White, Armstrong, and Tuwa—and 3 natural bridges—Sipapu, Kachina, and Owachomo. All are cut into Cedar Mesa sandstone that was laid down at the bottom of inland seas over 225 million years ago. Each bridge was carved in a sandstone wall that was once the bend of a stream. Over the centuries fast, sand-laden flood waters kept pounding against the walls, eventually breaking through them. Subsequent stream action and weathering widened the openings, and the bridges were formed. *Bridge View Drive*, an 8-mile loop road, begins at the visitor center and links the foot trails to the bridges. The first bridge to be seen is Sipapu, the longest, most mature, and the best proportioned of the 3. It rises to a height of 220 feet above the stream bed, with a span of 268 feet. The next, Kachina, is at a youthful stage in the life of a natural bridge. It is huge and bulky, with a height of 210 feet and a span of 206 feet. Flood waters in White Canyon are still enlarging the opening beneath the span. Owachomo, on the other hand, is at a late state of development, and is no longer subject to stream erosion—only erosion from rain, frost action, and sandblast. It is 106 feet high and has a span of 180 feet, and its life expectancy is shorter than that of the others.

For further information write: Canyonlands National Park, Moab, Utah 84532

RAINBOW BRIDGE NATIONAL MONUMENT
southeast Utah, just north of Arizona border, headquarters at Page, Arizona

Colorful, symmetrical Rainbow Bridge stands in one of the most remote, and until recently, inaccessible regions of the United States—the semidesert country of southeastern Utah. It is nestled among canyons carved by winding streams that flow from the northern slope of 10,388-foot Navajo Mountain to the Colorado River. The bridge, the largest known natural sandstone arch in the world, has a span of 278 feet and reaches a height of 309 feet above the floor of Rainbow Bridge Canyon. Its predominant color is salmon-pink, but there are dark streaks created by iron oxide or hematite. When rain hits the arch's upper portions, the hematite in the sandstone is washed down the sides where it remains. The hematite leaves long streaks of reds and browns. The coloring is most brilliant in the afternoon sun; an Indian legend maintained that the arch was a rainbow that was changed to stone.

This 160-acre national monument is now part of Glen Canyon National Recreation Area (*see*), and it may be reached by several routes. Two of the most popular are foot trails: a 14-mile walk from Rainbow Lodge, Arizona, and a 24-mile hike from Navajo Mountain Trading Post. There are many water approaches, including a trip of some 55 miles from either Wahweap or Halls Crossing to the landing in Bridge Canyon, from where there is an easy 1-mile hike up canyon to the fantastic bridge.

For further information write: Glen Canyon National Recreation Area, Box 1507, Page, Arizona 86040

Left: Flaming Gorge in Ashley National Forest. Right: Rainbow Bridge

SNOW CANYON STATE PARK
7 miles northwest of Saint George via State 18

This park contains Snow Canyon, a spectacular gorge, as well as the solidified remains of a large lava cone.

TIMPANOGOS CAVE NATIONAL MONUMENT
south from Salt Lake City via I-15 to junction with State 80, then east about 15 miles

Surrounded by Uinta National Forest (*see*), this monument covers 250 acres in **American Fork Canyon** on the northern slope of snow-capped 11,750-foot **Mount Timpanogos.** Timpanogos is probably an Indian word meaning "rock rivers," and the cave is actually a series of 3 caverns joined by man-made tunnels. They are reached via a trail that winds 1.5 miles from the visitor center to the cave entrance some 1,000 feet above the canyon floor. Along it are outstanding views of the **Wasatch Mountains, Utah Valley,** and **American Fork Creek** and canyon. The caverns, which developed along fault zones, were enlarged by the dissolving action of water on limestone that was laid down 330 million years ago as ooze at the bottom of an inland sea. Their interiors are decorated with pink filigreelike forms and sparkling white translucent crystals. In places the colors range from yellow through orange to brown. The array of cave formations, notably helictites and aragonite crystals, culminates in larger forms such as the **Great Heart of Timpanogos,** the **Giant's Comb,** fantastic **Chocolate Falls,** and **Father Times Jewel Box.** Tiny pools of water reflect the beauty of the cave.

For further information write: RFD 1, American Fork, Utah 84003

UINTA NATIONAL FOREST
central Utah, headquarters at Provo

The landscape ranges from gently rolling benchlands to rugged alpine zones in this 780,000-acre forest. The dominant tree species include Englemann spruce, aspen, and Douglas, white, and subalpine fir. The southernmost division of the forest is dominated by the **San Pitch Mountains.** The central area contains 11,871-foot **Mount Nebo** and the *Nebo Loop Road,* which runs from Nephi, along **Salt Creek,** then north to Payson. Just off the road is **Devil's Kitchen,** where the rock erosions resemble those in Bryce Canyon National Park (*see*). The loop also passes through an area inhabited by one of the state's largest elk herds. The forest's northernmost and largest division contains a portion of the **Wasatch Range** and innumerable other mountains. It includes the 10,750-acre **Mount Timpanogos Scenic Area** near Timpanogos Cave National Monument (*see*). Hiking trails leading to the summit of 11,750-foot **Mount Timpanogos** cross 5 major life zones, revealing the same climatic and vegetative changes that one would encounter on a journey from Provo to the Arctic Circle. The panoramas from the mountain heights include **Heber** and **Utah valleys**, the **High Uintas, Emerald Lake,** which lies like a jewel in a glacial cirque, and the Great Salt Lake (*see*), joined to **Utah Lake** by the **Jordan River.** The scenic area is skirted by the *Alpine Scenic Loop,* which includes part of State 80 and U.S. 91 and 189, linking **American Fork** and **Provo canyons.** The drive passes **Bridal Veil Falls,** which have a sheer drop of 450 feet. South of this scenic area is *Squaw Peak Trail* with its many exciting overlooks, and even farther south there is a scenic drive along **Right Fork Hobble Creek** and **Diamond Fork.** Over 1,000 miles of roads and over 1,000 miles of hiking trails penetrate this huge forest, a paradise for sportsmen.

For further information write: Superintendent, Provo, Utah 84601

WASATCH NATIONAL FOREST
northcentral Utah, south Wyoming, headquarters at Salt Lake City

This sprawling forest of some 870,000 acres encompasses the **Stansbury, Sheeprock, Wasatch,** and **Uinta mountain ranges.** The Wasatch Mountain highlands, formerly covered by ancient seas, are rich in fossil remains of dinosaurs and other creatures that once roamed the land. Much later, Indians hunted here and named the range Wasatch, meaning high mountain pass. In the 19th century trappers and explorers—Kit Carson, Jedediah Smith, William Ashley, Jim Bridger—explored this crossroads of history and roamed through its canyons and valleys. Pioneers, fortyniners, and Mormons passed through the valley of Great Salt Lake (*see*), some settling here, others moving farther west.

Major features in the Wasatch Mountains section of this forest include 10,242-foot **Porter Peak,** 9,026-foot **Mount Olympus,** and 11,319-foot **Twin Peaks,** as well as **Big and Little Cottonwood canyons.** The Uinta Mountains section, which extends slightly into Wyoming, is dotted with hundreds of lakes—**Castle, Washington, Big Elk, Bridger, Echo, Lost,** and **Pyramid. Mirror Lake,** less than 2 hours drive from Salt Lake City, is the gateway to the **High Uintas Primitive Area,** most of which lies in Ashley National Forest (*see*). **Bald Mountain,** whose summit may be reached by trail, rises 11,947 feet from the lake's west shore. It offers a superb view of this rugged land of lakes, streams, and mountains, some with 13,000-foot peaks. *Mirrow Lake Highway* offers a self-guided tour of the gateway area, and many trails lead into the wilderness. One of the great attractions on this scenic highway is the overlook at **Hayden Pass,** which divides the **Colorado River** and **Great Salt Lake** drainage systems. Nearby, **Hayden Peak** looms 12,485 feet above the area, where many streams originate. These converge to form 4 major rivers—the **Bear, Duchesne, Weber,** and **Provo,** each of which rises within a 2-mile radius. The forest is home to mule deer, elk, and the state's only moose herd, which numbers over 100. In remote areas there are bears, cougars, and coyotes and small creatures (marmot, beaver, marten, mink, and badger) are common.

For further information write: 4438 Federal Building, 125 South State Street, Salt Lake City, Utah 84111

ZION NATIONAL PARK
southwest Utah, headquarters at Springdale

This 320-square-mile park is some of the most spectacular and brilliantly colored sandstone and limestone canyon country in all of North America. Like Bryce Canyon and Canyonlands national parks *(see both)*, it is located in the scenic, arid plateau country of southern Utah. Here, the relentless forces of erosion—wind, rain, frost, and running water—have carved the land into steep-walled gorges and precipitous cliffs, lofty stone pinnacles, and templelike formations. Zion's spectacular desert-canyon landscape, with its famous sandstone monoliths, were created quite recently. They reveal only the last chapter in the region's geological history. However, the weather-scarred sedimentary rocks exposed here record over 225 million years of geological history, and date back to prehistoric periods when the region was covered with seas.

Zion Canyon, a twisting 2,500-foot-deep gorge almost 9 miles long, has brilliantly colored walls and sandstone cliffs. Their delicate pinks, reds, and whites, together with the fresh green of cottonwoods, ash, and maples that border the river, soften the imposing scene. The chasm was carved primarily by the down-cutting action of the running waters of the **North Fork of the Virgin River,** assisted by various geological agents. This seemingly placid river, which has been called "a moving river of sandpaper," has enormous amounts of sand and silt that have cut and scoured the canyon's walls and floors for hundreds and thousands of years.

Many points of interest can be reached or seen via the park's 20 miles of improved roadways. The *Zion Canyon Scenic Road* extends for 8 miles from the park's south entrance to the famous **Temple of Sinawava,** a huge natural amphitheater in a verdant oasis. This route is lined with many spectacular natural formations. Another picturesque park road is the *Zion-Mount Carmel Road* (State 15), which crosses the park from its eastern boundary westward to Zion Canyon junction. After leaving the eastern entrance one can see famous **Checkerboard Mesa,** where cracks run vertically and horizontally, cutting the rock into great blocks and making it vulnerable to erosion.

The park boasts some 155 miles of foot trails—gateways to its fantastic scenery. The most popular is *Gateway to the Narrows,* a mile-long foot path from the Temple of Sinawava to the famous **Narrows,** where Zion Canyon is only a few feet wide between perpendicular walls that loom about 1,500 feet above the stream bed. The *Emerald Pool Trail* leads to a small river formed by 2 waterfalls. A self-guiding trail starts at *Zion Canyon Scenic Drive,* about 5 miles up the canyon from the visitor center, and goes to fabulous **Weeping Rock.** Here springs filter from the canyon wall forming "tears" that drip from the cliff's face. The **Hanging Gardens** are on this trail. Springs seeping through porous rock have created an ideal environment for moisture-loving plants that thrive high up on the canyon wall above the footpath. *Canyon Overlook,* another self-guiding trail, leads to an excellent panorama atop **Great Arch.** *Hidden Canyon Trail* leads to Zion's "Shangrila," an almost inaccessible canyon. Among the other trails are the *East* and *West Rim trails* and the most difficult in the park, the *Lady Mountain Trail* to the top of a 6,540-foot mountain. From *Watchman Viewpoint Trail,* near the park's south entrance, one can see 6,555-foot **Watchman Mountain,** 3,887-foot **Springdale Mountain,** and Zion and **Oak Creek** canyons.

For further information: Superintendent, Springdale, Utah 84767

VERMONT

ASCUTNEY STATE PARK
midway between Windsor and Ascutney off U.S. 5

This park, on the state's eastern border with New Hampshire, covers over 1,500 acres on **Mount Ascutney.** A 4-mile-long paved road, one of New England's finest mountain parkways, leads close to the summit of the 3,144-foot mountain and winds its way from one scenic lookout to another. From *Connecticut View*, at 2,325 feet above sea level, one can gaze down upon the meandering **Connecticut River** and the New Hampshire hills. A hiking trail leads from the road's end to the mountaintop. From the vantage point of **Brownsville Rock** one can see the main range of the **Green Mountains,** the **White Mountains** of New Hampshire, and **Burke Mountain** in Darling State Park (*see*) 80 miles to the north. From another lookout point one can see most of southern Vermont.

BIG AND LITTLE EQUINOX MOUNTAINS
west of Manchester

The highest peak in the **Taconic Range,** 3,816-foot Big Equinox Mountain may be reached via the *Mount Equinox Skyline Drive.* This 6-mile-long toll road, which goes northwest from U.S. 7, passes 3,320-foot Little Equinox Mountain and continues on to the summit of Big Equinox, from where there is a magnificent view. *Road open May–Oct 15: daily 8–8; toll $3.00*

Left and below: waterfall and waterscene in Green Mountain National Forest. Top right: Mount Mansfield in spring

274

BUTTON BAY STATE PARK
6 miles west of Vergennes, just south of town of Basin Harbor
Situated on a high bluff overlooking Button Bay in Lake Champlain (*see*), this park offers fine views of New York's **Adirondack Mountains** to the west and the **Green Mountains** to the east. The bay is named for the button-shaped stones that have been loosened from the clay banks and which are found along the shore.

CAMEL'S HUMP STATE PARK AND FOREST
Huntington Center vicinity, off I-89
The main feature of this 12,850-acre preserve is **Camel's Hump Mountain**, a Registered Natural Landmark. The 4,083-foot mountain is significant because it illustrates the relationship between altitude and life zones. Its summit is covered with one of Vermont's largest extents of alpine-tundra vegetation. On the northern part of the peak there is a small meadow with a nearly pure stand of Bigelow's sedge. Between elevations of 2,800 and 3,800 feet there is a belt of northern fir forest, and at the lower edge of this zone there is a transition area of red spruce and birches. Below this, extending from 1,800 feet to 2,600 feet, is a northern hardwood forest. Many hiking trails lead to the Hump's summit, which is also traversed by the famous *Long Trail*. The views from the mountaintop include exceptional panoramas of New York's **Adirondack Mountains** and **Lake Champlain** (*see*) to the west, the **White Mountains** of New Hampshire to the east, and Vermont's **Green Mountains** north to Canada and south to Killington.

GREEN MOUNTAIN NATIONAL FOREST
western Vermont, headquarters at Rutland
This 240,000-acre forest embraces the main range of the Green Mountains, the dominant geographical feature of the state. A range of the **Appalachians**, they form a backbone down the center of Vermont from the Canadian line to the Massachusetts border. Their slopes and all but a few of their highest summits are covered with the dark evergreen of fir, pine, and hemlock and with deciduous maple, birch, and beech—the source of glorious color in autumn.

The forest is divided into 2 sections, stretching nearly the length of the state. One part begins at the Vermont-Massachusetts line and extends north to **Roaring Brook**; the other, more northerly unit encompasses an area roughly between **Blue Ridge Mountain** and **Mount Ellen**. The forest embraces important drainages in the **Lake Champlain** basin and at the headwaters of the **Connecticut** and **Hudson rivers**. It is also rich in plant and animal life.

Green Mountain contains many scenic roads and trails. One of the most striking drives is a 15-mile stretch of State 100 from north of Hancock to Warren. It is flanked by the trickling waters of the **White** and **Mad rivers**, and to the west and northwest there are spectacular views of Vermont's own **Presidential Mountains**. Large portions of the *Long Trail* and the *Appalachian Trail*, both National Scenic Trails, meander through Green Mountain along the heights of the peaks. The Long Trail, or "Footpath through the Wilderness," covers some 255 miles from the Massachusetts line to Canada. About 80 miles of it traverse this forest. In the southern unit, the Appalachian and Long trails follow the same path, but near Rutland the Appalachian Trail turns east to complete its journey across New Hampshire to northern Maine. Among the most popular short hikes from or on the Long Trail is the walk to the open summit of 4,052-foot **Mount Abraham**, 2½ miles from **Lincoln**

VERMONT

Gap. At the summit of **Brandon Gap,** on State 73, there is a short but steep climb to the top of the great cliff of 3,140-foot **Mount Horrid,** from where hawks are frequently sighted. From the summit of **Sherburne Pass** on U.S. 4, there are trails outside the forest's boundary to 3,957-foot **Pico Peak** and 4,235-foot **Killington Peak,** the second highest peak in the state after Mount Mansfield.

There are superb recreational opportunities in Green Mountain, including swimming, hunting, fishing, and riding on excellent trails. Ski facilities are outstanding, and such well-known and popular areas as Carinthia, Bromley, Glen Ellen, Haystack, Mount Snow, and Sugarbush are located at least partially in the forest.

For further information write: 151 West St, Rutland, Vt. 05701

GROTON STATE FOREST
access via road from U.S. 2 east of Marshfield or U.S. 302, 2 miles west of Groton

This 20,000-acre forest contains 4 separate campgrounds: New Discovery, Stillwater, Big Deer, and Ricker. It encompasses 6 bodies of water: ponds called **Kettle, Niggerhead, Osmore, Peacham, Ricker** or **Lund** and 3-mile-long **Lake Groton.** A road leads close to the summit of 1,958-foot **Owl's Head Mountain,** from where there is an excellent view of the forestland in the foreground, the **Green Mountains** to the west, and New Hampshire's **White Mountains** to the east. There are also some 30 miles of hiking trails leading to all the lakes and mountain peaks in the forest, including Owl's Head, **Kettle Mountain, Silver Ledge, Big** and **Little Deer.**

LAKE CHAMPLAIN
west Vermont, east New York, and south Quebec, Canada

For more than 2 centuries Lake Champlain lay directly in the path of the Anglo-French-American struggle for this part of the North American continent. Discovered and named by French explorer Samuel de Champlain in 1609, the beautiful waterway became the site of many forts and battles during the Colonial wars, the Revolutionary War, and the War of 1812. Today its shores are lined with resorts and good farming and apple-growing areas.

Situated in a broad valley between New York's **Adirondack Mountains** on the west and Vermont's **Green Mountains** on the east, this lake forms the New York-Vermont boundary for about 100 miles and extends northward into southern Quebec. About two-thirds of the lake's cubic area are in Vermont; it also contains a group of islands (**Grand Isle, Isle La Motte**) and a peninsula, which belong to Vermont. U.S. 2, off I-89, connects the islands with the mainland in Vermont, New York, and Canada, and several toll ferries cross the lake. Vermont's Champlain shoreline is lined with several state parks that offer excellent recreational facilities in lovely settings. Burton Island State Park is on 300-acre **Burton Island** at the entrance of **Saint Albans Bay.** It is accessible only by boat from the tip of **Hathaway Point** on the mainland. Sand Bar State Park, near Sandbar Bridge to Grand Isle, has a fine sand beach, and Grand Isle State Park, on the island's eastern shore, is also popular. Farther north, on the northern tip of Grand Isle, is North Hero State Park, which has an extensive lake shoreline. D.A.R. State Park, 1 mile north of Chimney Point Bridge on State 17, is located on a bluff overlooking this narrow part of the lake and offers splendid views. The Vermont side of **Missisquoi Bay,** the northeastern arm of the lake which extends into Canada, is the site of the **Missisquoi National Wildlife Refuge.**

276

MOLLY STARK STATE PARK
3 miles east of Wilmington, off State 9

Situated on the western slope of 2,415-foot **Mount Olga**, this park is threaded with hiking trails and is known for its mountain scenery and excellent views. The *Molly Stark Trail* (State 9) which crosses Vermont from east to west between Brattleboro and Bennington is very scenic, especially at **Hogback Mountain**. Both the park and the trail are named for the wife of General John Stark, who defeated the British at the Battle of Bennington in August, 1777.

MOUNT MANSFIELD STATE FOREST
main approach from State 108 between Stowe and Jefferson

This vast forest, which covers over 20,000 acres, is divided into 4 sections: the Smugglers Notch, Jefferson, Little River, and Underhill recreation sites. The forest also includes most of Mount Mansfield, the loftiest peak in Vermont. It is 4,393 feet high, about 5 miles long, and the center of one of the state's best-known ski areas. The mountain's profile resembles a human face turned toward the sky, and the various peaks are named **Forehead, Nose, Chin,** (the highest point), and **Adam's Apple.**

The most famous area of the forest is **Smuggler's Notch,** a deep gorge at the base of Mount Mansfield. During the War of 1812 and the Civil War, contraband goods and cattle were smuggled from Boston to Canada through the notch. There are several interesting rock formations at the top of the gorge, notably **Smuggler's Cave,** the **Refrigerator,** the **Hunter and the Dog,** the **Singing Bird, Elephant's Head,** and **Smuggler's Face.** The largest boulder in the chasm is **King Rock,** which fell from a high cliff in 1910 and which weighs about 6,000 tons. Many trails lead from the Smuggler's Notch area to Mount Mansfield's summit, which is also crossed by the famous Long Trail (*see Green Mountain National Forest*). The privately owned gravel *Mount Mansfield Toll Road* (entered on State 108, 6 miles northwest of Stowe) winds through heavily forested slopes to the summit, from where the visibility is usually between 50 and 70 miles across **Lake Champlain** to the **Adirondacks.**

OKEMO STATE FOREST
northwest via park road from State 103 at Ludlow

In the heart of the well-known ski area, this park contains foot trails to the summit of 3,343-foot **Okemo Mountain** and a road that stops just short of the mountaintop. The peak, which stands virtually alone, affords superb views of the **Adirondack Mountains** of New York, the **Green Mountains** of Vermont, and the **White Mountains** of New Hampshire.

QUEECHEE STATE PARK
off U.S. 4, west of Hartford

This lovely park is adjacent to famous **Queechee Gorge,** the mile-long chasm through which the **Ottauqueechee River** flows. The gorge, known sometimes as Vermont's Little Grand Canyon, can be well appreciated from the highway bridge on U.S. 4, which crosses the ravine near its midpoint and which is 162 feet above the water. The steep, nearly vertical walls of the ravine are dominated by hemlock and a sampling of other trees such as beech, sugar and red maple, red spruce, white pine, and yellow and white birch. The understory is characterized by hobblebush and mountain maple. The moist rock walls and ledges of the gorge are lined with flowering raspberry, wild columbine, violets, and asters.

VIRGINIA

ASSATEAGUE ISLAND NATIONAL SEASHORE. *See* MARYLAND

BLUE RIDGE PARKWAY

A unit of the national park system, this famous scenic highway extends 469 miles through the southern **Appalachians**. It connects 2 national parks—Shenandoah at its northern end and Great Smoky Mountains on its southern end; and traverses 3 national forests—George Washington and Jefferson in Virginia and Pisgah in North Carolina (*see all*). Joining the *Skyline Drive* at Shenandoah National Park, the parkway crosses the **Blue Ridge**, the eastern rampart of the Appalachians. Then, skirting the southern end of the massive **Black Mountains**, it goes through the **Craggies**, the **Pisgahs**, and the **Balsams** before ending at Great Smoky Mountains Park. It cuts through an ancient region of rugged mountains and deep, narrow coves where wild animals and vegetation abound.

In Virginia, scenic points include **Humpback Rocks**, named for their humped appearance. Near them, self-guiding *Greenstone Trail* offers an interesting walk through an oak-hickory forest. The short *Thunder Ridge Trail* leads to a superb view of the **Arnold Valley**, a mass of rhododendron in early June. At Fallingwater there is a loop trail along *Fallingwater Cascades*, and the Peaks of Otter Visitor Center houses exhibits showing the ecological rela-

Left: Natural Bridge. Top right: sand dunes in Seashore State Park. Below: South Fork of Shenandoah River in George Washington National Forest

tionships of the plants and animals in the so-called Southern Highlands. Farther south, trails and a road lead to the summit of **Roanoke Mountain,** which offers an impressive panorama. From **Roanoke Valley** one sees Roanoke, the largest city along the parkway. Other places to stop include *Smart View,* with trails and a woodland of dogwood; **Rocky Knob,** with trails; and **Groundhog Mountain,** which has an early mountaineer's cabin. A sampling of the many points of interest along the North Carolina segment of the parkway includes famous **Cumberland Knob,** with a loop trail to **Gully Creek Gorge.** From Flat Rock a trail leads to a lovely vista of **Grandfather Mountain** and **Linville Valley.** The **Linville Falls** area is a rugged, scenic region, famous as the habitat of the rare Carolina hemlock. Another parkway highlight is the **Craggy Gardens,** a 700-acre recreation area at an elevation of over 5,000 feet in the Great Craggy Mountains. The gardens are threaded with trails and are spectacular in June when the rhododendron bloom.

For further information write: Box 1710, Roanoke, Va. 24008

CUMBERLAND GAP NATIONAL HISTORICAL PARK. *See* KENTUCKY

DISMAL SWAMP, or GREAT DISMAL SWAMP
southeast Va. and northeast N.C., between Norfolk, Va. and Elizabeth City, N.C.
This swamp, once an impenetrable area of some 2,000 square miles, has been partially reclaimed and now covers only about 600 square miles. (George Washington surveyed it in 1763.) It is characterized by dense forests of pine, black gum, juniper and cypress, and a tangled undergrowth resting on spongy peat ground. The canals and ditches which thread the area are so overgrown that they resemble green tunnels. Near the swamp's center is peat-bottomed **Lake Drummond,** about 3 miles wide and 6 miles long, and the highest elevation in the swamp.

DIXIE CAVERNS
just west of Roanoke and Salem, on U.S. 11, U.S. 460, and I-81
These are the only caverns in beautiful **Roanoke Valley,** which lies between the **Blue Ridge** on the east and the **Alleghenies** on the west. They contain a variety of formations with fanciful names.

ENDLESS CAVERNS
3 miles south of New Market via U.S. 11, or exits 66 or 67 off I-81
Located in the lower west slopes of **Massanutten Mountain,** these caverns are known for their vivid natural coloring and variety of formations. Exploration by speleologists has failed to find an end to the labyrinthine passages.
Open daily: June 11–Labor Day 8–8; spring and fall 9–5; winter 10–5. Admission: adults $2.50, children (6–12) $1.25

GEORGE WASHINGTON NATIONAL FOREST
northwest Virginia and east West Virginia, headquarters at Harrisonburg, Va.
This million-acre forest in an area steeped in history includes 3 separate sections. It extends over 100 miles westward across the **Blue Ridge, Massanutten,** and **Shenandoah mountains** into the eastern upthrusts of the **Alleghenies** in West Virginia. (Here, our first President hunted deer and turkey and made some of the original surveys.) Predominantly a hardwood forest, George Washington was one of the first national forests to be established in the East. It is traversed by many self-guiding walks and trails, including a section of the *Appalachian.* Its natural wonders include unique

VIRGINIA

Massanutten Mountain, an isolated ridge standing right in the middle of the famous **Shenandoah Valley**. It is bordered by 2 forks of the **Shenandoah River,** characterized by its 7 bends, visible from the *Woodstock Tower*. The forest's highest point is 4,467-foot **Elliott Knob,** which may be reached via a 4-mile trail from State 42. *For further information write: Harrisonburg, Virginia 22801*

GRAND CAVERNS
just off U.S. 340 at Grottoes, between Elkton and Waynesboro
These enormous caverns (the floor of the **Grand Ball Room** alone covers 5,000 square feet) are famous for their travertine shields, unique blanket-draped formations projecting from the sidewalls. *Open daily: May–Sept 15, 8–8; Sept 16–Apr 30, 9–5. Admission: adults $2.50, children (6–13) $1.25*

GREAT FALLS OF THE POTOMAC. See DISTRICT OF COLUMBIA

JEFFERSON NATIONAL FOREST
southwest Virginia, headquarters at Roanoke
Covering 610,000 acres in the **Allegheny** and **Blue Ridge mountains** of Virginia, this forest stretches from the **James River** south to the Tennessee border. It is a haven for hikers, hunters, and fishermen, and is traversed by parts of the Blue Ridge Parkway (*see*) and the *Appalachian Trail*. Mount Rogers, at 5,729 feet, the highest point in the state, is within **Mount Rogers National Recreation Area.** This 154,000-acre tract resembles a Swiss alpine setting, with its rich valleys, high peaks, and vast open meadows with grazing sheep. *For further information write: Box 4009, Roanoke, Virginia 24015*

LURAY CAVERNS
just west of Luray on U.S. 211, exit 67 of I-81
These famous **Shenandoah Valley** caverns contain numerous massive and colorful formations. Aside from thousands of stalactites and stalagmites, reflected in the various lakes, there is the unique **Cathedral** with its Stalacpipe Organ—an organ that plays music by creating a stereophonic effect from the different stalactites. *Open daily: winter 9–4; spring and fall 9–6; summer 9–7. Admission: adults $2.50, children (7–13) $1.25*

NATURAL BRIDGE
at Natural Bridge, near Lexington on I-80 and U.S. 11
This arch, carved by nature from 36,000 tons of limestone, is 215 feet high, 90 feet long, and varies in width from 50 to 150 feet. It spans **Cedar Creek** and joins 2 mountains; U.S. 11 passes over it. The historic bridge was surveyed by George Washington, who carved his initials into it, and was once owned by Thomas Jefferson. *Open daily: Apr–Sept, 7–10; rest of year, 7–9. Admission: adults $2.70, children (6–12) 90¢*

NATURAL CHIMNEYS
a half mile north of Mount Solon, via State 42
These 7 erosion-carved stone towers, which resemble the turrets of a medieval castle, rise some 100 feet at the western edge of the **Shenandoah Valley.** The formations are named for the huge chimneys once used in the area for the smelting of iron ore. Their bases are pierced with natural tunnels, and cedars grace their tops. *Open daily: Mar–Nov 8–dark. Admission: adults $1.50, children (7–13) 75¢*

NATURAL TUNNEL STATE PARK
about 14 miles northwest of Gate City on U.S. 23, 58, and 421

The park's main attraction is a huge natural tunnel through the solid rock of **Powell's Mountain.** Carved through a limestone ridge over thousands of centuries, it is 100 feet high, 130 feet wide, and 900 feet long. A railroad and **Stock Creek** pass through the tunnel.

SEASHORE STATE PARK
on U.S. 60 at Cape Henry in Virginia Beach

Most of this park's 2,770 acres are preserved as the **Seashore Natural Area,** designated a Registered Natural Landmark in 1965. It is an area of lagoons filled with cypress trees, giant sand dunes, and an amazing variety of plants, with 40 miles of hiking trails. The landscape is a direct result of the ocean and wind forces, which together created parallel rows of dunes. Eventually, these became heavily wooded, and today there are 2 distinct types of forest: dogwood, pine, oak, hickory, and beech grow on the even-topped dunes; and a cypress-tupulo forest, which has achieved its maximum growth, in the intervening swamps and pools.

SHENANDOAH CAVERNS
near New Market, exit 68 off I-81, or 4 miles north and 1½ miles west of U.S. 11

Among the many Shenandoah Valley caves, these caverns are outstanding. They contain the rare "bacon" formation (the rock striations resemble a slab of bacon), and the **Grove of Druids.**
Open daily: summer 9–7; winter 9–5. Admission: adults $2.50, children (7–14) $1.25

SHENANDOAH NATIONAL PARK
headquarters 4 miles west of Thornton Gap, 4 miles east of Luray on U.S. 211

This 300-square-mile park lies astride an 80-mile segment of northern Virginia's **Blue Ridge Mountains.** Shenandoah, an Indian word meaning "Daughter of the Stars," is an apt name since the park embraces some of the highest, most scenic parts of these mountains. One of the best ways to enjoy its beauty is via the 105-mile *Skyline Drive*, which extends the entire length of the park along the ridge-crest, from the northern entrance at Front Royal to its southern exit at Rockfish Gap. In the south, it connects with the Blue Ridge Parkway (*see*). There are 75 overlooks along the drive, which afford magnificent panoramas of the rolling land of the **Shenandoah Valley** to the west and the wooded hills, orchards, and fields of the Piedmont on the east. Among the many fascinating features of the drive is **Marys Rock Tunnel,** which cuts through 660 feet of solid rock. Shenandoah's rolling landscape is filled with spur ridges and innumerable valleys through which run swift, cold streams with falls and cascades. A portion of the *Appalachian* and many other hiking and saddle trails lead up to summits and down into hollows. *For further information: Superintendent, Luray, Virginia 22835*

SKYLINE CAVERNS
at northern entrance of Shenandoah National Park, on U.S. 340

Formed millions of years ago by water slowly seeping through cracks and fissures in Dolomite limestone, these caverns contain many underground streams and cascades. Their major attraction is a group of rare white calcite formations called anthodites, or cave flowers, reputed to be the only such formations in the world.
Open daily: summer 8–8; winter 9–5. Admission: adults $2.50, children (7–13) $1.25

WASHINGTON

BEACON ROCK STATE PARK
4 miles west of Bonneville Dam on U.S. 830

This 4,049-acre park contains one of the world's largest monoliths, Beacon Rock, which rises 848 feet above the gorge formed by the **Columbia River** as it cuts through the **Cascade Range.** The rock's sheer escarpment looks impossible to climb, but an exciting trail leads to its summit, from where there is a superb view.

CHINOOK POINT
5 miles southeast of Fort Columbia Historical State Park via U.S. 101

In May, 1792, Captain Robert Gray discovered the mouth of the **Columbia River** and dropped anchor at Chinook Point. This ended the lengthy search for the legendary "Great River of the West" and gave the United States a legitimate claim to the Northwest. For years Chinook Point and adjacent **Scarboro Hill** served as landmarks for sailors navigating the dangerous entrance to the Columbia. National Historic Landmark

COLVILLE NATIONAL FOREST
north Washington, headquarters at Colville

Embracing almost 100,000 acres, this forest is filled with winding green valleys circled by rolling timbered slopes and several high peaks. It is dotted with many small lakes, such as **Little Pend Oreille, Pierre,** and **Sullivan,** all well-stocked with fish, and is traversed or bounded by several important waterways, including the **Pend Oreille, Kettle, Colville,** and **Columbia rivers.**
For further information: Federal Building, Colville, Wash. 98114

COULEE DAM RECREATION AREA
northeast Washington, headquarters at Coulee Dam

This 102,500-acre area, administered by the National Park Service, offers many outdoor activities such as swimming, water skiing, and boating. Grand Coulee Dam, one of the largest in the world, measures 550 feet in height, 500 feet in width at its bases, and 4,173 feet in length. This gigantic concrete structure is the key link in a great chain of dams, siphons, canals, and reservoirs that comprise the Columbia Basin Project, which harnesses the **Columbia River** for irrigation, power, and flood control. Grand Coulee, the northernmost of the many dams on the river, backs up **Franklin D. Roosevelt Lake.** This huge lake extends northward 145 miles to the Canadian border and has 31 recreation sites on its 660 miles of shoreline. A 3-hour drive from Coulee Dam to Kettle Falls by way of Fort Spokane affords scenic views of the countryside and lake, as does another drive (State 21) along the **San Poil River** from Keller Ferry to the old gold-mining town of Republic. The recreation area is noted for its unusual flora and fauna. Over 400 species of plants flourish here because of wide differences in climatic conditions.
For further information write: Box 37, Coulee Dam, Wash. 99116

CRAWFORD STATE PARK
14 miles northwest of Metaline Falls, near Boundary Dam

The principal attraction here is **Gardner Cave,** the largest limestone cavern in the state, with a total slope length of about 1,050 feet. A good trail leads north, up a small hill, to the cave's entrance; there are some 875 feet of passageway in the cave.

Left: Dry Falls of Grand Coulee. Top right: Mount Rainier. Below: glacial lake in characteristic North Cascades landscape

WASHINGTON

FEDERATION FOREST STATE PARK
about 17 miles east of Enumclaw on State 410 (Chinook Pass Highway)

This park consists of 612 acres of virgin timber. It contains an Interpretive Center whose primary purpose is to show the contrasts of nature found in Washington. Wide climatic differences occur across the state, and the flora varies from area to area. Washington includes 7 of the 10 general life zones found in the United States. The park is located in a transition area between the Coast Forest Zone—extending from the beaches of the **Pacific Ocean** inland through the **Puget Sound Basin** and upward into the lower hills of the **Olympic Mountains** and the lower western slopes of the **Cascade Range**—and the Mountain Forest Zone, which occupies the mountainous areas of eastern and western Washington to an elevation limit of about 5,000 feet. In the park, the *East Trail* winds along an ancient river terrace several feet above the present channel of the **White River**; the *West Trail* also follows the ancient river terrace. The forest is traversed by part of the famous *Naches Trail*, one of the first pioneer trails between eastern Washington and the Puget Sound country.

GIFFORD PINCHOT NATIONAL FOREST
southwest Washington, headquarters at Vancouver

This 1.35 million acre forest is named in honor of the first Chief of the United States Forest Service. It extends southward from the Mount Rainier National Park (*see*) almost to the Oregon line. In one area it borders **Columbia River Gorge**, the route of the 1805–6 Lewis and Clark expedition. The forest contains 2 prominent snow-clad peaks—9,677-foot **Mount Saint Helens**, which is volcanic; and 12,326-foot **Mount Adams**, second only to Mount Rainier in the Northwest. Gifford Pinchot forest lies along the western slope of the **Cascade Mountain Range** in rugged, heavily timbered terrain that is frequently drenched with rain and snow from moisture-laden clouds which originate over the **Pacific Ocean**. The landscape is covered with hundreds of alpine lakes and innumerable streams that flow from high glaciers to rivers such as the **Cowlitz, Yakima,** and **Columbia**—thousands of feet below.

About 2,150 miles of roads and 1,300 miles of hiking and riding trails penetrate this huge area. The *Pacific Crest National Scenic Trail*, closed to motorized travel, traverses the whole length of the forest. It goes along the summit of the Cascades from **Carlton Pass** in the north to the Columbia River in the south.

The 82,680-acre **Goat Rock Wilderness**, in the northeast section of the forest, extends into a portion of Snoqualmie National Forest (*see*). It is a rugged and beautiful region of flinty pinnacles (the habitat of mountain goats) and icy snowfields and glaciers, surrounded by flower-filled meadows.

The 42,111-acre **Mount Adams Wilderness** is located on the forest's eastern edge. The sides of Mount Adams are strewn with glaciers, and the lower slopes are covered with a large variety of trees, shrubs, and flowers. The mountain is also surrounded by vast fields of wild huckleberries. **Bird Creek Meadows**, just outside the wilderness on Mount Adams' southern slope, is an outstanding scenic area famous for its colorful display of native flowers.

The **Spirit Lake–Mount Saint Helens Area** on the forest's west flank has a self-guiding nature trail that describes an ancient forest buried by pumice during volcanic eruptions of Mount Saint Helens. *For further information write: Box 449, Vancouver, Wash. 98660*

WASHINGTON

GINKGO PETRIFIED FOREST STATE PARK
29 miles east of Ellensburg on U.S. 10 (I-90), then north

This forest preserves thousands of logs petrified in lava flows, including logs of the ginkgo tree, rarely found as fossil wood. The logs lie in drift piles where they were washed onto the shores of ancient lakes and swamps probably 15 million years ago. Over 200 tree species have been identified, including swamp-loving trees as well as upland species that were floated to the lowlands. The fossils lack roots, limbs, and bark, indicating that the trees were abraded by floodwater during their transport from the highlands to lakeshores and swamps. The site overlooking the **Columbia River** is distinctive because of the large number of genera and species represented and also because fossils are rarely preserved in lava flows as they are here. Registered Natural Landmark

GRAND COULEE

Grand Coulee is an ancient bed of the **Columbia River.** It extends for 50 miles from the town of Grand Coulee to **Soap Lake,** a highly mineralized body of water whose black basalt cliffs reveal its volcanic origin. Grand Coulee is a natural wonder of the Columbia River Basin, which has been shaped by volcanic activity, glaciation, and water erosion. Millions of years ago successive floods of lava filled the basin and diverted the Columbia River into a big westward bend. Then Ice Age glaciers advanced south from Canada and reached the lava plateau of central Washington. About 10,000 years ago this ice blocked the bend, damming the present site of Grand Coulee Dam. Later the Columbia overflowed its banks and spilled across the plateau in a series of huge floods. The erosional power of this vast body of water was tremendous, and the lava and softer lake sediments on the plateau were carved into a series of gashes called the Channelled Scablands. The largest and most spectacular of these was Grand Coulee, through which the Columbia flowed. However, because subsequent events (notably the deformation of the lava beds, the advance and recession of the glacial ices, the cutting of a new course of the Columbia, and the formation and retreat of waterfalls) the Columbia returned to its present channel. Grand Coulee was left dry, and only a flat depression lined by 1,000-foot perpendicular basalt walls remained. Only in the 20th century has artificial damming (*see* Grand Coulee Recreation Area) turned parts of the dry channel into storage reservoirs.

One of the most startling remnants of ancient Grand Coulee is **Dry Falls** in Sun Lakes State Park, 6 miles southwest of Coulee City. At 35-mile-wide Dry Falls the prehistoric Columbia plunged more than 400 feet over curving cliffs from the upper Grand Coulee before continuing to the Pacific. Registered Natural Landmark

KAMIAK BUTTE STATE PARK
12 miles north of Pullman via State 27

This 298-acre park features Kamiak Butte which towers above the surrounding wheat fields. Some geologists believe that the butte is the surviving peak of a prehistoric mountain range that was engulfed by a lava flow. Its rocky slopes are covered with nearly every type of tree native to the Northwest.

KANIKSU NATIONAL FOREST. *See* IDAHO

LAKE CHELAN NATIONAL RECREATION AREA. *See* NORTH CASCADES NATIONAL PARK

A ferry winds its way through the San Juan Islands.

MIMA MOUNDS
west of Little Rock, off State 121

This 620-acre state-owned tract preserves a group of remarkable mounds that look like haycocks on a meadow or segments of spheres nearly buried in the earth. They range in height from barely perceptible lumps to a maximum of 7 feet and have an average base diameter of 20 feet. They occur on a prairie that was formed by outwash of the continental ice sheet during the late Pleistocene epoch, or Ice Age. Scientists are not sure how the mounds were formed, but the rodent theory (the burrowing of gophers) is generally accepted. Registered Natural Landmark

MOUNT BAKER NATIONAL FOREST
northcentral Washington, headquarters at Bellingham

This 1,282,962-acre forest encompasses some of the state's most primitive regions. Majestic 10,778-foot **Mount Baker** dominates the northwestern sector, and 10,528-foot **Glacier Peak** (glaciers radiate in all directions from its summit) stands remote and beautiful in the southeast. These are 2 of the state's 5 isolated peaks of volcanic origin—the others are **Mounts Rainier, Saint Helens,** and **Adams.** Mount Baker was known to the Indian peoples of the region as Koma Kulshan, or white, steep mountain. In 1792 the English explorer Captain George Vancouver, still searching for the elusive Northwest Passage, named Mount Baker after a crew member who was reputedly the first to spot the mountain. Now classified as a dormant volcano, Mount Baker still emits sulphurous fumes, and in 1854 it covered the countryside with ashes. Glacier Peak dominates 458,505-acre **Glacier Peak Wilderness,** deeply penetrated by river valleys and covered with jutting glacier-carved peaks. The wilderness extends eastward into Wenatchee National Forest (*see*) and is traversed by a portion of the *Pacific Crest National Scenic Trail.* Mount Baker Forest also includes a portion of the **Paysayten Wilderness** (*see Okanogan National Forest*).

The most characteristic feature in this forest is its glaciers, the large fields of snow forever grinding slowly down the mountainsides. Of the approximately 1,000 glaciers within the contiguous United States, 674 are in Washington State. Of these, 390 are found in Mount Baker Forest and adjacent North Cascades National Park (*see*).

For further information write: Federal Office Building, Bellingham, Wash. 98225.

MOUNT RAINIER NATIONAL PARK
about 58 miles southeast of Tacoma, headquarters at Longmire

Washington's highest point and its largest and best-known landmark, 14,408-foot Mount Rainier, is part of the **Middle Cascade Range**. This remarkable mountain stands as an isolated cone towering more than 9,000 feet above the ridges of the surrounding Cascade peaks. It is a dormant volcano; its last eruption probably occurred about 2,000 years ago. Rainier's summit bears 3 distinct peaks: 14,112-foot **Liberty Cap** on the north; 14,150-foot **Point Success** on the south; and 14,408-foot **Columbia Crest**, the highest elevation in the whole Cascade Range, on the east.

More than a tenth of the park's 378 square miles is covered by ice—part of the extensive system of alpine glaciers that radiates from the mountain's lofty summit. The glaciers, 26 of which are important enough to be named, extend down Mount Rainier's deeply furrowed slopes; together they constitute one of North America's largest single-peak glacier systems. Six glaciers originate in the summit ice cap: **Nisqually, Ingraham, Emmons, Winthrop, Kautz,** and **Tahoma.**

Mount Rainier National Park contains 4 visitor centers, which are near the entrances and which serve as starting points for the park's many trails and roads. Most places of interest may be reached via the park's 140 miles of roads.

Mount Rainier Park's 300 miles of hiking trails are exciting and rewarding. The famous *Wonderland Trail*, which completely encircles Mount Rainier, traverses almost 90 miles of Pacific Northwest backcountry. It crosses virgin forest, alpine meadows, and glistening snowfields, thus offering samples of the varied park terrain. Other trails include the famous *Paradise Glacier Trail* on which the average visitor can actually get out on glacial ice and see the ice caves for which Paradise Glacier is so famous. The caves, started by summer melting and carved by air flow, are usually open in late August and September. They are constantly changing in size and shape. A number of interesting trails originate in the Sunrise Area. The *Emmons Vista Self-guiding Nature Trail* explores an area between the forested lower slopes and the treeless snowfields of Mount Rainier. Its main attraction is Emmons Glacier, which flows down the mountain's northeast flank and which is the largest glacier on the mountain, measuring 5 miles in length and 1 mile in width. Information about the many trails, mountain climbing, and skiing is available at the various visitor centers.

For further information: Superintendent, Longmire, Wash. 98397

MOUNT SPOKANE STATE PARK
34 miles northeast of Spokane via U.S. 2

Mount Spokane is situated in this 20,771-acre park, the largest in the state system. An improved road leads to the mountain's 5,881-foot summit, which offers spectacular views of Spokane, the mountains of Washington and Idaho, and 17 lakes.

NISQUALLY DELTA
15 miles east of Olympia and 20 miles southwest of Tacoma via I-5

Over the past 30,000 years the **Nisqually River** has built up a delta of some 4,000 acres where it flows into Puget Sound (*see*). About 2,765 acres of the delta are relatively undisturbed and have been designated a Registered Natural Landmark. The other 1,035 acres of the delta, between the river on the east and **McAllister Creek** on the west, have been diked to provide pastureland for a dairy farm.

Nisqually Delta—made up of mud flats, salt marshes, and shrub-covered riverbanks—has a tide range of over 16 feet. The area is the only natural nesting place for migratory waterfowl in the southern Puget Sound region.

NORTH CASCADES NATIONAL PARK and ROSS LAKE AND LAKE CHELAN NATIONAL RECREATION AREAS
northcentral Washington, headquarters at Sedro Woolley

This national park complex covers 1,053 square miles and contains 4 distinct sections: the North and South Units of the National Park and Ross Lake and Lake Chelan National Recreation Areas. Together they conserve an outstanding portion of the **North Cascade Range.** The Cascades, often called the American Alps, extend from south of California's Lassen Volcanic National Park (*see*) north to Canada's **Fraser River.** The array of alpine scenery in the 4 sections is unmatched in the conterminous 48 states. It includes over 150 active glaciers, hundreds of jagged peaks, great ice aprons and ice caps, hanging valleys, waterfalls and alpine lakes nestled in glacial cirques, and deep glacier-carved canyons.

North Cascades is a true wilderness park with just 1 paved and 2 dirt roads; its vast expanses must be explored via 345 miles of hiking and horse trails. (Professional guides and packtrain services are available.) The park's Northern Unit contains massive **Mount Shuksan,** whose 9,127-foot summit may be reached by trail. This mountain is strewn with glaciers, notably **White Salmon, Hanging, Upper Curtis, Lower Curtis, Sulphide, Crystal, East Nooksack, West Nooksack,** and **Price.** The latter is above **Price Lake,** which drains into the north fork of the **Nooksack River.** East of Mount Shuksan, across the valley of the **Baker River** and its tributaries, its glacier-covered **Picket Range,** the dominant feature of the Northern Unit. This range bristles with peaks such as 8,236-foot **Mount Challanger** with its **Challanger Glacier.** The Southern Unit is centered around **Eldorado Peaks,** rugged highlands cloaked with a massive, living glacier and dominated by 8,868-foot **Eldorado Peak.** Farther south in this unit is famous **Cascade Pass** between the **North Fork of the Cascade River** and the **Stehekin River.** To the northeast is **Mount Logan.** The park's 2 units are separated by **Ross Lake Recreation Area,** which contains 3 man-made lakes—12,000-acre **Ross Lake,** 910-acre **Diablo Lake,** and 210-acre **Gorge Lake,** all created by impounding sections of the **Skagit River.** This recreational area also includes glaciers, forested valleys, and mountain peaks. **Big Beaver Valley** on the west shore of Ross Lake contains beaver ponds, marshes, and a stand of western red cedar over 1,000 years old. **Thunder Creek Valley** near Diablo Lake contains a rain forest of giant conifers, 250 feet tall. The Lake Chelan National Recreation Area, south of the park's Southern Unit, includes the southern half of Stehekin Valley and the northernmost 5 miles of **Lake Chelan.** This glacier-carved lake is 1,500 feet deep, between 1 and 2 miles wide in most places, and 55 miles long. It is a true inland fiord that winds northwestward between the **Chelan Mountains** on the west and the **Sawtooth Ridge** on the east. It is an exceptionally scenic waterway and provides boat access to the park's southern entrance. A road runs from the village of Stehekin on the northeastern shore of the lake, 24 miles to the head of Stehekin Valley, just below Cascade Pass. However, the main park approach is from the west via State 20 from Burlington; when completed, *North Cross Highway* (State 20) will provide access from the east. *For further information write: Sedro Woolley, Wash. 98284*

OKANOGAN NATIONAL FOREST
northcentral Washington, headquarters at Okanogan

Okanogan, formerly the Chelan National Forest, covers 1,520,456 acres of breathtaking, rugged scenery with ample opportunities for hiking, horseback riding, skiing, hunting, fishing, and mountain climbing. It is in a rough triangle formed by the Canadian border on the north, the **Cascade Range** on the northwest, and the **Columbia** and **Okanogan rivers** on the east. There are smaller sections of the forest east of the Okanogan, several of which are clustered around **Aeneas Valley.** Ponderosa pine predominate; and the forest region is rich in marine fossils because the area was once the bottom of a prehistoric sea. Okanogan also has many county roads and some 1,200 miles of forest roads, but there are many remote areas in the west and northwest that can only be reached by trail. The *Pacific Crest National Scenic Trail,* which goes from Mexico to Canada, crosses the northwest portion of Okanogan and offers superb mountain scenery. Much of this back country is in the 505,524-acre **Pasayten Wilderness,** which extends into Mount Baker National Forest *(see).* This wilderness is filled with alpine meadows, towering peaks, glacial streams, all penetrated by over 500 miles of trails (motorized vehicles are not permitted).

For further information write: Supervisor, Okanogan, Wash. 98840

OLYMPIC NATIONAL FOREST
Olympic Peninsula in northwest Washington, headquarters at Olympia

Like neighboring Olympic National Park *(see),* which it very nearly surrounds, this 651,226-acre forest has all the unique characteristics of the **Olympic Peninsula.** It contains an unusual blending of marine climate; lush, fast-growing Olympic rain forest vegetation; rushing glacial streams; as well as ice- and water-carved peaks and valleys. Aside from the towering trees, notably Douglas fir, western hemlock, Sitka spruce, and western red cedar, the most dominant feature of this forest is roaring water. Water splashes against rocky walls of narrow canyons as it winds its way down forested slopes from the melting highcountry snowfields to the sea. Fishing, especially for salmon, is excellent in Olympic's many streams, ponds, and backcountry high lakes, such as **Silver, Karnes,** and **Mildred.** Wildlife, such as deer, bear, cougar, elk, and a host of smaller mammals, is abundant.

Innumerable roads penetrate the forest, and many are spurs of U.S. 101, the main highway around Olympic Peninsula. One of the most inspiring roads climbs to the top of 3,000-foot **Mount Walker,** near Quilcene. The mountain, whose slopes are brightened with rhododendron, affords spectacular views of **Puget Sound** and the **Olympic Mountains.** Over 180 miles of trails meander through the varied forest settings. Many penetrate the higher reaches, such as the area around 5,701-foot **Mount Jupiter,** west of Seal Rock. Here one can walk along the ridge and admire the surrounding valleys and mountains. Other climbs lead to **Baldy Ridge,** in the forest's northernmost unit, and **Marmot Pass,** north of Mount Jupiter, where one can see mountain goats on rocky lookout points. Other trails lead over spongy moss and fern on rain forest floors as they penetrate groves of giant Douglas firs. One can admire **Willaby Creek** as it rushes through an Olympic rain forest just south of **Lake Quinault.** A different type of experience is available at **Seal Rock Beach** on **Hood Bay,** probably the only place in the national forest system where a visitor can gather his own oysters.

For further information: Federal Building, Olympia, Wash. 98501

WASHINGTON

OLYMPIC NATIONAL PARK
northwest Washington, headquarters at Port Angeles

This national park, the westernmost in the conterminous United States, covers 1,400 square miles in the central portion and western edge of the **Olympic Peninsula.** It is almost entirely surrounded by Olympic National Forest (*see*) and is famous for its extremely varied flora and fauna. The park's 50-mile-long strip of **Pacific Ocean** coastline extends from **Cape Alava** to Kalaloch campground. It is wave-scarred, and bears a strong resemblance to the rugged shoreline of Maine's Acadia National Park (*see*). The coastline is divided into a series of promontories or headlands separated by coves and inlets and is characterized by sea caves, sea arches, beaches, sand barriers, and offshore rocks, where seals often take the sun. In places the sand beaches alternate with dense forests that reach the waterline. This Pacific strip is accessible from U.S. 101 at Kalaloch and by spur roads leading to the mouth of the **Hoh River,** to the fishing village of La Push at the mouth of the **Quileute River,** and to **Rialto Beach.** The rest must be explored on foot or on horseback.

The other, much larger, section of the park is a vast wilderness region around 7,965-foot **Mount Olympus,** the highest peak of the **Olympic Range.** The park's Olympic mountains contain at least 60 glaciers, covering an aggregate area of about 25 miles. Six of them —**Hoh, Blue, White, Hubert, Jeffers,** and **Hume**—flow down the icy slopes of Olympus. Other Olympic peaks that still support glaciers include **Mounts Carrier** (6,995 feet), **Tom** (7,048 feet), **Christie** (6,179 feet), **Queets** (6,480 feet), and **Anderson** (7,332 feet). Few roads penetrate this mountain region, but there are some 600 miles of hiking and riding trails, most of which follow stream courses.

The Olympic Range contains 2 main sections: the wet area which roughly faces the park's western boundary and which traps the moisture-laden air from the Pacific; and the dry sector, along the park's eastern side, where the peaks are separated by short, steep river canyons. The west side of the peninsula has the wettest winter climate in the conterminous United States, and in some places yearly precipitation often exceeds 140 inches. This does not include the heavy annual snowfall that blankets the high country and especially Mount Olympus. In contrast, the northeast corner of the peninsula, especially **Sequim Valley** (outside the park), is one of the driest places on the West Coast.

The extremely moist conditions that have existed for centuries in Olympic's western valleys have led to the development of fantastic coniferous rain forests located in the valley of the **Hoh, Queets,** and **Quinault rivers.** The undergrowth is abundant and luxuriant and includes moisture-loving fungi, mosses, liverworts, and ferns. The moss-festooned trees often reach record size.

The park has 3 visitor centers: The Pioneer Memorial Museum near Port Angeles, the Storm King Visitor Center at **Lake Cresent,** and the Hoh Rain Forest Visitor Center.

For further information: 600 E Park Ave, Port Angeles, Wash. 98362

PALOUSE FALLS STATE PARK
17 miles southeast of Washtucna off State 26

The spectacular Palouse Falls plunge 198 feet from a rocky gorge into a great rimrock basin below. From here the **Palouse River** travels southward to join the **Snake River.** A park trail leads from the falls down to the river, and in the basaltic bluffs at the base of the canyon one can see caves that the Palouse Indians once used for shelter and storage.

Glacier and Hoh River rain forest on Olympic Peninsula

POINT OF ARCHES
10 miles south of Cape Flattery

Cape Flattery is a spectacular neck of land at the northwest tip of the Olympic Peninsula. The Pacific Ocean is on the west, the Strait of Juan de Fuca is on the east, and lonely rockbound Tatoosh Island with its lighthouse stands just offshore. Below, the wild surf pounds away at the cliff face, carving great sea caverns and blow holes. Point of Arches, which may be reached only by jeep or rugged hiking, is one of the most beautiful, unspoiled stretches of beach in the state. It features wave-cut arches, craggy offshore rocks, tunnels, inlets, and tidal pools. Cliffs and jutting headlands rise from the beach or the sea. Adjacent to these headlands there are uplands forested with coniferous trees such as hemlock, cedar, and spruce, intermixed with scattered broad-leaved trees, shrubs, and an understory of huckleberry and ferns. The sandy beaches and tidal pools are populated with a variety of creatures—anemones, limpets, burrowing mollusks, snails, crabs, barnacles, and algae. In April, large pods of gray whales may be seen cavorting offshore. Point of Arches preserves a fine example of a sea-sculptured, rocky shoreline and a fully developed upland environment. Registered Natural Landmark

PUGET SOUND
northwest Washington

Puget Sound is a deepwater inlet of the Pacific Ocean, connected to the Pacific by the Strait of Juan de Fuca. Officially, it extends about 100 miles from Admiralty Inlet, its entry and northernmost portion, to Olympia. However, in popular usage the name has come to mean the salty inland seas to the north as well. Thus the San Juan Islands (*see*), although not technically in the sound, are often considered part of it. Puget Sound branches into Hood Canal, a western arm that separates the Olympic and Kitsap peninsulas. It is a paradise for sailors and is dotted with over 300 islands the largest of which is Whidbey (*see*). The sound contains many good harbors and its shoreline and islands are the sites of many state parks and resorts. Dash Point State Park, northeast of Tacoma, offers swimming, fishing, and clamming, as do Eagle Island State Park, between Anderson and McNeil Islands, and Camano Island State Park. Several toll ferries link the mainland, the islands, and Vancouver Island.

WASHINGTON

ROSS LAKE NATIONAL RECREATION AREA. *See* **NORTH CASCADES NATIONAL PARK**

SAN JUAN ISLANDS

These islands are actually a partially submerged archipelago between the mainland of Washington State and Vancouver Island, British Columbia. They are scattered in the arm of the Pacific that reaches northward from Puget Sound; not counting the innumerable islets, rocks, and reefs, there are over 170 islands in the group. The largest are **San Juan, Orcas,** and **Lopez.** With their harbors, coves, and beaches, the San Juans are very popular vacation spots. At low tide their beaches offer a wealth of sea life—great sea urchins, bright orange sea cucumbers, crimson sea plumes, sea anemones, jellyfish, scuttling crabs, clams, mussels, and long strips of kelp. Inland, many islands have trout-filled lakes. Some islands are privately owned, and many are uninhabited. At Moran State Park on Orcas Island there is trout fishing in **Cascade, Mountain,** and **Twin lakes;** a paved road leads to the summit of **Mount Constitution,** at 2,409 feet the highest point in the San Juans. There are many other state parks that are accessible only by boat or which are still undeveloped. San Juan Island is the site of the San Juan Island National Historic Park, which commemorates the bloodless "Pig War" of 1859 between the United States and Great Britain over sovereignty in the San Juan Islands area. Peaceful arbitration of the dispute in 1872 placed the islands within United States limits.
For further information write: Box 549, Friday Harbor, Wash. 98250

SEQUIM BAY STATE PARK
4 miles south of Sequim via U.S. 101

This 90-acre park on **Sequim Bay** offers swimming, clamming, and boating in a setting of towering trees and native shrubbery. By a quirk of nature the Sequim area is one of the driest areas on the **Pacific Coast,** even though it is only a few miles away from one of the wettest spots in the United States (*see Olympic National Park*).

SNOQUALMIE NATIONAL FOREST
westcentral Washington, headquarters at Seattle

This vast 1.2 million-acre forest partially surrounds Mount Rainier National Park (*see*). It stretches southward along the scenic **Cascade Mountains** from **Stevens Pass** to south of **White Pass** and includes a portion of the Goat Rocks Wilderness (*see Gifford Pinchot National Forest*). Like many other national parks and forests in Washington, Snoqualmie offers the 2 extremes of state geography and climate, with the Cascade Crest as the divider. West of the high summit peaks, moisture-laden clouds from the **North Pacific** deposit huge amounts of snow and rain. This precipitation stimulates lush forest growth of Douglas fir, western hemlock, and western red cedar. East of the crest there are open stands of golden-barked ponderosa pine and other species that prefer drier and sunnier conditions.

Sightseers may drive over 1,700 miles of forest roads and hike or ride over 1,200 miles of trails. The *Pacific Crest National Scenic Trail* runs the length of the forest along the summit of the Cascade Mountains. Attractions in the northern part include **Sunset, Bridal Veil, Eagle, Alpine** and **Deception falls.** In the southern section, the *Mather Memorial Parkway* (State 410) follows the **Naches** and **Pleasant rivers** through a scenic region.
For further information write: Supervisor, Seattle, Wash. 98104

STEPTOE BUTTE STATE PARK
14 miles north of Colfax via U.S. 195

Steptoe Butte, a pyramid-shaped bulk, covers about 200 acres and rises 1,000 feet above the surrounding plateau to an elevation of 3,613 feet. The butte is an example of a geological formation that is an isolated mountain peak of older rock surrounded by basalt; all such buttes are given the generic name "steptoe." This one is the most outstanding of the several steptoes in eastern Washinton. There is a drive to the summit from where there is a magnificent view. Registered Natural Landmark

UMATILLA NATIONAL FOREST. *See* OREGON

WENATCHEE NATIONAL FOREST
central Washington, headquarters at Wenatchee

This forest encompasses nearly 2 million scenic acres. It stretches from the alpine beauty of the **Cascade Crest** in the west to the semi-arid hills bordering the mighty **Columbia River** on the east, and from the **Stehekin Valley** in the north to the **Yakima River** and Ellensburg area in the south. In the language of some Indian peoples Wenatchee means "good place," and in other Indian tongues it means "river issuing from a canyon." Both translations are appropriate, the latter in particular since the Wenatchee River issues from **Tumwater Canyon** as a wild torrent of white water and heads toward a rendezvous with the Columbia River, just northeast of the town of Wenatchee. Water is one of the greatest attractions of this national forest. Six major lakes—**Keechelus, Kachess, Cle Elum, Entiat, Wenatchee,** and **Chelan**—supply 44,000 acres of water for swimming, waterskiing, and boating. The largest of these is Lake Chelan, which extends 55 miles through a deep trough left by a glacier from Chelan in the south to the Stehekin Valley. The upper end of the fiordlike lake, the largest natural lake in the state, is in the Lake Chelan National Recreation Area (*see North Cascades National Park*). In addition, Wenatchee contains over 130 smaller lakes and hundreds of miles of roaring streams filled with trout. There are over 1,500 miles of forest roads and more than 1,900 miles of trails. The *Cascade Crest Trail*, part of the *Pacific Crest National Scenic Trail*, closely follows the Cascade summit in the forest.

For further information write: Supervisor, Wenatchee, Wash. 98801

WHIDBEY ISLAND
northwest Washington, in Puget Sound

This island, which is over 40 miles long, is the largest in **Puget Sound** (*see*) and one of the largest in the United States. It was discovered in 1792 by Joseph Whidbey, a member of Captain George Vancouver's expedition in search of the Northwest Passage. At the island's north end is scenic **Deception Pass**, a narrow, swift tidal strait separating Whidbey from **Fidalgo Island.** Vancouver named the pass after he learned that it was an open channel rather than a closed harbor. The strait, whose walls are 182 feet high, is spanned by a lovely 1,350-foot-long bridge to Fidalgo Island, which in turn is linked by bridges to the mainland. Deception Pass State Park, 8 miles north of Oak Harbor, is noted for its overhanging cliffs and intervening beaches, and offers hiking and nature trails as well as swimming, fishing, clamming, and oystering. South Whidbey, 10 miles south of Coupeville, is another developed state park on the island.

WEST VIRGINIA

BABCOCK STATE PARK
just south of Clifftop via U.S. 19, then west

A rugged, 3,637-acre park, Babcock is noted for its many scenic views of **New River Canyon,** one of the most spectacular gorges in the East. Sixty miles long and over a thousand feet deep in many places, this chasm also runs through Hawks Nest State Park (*see*). At Babcock 2 mountain streams have formed a Y-shaped ravine by slashing their way through a 2,600-foot-high plateau.

BERKELEY SPRINGS
Berkeley Springs Park, Berkeley

These springs, at the foot of **Warm Springs Mountain,** have long been famous for their curative powers. They were visited by George and Martha Washington. The water flows at the rate of 2,000 gallons per minute and maintains a constant temperature of 74°.

BLACKWATER FALLS STATE PARK
4 miles southwest of Davis on State 32

Surrounded by Monongahela National Forest (*see*), this 1,688-acre park contains amber-colored **Blackwater River,** which plunges over a 57-foot ledge to form Blackwater Falls. Below the waterfall, the stream makes a turbulent drop through a narrow, 500-foot-deep gorge filled with huge boulders.

Left: owl in Monongahela National Forest. Top right: Potomac panorama. Bottom: Blackwater Falls in winter

CATHEDRAL STATE PARK
just east of Aurora on U.S. 50, or 4 miles west of junction with U.S. 219

The park's majestic, centuries-old hemlocks, towering 80 to 90 feet skyward with circumferences up to 21 feet, evoke a sense of reverence such as an ancient cathedral might inspire. They stand close together in a virgin forest and create a vaultlike effect as the sun's rays penetrate only in thin shafts of light. These giants are remnants of a heavily-logged tree that was once common on the slopes of the eastern highlands. Registered Natural Landmark

CRANESVILLE SWAMP NATURE SANCTUARY
9 miles north of Terra Alta by local road

Cranesville Swamp covers about 560 acres and straddles the Preston County, West Virginia, and Garrett County, Maryland, line. Approximately 259 acres of it are a Registered Natural Landmark open to the public and owned by a national nonprofit organization dedicated to the preservation of our vanishing natural lands. The history of the swamp dates back some 10 to 25 thousand years during the Pleistocene epoch or Ice Age. During this period, when the North American continent became covered with ice, the northern or boreal forest retreated south ahead of the advancing ice sheet. When the glacier finally retreated and the climate became warmer, the northern forest advanced northward to where it exists today. In the Cranesville Swamp area a small tract of this once-vast northern forest remains a relict colony, a phrase used by botanists. This remnant survived because of local conditions similar to those found several hundred miles to the north.

For further information write: The Nature Conservancy, 1800 North Kent Street, Arlington, Virginia 22209

GRANDVIEW STATE PARK
east of U.S. 21 and 19 near Beckley

This 878-acre park offers a spectacular 7-mile view of the **Horseshoe Bend** of the **New River.** One can also see the river's canyon, which is 1,400 feet deep here and which also may be observed in Babcock and Hawk's Nest state parks (*see both*).

HANGING ROCKS
4 miles north of Romney on State 28

These perpendicular cliffs tower nearly 300 feet above the **South Branch of the Potomac River** and offer a view of the valley below.

HARPERS FERRY NATIONAL HISTORICAL PARK
eastern West Virginia and southwest Maryland, headquarters at Harpers Ferry

Harpers Ferry is strategically located on a point of land at the confluence of the **Shenandoah** and **Potomac rivers** and is surrounded by the **Blue Ridge Mountains.** The town was the theater of many important events from the early Federal period to the end of the Civil War. But it is best known as the site of John Brown's unsuccessful raid on the federal arsenal in 1859.

The national historical park comprises 4 separate tracts of land. The one in downtown Harpers Ferry contains the visitor center and the **Point,** the actual meeting place of the 2 rivers and the heart of the town during the Civil War. This section also contains **Jefferson Rock,** where Thomas Jefferson stood in 1783. He surveyed the splendid scenery and mountains and declared that the view was "stupendous," and "worth a voyage across the Atlantic." The Maryland Heights section in Maryland is traversed by the *Blue*

WEST VIRGINIA

Blazed Trail. The Bolivar Heights and Loudoun Heights sections, linked by U.S. 340, are in West Virginia. The *Loudoun Heights Trail* connects with the *Appalachian Trail*. There are guided tours of this historic area, which contains several restored buildings. Hiking, mountain climbing, fishing, and boating are also available. *For further information write: Box 117, Harpers Ferry, W. Va. 25425*

HAWKS NEST STATE PARK
about 3 miles east of Gauley Bridge on U.S. 60

Set amidst majestic mountain scenery, this is one of the state's most popular parks. Before this area was populated, fish hawks nested in the high precipices. From lofty **Gauley Mountain** there is a spectacular overlook onto scenic **New River Canyon** more than 500 feet below. This gorge, which may also be admired from Babcock State Park (*see*), has sheer vertical walls. A new aerial tramway leads from Hawks Nest Lodge to the bottom of the canyon.

LOST WORLD
Lewisburg, about 2 miles from center of town

Located underneath the famous **Greenbrier Valley**, noted for its towering ridges and serene rolling hills, this newly opened cavern contains a series of gigantic underground chambers. The rooms are filled with colorful rock formations, some resembling birds, fish, animals, and people. These and many other shapes are carved out of tiny diamondlike crystals and huge stalagmites. Scenic trails take the visitor along a prehistoric ocean floor, over a subterranean mountain of rock, and to an ancient beach over 3 million years old. *Open Apr 15–Oct 31: daily 9–dark. Admission fee charged*

MONONGAHELA NATIONAL FOREST
eastern West Virginia, headquarters at Elkins

Monongahela stretches across 820,000 acres of the **Allegheny Mountain Range** in a vast sprawling region of mountain peaks, soft lowland valleys, windswept plateaus, rocky outcrops, and swift tumbling rivers. The forest is edged with gracefully rolling pasture lands, known locally as sods. These once-forested areas were cleared for agriculture by early pioneers, and the hardy grass cover has developed naturally.

Monongahela, which is threaded with many hiking trails and scenic roads, contains several outstanding recreation areas. The **Spruce Knob-Seneca Rocks National Recreation Area** covers 100,000 acres and is divided into 2 units. The Spruce Knob Unit is dominated by 4,862-foot **Spruce Knob**, the highest point in the state, which is topped by an observation tower. The Seneca Rocks Unit contains towering quartzite formations that rise nearly 1,000 feet at the mouth of **Seneca Creek**. Near Seneca Rocks are similar formations called **Champe Rocks, Blue Rock,** and **Chimney Rock.** This unit also includes **Smoke Hole**, a gorge through which the **South Branch of the Potomac** flows for 20 miles.

Stuart Recreation Area, about 5 miles east of Elkins, is fringed by **Shavers Fork**, an excellent trout stream, and contains an interpretive forest trail. Stuart Memorial Drive leaves U.S. 33 at Stuart Recreation Area to climb 2,000 feet to the 4,008-foot summit of **Bickle Knob.** The drive continues along the tops of high ridges eastward through forests to **Bear Heaven Recreation Area** and terminates at **Alpena Gap** picnic area, where U.S. 33 crosses **Shavers Mountain.** Farther south is **Gaudineer Scenic Area**, which contains a 130-acre remnant of the once-huge virgin spruce forest that covered the region. This small stand, about 250 years old, includes

296

spruce that tower 100 feet and grow to 35 inches in diameter. The **Blue Bend Recreation Area,** on **Anthony Creek** in the southern part of the forest, offers guided tours along an interpretive trail. Northeast of here is **Lake Sherwood Recreation Area,** which holds the largest lake in Monongahela.

For further information write: Elkins, West Virginia 26241

MONT CHATEAU STATE PARK
northeast of Morgantown on State 73

This park, which adjoins the Cooper's Rock State Forest, offers fishing and swimming in 14-mile-long, fiordlike **Lake Cheat,** between the **Cheat** and **Monongahela rivers.**

NORTH BEND STATE PARK
2 miles east of Cairo on State 31

The picturesque valleys and lush wooded hills of this 1,402-acre park are covered with outstanding rock formations, such as the **Old Stone Face.** Along nature trails (*Castle Rock, Giant Tree,* and *Lonesome Pine*) one can observe the park's unusual flora and fauna. The meandering **North Fork of the Hughes River** is well-stocked with muskie and smallmouth bass.

SENECA CAVERNS
3 miles from U.S. 33 at Riverton

Situated in the **Potomac Highlands** and surrounded by Monongahela National Forest (*see*), these caverns once served as a place of refuge for the Seneca Indians. The deepest chamber is 165 feet underground, and the closest one to the earth's surface is only 25 feet below. All the living, growing stone formations have been fashioned over thousands of years by drops of water trickling through the roof of the caverns.

Open Apr–Oct: daily 7–9; weekends only in Nov. Admission: adults $1.75, children (6–12) 75¢

SMOKE HOLE CAVERN
8 miles west of Petersburg on State 4 and 28

Named by the Seneca Indians, who used it as a place for smoking meat, this cavern was later used for ammunition storage during the Civil War. According to legend millions of dollars in gold are stashed away in its secret recesses. Among the many ancient formations here are what is reputed to be the longest ribbon stalactite in the world and rare limestone coral.

TOMLINSON RUN STATE PARK
near Pughtown, about 2 miles south of U.S. 30 junction with State 2

Situated in the narrow neck of West Virginia east of the **Ohio River,** between Ohio and Pennsylvania, this park covers 1,398 acres. It is a wilderness area filled with forested hills, overhanging cliffs, and rare wildlife. It includes a 28-acre lake and 4 fishponds.

WATOGA STATE PARK
southwest of Huntersville, via secondary road

West Virginia's largest state park, 10,057-acre Watoga, is also one of the oldest and most popular. It is surrounded by Monongahela National Forest (*see*) and contains high altitude forestland, 11-acre **Watoga Lake,** and the 400-acre Brook Memorial Arboretum. The park is crisscrossed by trails leading to scenic views, and, like the adjoining Calvin Price State Forest, is a wilderness area abounding in wildlife. In summer park naturalists conduct nature hikes.

WISCONSIN

AMNICON FALLS STATE ROADSIDE PARK
5 miles southeast of Superior on U.S. 2

This 816–acre park is situated on the banks of the **Amnicon River**. The swift-flowing stream forms several waterfalls as it plunges over a series of precipices before dropping over a 20-foot wall.

APOSTLE ISLANDS NATIONAL LAKESHORE
off Bayfield Peninsula in southern Lake Superior, headquarters at Ashland

The scenic Apostle Islands are scattered over about 1,000 square miles of the fresh, blue waters of **Lake Superior**. Not counting **Long Island**, which lies off Chequamegon Point in **Chequamegon Bay** and which is sometimes included in the group, there are 22 Apostle Islands. They are heavily forested with stands of second-growth mixed hardwoods and pine, and are generally gently sloping land masses without distinctive landmarks. Their shores are characterized by steep walls with many cliffs, where wave erosion has often carved sea caves and picturesque pillars and arches. There are also many protected bays and inlets lined with lovely sand beaches.

Eons ago the Apostles were a solid part of **Bayfield Peninsula**, a blunt-tipped, lofty-ridged finger of land that juts about 20 miles into the western end of Lake Superior. Weathering and the scourings and gougings of 4 glaciers carved out the archipelago, which is about 30 miles long and 80 miles wide. The islands rise to heights

Left: Big Manitou falls in Pattison State Park. Top right: Saint Croix National Scenic River. Bottom: north woods in winter

varying between 50 and 480 feet. The smallest is **Little Manitou,** only a few yards in size. The largest is **Madeline Island,** which covers about 14,000 acres.

The islands, once home to the Chippewa Indians, later served as resting places for French and English explorers and traders. Today they are windswept and remote places of beauty, with miles of beach and lake-facing rocks. Twenty of the Apostles are now included in recently established Apostle Islands National Lakeshore, which is still being developed. It covers approximately 42,185 acres, and land is still being acquired. The lakeshore contains an 11-mile strip on the northwest portion of Bayfield Peninsula and all the Apostles except Madeline and Little Manitou. The 20 islands within the lakeshore include **Stockton,** the second largest, often called **Presque Isle;** and **Devils Island,** Wisconsin's northernmost body of land, the site of an important Lake Superior lighthouse.

For further information write: 206 6th Ave, Ashland, Wis. 54806

CAVE OF THE MOUNDS
between Mount Horeb and Blue Mounds on U.S. 18 and 151

Formed by the action of subterranean water, this cavern is renowned for the variety and unusually brilliant coloring of its formations— mainly stalactites, stalagmites, and helictites. In one chamber there are huge quantities of cave onyx as well as several specimens of an extremely rare formation of crystallized white limestone with black stripes formed by deposits of manganese oxide.

Daily tours: summer 8–6:20; May, Sept, Oct 9–4:20. Admission: adults $1.50, children (5–11) 50¢

CHEQUAMEGON NATIONAL FOREST
northcentral Wisconsin, headquarters at Park Falls

This 837,567-acre forest is named for a nearby body of water, Lake Superior's **Chequamegon Bay.** Chequamegon—a Chippewa word meaning "place of shallow water"—is a forest with over 400 lakes that dot the gently rolling hills of the north woods region of Wisconsin. The forest contains 464 miles of rivers and streams and 4 major waterways: the **Chippewa, Namekagon, Flambeau,** and **Yellow rivers,** which were used extensively by Indians and fur traders. Today the Flambeau and Chippewa are particularly appealing to canoeists. The dominant timber species are hardwoods and conifers with extensive pine and spruce plantations. Chequamegon is rich in animal life, including black bear, white-tailed deer, fox, coyote, bobcat, raccoon, beaver, and other game. Ruffed grouse and woodcock are plentiful; and the fishing is good, especially for muskie, pike, bass, walleye, trout, and panfish. There are numerous scenic drives and trails. Forest Highway 32, the *Wilderness Drive,* is particularly beautiful in September when the foliage is a blazing mass of reds, yellows, and oranges. The scenic *North Country Trail* traverses the northern half of the forest. Its eastern section winds through the **Penokee Hills,** a region of high granite ridges and steep-walled valleys drained by many, clear swift streams.

For further information write: Supervisor, Park Falls, Wis. 54552

COPPER FALLS STATE PARK
4 miles north of Mellen off State 13 or 169

This rugged, picturesque park contains 1,796 acres forested with hemlock and hardwoods. At Copper Falls the raging, reddish waters of the **Bad River** plunge over the **Keweenawan Trap Ledge** into a 65-foot deep gorge in a tumult of copper foam.

WISCONSIN

CRYSTAL CAVE
1 mile southwest of Spring Valley on State 29

This cave contains numerous chambers and passages carved by a subterranean river. Attractions include colorful formations, mineral veins, and fossils.

Tours daily: Mar–Nov 8–8; spring and fall 9–6. Admission: adults $1.75, children (under 14) 90¢

DELLS OF THE EAU CLAIRE RIVER COUNTY PARK
18 miles east of Wausau on State 52

This 152-acre park is famous for the unusual rock formations carved by the Eau Claire River. For a short distance the river flows quietly over granite boulders, but then it races over fingerlike masses of rock worn smooth by the water's action. Finally, the Eau Claire cascades down a rocky gorge in a series of falls. The park is criss-crossed with trails that overlook the rapids.

DEVIL'S LAKE STATE PARK
3 miles south of Baraboo via State 123

This park covers 3,820 acres of great natural beauty in the **Baraboo Range** of southcentral Wisconsin. Its main feature, oval-shaped Devil's Lake, is hemmed in on 3 sides by a horseshoe of spectacular cliffs rising 400 to 500 feet above the waters. These purple-hued quartzite rocks and escarpments of the Baraboo Range are covered with a heavy blanket of white pines. Millions of years ago the Range was a series of high peaks. They were eroded down to their present size by winds, rain, and the waves of preglacial seas. When the continental ice sheet moved down over Wisconsin from the north, the ancient crystalline ramparts of the Baraboo Mountains slowed its progress, and great chunks of ice were shunted off to the north and the south. Then, before the glacier could completely cover the area, its forward movement ceased and the ice sheet began to retreat. Devil's Lake was formed when glacial debris blocked both ends of a gorge that had been carved through the Baraboo Range by the **Wisconsin River**. The lake now fills the basin thus formed.

DOOR COUNTY PENINSULA
northeast Wisconsin, access via States 42 and 57

This rugged, slender finger of land is one of the most unusual resort areas in the Great Lakes region. Its eastern shore is washed by **Lake Michigan,** its western shore by the waters of **Green Bay.** With its numerous bluffs, bays, harbors, coves, beaches and offshore islands, the peninsula resembles a New England landscape. Door Peninsula is bisected by **Sturgeon Bay** and a ship canal linking Lake Michigan and Green Bay. The county takes its name from the ½-mile-wide channel at its northern end, which the French named Portes des Morts Strait (Death's Door Strait) because of its navigational hazards. Across this perilous body of water lies **Washington Island,** which is heavily wooded. Rock Island State Park, located off the northeastern tip of Washington Island, may be reached only by boat.

EAGLE CAVE
4 miles east of Blue River on State 60, then 3 miles north

This cave is noted for the variety of its rock formations. It is surrounded by a scenic area that is threaded with hiking trails.

Open May–Oct: daily 9–5; rest of year, Sat and Sun. Admission: adults $1.50, children 75¢

GOVERNOR DODGE STATE PARK
3 miles north of Dodgeville on State 23

Famous for its rocky promontories, this park covers 5,029 acres. Its rough terrain was carved by hundreds of centuries of water erosion working on sandstone and limestone deposited by prehistoric seas. Massive walls of sandstone greet the visitor at every turn. The main park valley has been dammed to form lovely Y-shaped, **Cox Hollow Lake,** which is bordered by bluffs and sheer cliffs.

ICE AGE NATIONAL SCIENTIFIC RESERVE

This reserve is composed of outstanding areas of glacial features scattered across Wisconsin. The Pleistocene epoch, or Ice Age, has left its vivid imprints across the landscape of the northern half of America from the Atlantic to the Rockies. Glaciation in North America began about 1 million years ago when an ice cap formed in the vicinity of Labrador and Hudson Bay. The increasing weight of the ice pressed it forward, and soon a blanket of ice thousands of feet thick was sweeping slowly southward across America as far as the Ohio and Missouri rivers.

As the great ice sheet moved, it scoured, scratched, grooved, and eroded the landscape over which it passed. Soil and rock fragments of all shapes and sizes were collected, swept along in the ice, and then deposited farther south. The rock debris, known as glacial drift or till, was deposited by the glaciers at depths ranging from a few inches to hundreds of feet. As the ice sheet advanced, this drift was sometimes pushed or dumped into moraines—long hills that mark the edges of the ice pathways. When the glaciers melted, even more material was deposited across the land, forming gently undulating ground moraines or till plains. Other glacially-formed landscape features found in Wisconsin include narrow ridges called eskers; conical masses known as kames; oval hills tending in the direction of the ice movement and known as drumlins; and large depressions, often filled with lake waters, called kettleholes.

The Ice Age National Scientific Reserve covers 32,500 acres across the state. The reserve, which is to be administered by the state in cooperation with the Department of the Interior, is a long-term project whose development will progress as funds become available. The comprehensive plan for future development calls for an Ice Age Trail (for hiking, riding, and biking) about 600 miles long to connect the 9 units of the reserve. The trail would generally follow the marks left by the end of the glacier across the state.

For further information write: National Park Service, Northeast Region, 143 Third Street, Philadelphia, Pa. 19106

INTERSTATE STATE PARK
on U.S. 8 at Saint Croix Falls

The oldest of Wisconsin's state parks, Interstate was created in cooperation with Minnesota in 1900. The Wisconsin portion lies on the east side of the famous Dalles of the Saint Croix River (*see Minnesota*), a scenic gorge with 200 foot high walls. The seething Saint Croix is lined with red cliffs and pine-covered terraces; many hiking trails penetrate both sides of the park. The **Old Man of the Dalles,** a dour-looking rock profile, dominates the Wisconsin bank where the river turns southwest.

LAKE WINNEBAGO
eastcentral Wisconsin

This lake, which is one of the largest inland bodies of fresh water in the United States, is about 30 miles long and between 5 and 10 miles wide. Because the **Fox River** enters it at the northern end and leaves it at its western shore, the Winnebago was a basic link in the pioneer route across Wisconsin to the Mississippi River. High Cliff State Park, containing 894 acres of timberland, is on the lake's northeast shore.

MENOMINEE COUNTY
5 miles north of Shawano

This 234,902-acre county was until recently the Menominee Indian Reservation. It is now operated by its Indian residents, and is the first county of its kind in the United States. The county, much of which is rugged forestland, is traversed in its eastern half by over 20 miles of the wild, scenic **Wolf River,** eligible for inclusion in the National Wild and Scenic Rivers system. The river, which is practically undeveloped but open to the public, is noted for its excellent whitewater canoeing and its many scenic tributaries, rapids, and waterfalls such as **Keshena Falls.** The Wolf is closely paralleled by State 55, a highly picturesque route.

For further information: Menominee Enterprises, Neopit, Wis. 54150

NICOLET NATIONAL FOREST
northeast Wisconsin, headquarters at Rhinelander

This forest covers some 649,000 acres in the lake district of northern Wisconsin. It is named in honor of Jean Nicolet, the French explorer who arrived in Green Bay in 1634, and was the first white man in Wisconsin. The forest has over 10 miles of self-guiding walking tours, as well as 95 miles of self-guiding auto tours with interpretive stops and signs that explain the forest's vegetation and wildlife. Common tree species include pine, spruce-balsam, sugar maple, oak, and white and yellow birches; there are also balsam-cedar-spruce swamp forests. The 1-mile-long *Butternut Lake Forest Trail,* which begins at the Franklin Lake Campground, passes glacier-formed **Tamarack Swamp,** a deer trail, a natural arch, an awesome stand of ancient hemlocks known as the **Hemlock Cathedral,** and the **Avenue of Giants,** lined with 400-year-old giant white pines. The forest has 844 miles of fishing streams and 367 lakes.

For further information write: Federal Office Building, Rhinelander, Wis. 54501

PATTISON STATE PARK
10 miles south of Superior on State 35

This 1,365-acre park is located high above the Lake Superior basin. It contains Wisconsin's highest waterfall, **Big Manitou Falls,** which the Indians called Gitchee Monido, or Falls of the Great Spirit. They are formed when the **Black River** rushes over a ledge and plunges 165 feet through a narrow sandstone notch.

RIDGES SANCTUARY
a half mile north of Bailey's Harbor, Door Peninsula

This sanctuary was established to protect and cultivate wildflowers. It includes 26 of the 45 species of orchids that have been identified in the state. In addition, the Ridges encompasses an unusual geological formation—some 16 sand ridges that progress inland from the shoreline of **Lake Michigan.** The site enables the visitor to observe the complete ecological succession from sand and water on the lakeshore to a fully mature boreal forest that thrives farther inland. Registered Natural Landmark

ROCHE A CRI STATE ROADSIDE PARK
2 miles north of Friendship via State 13
> The main feature here is Roche a Cri, which stands some 300 feet above the surrounding green plain. One of the best known landmarks of Wisconsin's great crescent-shaped central plain region, it is one of the many rocks that still stand on the sand flats in the former bed of ancient glacial Lake Wisconsin.

SAINT CROIX NATIONAL SCENIC RIVERWAY
east Minnesota and northwest Wisconsin, headquarters at Saint Croix Falls, Wis.
> The riverway, part of the recently established National Wild and Scenic Rivers system, consists of approximately 200 miles along the upper Saint Croix and its tributary, the **Namekagon**. The area to be included begins at Saint Croix Falls, Wisconsin, and follows the Saint Croix upstream to Gorden, Wisconsin. This section of the river forms the boundary between Minnesota and Wisconsin. The Namekagon, which lies entirely in Wisconsin, rises in Namekagon Lake in the northwest part of the state, and flows 98 miles to its confluence with the Saint Croix east of Riverside.
>
> The National Park Service plans to acquire a total of 62,736 acres of land along the shores of these 2 rivers by June, 1973. The Northern States Power Company, the largest single landowner along both sides of the upper Saint Croix, has led the way in developing this scenic riverway by agreeing to donate approximately 25,000 acres of its property to the federal government. In the meantime, the company has established 70 miles of camping areas and access points along the Saint Croix, all of which have been kept primitive in order to preserve as much as possible of the unspoiled nature of the area. The Minnesota sites include the areas where the **Sunrise** and **Snake rivers** flow into the Saint Croix. The Wisconsin sites include Nelson's Landing, near the head of **Kettle Rapids.**
>
> *For further information: Box 579, Saint Croix Falls, Wis. 54024*

WISCONSIN DELLS
southcentral Wisconsin, access via I-90
> This picturesque gorge was formed by the **Wisconsin River** cutting its way through soft sandstone cliffs and carving the rock into strange formations and shapes. The channel is about 8 miles long and some 150 miles deep; a dam divides the river into areas known as the Upper and Lower Dells. The Dells may be explored by several different boat trips as well as by trails along the riverside and on the crests of the 90-foot cliffs.

WYALUSING STATE PARK
12 miles south of Prairie du Chien via U.S. 18
> This historic 2,575-acre park contains the site where on June 17, 1673, Father Jacques Marquette and Louis Joliet are presumed to have discovered the **Mississippi River** at its junction with the **Wisconsin**. The French explorers had traveled up the Fox River from Green Bay and then had made an easy portage to the Wisconsin, which flows south and west to the Mississippi. They are the first white men known to have traveled the upper Mississippi, and the route they established between Green Bay and Prairie du Chien, the Fox-Wisconsin Waterway, was the main trade route—especially for fur traders and log-rafting lumberjacks—for the next 150 years. Wyalusing, which lies high in the hills above the Mississippi, offers a commanding view over the mighty river west to Iowa and north across the level plain to Prairie du Chien.

WYOMING

AYERS NATURAL BRIDGE
Ayers Park, 12 miles west of Douglas on I-25, then 5 miles south
> This natural stone archway, 30 feet high and 50 feet wide, was formed by **La Prele Creek**, which wore its way through the rock.

BIGHORN CANYON NATIONAL RECREATION AREA. *See* MONTANA

BIGHORN NATIONAL FOREST
northcentral Wyoming, headquarters at Sheridan
> This forest, which is about 80 miles long and 30 miles wide, is located in the heart of the **Bighorn Mountains,** which lie east of the **Continental Divide.** The range rises abruptly out of the Great Plains and extends from southern Montana south through northcentral Wyoming. The forest is drained by the **Bighorn, Tongue,** and **North Fork of the Powder rivers,** all tributaries of the **Yellowstone River.** The dominant timber species is lodgepole pine. Other important conifers include ponderosa and limber pine, Douglas and alpine fir, Engelmann spruce, and Rocky Mountain red cedar. Broadleaf trees are aspen, cottonwood, and narrowleaf cottonwood.
>
> One of the major attractions is the **Cloud Peak Primitive area,** which is in the forest's southern half, and which includes some 137,000 acres in the most rugged portion of the Bighorn Range. The area is named for its highest point, 13,165-foot Cloud Peak. The lowest elevation in the wilderness is at the **Main Fork of Paintrock Creek,** which lies about 8,500 feet above sea level. There are many lakes in this area, the largest being jewel-like **Lake Solitude,** unexcelled in lonely grandeur. All told, there are 256 fishing lakes and 49 miles of fishing streams. The whole wilderness is traversed by good trails and is an ideal setting for saddle and pack trips.
>
> The northern part of the forest is traversed by many trails and roads. U.S. 14 crosses 9,033-foot **Granite Pass** and travels through scenic **Shell Canyon.** U.S. 14A passes through **Five Springs Canyon,** passes by 9,956-foot **Medicine Mountain,** and nearly reaches Medicine Wheel, a curious prehistoric structure, probably used by the Indians for religious ceremonies. U.S. 16, at the forest's southern end, goes across 9,666-foot **Powder River Pass** and through beautiful **Tensleep Canyon.**
> *For further information write: Supervisor, Sheridan, Wyo. 82801*

BLACK HILLS NATIONAL FOREST. *See* SOUTH DAKOTA

BOAR'S TUSK
27 miles north of Rock Springs
> This volcanic formation, about 400 feet high, looms up from barren terrain east of U.S. 187, from where it is visible.

BOYSEN STATE PARK
on U.S. 20, 14 miles northwest of Shoshoni
> This park is situated on the east shore of Boysen Reservoir, created by Boysen Dam on the **Wind River.** The reservoir contains about 18,000 surface acres of water. It stretches from the sagebrush flats, east of Shoshoni, north to the dam, which is located at the head of famous **Wind River Canyon.** At the canyon, formed by the river as it flows through the **Owl Creek Mountains,** the Wind becomes the **Big Horn River.** U.S. 20, which runs through the canyon, was

Left: Devils Tower. Top right: packtrain trip in Wind River Range. Below: Grand Teton National Park

blasted from the rock and in 3 places actually tunnels through the solid granite of the Owl Creek Mountains. The 2,000-foot-high canyon walls line the highway and reveal remarkable rock formations, rich in geologic history. Boysen State Park is surrounded by the Wind River Indian Reservation, home grounds for both Shoshone and Arapahoe peoples and the only Indian reservation in the state.

BRIDGER NATIONAL FOREST
west Wyoming, headquarters at Kemmerer

This forest covers 1,700,000 acres in 2 divisions: the western, or Wyoming Division, and the eastern or Bridger Division, which contains portions of the **Wind River Range** and the **Bridger Wilderness.** The forest was named for Jim Bridger, a famous mountain man, explorer, and a partner in the Rocky Mountain Fur Company that prospered during the early 1800s. The Wyoming Division extends southward from the **Grand Canyon of the Snake River.** It includes parts of or all of the **Salt River Range, Porcupine Ridge,** and the **Wyoming Range.** This section abounds in creeks and rivers, and is almost bisected from north to south by **Greys River.** One of the most interesting features of this division is **Periodic Spring,** about 5 miles east of Afton. During late summer this spring completely shuts itself off every 18 minutes, and then builds up until ice-cold torrents gush forth. The canyon leading to the spring is unusually scenic. The southern end of the Wyoming Division is traversed by the *Lander Cut-off* of the *Oregon Trail.* This historic route was constructed in 1858 by Colonel Frederick Lander. It was the first engineered road west of the Mississippi and was traveled by pioneers headed for Oregon or the California gold mines.

The forest's Bridger Division includes 383,000-acre Bridger Wilderness, a scenic wildland dotted with over 1,300 lakes. A plentiful supply of rainbow, easternbrook, cutthroat, golden, Mackinaw trout, and some whitefish and Montana grayling await the angler. This 90-mile-long wilderness is roadless, but is traversed by about 500 miles of trails for horseback riding and hiking. The terrain is rough and rugged, and is appealing only to experienced and hardy hikers. The eastern boundary which separates the Bridger Division from Shoshone National Forest (*see*) is formed by the Wind River Range. All along the **Continental Divide** are huge, "live" glaciers, and massive granite outcrops popular with mountain climbers. Elevations range as high as the 13,785-foot peak of Wyoming's highest point, **Gannett Peak,** which straddles the Divide and extends partly into Shoshone National Forest. The tundralike highcountry is ablaze in many places with wildflowers. Other attractions in the Bridger Division include **Lower Green River Lake,** overshadowed by 11,679-foot **Square Top Mountain** and surrounded by many trails. **Fremont Lake,** just west of the Elkhart Park entrance to the wilderness, is one of the state's largest lakes and is noted for its large fish, including the record-breaking mackinaw weighing over 40 pounds. **Fortification Mountain,** the center of a popular winter sports area, is near the lake. **Kendall Warm Springs,** on the Green River in the northeast section of this division, maintains a constant temperature of 84.4° and is the only place in the world where the tiny Kendall Dace is found. These fish are barely 2 inches long when full grown. *For further information write: Supervisor, Kemmerer, Wyo. 83101*

CASTLE GARDENS PETROGLYPH SITE
about 28 miles south of Moneta on U.S. 20-26

These "gardens" are situated in a valley whose eastern side is filled with gleaming white ledges and multicolored sandstone formations. The stone is eroded into strange shapes—cones, shelves, minarets, and spires—many of which rise almost 100 feet from the ground. Some of the wind- and rain-carved rocks resemble giant red toadstools, precariously supported by thin stems. In combination with the natural landscape, these formations suggest a medieval castle surrounded by gardens. The site also contains cliffs, 6 miles long and 1 mile wide, and between 10 and 100 feet high. The vertical face of these walls is covered with numerous well-preserved Indian petroglyphs, including many depictions of water turtles. The age and specific meaning of the pictographs is not known. National Historic Landmark

CROOKED CREEK NATURAL AREA
15 miles northeast of Lovell

This 160-acre tract features a ridge that rises several hundred feet above the surrounding **Crooked Creek Valley.** The ridge has produced fossils of land vertebrates that lived in the early Cretaceous period, which began some 135 million years ago. The northeast-facing cliff of this ridge has yielded nearly entire skeletons of a primitive duckbill and of a small carnivore as well as many other fossils of significance. Registered Natural Landmark

DEVILS TOWER NATIONAL MONUMENT
northeast corner of Wyoming, on State 24, 7 miles north of U.S. 14

Devils Tower, noted for its beauty and grandeur, is an ancient lava dome with fluted sides. Situated where the pine forest of the Black Hills (*see South Dakota*) merges with the grasslands of the rolling plains, it looms 1,280 feet above the **Belle Fourche River.** In 1906 Devils Tower was proclaimed the country's first national monument. This imposing, stump-shaped cluster of rock columns measures 1,000 feet across its base and tapers to 275 feet at its top. It rises 865 feet above its forested moundlike base and is 5,117 feet above sea level, making it the tallest rock formation of its kind in the United States. Geologists believe that the monolith was formed by molten rock that was forced into a dome-shaped mass as it thrust its way upward through the earth's crust. Its rock was formed by the cooling and crystallization of the once-molten materials. The tower's most striking feature, its fluted columns, are actually the cracks that appeared as the volcanic dome cooled. These columns were then covered over with softer sedimentary rock, but erosion mainly by the Belle Fourche River, long ago wore away this softer material and exposed the columns. The force of gravity, coupled with the effects of freezing and thawing of water in the dome's crevices and joints, has caused some of the eroded columns to fall off the tower. (None has fallen off in recent years.) The tower is encircled by the *Tower Trail*, a self-guiding nature walk that passes several fallen columns. The monument, which covers about 2 square miles, is also a natural exhibit of botanical plant succession from bare rock to a fully mature forest. The tower is covered with a few bright patches of lichens and mosses. As soil forms from the rock, and as dust settles in the crevices, grasses begin to grow. Then, wildflowers, shrubs, and finally trees—notably ponderosa pine, juniper, and quaking aspen—appear. Prairie dogs, white-tailed deer, and small mammals such as cottontails and chipmunks may be seen within the monument, which is frequented by a variety of birds, including hawks and falcons.
For further information: Superintendent, Devils Tower, Wyo. 82714

WYOMING

FLAMING GORGE NATIONAL RECREATION AREA. *See* **ASHLEY NA-
TIONAL FOREST, UTAH**

FOSSIL FISH BEDS
about 10 miles west of Kemmerer, off U.S. 30 N
> This site contains what is reputed to be the world's largest deposit
> of fossilized fish. The fish once lived in the inland sea that covered
> the area, perhaps 40 or 50 million years ago. The fossils lie in low
> cliffs and are buried under some 35 feet of shale and calcite. How-
> ever, since the turn of the century, fossil hunters have blasted away
> at the protecting layers in many parts of the hill, and some of the
> fossils are now preserved in a museum.
> *Museum open: June 1–Sept 1, Mon–Fri noon–9*

GRAND TETON NATIONAL PARK
westcentral Wyoming, headquarters at Moose
> This 485-square-mile park contains 2 major attractions: the lofty,
> snow-flecked peaks of the Grand Tetons and their basin, famous in
> Wyoming history as **Jackson Hole** ("hole" was the word for valley in
> fur-trader slang). The Grand Tetons, which appear to change color
> from shades of gray to blue to purple, are a symmetrical, majestic
> range that has always enthralled visitors. In 1819 a group of French-
> Canadian fur trappers saw the mountains from the west, and de-
> scriptively called 3 of the most prominent peaks "Les Trois Tetons"
> —or the three breasts. Today these 3 are known as the **Grand**
> (13,770 feet), the **Middle** (12,804 feet), and the **South** (12,514 feet)
> **Tetons,** and the French name is applied to the whole range which
> includes 12 other peaks over 11,000 feet high. The range itself is
> relatively small, extending some 40 miles from north to south. The
> snowfields and small glaciers that cover the peaks, and the canyons
> and moraines that rim the large lakes in Jackson Hole, are all rem-
> nants of the forces that molded the landscape during the Ice Age.
> The peaks rise in stunning abruptness over the lake-studded basin.
> Alpine lakes fill the many hollows below the summits, and their out-
> lets enter the larger lakes lying close to the base of the range.
> These large lakes are **Jackson, Leigh, Jenny, Bradley, Taggart,** and
> **Phelps.** All are nestled in dense forests outside the mouths of the
> series of canyons that separate the mountains. With so much stun-
> ning scenery compressed into such a small area, it is not surprising
> that large numbers of Indians, trappers, and settlers were attracted
> to the Jackson Hole area early in the 19th century. The "hole,"
> which was named for mountain man David Jackson, is a high
> mountain valley, about 50 miles long and between 6 and 12 miles
> wide. It is bisected by a meandering segment of the swift-flowing
> **Snake River;** professionally guided float trips down the river in
> rubber rafts may be arranged with several local concessioners.
> These exhilarating excursions afford beautiful views of the Tetons
> and the park's wildlife. The valley is encircled by several mountain
> ranges: on the west it is bounded by the towering Teton spires; on
> the north by the high plateaus of Yellowstone National Park (*see*),
> and on the east and the south by the **Mount Leidy highlands** and
> the **Gros Ventre Mountains.** Man-made **Jackson Lake,** which fills
> a glacier-carved basin, occupies a large part of Jackson Hole. Each
> year thousands of American elk (wapiti) winter in the snow-covered
> valley; some summer in Yellowstone and begin migrating south in
> the fall. Other large animals that may be seen in the park are moose,
> bear, mule deer, bighorn sheep, and pronghorn antelope.
> *For further information: Superintendent, Moose, Wyo. 83012*

Rugged terrain in Shoshone National Forest (see page 311)

HELL'S HALF ACRE
44 miles west of Casper on U.S. 20 and 26

Often called Baby Grand Canyon, Hell's Half Acre is actually a 320-acre chasm filled with freakish shapes carved out of shale and sandstone by the eroding forces of wind and rain. The deep caverns, crevices, towers, spires and other indescribable shapes are all highly colored, adding to the weird effect of the region, which is also known as Devil's Kitchen. The Indians used the depression as a buffalo trap. Today it is maintained as a local park, and trails meander among the strange figures.

HOT SPRINGS STATE PARK
on the edge of Thermopolis, access via U.S. 16, 20, and 26

This 956-acre park, located on the banks of the **Big Horn River**, includes 4 major hot springs and hundreds of small ones, some of which flow directly into the river. **Big Horn Hot Spring** flows at the rate of 18,600,000 gallons of mineral water per day and is the world's largest single mineral hot spring; it maintains a constant temperature of 135°, and the beautiful terraces and mineral cones formed by its water are an ideal prelude to the nearby wonders of Yellowstone National Park (*see*).

INDEPENDENCE ROCK
53 miles southwest of Casper on State 220

Known as "the great registry of the desert," this huge, gray-brown monolith was a famous landmark on the Oregon Trail. It lies on the north bank of the **Sweetwater River** and is 193 feet high with a base that covers 27 acres. The rock is inscribed with thousands of names, many painted, carved, or written on its surface by pioneers on their way west. Its sides are also covered with striations left by glacial action during the Ice Age. National Historic Landmark

WYOMING

KEYHOLE STATE PARK
8 miles north of I-90 between Moorcroft and Sundance

This park is situated on the southeast shore of Keyhole Reservoir—an impoundment of the **Belle Fourche River**—and is within sight of Devils Tower National Monument (*see*). The surrounding mountains comprise the western boundary of the famous Black Hills of South Dakota (*see*), which actually extend into northeastern Wyoming. Wildlife such as antelope, deer, elk, and wild turkey are common in the area.

MEDICINE BOW NATIONAL FOREST
southeast Wyoming, headquarters at Laramie

This 1,060,000-acre forest is divided into 4 separate sections. The northernmost division contains part of the rugged **Laramie Mountains**, including their highest point, 10,272-foot **Laramie Peak**, a noted Oregon Trail landmark. To the southeast lies the forest's smallest division, Pole Mountain. It includes the **Sherman Mountains**, unusual rocky ridges rising above the Laramie Mountains that are famous for their grotesque, erosion-caused rock configurations, and the Pole Mountains, noted for their strange rock formations in the vicinity of Vedauwoo Interchange. Vedauwoo is a Cheyenne Indian word meaning "earthborn," and the Indians believed that the jumbled mass of strange rocks in this area had been created by playful spirits of man and animals. To the west of the Pole Mountain Division is the Medicine Bow Division, the largest of the 4 sectors. It contains much of the Wyoming portion of the **Medicine Bow Mountains**, which extend north-northwest from Cameron Pass, Colorado, to the town of Medicine Bow. Locally, that part of the Medicine Bow Range just west of Centennial, Wyoming, in Albany and Carbon counties, is known as the **Snowy Range.** Even in late summer, many of its craggy mountain peaks are covered with snow. State 130, a scenic route known as the *Snowy Range Road*, goes through these mountains, passing near 12,013-foot **Medicine Bow Peak**, one of the highest points in the Medicine Bow Range. The timber cover of the Snowy Range is characteristic of this section of the Rocky Mountains. At lower elevations, up to 9,500 feet, lodgepole pine cover the slopes. Above 9,500 feet, Engelmann spruce is dominant. Above 10,500 feet, the spruce forest thins out to alpine and subalpine cover, characterized by large open grass parks with scattered shrubby growths of timberline spruce and fir. The lake-filled Snowy Range also contains the headwaters of the numerous streams that irrigate the valleys of the **Little Laramie** and **North Platte rivers.** The westernmost, Hayden, division of the forest spans a portion of the **Continental Divide,** and includes 9,915-foot **Battle Pass** and 11,004-foot **Bridger Peak,** both along the Divide. Other points of interest in this division are 10,979-foot **Blackhall Mountain,** which has a lookout tower, 10,303-foot **Green Mountain,** and 10,784-foot **Vulcan Mountain.** The forest also includes a winter sports area at Happy Jack, east of Laramie; the Medicine Bow Ski Area on State 130 near Ryan Park; and the Snowy Range Ski Area on State 130 just west of Centennial.
For further information write: Box 3355, Laramie, Wyo. 82701

NAMES HILL
on Green River, 5 miles south of La Barge and just west of U.S. 189

Like Register Cliff and Independence Rock (*see both*), Names Hill is inscribed with signatures and messages left by 19th-century pioneers on their way to California. The earliest dated name on this site is from 1822, earlier than any dated inscription on either of the other 2 locations. In 1844 Jim Bridger, the famous fur trapper and mountain man, left his name here.

NATIONAL ELK REFUGE
immediately northeast of Jackson on U.S. 26, 89, 187

This famous refuge, which is situated in Jackson Hole, is the winter home of the nation's largest herd of American elk (wapiti), which is estimated to contain between 7,000 and 10,000 animals. The refuge is also home to moose, native deer, pronghorn antelope, and buffalo. During the summer, when the elk migrate to the meadows of higher mountain regions, especially in Teton National Forest and Yellowstone National Park (*see both*), a small herd may be seen in a pasture 3 miles north of Jackson. During winter months visitors may take sleigh rides through the refuge and observe the elk.
Open daily: 8–4:30. Admission: adults $1.50, children 75¢

PETRIFIED FOREST
about 30 miles north of Medicine Bow via State 487, then local road

This 2,560-acre tract is situated on the east bank of the **Little Medicine Bow River**. The forest contains the petrified remains of subtropical trees estimated to be 50 million years old. It is made up of the simplest kind of petrified wood in which silica has replaced the tree tissues. Only a little of the wood is agatized.

RED DESERT
north of I-80, west of Rawlins

This vast, treeless high-altitude desert, located in a break on the **Continental Divide,** is noted for its beautiful colors, which change hourly according to the brilliance and direction of the sunlight. Although the region seems barren, it is the wintering place for thousands of sheep. The **Great Divide Basin** is an eastward continuation of the Red Desert. The basin is a vast area of gray salt soil covered in some places with greenish-gray shrubs. Patches of alkali alternate with clumps of sage and greasewood. To the southeast of the Great Divide Basin lie the **Medicine Bow Mountains.**

REGISTER CLIFF STATE HISTORIC SITE
1¼ miles southwest of Guernsey on U.S. 26

This cliff was one of the Wyoming landmarks along the Oregon-California Trail, on which emigrants carved their names and left messages and greetings for each other. The 2 other sites are Names Hill and Independence Rock (*see both*). Register Cliff, which looms above the **North Platte River,** contains about 700 names that are still legible; one is dated 1842. At the foot of the cliff is a lovely meadow that served as a resting place for the pioneers. The nearby Oregon Trail Ruts State Historical Site preserves some of the ruts worn into the rock by the wagon wheels of the mid-19th-century emigrants. Several of the ruts are between 5 and 6 feet deep.

SHOSHONE NATIONAL FOREST
northwest and westcentral Wyoming, headquarters at Cody

In 1891 Shoshone became the first timberland in the United States to be reserved under the national forest system. Today it covers nearly 2½ million acres and embraces portions of 2 Rocky Mountain Ranges—the **Absaroka** and **Wind River ranges.** Shoshone is a true wilderness forest, marked by many glaciers and abounding in rugged mountains as well as hundreds of lakes and miles of trout streams. Its northern portion contains the **North** and **South Absaroka wilderness areas** as well as the **Stratified Wilderness Area,** famous for its forest of standing petrified tree trunks at the head of **Frontier Creek.** This division includes the **Carter Mountains,** spectacular **Wapiti Valley,** scenic **Clark's Fork Canyon of the Yellowstone River,** and the **North Fork of the Shoshone River Canyon.** The forest's southern portion contains 2 units. The northern section is dominated by **Glacier Wilderness Area,** so named because it contains some of the largest living glaciers in the continental United States, including **Downs, Gannett, Dinwoody, Fremont,** and **Bull Lakes glaciers.** This unit is located on the eastern slope of the Wind River Range and on the southern slope of the Absaroka Range; it includes the headwaters of the famous Wind River. The western boundary of this unit is formed by the **Continental Divide** and is lined by famous and historic peaks and passes. Strategically located, 9,210-foot-high **Union Pass** is the core area from which 3 great Wyoming mountain ranges rise: the Wind River to the southeast, the **Gros Ventre** to the west, and the Absaroka to the north. The pass also offers easy passageway among the headwaters of 3 great river systems—the **Colorado,** the **Columbia,** and the **Missouri.** It was an important crossing point, especially for fur traders. A little south of Union Pass are many other famous peaks including 13,344-foot **Downs Peak;** part of 13,785-foot **Gannett Peak,** the highest point in Wyoming; and 13,370-foot **Fremont Peak.** The southern section of this division contains the **Popo Agie Primitive Area,** which also extends east from the Continental Divide. The area's rugged terrain was formed by centuries of glacial action.

For further information write: Supervisor, Cody, Wyo. 82314

SINKS CANYON STATE PARK
southwest of Lander via State 131

This park, which adjoins a section of Shosone National Forest (*see*), features the famous Sinks, where a fork of the **Popo Agie River** mysteriously disappears into a gaping subterranean cavern in the south wall of **Sinks Canyon.** The water emerges nearly half a mile farther down the canyon in a series of deep, crystal-clear springs that flow out from under the north canyon wall. The spring pool, known as the **Rise of the Sinks,** is a closed-to-fishing zone, where one can admire hundreds of huge rainbow trout. The rest of the Popo Agie River, above the Sinks and below the Rise, offers excellent public fishing. Sinks Canyon is a nature park, with hiking trails, informative signs, and many scenic lookouts.

SOUTH PASS
about 10 miles southwest of South Pass City on State 28

In 1824 Jedediah Smith and Thomas Fitzpatrick, both famous mountain men, took a party over South Pass and established the regular use of this broad level valley in transcontinental travel. (The first recorded white men to actually use the pass were Robert Stuart and his group of Astorian fur traders on their return exploration trip from the Pacific in 1812.) Located in the **Wind River Range,** 7,550-foot South Pass was the easiest passageway through the **Rocky Mountains.** The Oregon-California Trail crossed the **Continental Divide** here, and the pass was used more than any other route by westbound settlers. It also played a significant role in the development of the fur and mining trades, western exploration, and the establishment of effective American claim to the Pacific Northwest. Registered Historical Landmark

TARGHEE NATIONAL FOREST. *See* IDAHO

TEAPOT ROCK
south of Midwest via U.S. 87

This odd rock formation is near Teapot Dome, which lent its name to a famous oil lease scandal during the administration of President Warren G. Harding. Teapot Rock actually resembles a disfigured human hand rather than a teapot. It is made of eroded sandstone, and measures 75 feet in height and 300 feet in circumference.

TETON NATIONAL FOREST
northwest Wyoming, headquarters at Jackson

This forest covers 1,700,781 acres of mountainous terrain. It is bordered by Grand Teton and Yellowstone national parks (*see both*) and surrounds famous **Jackson Hole,** the glacial valley adjoining Wyoming's **Teton Range.** The location of the forest—partly on the **Continental Divide**—makes it an important water-yield area; average annual precipitation in the form of rain and snow is about 24 inches. More than 1,000 miles of streams and 2,000 acres of mountain lakes offer excellent trout fishing. Wildlife is another major forest attraction. In summer visitors are apt to spot the rare trumpeter swan, sandhill cranes, grouse, several species of hawk, bald and golden eagles, black bears, beavers, martens, bobcats, otters, and mink. Elk, mule deer, and moose may also be seen.

Teton Wilderness, 563,500 acres in the northern portion of this national forest, is a region of coniferous meadows, lakes and streams, and broad valleys. Along the Continental Divide, which traverses its eastern portion, there are numerous steep canyons and barren alpine tracts where snowfall is common even in the middle of summer. Wilderness elevation ranges from 7,500 feet to 12,165 feet at **Younts Peak,** the highest point in the forest, situated at the head of the **Yellowstone River.** Scenic **Yellowstone Meadow**—1 mile wide and 7 miles long—traversed by the meandering Yellowstone River, is a favorite spot for big game; it lies just south of **Bridger Lake** near the northern boundary of the wilderness. Another major attraction is 8,200-foot **Two Ocean Pass,** a Registered Natural Landmark. This pass, a small meadow area on the Continental Divide, contains **Two Ocean Creek,** which divides and spills into **Atlantic** and **Pacific creeks.** The waters that enter Pacific Creek flow west into the Snake River and eventually end up 1,353 miles from the pass in the Pacific Ocean. The waters that enter Atlantic Creek flow into the Yellowstone River and eventually drain into the Atlantic Ocean, 3,488 miles from the pass.

The southern portion of the forest contains part of the **Wind River Range** as well as much of the **Hoback River** with its scenic canyon. The dominating features of this southern part, however, are the **Gros Ventre River** and the **Gros Ventre Range,** whose prominent peaks include 11,525-foot **Triangle,** 11,645-foot **Darwin,** 11,730-foot **Doubletop** (the highest in the range), and 11,130-foot **Hodges.** About 6 miles up the Gros Ventre River, above the community of Kelly, is the **Gros Ventre Slide Geological Area.** The area preserves the remnants of a huge slide that occurred on June 23, 1925. An entire mountain broke loose and in just a few minutes an estimated 50 million cubic yards of earth, rocks, and trees rushed downward into the valley of the Gros Ventre River.

For further information write: Supervisor, Jackson, Wyo. 83001

WASATCH NATIONAL FOREST. *See* UTAH

YELLOWSTONE NATIONAL PARK
northwest Wyoming, northeast Idaho, and southwest Montana, headquarters at Mammoth Hot Springs, Wyoming

On March 1, 1872, Yellowstone became America's first national park; now, after 100 years it is the undisputed queen of the national system. Yellowstone is a wonderland of spouting geysers, boiling hot springs, sputtering mud volcanoes, colorful canyons, waterfalls, and wildlife. The largest national park, it contains over 3,400 square miles and extends into Montana on the north and west and Idaho on the southwest. The first white American to explore this huge area was John Colter, a veteran of the Lewis and Clark Expedition who arrived at present-day Yellowstone in 1807.

Most of the park's landscape is the result of volcanic activity, later altered by glaciers and the forces of erosion. Its central portion is a broad, level volcanic plateau with an average elevation of about 8,000 feet above sea level. Bordering the plateau on the south, east, and northwest are mountain ranges (mainly the **Gallatin** and the **Absaroka**), whose peaks and ridges rise between 2,000 and 4,000 feet above the enclosed tableland. The park is traversed from north to south by the **Yellowstone River,** and the **Continental Divide** winds diagonally across its southern half.

There are over 500 miles of roads in Yellowstone, and most of the major attractions are adjacent to the 142-mile-long *Grand Loop Road.* There are also several drives that lead off the Loop to points of special interest. Yellowstone also contains more than 1,000 miles of trails. Among the most popular are the *Shoshone Lake Trail* in the Old Faithful area and the *Howard Eaton Trail* (the park's longest), which follows the Grand Loop fairly closely. Many trails lead into the remote backcountry area.

The Grand Loop takes visitors to the major hydrothermal features —the world-famous geysers, hot springs, mud pots, mud volcanoes, and mud geysers. Most of these are concentrated in an area north of **Old Faithful Geyser,** but there are more than 10,000 hydrothermals elsewhere in the park. The most famous of the park's varied attractions, geysers are special types of hot springs that intermittently erupt a column of steam and hot water. The geyser basins and the park's other thermal oddities are remnants of the ancient volcanic period that occurred about 50 million years ago. In the basin area heat still remains in the rocks beneath the earth's crust. As water seeps into these hot regions it is changed into steam, and when

From left to right in Yellowstone: Old Faithful, Grand Canyon of the Yellowstone River, snowscape

enough pressure builds up, the steam seeks a way out. It may reach the atmosphere again as a jet of steam visible only when it condenses to vapor at some distance above the ground; in this case it is called a steam vent or fumarole. If its exit is clogged by incoming liquid water, the steam pushes the water out of the way and a geyser eruption takes place. The park has over 100 active geysers and some 3,000 noneruptive hot springs. Old Faithful is the most famous geyser even though it is not the largest or most powerful in the park. It has become Yellowstone's trademark because of its relative regularity—it erupts at intervals of between 61 and 67 minutes, although it has been known to deviate from this schedule. A typical eruption begins with a few short spurts of water. Within a matter of minutes a towering plume of over 10,000 gallons of boiling water is rocketing as high as 170 feet skyward. It plays at maximum height for about 20 seconds and then the eruption decreases in intensity. Boardwalks wind through many of the park's hydrothermal basins, several of which have self-guiding trails. Such trails are found at **Mud Volcano** (a crater opening through which steam rises to the surface and which periodically becomes choked with a gurgling mass of mud); **Norris Geyser Basin**; and **Fountain Paint Pots** (a unique hot spring consisting of depressions filled with boiling mud and a small amount of water and kept in an almost continual state of agitation by escaping gases and steam).

The awesome **Grand Canyon of the Yellowstone River** is southwest of **Mammoth Hot Springs**. This gorge is one of the park's most impressive features, especially when seen from the magnificent view points that line both rims. These points include *Artist, Inspiration, Grandview,* and *Lookout.* From Artist Point one can see the famous **Lower Falls of the Yellowstone** as it plunges 308 feet into the foaming river. The **Upper Falls,** located a short distance upstream from the Lower Falls, is a lofty 109-foot cascade that marks the beginning of the canyon, which stretches northward 24 miles. The chasm ranges in depth from 800 to 12,000 feet and is 1,500 feet wide in places. Its walls are predominantly yellow (hence the park's name), but red, brown, orange, pink, and white add to the rainbow of colors. The Yellowstone River extends south from the canyon to **Yellowstone Lake,** which lies at 7,731-feet above sea level. The lake is an immense body of water, whose shoreline is over 100 miles long, making it the largest high-altitude lake in the United States. *For further information: Yellowstone National Park, Wyo. 82109*

National Park Service Properties Described in this Guide

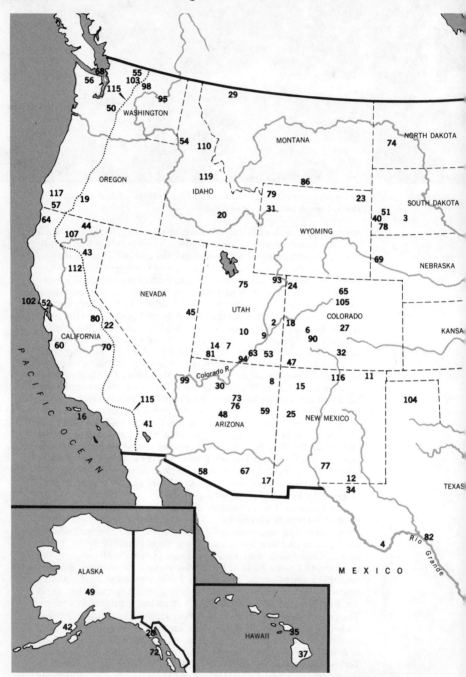

The numbers on this map are keyed to the lists on the next two pages. The numbers are placed on the sites of the national parks, monuments, memorials, lakeshores, seashores, recreation areas, scenic riverways, trails and parkways included in this

CANADA

MINNESOTA

L. Superior

39

83

118

WISCONSIN

120

MICHIGAN

106

L. Huron

L. Ontario

NEW YORK

VT.

N.H.

MASS.

CONN.

R.I.

87

MAINE

108

61

IOWA

L. Michigan

97

L. Erie

PENNSYLVANIA

91

92

N.J.

ILLINOIS

INDIANA

OHIO

WEST VIRGINIA

36

13

MD.

DEL.

85

MISSOURI

Ohio R.

KENTUCKY

46

71

VIRGINIA

109

Missouri R.

114

111

TENNESSEE

21

33

NORTH CAROLINA

88

89

KLAHOMA

ARKANSAS

38

Mississippi R.

113

66

108

SOUTH CAROLINA

GEORGIA

62

84

MISSISSIPPI

ALABAMA

LOUISIANA

96

96

FLORIDA

ATLANTIC OCEAN

100

Gulf of Mexico

26

5

guide. These properties, all administered by the National Park Service, sometimes
extend into several states. They are listed here, however, only under the state containing their description in this book.

A. National Parks, Monuments, and Memorials

1 Acadia Natl Park, Maine
2 Arches Natl Park, Utah
3 Badlands Natl Monument, S. Dak.
4 Big Bend Natl Park, Texas
5 Biscayne Natl Monument, Fla.
6 Black Canyon of the Gunnison Natl Monument, Colo.
7 Bryce Canyon Natl Park, Utah
8 Canyon de Chelly Natl Monument, Ariz.
9 Canyonlands Natl Park, Utah
10 Capitol Reef Natl Park, Utah
11 Capulin Mountain Natl Monument, N.M.
12 Carlsbad Caverns Natl Park, N.M.
13 Catoctin Mountain Park, Md.
14 Cedar Breaks Natl Monument, Utah
15 Chaco Canyon Natl Monument, N.M.
16 Channel Islands Natl Monument, Calif.
17 Chiricahua Natl Monument, Ariz.
18 Colorado Natl Monument, Colo.
19 Crater Lake Natl Park, Ore.
20 Craters of the Moon Natl Monument, Idaho
21 Cumberland Gap Natl Historical Park, Ky.
22 Devils Postpile Natl Monument, Calif.
23 Devils Tower Natl Monument, Wyo.
24 Dinosaur Natl Monument, Colo.
25 El Morro Natl Monument, N.M.
26 Everglades Natl Park, Fla.
27 Florissant Fossil Beds Natl Monument, Colo.
28 Glacier Bay Natl Monument, Alaska
29 Glacier Natl Park, Mont.
30 Grand Canyon Natl Park and Monument, Ariz.
31 Grand Teton Natl Park, Wyo.
32 Great Sand Dunes Natl Monument, Colo.
33 Great Smoky Mountains Natl Park, Tenn.
34 Guadalupe Mountains Natl Park, Texas
35 Haleakala Natl Park, Maui, Hawaii
36 Harpers Ferry Natl Historical Park, W. Va.
37 Hawaii Volcanoes Natl Park, Hawaii
38 Hot Springs Natl Park, Ark.
39 Isle Royale Natl Park, Mich.
40 Jewel Cave Natl Monument, S. Dak.
41 Joshua Tree Natl Monument, Calif.
42 Katmai Natl Monument, Alaska
43 Lassen Volcanic Natl Park, Calif.
44 Lava Beds Natl Monument, Calif.
45 Lehman Caves Natl Monument, Nev.
46 Mammoth Cave Natl Park, Ky.
47 Mesa Verde Natl Park, Colo.
48 Montezuma Castle Natl Monument, Ariz.
49 Mount McKinley Natl Park, Alaska
50 Mount Rainier Natl Park, Wash.
51 Mount Rushmore Natl Memorial, S. Dak.
52 Muir Woods Natl Monument, Calif.
53 Natural Bridges Natl Monument, Utah
54 Nez Perce Natl Historical Park, Idaho
55 North Cascades Natl Park, Wash.
56 Olympic Natl Park, Wash.
57 Oregon Caves Natl Monument, Ore.
58 Organ Pipe Cactus Natl Monument, Ariz.
59 Petrified Forest Natl Park, Ariz.
60 Pinnacles Natl Monument, Calif.
61 Pipestone Natl Monument, Minn.
62 Platt Natl Park, Okla.
63 Rainbow Bridge Natl Monument, Utah
64 Redwood Natl Park, Calif.
65 Rocky Mountain Natl Park, Colo.
66 Russell Cave Natl Monument, Ala.
67 Saguaro Natl Monument, Ariz.
68 San Juan Island Natl Historical Park, Wash.
69 Scotts Bluff Natl Monument, Nebr.
70 Sequoia and Kings Canyon Natl Parks, Calif.
71 Shenandoah Natl Park, Va.
72 Sitka Natl Monument, Alaska
73 Sunset Crater Natl Monument, Ariz.
74 Theodore Roosevelt Natl Memorial Park, N. Dak.
75 Timpanogos Cave Natl Monument, Utah
76 Walnut Canyon Natl Monument, Ariz.
77 White Sands Natl Monument, N.M.
78 Wind Cave Natl Park, S. Dak.
79 Yellowstone Natl Park, Wyo.
80 Yosemite Natl Park, Calif.
81 Zion Natl Park, Utah

B. National Lakeshores, Seashores, and Recreation Areas

82 Amistad Natl Recreation Area, Texas
83 Apostle Islands Natl Lakeshore, Wis.
84 Arbuckle Natl Recreation Area, Okla., *see listing for* Platt Natl Park

85 Assateague Island Natl Seashore, Md.
86 Bighorn Canyon Natl Recreation Area, Mont.
87 Cape Cod Natl Seashore, Mass.
88 Cape Hatteras Natl Seashore, N.C.
89 Cape Lookout Natl Seashore, N.C.
90 Curecanti Natl Recreation Area, Colo., *see listing for* Black Canyon of the Gunnison Natl Monument
91 Delaware Water Gap Natl Recreation Area, Penn.
92 Fire Island Natl Seashore, N.Y.
93 Flaming Gorge Natl Recreation Area, Utah, *see listing for* Ashley Natl Forest
94 Glen Canyon Natl Recreation Area, Utah
95 Grand Coulee Natl Recreation Area, Wash.
96 Gulf Islands Natl Seashore, Miss.
97 Indiana Dunes Natl Lakeshore, Ind.
98 Lake Chelan Natl Recreation Area, Wash., *see listing for* North Cascades Natl Park
99 Lake Mead Natl Recreation Area, Ariz.
100 Padre Island Natl Seashore, Tex.
101 Pictured Rocks Natl Lakeshore, Mich.
102 Point Reyes Natl Seashore, Calif.
103 Ross Lake Natl Recreation Area, Wash., *see listing for* North Cascades Natl Park
104 Sanford Natl Recreation Area, Tex.
105 Shadow Mountain Natl Recreation Area, Colo., *see listing for* Rocky Mountain Natl Park
106 Sleeping Bear Dunes Natl Lakeshore, Mich.
107 Whiskeytown-Shasta-Trinity Natl Recreation Area, Calif.

C. National Scenic Riverways, Trails, and Parkways

108 Appalachian Natl Scenic Trail. *See listings under various states as follows*—Me: Baxter and Grafton Notch state parks. N.H: Crawford Notch and Franconia Notch state parks. Ver: Green Mountain Natl Forest. Mass: Beartown State Forest, Mount Greylock State Reservation. Conn: Macedonia Brook State Park, Mohawk State Forest. N.Y: Palisades Interstate Park. N.J: High Point State Park, Stokes and Worthington state forests. Penn: Delaware Water Gap Natl Recreation Area. W. Va: Harpers Ferry Natl Historical Park. Va: George Washington and Jefferson natl forests, Shenandoah Natl Park. Tenn: Cherokee Natl Park. N.C: Nantahala and Pisgah natl forests. Ga: Amicalola Falls State Park, Chattahoochee Natl Forest.
109 Blue Ridge Natl Scenic Parkway, Va.
110 Clearwater (Middle Fork) Natl Wild and Scenic River, Idaho
111 Eleven Point Natl Wild and Scenic River, Mo.
112 Feather (Middle Fork) Natl Wild and Scenic River, Calif., *see listing for* Plumas Natl Forest
113 Natchez Trace Natl Scenic Parkway, Miss.
114 Ozark Natl Scenic Riverways, Mo.
115 Pacific Crest Natl Scenic Trail. *See listings under various states as follows*—Wash: Gifford Pinchot, Mount Baker, Okanogan, Snoqualmie, and Wenatchee natl forests. Ore: Crater Lake Natl Park; Mount Hood, Rogue River, Umpqua, Willamette, and Winema natl forests. Calif: Angeles, Cleveland, Eldorado, Plumas, San Bernardino, Sequoia, Shasta-Trinity, Sierra, Stanislaus, and Tahoe natl forests; Devils Postpile Natl Monument; John Muir Trail in Sequoia and Kings Canyon natl parks.
116 Rio Grande Natl Wild River, N.M.
117 Rogue Natl Wild and Scenic River, Ore, *see listing for* Siskiyou Natl Forest
118 Saint Croix Natl Wild and Scenic River, Wis.
119 Salmon (Middle Fork) Natl Wild and Scenic River, Idaho, *see listing for* Salmon Natl Forest
120 Wolf Natl Wild and Scenic River, Wis., *see listing for* Menominee County

ACKNOWLEDGMENTS AND PICTURE CREDITS

The editors wish to express their deep gratitude to the many individuals in the National Park Service, United States Forest Service, and in the state tourist offices for their generous help in providing text information and pictorial material. Unless otherwise indicated, the picture credits are listed below in the same order they are described in the captions. To simplify the listing, abbreviations for state names and the following abbreviations are used:

AA—American Airlines
NPS—National Park Service
USFS—United States Forest Service

1 N.C. Wildlife Resources Comm. 2–3 Union Pacific Railroad. 4 USFS. 7 NPS. 8 USFS, Cathedral Caverns. 12 USFS, USFS, Candian Government Photo Center. 12 below and 15 (left) Alaska Dept. of Economic Development & Planning. 15 right NPS. 19 NPS. 22 USFS. 24 AA, Ariz. Dept. of Library & Archive, AA. 27 USFS. 31 AA. 33 USFS. 35 USFS, Ark. Publicity & Parks Comm. 37 NPS. 38 NPS, USFS, USFS. 40–41 NPS. 42, 45 NPS. 46 USFS, AA. 49 NPS. 50, 51 USFS. 53 NPS. 54 USFS. 55 NPS. 56–57 NPS, NPS, NPS, AA. 58 NPS, NPS; (right and below) Colo. Dept. of Public Relations. 61 NPS. 62, 65 Colo. Dept. of Public Relations. 67 Colo. Visitors Bureau. 68 USFS. 70 Conn. Dept. of Environmental Protection, Conn. Development Comm. 73 (left), 74 Del. Bureau of Travel Development. 73 (right) Delaware Wild Lands, Inc. 75 NPS. 76 Fla. Dept. of Natural Resources, USFS, NPS. 79 NPS. 80–81 Fla. Dept. of Commerce. 83 USFS. 85 Ga. Dept. of Industry & Trade. 86, 87 USFS. 88 Hawaii Visitors Bureau, NPS, AA, AA. 91 Hawaii Visitors Bureau, NPS. 94 AA. 95 NPS. 97 AA. 98, 101 (right) Idaho Dept. of Commerce & Development. 101 (left) NPS. 103 USFS. 107 (left), 109 Ill. Dept. of Conservation. 107 (right) USFS. 110 Ind. Dept. of Natural Resources © Outdoor Indiana, NPS. 113 Iowa Development Comm., USFS, NPS. 116 Kans. Dept. of Economic Development. 117 USFS. 118 Ky. Dept. of Public Information, AA, NPS. 122 La. Wild Life & Fisheries Comm., USFS. 124 Wendy Buehr, (top right and center) Maine Dept. of Economic Development, NPS. 126 Maine Forestry Department. 129 Maine Dept. of Inland Fisheries & Game. 131 NPS (left), 133 Md. Dept. of Economic Development. 131 (right) USFS. 135 USFS, AA. 137 USFS, NPS. 139 NPS, Mich. Dept. of Conservation. 142 Mich. Dept. of Natural Resources. 143 NPS. 144 Grant Heilman, USFS, NPS, USFS. 146, 148–149 Minn. Dept. of Natural Resources, USFS, NPS. 151 NPS. 152 NPS, USFS. 154 Mo. Tourism Comm., USFS. 158 Bureau of Sport Fisheries & Wildlife, Mont. Highway Comm., USFS, USFS. 161 USFS. 162 USFS, NPS. 166, 169 Nebraskaland Magazine. 168 NPS. 170 USFS. 172–173 NPS, USFS. 175 USFS, State of N.H. Photo by Dick Smith. 176, 177 State of N.H. Photo by Dick Smith. 178 State of N.H. Photo by Geo. Hagopian. 179 USFS. 180 Palisades Interstate Park, NPS. 182 North Jersey Conservation Foundation. 184 NPS, NPS, N. Mex. Dept. of Development, USFS. 186 NPS. 187 USFS. 188–189 N. Mex. State Tourist Bureau. 192 (left and top right) N.Y. State Dept. of Commerce, USFS. 194 USFS. 195 NPS. 196 N.Y. State Dept. of Commerce. 200 NPS, USFS, USFS. 203 USFS. 204–205 N.C. Dept. of Natural and Economic Resources, NPS, USFS. 207 USFS, N. Dak. Travel Dept. 208 N. Dak. Game & Fish Dept., USFS. 210, 212, 213, 215 Ohio Development Dept. 216 USFS, Mike Shelton–State of Okla. 219 USFS. 220 USFS, USFS, Oreg. State Highway Dept. 223 USFS, Oreg. State Highway Dept. 225 USFS. 228 USFS, Oreg. State Highway Dept. 231 The Greater Erie Chamber of Commerce, USFS. 233, 234 NPS. 237 R.I. Development Council. 239 S.C. Dept. of Parks, Recreation & Tourism, Sea Pines Company. 242 USFS, NPS, S. Dak. Dept. of Game, Fish & Parks, NPS. 247 USFS, S. Dak. Dept. of Highways. 248 USFS, Tenn. Conservation Dept., USFS. 251, 253 Tenn. Conservation Dept. 254 NPS, NPS, USFS, NPS. 258 Natural Bridge Caverns, NPS. 260–261 USFS. 262 NPS, NPS, Utah Travel Council, NPS. 266 NPS. 271 Union Pacific Railroad, NPS. 274 USFS, Vt. Development Dept., USFS. 278 (left and top right) Va. State Travel Service, USFS. 282 (top left) 286, 291 (right) Wash. State Dept. of Commerce & Economic Development. 282 (right and below) NPS, NPS. 291 (left) USFS. 294 USFS, (right top and bottom) W. Va. Dept. of Commerce. 298 (left and below) Wis. Natural Resources Dept., (top right) USFS. 304 NPS, Union Pacific Railroad, NPS. 309 USFS. 314–315 NPS, USFS, NPS. 316–317 map by Francis & Shaw